HENRY MOORE

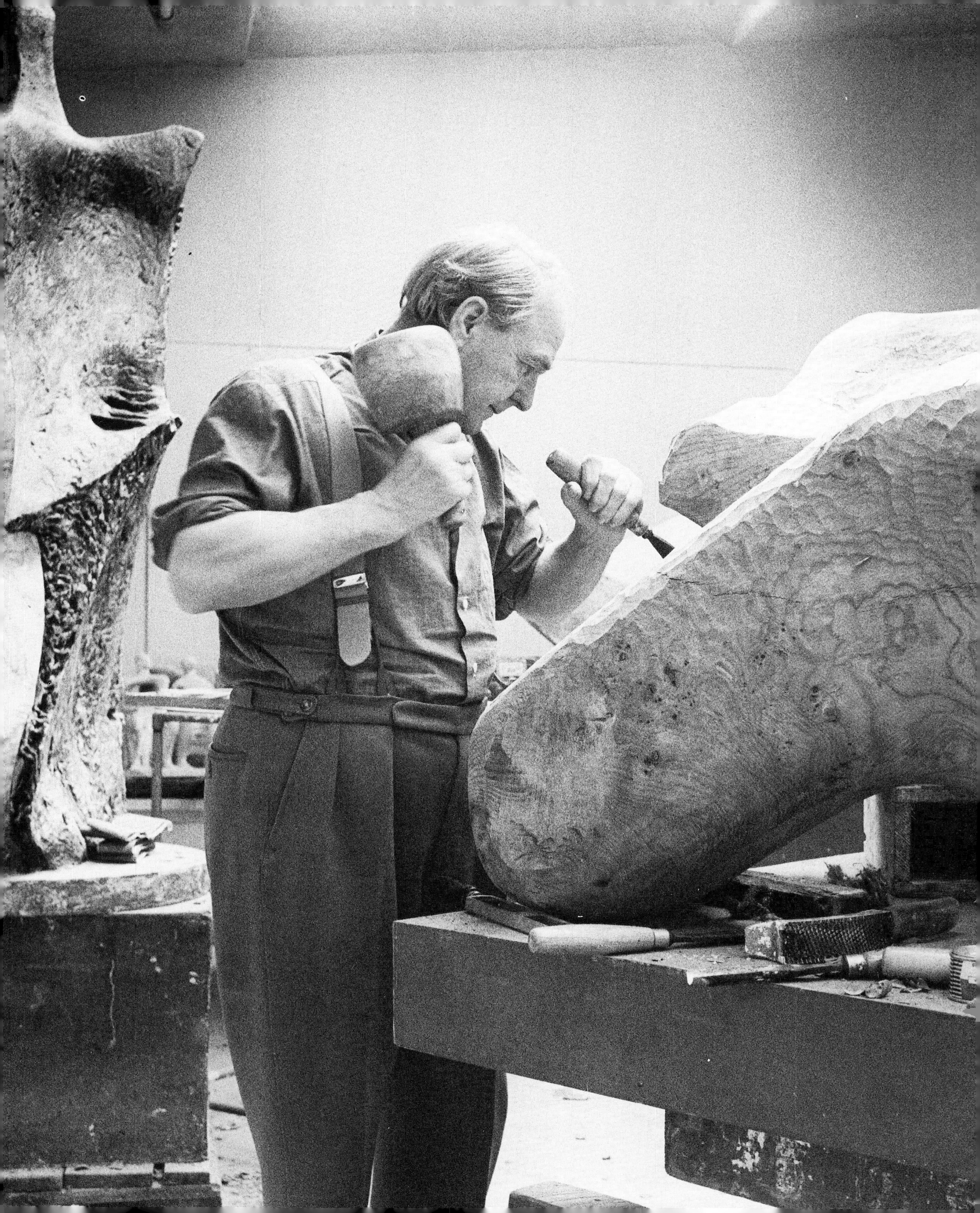

HENRY MOORE

1898 - 1986

AG NSW

ART GALLERY OF NEW SOUTH WALES

Published by the Trustees of the
Art Gallery of New South Wales
on the occasion of the exhibition
Henry Moore, 1992.

Compiled by David Mitchinson
and Nick Waterlow.
Edited by Angela Dyer.

National Library of Australia
Cataloguing-in-Publication entry
Henry Moore.

Bibliography.
ISBN 0 7305 9629 X.

Catalogue designed by
Spatchurst Design Associates,
Sydney.

Printed by Beaver Press, Sydney.

Distributed by the
Art Gallery of New South Wales,
Art Gallery Road, The Domain,
Sydney, Australia, 2000.

Photographic credits

Henry Moore Foundation
photographs by Brian Coxall
and Michel Muller

Inside front cover
John Hedgecoe

p.2 Errol Jackson

p.8 Bo Boustedt

p.11 © Lee Miller Archives

p.16 right: Errol Jackson

p.17 Royal Academy of Arts,
London

pp.19, 20 John Hedgecoe

p.22 Bo Boustedt

p.23 Michel Muller

p.24 Bo Boustedt

p.25 Geoffrey Shakerley

p.26 Michel Muller

p.27 Geoffrey Shakerley

p.28 Bo Boustedt

p.30 Bo Boustedt

p.82 Saidman

p.110 Lidbrooke

p.134 © J. S. Lewinski

Contents

Acknowledgements

This exhibition was selected and organised by David Mitchinson, Curator of the Henry Moore Foundation, and Nick Waterlow OAM, Consultant Curator to the Henry Moore Foundation.

Works were kindly lent by the following:

The Henry Moore Foundation, Much Hadham

Art Gallery of New South Wales, Sydney

Arts Council of Great Britain,
The South Bank Centre, London

The British Council, London

Leeds City Art Galleries

Carol and Tony Berg

Joanna and Edmund Capon

Private collection

The assistance of the following in the preparation of the exhibition and the catalogue is gratefully acknowledged:

The Henry Moore Foundation: Jean Askwith
Margaret McLeod, Julie Summers, Malcom Woodward

Hotel Inter • Continental, Sydney:
Wolfgang Grimm, General Manager; Melanie Baker

Parker Pen (Aust.) Pty. Ltd:
U. de Traubenberg, Managing Director

Arts Council Collection, London: Jill Constantine

The British Council, London: Diana Eccles

Leeds City Art Galleries: Alexander Robertson

Dr Susan Compton, London

Trevor and Esther Hayter, Sydney

The Henry Moore Foundation was established in 1977 'to advance the education of the public by the promotion of their appreciation of the fine arts and in particular the works of Henry Moore'.

The Foundation is centred at Perry Green, near Much Hadham in Hertfordshire, where Moore lived and worked for over forty years until his death in 1986. Here the Foundation maintains its permanent collection of works by Moore: sculptures and original plasters, drawings and sketchbooks, lithographs and etchings – over 12,000 pieces in all.

The Foundation is actively involved in the organisation of Henry Moore exhibitions throughout the world. Financial support is given to public galleries and other institutions, for exhibitions, sculpture acquisitions and conservation, research and publications, as well as providing fellowships and bursaries for sculptors and printmakers.

In 1988 the Foundation established the Henry Moore Sculpture Trust at Leeds, in Moore's native Yorkshire, where it also runs the Centre for the Study of Sculpture; a building programme is under way in Leeds to provide space for these expanding activities. The Foundation also supports a studio for sculptors to work in situ at Dean Clough in Halifax, and helps to fund the Yorkshire Sculpture Park, near Wakefield.

At Perry Green the Foundation continues to look after Moore's studios and to maintain the landscape of informal gardens and fields in which the artist liked his sculptures to be displayed, where they may be seen and shared by all.

Preface

SIR ALAN BOWNESS

Director
The Henry Moore
Foundation

For many people, this exhibition must be a dream realised. Australia was one of the first countries to recognise Moore's importance with a major exhibition in 1947-48, but until today no second retrospective has ever taken place. This is a curious fact, on which Nick Waterlow comments in his catalogue essay, and means that a large part of the artist's work has never been seen in Australia. Maybe this is no bad thing. In Europe and America there have been so many opportunities to look at Moore's sculptures that overfamiliarity may have resulted. To see a large body of work together for the first time must be a revelation.

Henry Moore has long taken his place among the great sculptors of the twentieth century. Now that we can see his work as a whole, certain things become clearer. He had a gift for creating three-dimensional objects, alive from every angle, that was second to none. He alone had the opportunities to work on a monumental scale, so that his sculpture consistently breaks the bounds of the museum gallery to stand in an open public space. His art seems to carry a universal humanist message that speaks to everyone, regardless of race or clan or sex. Susan Compton, in her illuminating essay in this catalogue, well describes what she rightly calls the 'deeper reality' of Moore's work.

The Henry Moore Foundation exists to help people to a deeper understanding of sculpture, and in particular of the work of Henry Moore. The artist left a large collection of his sculptures, drawings and graphics to the Foundation, and since the early 1980s a very impressive programme of travelling exhibitions has been arranged: Japan, India and Russia in the recent past; Germany, France and Australia this year; Hungary and Czechoslovakia in the near future.

Our friends in Australia have long been asking for a Moore exhibition, but the logistics and the costs are daunting. We had hoped to curate a show that could tour to several cities, and Arts Exhibitions Australia, under the direction of Robert Edwards, did much towards this end. Unfortunately despite much effort it proved impossible, and we were extremely grateful when one of the Directors involved, Edmund Capon of the Art Gallery of New South Wales, stepped forward to rescue the exhibition and make sure that it was at least shown in Sydney.

The Foundation's Curator, David Mitchinson, and I would particularly like to thank Mr Capon for his enterprise and co-operation. It has been a pleasure for our team to work with his to produce the exhibition and its fine catalogue.

The Foundation also owes a very special debt to Nick Waterlow, Director of the Ivan Dougherty Gallery and Senior Lecturer at the University of New South Wales, College of Fine Arts. At an early stage we asked Mr Waterlow to be the Foundation's adviser for the Australian exhibition: he has helped with the selection, given us invaluable advice and contributed a most interesting essay to the catalogue. The Foundation would also like to thank Susan Compton, who in 1988 curated the 90th birthday exhibition of Moore's work at the Royal Academy in London, for her original catalogue essay.

To all our friends and colleagues at the Art Gallery of New South Wales who have been involved with this exhibition go our grateful thanks.

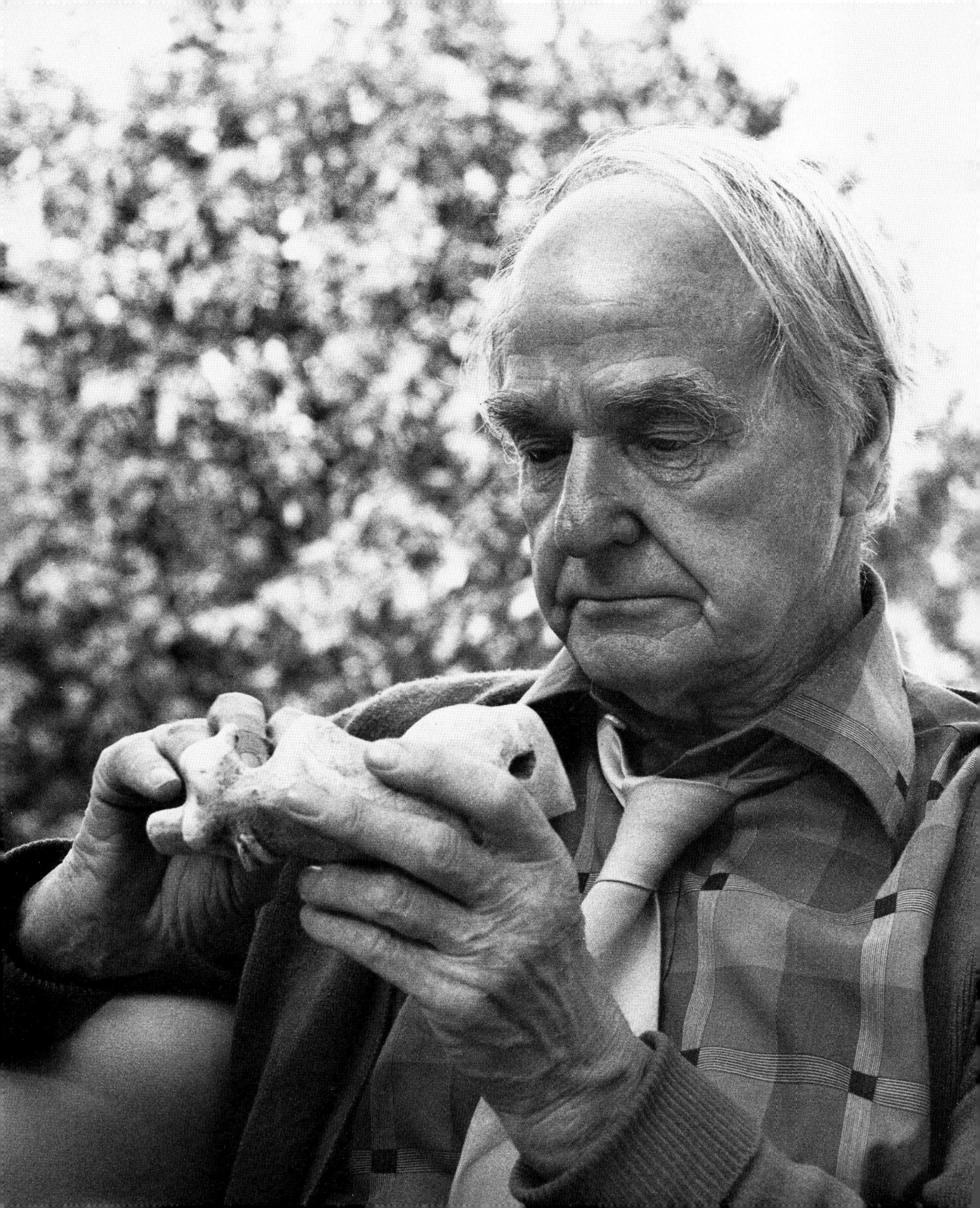

Preface

EDMUND CAPON

Director
Art Gallery of
New South Wales

The most poignant recollection of my first meeting with Henry Moore was those hands. As we sat in the drawing room of Hoglands, surrounded by the intimate bric-à-brac that we all accumulate, only in Moore's case it included somewhat up-market bric-à-brac such as Degas drawings, his hands were constantly busy: feeling, sensing, familiarising with, the textures and shapes of stones and pebbles.

We all know and acknowledge Henry Moore as the greatest figurative sculptor of the twentieth century, but it is the dimension of human experience that he brought to his art that so distinguishes his work. There is in every form, every turn, every manipulation of Moore's that quality of the human spirit, however seemingly abstract the final form may be. So powerful and so intrinsic is that quality of humanity that his work has truly assumed the mantle of a universal language. Even in the more abstracted works, which may have their origins in the inspiration of something so humble as a gnarled root, there is that mysteriously powerful sense of twisting or stretching limbs that echoes the striving aspirations of mankind.

It is just this quality of humanity, so deeply instilled in Moore's work, that makes it, firstly, so approachable and, secondly, so familiar. We in Australia have seen remarkably little of Moore's work, one semi-retrospective in 1947-8, but since then little more than haphazard glimpses. And yet it does not seem so unfamiliar, or perhaps more accurately, so unnatural. The strength and honesty of the dynamics of Moore's sculptures are the natural consequence of those hands, feeling the beauty and rhythms of natural forms and translating them into a universal experience that we all can enjoy and to which we can all respond. The intimacy of those moments of original and personal inspiration, still not lost in the monumental works for which he is renowned, are constantly captured in his drawings: works of such resounding humanity that none but the most abject philistine could fail to be moved.

A retrospective of the work of Henry Moore needs no justification; he is simply one of the most outstanding and universal artists of the twentieth century. That the exhibition has finally come to fruition is due to the extraordinary co-operation of the Henry Moore Foundation, its Director Sir Alan Bowness and Curator David Mitchinson, and indeed all the staff of the Foundation. This exhibition has been mooted and discussed for well over five years, but the demands on the Moore Foundation's resources in providing and co-operating with other exhibitions around the world is such that only now have we been able to fulfil that long-held ambition.

To the Trustees of the Moore Foundation, the Director and the staff, we express our gratitude for their wonderful co-operation and financial support in making this exhibition a reality. A special note of thanks to Dr Susan Compton for her wise and enlightening introduction to the catalogue and to the Australian Curator, Nick Waterlow, whom it has been a pleasure to work with again. Finally our thanks once again to the Hotel Inter•Continental Sydney and its General Manager, Wolfgang Grimm, for their continuing support.

Henry Moore: Links with Australia

NICK WATERLOW

'To be an artist is to believe in life'[1]

NOTES FOR THIS ESSAY MAY BE FOUND ON PAGE 208

Henry Moore is widely regarded as one of this century's greatest artists. But is that really the case in Australia?

It is true that the amount of literature on Moore is enormous and that a number of key works are located at a variety of interior and outdoor situations in public collections here, and that Michelangelo, Rodin and Moore even personify for some Australians the essence of sculpture.[2] Yet the last major exhibition of his work toured Australia in 1947 and 1948, encouraged by Hal Missingham, then Director of the Art Gallery of New South Wales (and from which incidentally one work returns, the Cumberland alabaster *Composition*, cat.22). An exhibition of bronzes visited New Zealand in 1956 and 1957, but not Australia. The exhibition *Recent British Sculpture* that toured in 1963 included only five works of Moore from 1956 to 1960 and since then there has been only the exhibition of *Portfolio Prints 1950-1981*, amplified by a small number of working models, that opened its peregrination at the Newcastle Region Art Gallery last year and will be seen at the S. H. Ervin Gallery in Sydney immediately prior to this exhibition. A few other works have appeared in public exhibitions, such as *Family Group* 1948-49 (LH 269) in the Botanic Gardens in 1956, but not a great number.

There was a time in the 1970s and 1980s when it was almost *de rigueur* for major art galleries and private collectors to own a substantial Moore. His reputation then spread far and wide as key works were placed in prominent public spaces throughout much of the world. His work took on the status of a sculptural imprimatur or logo that was universally impressed on our consciousness. Those massive bronzes perhaps gave people the impression that they knew a great deal not only about Moore's art but about the artist himself and his intentions.

I too had harboured such confident beliefs and indeed only had them shaken from me, quite abruptly and without premeditation, at the Royal Academy commemorative exhibition of 1988 and at the British Museum's parallel display of the Shelter sketch-books. What I experienced did not accord with my expectations. Firstly I had not believed I needed to increase my knowledge about the roots of Moore's thinking or his art, but these two exhibitions impressed upon me the absolute necessity of this information, more so for this artist than almost any other. The seeming impregnability of many of the bronze sculptures and the distance from their source was dispelled by the related drawings at the Royal Academy and by the remarkable example and range of the preceding carvings in wood, stone and marble, as well as the castings in lead. These too were fully understood in the context of the relevant earlier drawings. It was as though a full orchestra and a chamber group were simultaneously producing in relationship the complete and true sound of the composer. I remember a quote by Moore which I saw at the exhibition that shed crucial light on his search: 'the great (the continual, everlasting) problem (for me) is to combine sculptural form (Power) with human sensitivity and meaning i.e. to try to keep Primitive Power with humanist content.'[3]

The Shelter drawings at the British Museum brought Moore the humanist to the fore; I do not recall any more poignant images expressing wartime London. Kenneth Clark saw some of these sketches in his capacity as chairman of the War Artists' Advisory Committee and recommended Moore as an Official War Artist, which he duly became. 'Until my shelter drawings during the war,' Moore wrote later, 'I never seemed to feel free . . . to mix the Mediterranean approach comfortably with my interest in the more elementary concept of archaic and primitive peoples'.[4]

These drawings were exhibited by Kenneth Clark, as Director, at London's National Gallery, and they brought a larger and more sympathetic audience than before to Moore's work. There were also at the British Museum some key drawings from another War Artist series that helped establish Moore as a remarkable artist in the humanist tradition: the coalmining studies he made in Wheldale Colliery where his father had worked in Castleford, Moore's birthplace. Also exhibited was the astonishing work *Crowd Looking at a Tied-up Object* 1942 (HMF 2064), which preceded Christo's wrappings by a long chalk. On display in the exhibition was *Art in Australia* of September 1941 featuring Herbert Read's 'The Drawings of Henry Moore'.

Why did Read, who did not visit Australia until the early 1960s, choose this magazine for such a seminal essay? Peter Bellew, the editor in 1941-42, sent copies of his first four issues to Read who was enormously impressed that in such a dark age the support for modern art was continuing unabated in this far-flung quarter. Kenneth Clark, a fellow supporter of modernism, also believed 'the new *Art in Australia* is unquestionably the best art magazine being published today anywhere in the world.'[5] Read wrote that 'Henry Moore's drawings played the same part in the establishment of his reputation that the notes which T. S. Eliot added to *The Waste Land* did in similar circumstances'.[6] Read continued that the 'shelter drawings form the most authentic expression of the special tragedy of this war – its direct impact on the ordinary mass of humanity, the women, children and old men of our cities'.[7] But the kernel of the essay was the author's defence of Moore the modernist against those who had accused him of returning with these drawings to the style of the academic. 'The whole meaning and substance of his past work is implicit in this new work. Any division between the new and the old is arbitrary and illogical',[8] argued Read. Britain, during the war effort, had all but abandoned modernism, but Read found one of the very few outposts maintaining this energy in which to express his pertinent defence of one of its champion artists.

Henry Moore in the London Underground in 1943 during a re-creation of the wartime scene for a film, *Out of Chaos*.

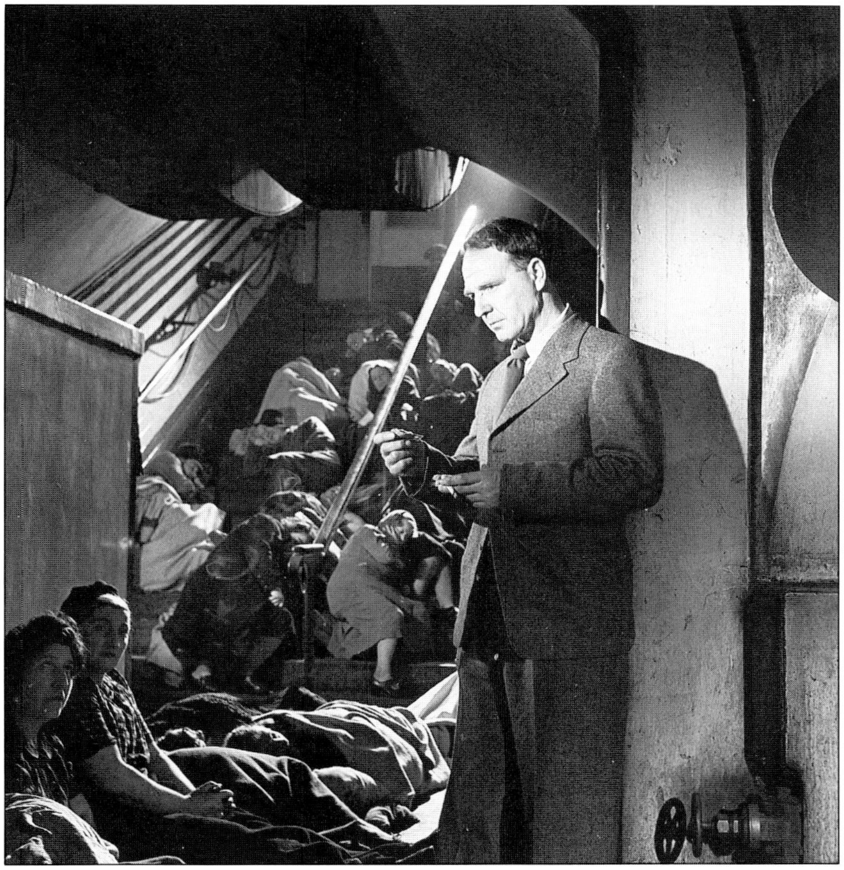

The most perceptive review of the 1947-48 Moore exhibition, that came from the United States and visited every Australian state apart from Queensland and the Northern Territory, was by Bernard Smith, originally published in *Hermes*, the University of Sydney magazine, and reprinted in his recent book *The Critic as Advocate*.[9] He referred to 'The Sculptor's Aims', an article by Moore published in *Unit One* in 1934;[10] the first point Moore made was the necessity for the sculptor to be true to the material, that stone for example 'should keep its hard tense stoniness'.[11] Smith disagreed, arguing that 'as soon as a sculptor begins to carve or model in his material he begins to invest that material with values it did not possess before . . . he is always turning his material from what it is to what he wants it to be. Indeed the sceptic may suggest that the best way to allow a piece of stone to be true to its material is to leave it alone'.[12] Smith believed Moore's development in artistic stature was achieved through his ability to modify in practice his sculptural precepts, and that during the war years 'his art leapt suddenly to the challenge of a human situation that had never before found expression in art, and his work achieved greatness where before it had only achieved perfection'.[13] He was referring to the Shelter drawings which combined 'formal perfection with direct social relevance'.[14]

The British Council brought this review to Moore's attention, and he requested a meeting with Smith who was in England at the time. Smith visited Perry Green, the artist's home in Hertfordshire, on 18 January 1949. His diary entry recalls Moore as a down-to-earth Yorkshireman at one with his surroundings, with an inner sense of direction and an awareness of his ability to communicate it through his work. Moore was, incidentally, repairing a sculpture damaged on the recent overseas exhibition tour. An interesting point made to Smith at the time by Moore, the public artist, was that he 'felt it desirable to accept official commissions such as the 1944 *Madonna and Child* (cat. 71) for the church of St Matthew, Northampton, every so often, because the artist could then seek to create a true compromise between his own personal vision and the popular taste'.[15]

The 1963 exhibition *Recent British Sculpture* was dominated not by the five Henry Moores[16] but by Kenneth Armitage, Eduardo Paolozzi and other younger sculptors; but whenever major purchases were made, particularly by the public galleries and National Capital Development Commission, Moore's name again came to the fore in Australia. There are a number of important works in public collections that should be named. The Australian National Gallery possesses the monumental bronze *Hill Arches* 1973 (LH 636; see cat. 139), on display in the sculpture garden, and the smaller *Head of a Girl* (LH 56) made in plaster of 1928. The National Gallery of Victoria has the monumental bronze *Draped Seated Woman* 1957-58 (LH 428) as well as a bronze *Family Group* 1947 (LH 267) and a key work of 1930, *Half-Figure* (LH 91) in Ancaster stone, the first public gallery purchase in Australia through the Felton Bequest in 1948. Eric Westbrook, Director of the National Gallery when *Draped Seated Woman* was purchased, had mounted one of the first Moore retrospectives as Director of Wakefield City Art Gallery in 1949. In 1951, when with the British Council, Westbrook took the first of Moore's exhibitions to Athens and visited Olympia with the artist. The Art Gallery of South Australia owns *Seated Figure against Curved Wall* 1956-57 (LH 422), the Art Gallery of Western Australia has the large bronze *Reclining Figure* 1956 (LH 402), Queensland Art Gallery possesses a cast of *Maquette for Reclining Figure: Prop* 1975 (cat.164) and the Art Gallery of New South Wales has the large bronze *Reclining Figure: Angles* (cat.163) located in front of the building and *Helmet Head No. 2* (cat.90) in bronze. These two works form part of this exhibition, as do two drawings from the Gallery's collection, including the remarkable 1933 *Reclining Figure: Drawing for Sculpture* (cat.30). The large bronze *Two Piece Reclining Figure No.9* 1968 (LH 576) sits on the National Library Terrace in Canberra, and the University of Adelaide has *Reclining Connected Forms* 1969 (LH 612). A number of drawings add to these holdings in public collections, and there are several works of sculpture and some drawings in private hands. The Sydney gallery owner Rex Irwin, an advocate of Moore, has been responsible through his exhibitions for the availability of some of the important privately owned works.

William Ohly, a friend of Henry Moore, owned after the war the Abbey Arts Centre in Cockfosters near London which became a residential centre for artists and writers including Australians such as Robert Klippel, James Gleeson, Noel Counihan, Leonard French, Bernard Smith and Inge King. Ohly also ran the Berkeley Galleries in London where Klippel first set eyes on Moore bronzes in 1947. Moore often visited The Abbey where he saw the work of Klippel and Gleeson, both of whom he invited to Perry Green for New Year's Day 1948. Klippel was a close friend of the Tasmanian-born sculptor Oliffe Richmond, the first Australian assistant, in 1948-49, to Henry Moore. He apparently was such a good carver that the *Time/Life Screen* panel (see cat.100) he had worked on needed to have the edges roughed up by Moore. Richmond was followed as assistant from 1949 to 1953 by the New Zealander Alan Ingham, who also worked on a *Time/Life* panel as well as the *Reclining Figure: Festival* (see cat.92), *Helmet Head No. 2* (cat.90) and *King and Queen* (cat.101). He also experimented with Moore in bronze casting and was responsible for installing a foundry at Perry Green. Anthony Caro was a fellow assistant and Ingham remembers them adapting a music hall song that began 'Don't have any more, Mrs Moore' to 'Don't do any more, Mr Moore, or else you'll have to rent the house next door'. Moore's other Australian assistants were Owen Broughton 1950, Stephen Walker 1953-54, Daryl Hill 1954, Lenton Parr 1955-56, Neil Stocker 1960-62, Ron Robertson-Swann 1963-65, Graham Gilchrist 1968-70, who worked on the enlarging of *Oval with Points* (cat.130), and Tom Fantl 1977-78. Ron Robertson-Swann felt that Moore liked the Australians because they were hard working, honest and direct, and had a sense of humour. Stephen Walker agreed the Australians worked hard, as they generally had a limited time and wanted to make the most of it. From my discussions with Moore's assistants it is clear they learned considerably from the experience and each described a variety of personal and generally warm memories, but it was Lenton Parr who so aptly summed up Moore's professional achievement. 'He was', Parr said, 'the last of the great humanist artists from the Greek and Roman eras through the Renaissance to this century.'[17]

It is difficult to gauge the impact, during Henry Moore's lifetime, of his ideas and work on this country and its artists, though it would appear to be less than for instance in the United States, Canada, Europe and Japan, where his work achieved enormous prominence and his ideas held considerable sway. But Charles Wilmot, the British Council's chief representative here during the 1947-48 exhibition, wrote that it 'had been an inspiration to Australian artists',[18] which undoubtedly it was. (It also produced a cartoon by Molnar that became a favourite of the artist.) As a result of the exhibition and during the 1950s Moore's influence was pervasive, and Lyndon Dadswell was one artist who clearly revealed the former's traces, as did Oliffe Richmond who was living in England. But each emerged to establish his own identity, in particular Richmond with his later pieces in wood. Although artists like Robert Klippel and many others were inspired by the seemingly extreme modernist position adopted by Moore's sculpture at a time of considerable conservatism in Australia, almost none chose to tread a similar path.

DAILY TELEGRAPH · 8TH DECEMBER 1947

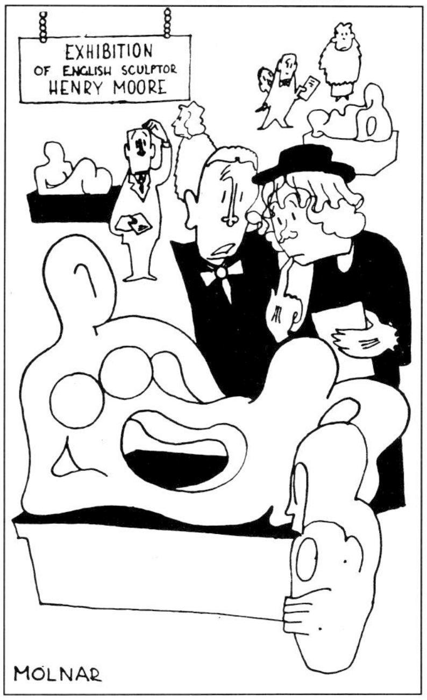

'This reminds me, dear. Did you post our Christmas food parcels to Aunt Matilda?'

The bulk of the Australian assistants to Moore did not emerge as followers though they undoubtedly gained a great deal from his presence. Lenton Parr, for instance, felt that Moore was such a remarkable composer of figures and such a master of the materials he chose to use, that he himself could not compete in these areas and so moved towards the non-representational use of steel. (He also remembered a New Zealand press article in 1956 headed 'Moore – Genius or Madman?' reaching Perry Green, much to Moore's amusement. Auckland's mayor said, 'I have never seen the art gallery so desecrated by such a nauseating sight'[19] – which must have contributed greatly to the attendances at the exhibition.) Stephen Walker and Ron Robertson-Swann, in very different ways and for quite different reasons, developed ideas that Moore's work did not propagate, as had Caro and his contemporary Phillip King, who had also been assistants to Moore. It was King and Caro who later recommended Robertson-Swann for this same position.

On the broader front the promotion of Moore by the mother country as her most brilliant artist since Constable and Turner as well as the world's greatest sculptor brought out a colonial cussedness and a feigned lack of interest. Now, almost six years after Henry Moore's death, this exhibition makes it possible for the depth and breadth of his important vision to find sufficient resonance here for a lasting response. Now his work can be approached directly, in all its variety and its intimacy, less obscured by the aura created around its maker.

There are many reasons, I believe, why his work and its sources need to be actively present in Australia today. The first derives from Lenton Parr's summing up of Moore. He beyond all other sculptors of this century – and I think for example of Brancusi, Arp, Giacometti, Hepworth, Calder, David Smith, Noguchi and Caro – drew together the consequential elements of the primitive, the classical and the modern and united them in a complete and resolved way and from the perspective of a humanist. His work reminds us, at a time when much art addresses only a limited audience, that there remain subjects of common human interest that are far from exhausted, as it also does at a time of questioning cultural identity, that vital aspects of our shared cultural origins live and are not only relevant but are also of use today. The second is the inspiration derived from sharing Moore's constant search for meaning, ranging from the intimate and deeply personal experience to the universal, and also from the way in which he carefully selected those materials best suited to the subject and from which emerged the form most fully expressive of his perception. The third is his ability to overcome narrative, transcend the specific but maintain the essence, indeed the spirit, of the subject whether it be mother and child, reclining figure, warrior, animal, ancient monument, natural or organic form. Fourthly, his work vitally reminds us, in an increasingly materialistic, mechanistic and spiritually valueless society, of links with what Carl Jung termed the 'collective unconscious'. Moore wrote: 'There are universal shapes to which everybody is subconsciously conditioned and to which they can respond if their conscious control does not shut them off'.[20]

Moore in his own words created a 'common world language of form' to express his belief that 'art is a universal activity with no separation between past and present'.[21] He also triumphantly created a life's work that brings to the attention of so many people in so many parts of the world timeless forms that make sense of our short span on this troubled earth.

Henry Moore: The Deeper Reality

SUSAN COMPTON

Henry Moore is the sculptor who has done most to recreate our awareness of the human image in the twentieth century. We instantly recognise a figure by Moore, be it a monumental bronze or a tiny study in terracotta, a sketch or a finished drawing. His preferred subject was the human form, usually female, and he was constantly imagining Woman afresh, penetrating her inner secrets that had lain unrecognised by sculptors of the past. Whether we live in Australia, Japan, America or Britain his idiom is accessible now to all. Yet this was not always the case. In order to arrive at a new vision at the begininng of his career Moore had to turn away from the models held up to art students in Britain in the 1920s – sculpture from classical times and from the Renaissance. He responded more deeply to the gravity and universality that he found in other carvings in the British Museum, where he spent much of his free time. There he studied works which were not always considered by his teachers to be art, but simply objects, placed in the museum as a record of cultures with little relevance to their own. These carvings convinced Moore that in recent times sculptors had debased their art by making it superficially lifelike – he wanted a return to 'truth to material' where stone looked like stone and not like flesh. When he first saw two reliefs from the eleventh century in Chichester cathedral he described them as just what he wanted 'to emulate in sculpture: the strength of directly carved form, of hard stone, rather than modelled flowing soft form'.[1]

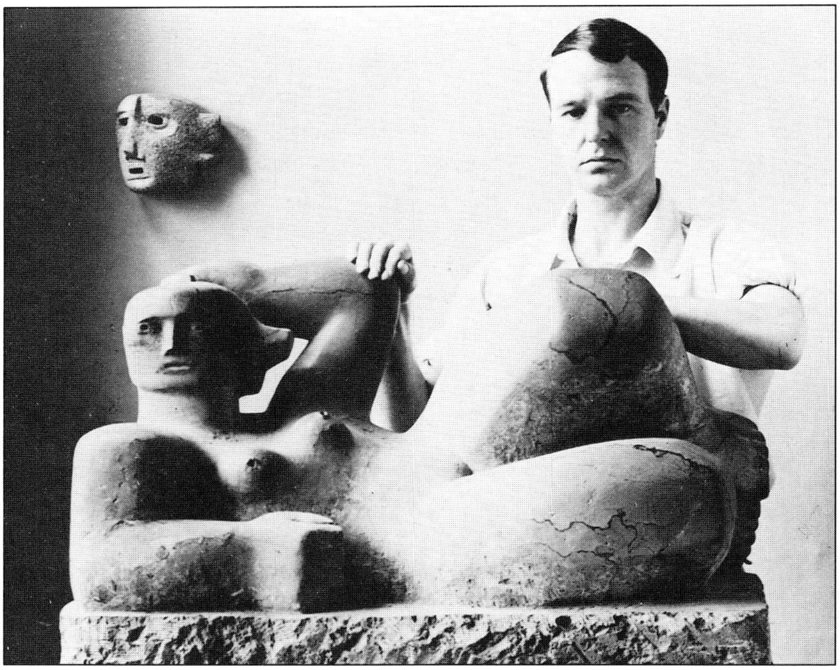

Henry Moore in his studio *c.*1930 with **Reclining Figure** 1929; on the wall is **Mask** 1930.

NOTES FOR THIS ESSAY MAY BE FOUND ON PAGE 208

Surprisingly, perhaps, in order to achieve his aim Moore began from the human form, painstakingly observed: his early drawings confirm his close attention to the model posing in the studio in all its three-dimensional reality. Later he began to draw more inventive compositions, capable of furthering his new approach to sculpture. Some of his early carvings are directly inspired by pre-Columbian, Sumerian or Egyptian art, but, whereas the ancient figures are static, Moore added a subtle turn of the head or twist of the torso (cats.18, 19, 20). Each one shows a different facet of his struggle to create a new monumental language in which the material remained true to itself; each figure receives its vitality from the tradition of the distant past. Among the sculptors of his day he admired the work of Constantin Brancusi, a Romanian who had settled in Paris and was renowned for his simple, effective images, especially of birds and heads. Moore said that Brancusi made us 'shape-conscious', though he felt his own generation could 'begin to open out. To relate and combine together several forms of varied sizes, sections and directions into one organic whole'.[2] His two small heads (cat.17) can be seen as an attempt to build on the foundations of Brancusi and ancient Cycladic art (which he had admired in the British Museum). *Woman with Upraised Arms* (cat.9) gives a strong sense of the stoniness of a block of stone; she seems to draw inspiration from a distant era when humans were more directly in touch with Nature.

Today we perceive these carvings as the early work of a gifted sculptor, and it is hard to understand why, when Moore began to exhibit in London, his suitability as an art teacher was questioned – it was seriously suggested that he might corrupt the young. As a result, he felt obliged to resign his post at the Royal College of

Art,[3] but this freedom enabled him to make far more radical inventions in the 1930s. His new creations – of which cat.31 is one of the most extreme – were, however, equally misunderstood and ridiculed in London by all but a few individuals. Those who appreciated Moore's inventions had already accepted the changes that Picasso and others had brought about in art in Paris, and Moore himself soon became interested in Surrealism, a movement that provided artists and writers with a new approach to the act of creation, derived from their interest in psychoanalysis.

Psychology – especially its implications for art – was very widely discussed by writers and artists in Western Europe in the 1920s and 1930s. Sigmund Freud's assertion that dreams, jokes and errors ('Freudian slips') are a key to the unconscious mind provided Surrealist artists with tools for creation; Carl Jung's recognition of a universal world of archetypal images and a collective unconscious allowed artists new interpretations of ancient myths. Instead of planning a work of art in advance, the Surrealist preferred to allow the unconscious mind free play: by loosening the control of the conscious intellect, art could be formed by automatism rather than choice, doodle rather than deliberation. Unusual objects often provided the artist with a starting point: a new form (a 'chimera') came into being by the substitution of one thing for another.

The creative possibilities of this method evidently intrigued Moore, though he did not commit himself entirely to Surrealism or to his subconscious mind. In the 1930s he worked as relentlessly as he had done in the previous decade, covering pages of sketchbooks with ideas for sculpture. A bone or a pebble could give him a starting point, its shape leading him to new ways of imagining the human form (cats.25, 26). His favourite subjects were already the Reclining Figure and the Mother and Child because they gave him a subject devoid of storytelling, though he did not remain content with their familiar appearance – even mediated through older forms of art. He sensed the wholeness of Creation. The evolution of life captured his imagination: the relationship of mother and child required an earlier stage, the womb, the foetus and, before that, the egg. Diagrams from human anatomy books suggested to Moore free ways of interpreting the cavities of the Reclining Figure. He now began linking his renderings of mankind – considered the highest form of life – to life in some of its most primitive aspects. He delved into biology textbooks to find the simplest of organic forms. Nevertheless, his arrangement of these elements retained strong allusions to heads, arms, bodies and legs, so that the resulting sculpture – however incomplete and distorted – marries our awareness of the material in which it is made with our recognition of the human state. We may be hard pressed to see beyond the stone in a carving such as cat.32, but we instinctively identify the two forms of cat. 37 as related to the heads of a Mother and Child.

We can more easily appreciate Moore's vision today than was possible half a century ago because we feel less threatened by it. With our new interest in the totality of Creation and our minds fed by television films about natural history we can follow him in his attempt to convey the life force which underlies all organic Creation. For Moore, this was not an abstract idea but a concrete reality: he saw a wholeness in Nature denied to those who set out simply to make a represention of the externals of ideal human beauty. In the 1930s, when totalitarian regimes were idolising the physical perfection of athletes and 'ideal man', he was exploring Nature in all her manifestations, including her imperfections which he transformed into a new kind of beauty. We may remember a stanza by T.S. Eliot, first published in 1936: 'Out of the formless stone, when the artist unites himself with stone,/ Spring always new forms of life, from the soul of man that is joined to the soul of stone;/ Out of the meaningless practical shapes of all that is living or lifeless/ Joined with the artist's eye, new life, new form, new colour'.[4] Moore rejected the dualism which pervaded culture in the West, where mind and body, spirit and matter, life and death, inner and outer, have been seen as direct opposites for so many centuries. It is only in recent years that we have begun to understand the interrelationship of the part and the whole; we are gradually becoming aware of a lack of wholeness in our own lives and in our world. Now we are astonished that Moore was able with such foresight to create sculptural equivalents of the human body, which reflect our physiological shortcomings and our psychological incompleteness and at the same time link the human form with Nature in her entirety – even the very rocks themselves.

Moore's way of working became more direct in the later 1930s when he acquired a small cottage in the countryside adjoined by a large area of rough grass, which formed a landscape in miniature. There he placed stones, brought from a quarry far away, setting them upright in the ground; he then made drawings in which he imagined how he would carve them (cat.39). At the same time he began to photograph his small models (maquettes) in silhouette against the landscape; the

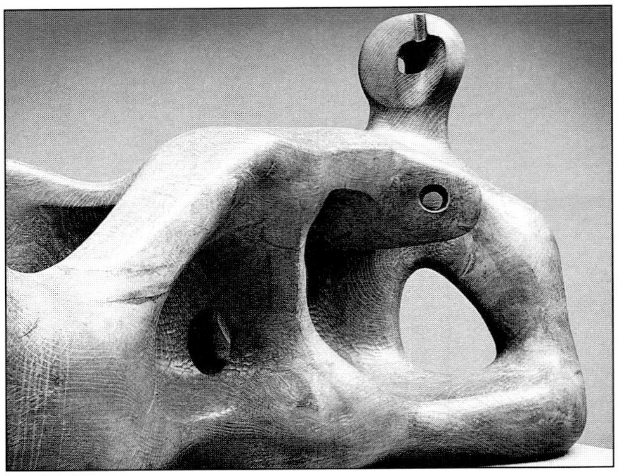

Reclining Figure 1939 (LH 210) carved in elm wood.

resulting print gave him an idea of how the tiny figure would look if he chose to enlarge it (cat.76). A rare sheet of drawings (cat.43) shows that he was already thinking about precise places for his work – at the base of the page one compartment is inscribed: 'Setting for sculpture – in orchard'. Moore also began a dialogue with Nature herself, for he labelled another compartment: 'wide expanse of sky' and yet another, 'Sheep or cows in field as background perhaps for sculpture'.

With hindsight it is easier to connect the last statement with Moore's sculptures from the 1970s – one of which he named *Sheep Piece* (see cat.138) – but in the 1930s he had already been asked by an architect to make a figure for a particular outdoor setting. This was a terrace from which there was a panoramic view of grass-covered hills, the South Downs in Sussex. The final carving in green Hornton stone (see below; today in the Tate Gallery, London) closely resembles the preliminary maquette exhibited (cat.47). We can recognise Moore's figure as a reclining woman because of its head-like form balanced on shoulders and breasts, though her thickened arms are joined to the hips and there is a large hole where we would expect to find the womb. In the original setting, where the stone figure endlessly contemplated the distant hills and valleys, she appeared to echo the contours of the landscape and belong to the Earth as much as to the human race.

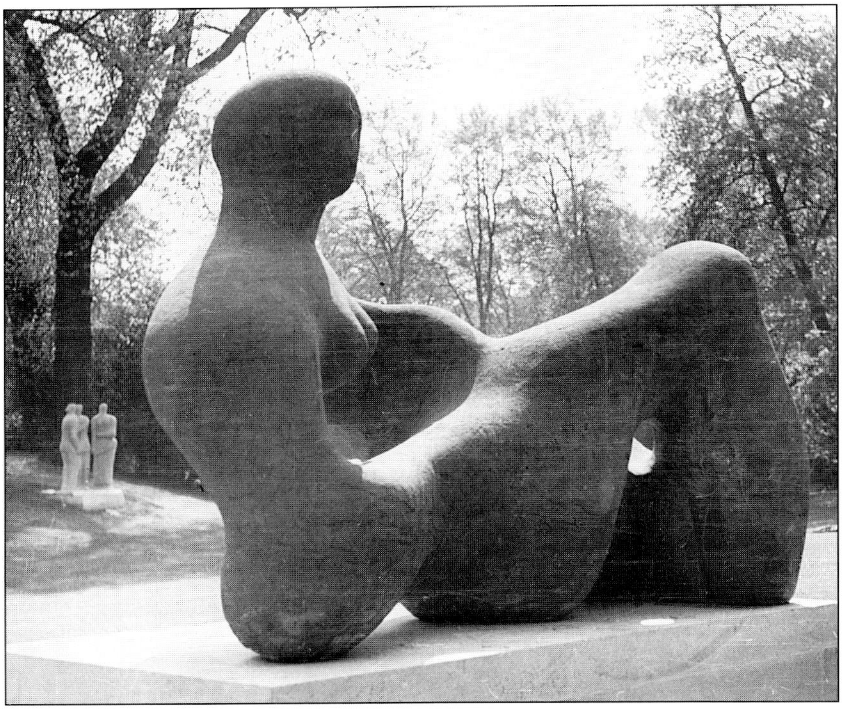

Recumbent Figure 1938 (LH 191) photographed in Battersea Gardens, London, with **Three Standing Figures** 1947-48 (LH 268) in the background.

Alongside connections with Nature the figure has mythical qualities, for, while engaged in creating her, Moore seems to have pondered on Creation as described poetically in the Bible. As he worked with clay to form the maquette he may have known that the verb chosen in Hebrew for God's creation of man is the one used to describe the potter's working with clay. The Hebrew word for mankind (*Adam*) is very close to the word for red earth (*Adamah*) and the story of Creation told in the first two chapters of the Book of Genesis emphasises that man and woman are a part of Nature and responsible for looking after the world. We can perhaps imagine Moore's mythical woman as the fleshing out of Adam's rib as told in the story of the creation of Eve. The biblical connection is strengthened by a second figure from the same year (cat.48) in which Moore carved a breast-like form that doubles as the head of Eve's tempter, the Serpent. The version shown here is the maquette for a large elmwood carving (see above; now in the Detroit Institute of Arts); it was destined for an indoor site, a round-headed niche, so its cave-like body provides its own mysterious spaces instead of suggesting the hollows of a natural landscape.

During the late 1930s Moore's work remained highly inventive and he had numerous ideas for sculpture, including the powerful stringed figures discussed elsewhere in this book (see p.51). But at the same time there seemed to be a danger of a sort of sterility: his art risked becoming an art for its own sake. He was rescued from this potential impasse by the outbreak of war in Europe in 1939, the fall of France in 1940, and the bombing raids which began nightly to destroy London. The threat of invasion was real and his house in the country was perilously near the coast of Kent; his studio in London was damaged by bombs. In the confusion of 1940, when carving became impractical, he unexpectedly came upon new subject matter. He took the Underground train home late one night and saw the station platforms being used as shelters from the air raids. Huddled together and enveloped in blankets were figures, seated and lying on the platforms in scenes which inspired him to make powerful drawings. He felt he could not stand on the platform and draw people sleeping but he spent many hours watching them and making notes, finding that he could restore a degree of realism both to his figures and drapery. Indeed, Moore later said that the experience of contemplating these innocent victims of warfare revived a humanist viewpoint in his art. He was no stranger to the dangers of war himself, for he had been fortunate not to lose his sight when, as a young soldier during the First World War, he was gassed in the trenches of northern France before ever he went to art school. The drawings of shelterers in the Underground, which he made in 1940-42 as an Official War Artist, are among his best-known images; he combined wax crayons and water colour, pen and ink and gouache in compositions which convey the comradely spirit of people facing a common danger during those fearful nights. When an exhibition of Moore's work was held in 1941 at the National Gallery in London, on walls bare of its historical treasures (sent away for safe keeping out of reach of bombs), his drawings captured the spirit of the moment so well that the public – usually wary of modern art – took the artist to its heart.

Madonna and Child
1943-44 in
St Matthew's church,
Northampton.

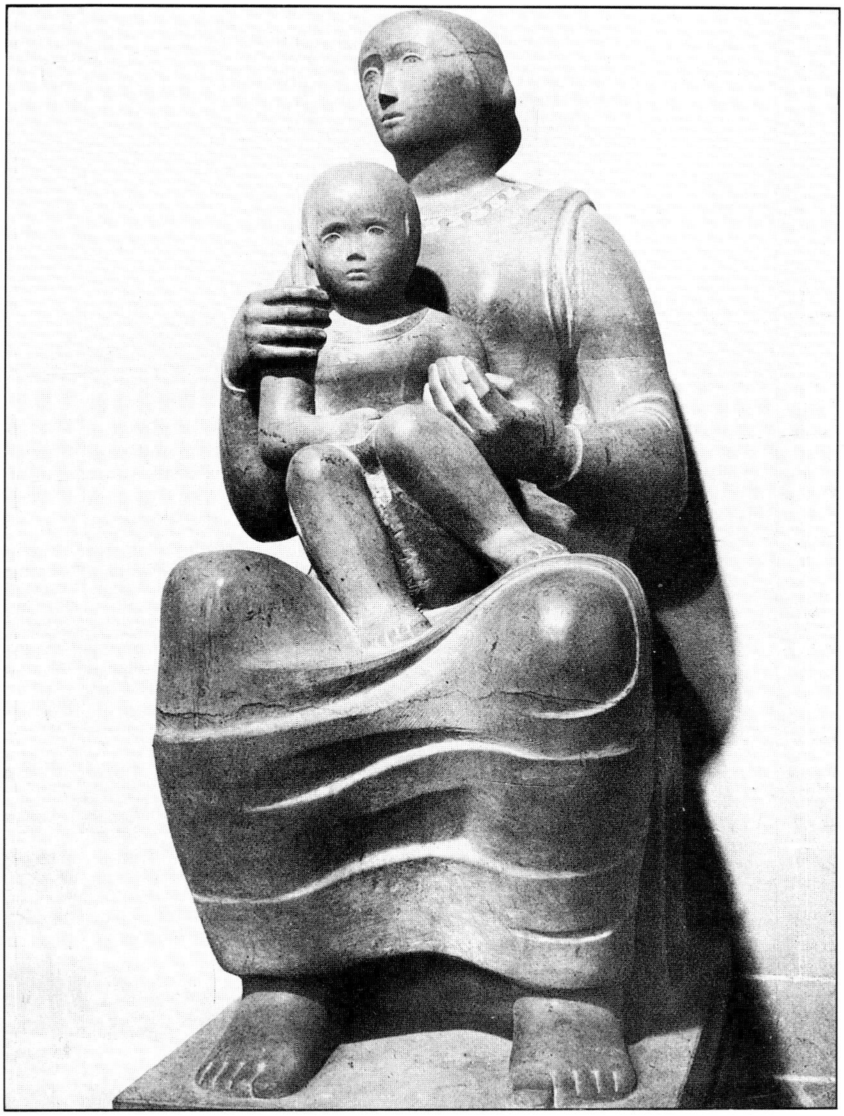

At this time Moore was invited to carve a Madonna and Child for St Matthew's church, Northampton, and thus found himself addressing one of the most celebrated images of Western sculpture, which, in its basic form of Mother and Child, had fascinated him for twenty years. In 1944 he listed differences which seemed to him to distinguish a Madonna and Child from its non-religious counterpart: he felt that 'austerity and nobility' and even 'grandeur' were the necessary qualities for the religious image; he made a number of small models, and the second of the two included here (cats.70, 71) he deemed to have the appropriate 'quiet dignity and gentleness'.[5] Unlike a great deal of his earlier work the resulting Northampton *Madonna and Child* 1943-44 (LH 226) makes the viewer aware that Moore belongs firmly in the tradition of Western sculpture. Today it is more acceptable than it seemed when first installed in the church, when it was criticised for being distorted, even irreverent. The degree of representation in this group is exceptional, and when, in 1949, Moore was asked to carve a Family Group symbolic of discovery for the forthcoming Festival of Britain,[6] although he had already worked on the theme of the Family (cats.58, 72, 73, 74, 85) he submitted instead his own 'discovery' in the form of the *Reclining Figure*: *Festival* (overleaf; see cat.92). This does not resemble a figure as we can see it, but its bone-like structure and cave-like spaces symbolise the uneasy years following the end of the war as surely as the Shelter drawings had symbolised the war itself. Moore captured the prevailing need to rethink the basis of Western civilisation, which had been so deeply challenged by the war and the grim revelations of destruction of peoples and cities after the cessation of hostilities. A mood of uncertainty bordering on fear continues in drawings such as cat.84, in which the two figures reflect the new threat of nuclear warfare.

The humanism that Moore had rediscovered in the depths of wartime was not entirely lost to him when in 1953 he made *Draped Reclining Figure* (cat.96).

Drapery had played an important role in the Shelter drawings, cocooning the figures inside the tunnels, but he now found a connection between drapery and the landscape. He connected the 'folds, here small, fine and delicate, in other places big and heavy, with the form of mountains, which are the crinkled skin of the earth.'[7] He was here taking up an idea originally put forward by Henri Gaudier-Brzeska (the young French-born sculptor who had worked for a few years in Britain before being killed in the trenches in 1915), whose work had influenced Moore's early carving of *Dog* (cat.3). Gaudier had insisted that 'sculptural energy is the mountain', and Moore came increasingly to identify literally with this quotation[8] and to integrate his own figures with his experience of Nature, more particularly of the landscape. The culmination was the invention of two- and three-part reclining figures at the very end of the decade. Before then, he explored themes which had germinated in the late 1930s but had been put aside because of the war. One of the most fruitful was one form enclosed by another – to be seen in the 1938 drawing *Sculptural Ideas: Hollow Form* (cat.42), and in the 1940 sculpture *The Helmet* (cat.56). Ten years later Moore made more Helmet Heads (cats.89, 90), again with the interior unrelated to the protective exterior; he went on to develop the theme in the *Upright Internal/External Form* (LH 297a; see cat.93). Although the concept may seem 'abstract', the latter sculpture has an affinity to an Egyptian mummy in its case, to the soft part and shell of a mollusc, or even to a child in the womb. Moore openly suggested the last relationship in his drawing for sculpture (cat.88) though in the final work he made no concession to male or female. None the less, one writer identified *Upright Internal /External Form* as an illustration of the human being – the 'container and the contained, mother and child, body and soul', taking the analogy even further by describing the internal form as the psyche – the distinguishing mark of humans, the mind, soul, or spirit itself.[9]

The plaster for **Reclining Figure: Festival** 1951 (LH 293), photographed by the artist

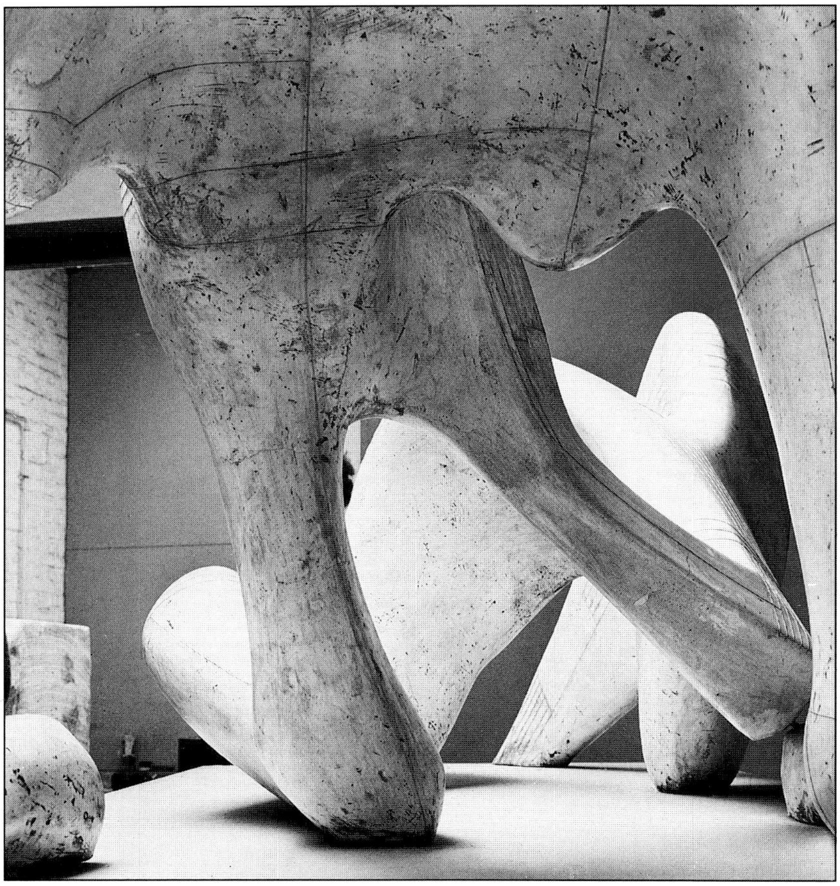

This interpretation, made by a Jungian analyst, may seem exaggerated. Indeed, the writer devoted his book to finding links between Moore's work and the collective unconscious and its universal myths. He noticed the conjunction of three figures – to be seen in the first compartment of the etching *Figures in Settings* (cat.86) – and he identified them with the Three Fates of ancient Greek myth. Such an interest, however, has to do with Moore's studying Greek mythology rather than tapping into a collective unconscious. In the 1940s he made illustrations for a 'modern Odyssey' by the poet Edward Sackville-West,[10] and a few years later he made a set of etchings based on the story of Prometheus as told by Goethe.[11] His interest continued, for he named a head 'Cyclops' (cat.123) in the 1960s, and when in the 1980s a tapestry was made from an earlier drawing he named it *Three Fates* (cat.184).

As a result, possibly, of thinking about Greek mythology and of a visit to Greece in 1951, Moore turned in the 1950s to the male figure on its own. His *Fallen Warrior* (see cat.103) is one of three Warriors made at the time, though he returned to the theme in the early 1970s when he was invited to provide a monumental sculpture for a public site in the German town of Goslar (see cat.151). His Warriors are never victorious – their only weapon is a shield, they are forever caught on the defensive, they stand as allegories of the failure of brute strength. Indeed, his male figures are emasculated: he remained uncertain about representing the male sexual organ (so often hidden by fig-leaves in Western sculpture). It is barely present in his figures of Warriors and other figures that we read as 'male', such as the taller of the *Two Three-Quarter Figures on Base* (cat.127) and the *Male Torso* (cat.176) of 1980.

Moore drew Man when he chose, for instance at top left of a page of sketchbook studies (cat.83) for wooden figures. The Man is, however, insignificant in comparison with the central bone-like form that we read as the trunk of a human figure, but above the head of the figure on the right (apparently a female) he has drawn a curious device which reminds us of a penis, a fish, a serpent, or, perhaps, an airship. Such substitutions are typical of Surrealist art. Working under the influence of Freud, Surrealists often invented visual metaphors that verge on fetishism, the theory being that the brain excludes certain things because they are too dangerous, so the artist represents them by means of forms that are analogous in appearance. Moore's metaphors are usually different – we have already met his use of a Helmet as a head and seen the complex relationship of his figures to bones and stones. In the 1950s the resemblance to stones was more important to the artist than any consideration of 'maleness' as such: the genesis of the seated *Warrior with Shield* (LH 360) was a found object, a flint, and another stone, barely transformed, provided the head of the King in cat.101; yet another provided the *Animal Head* (cat.94). These transformations are more like magic than fetishism – Moore worked less in the vein of Surrealism than in an English tradition. His antecedents are found in the eighteenth-century watercolourist Alexander Cozens, who generated imaginery landscapes from blots on his paper, or the visionary artist and poet William Blake, who obtained colour and texture by pressing one painted sheet of paper upon another before the first had dried. Like Moore, these artists celebrate the totality of Nature instead of avoiding dangerous areas. Moore's males do not flaunt their sexuality: he chose a defensive Warrior as a symbol of non-aggression not of sexual impotence.

In the 1950s Moore explored several alternative sources for his art. He returned to antiquity with the

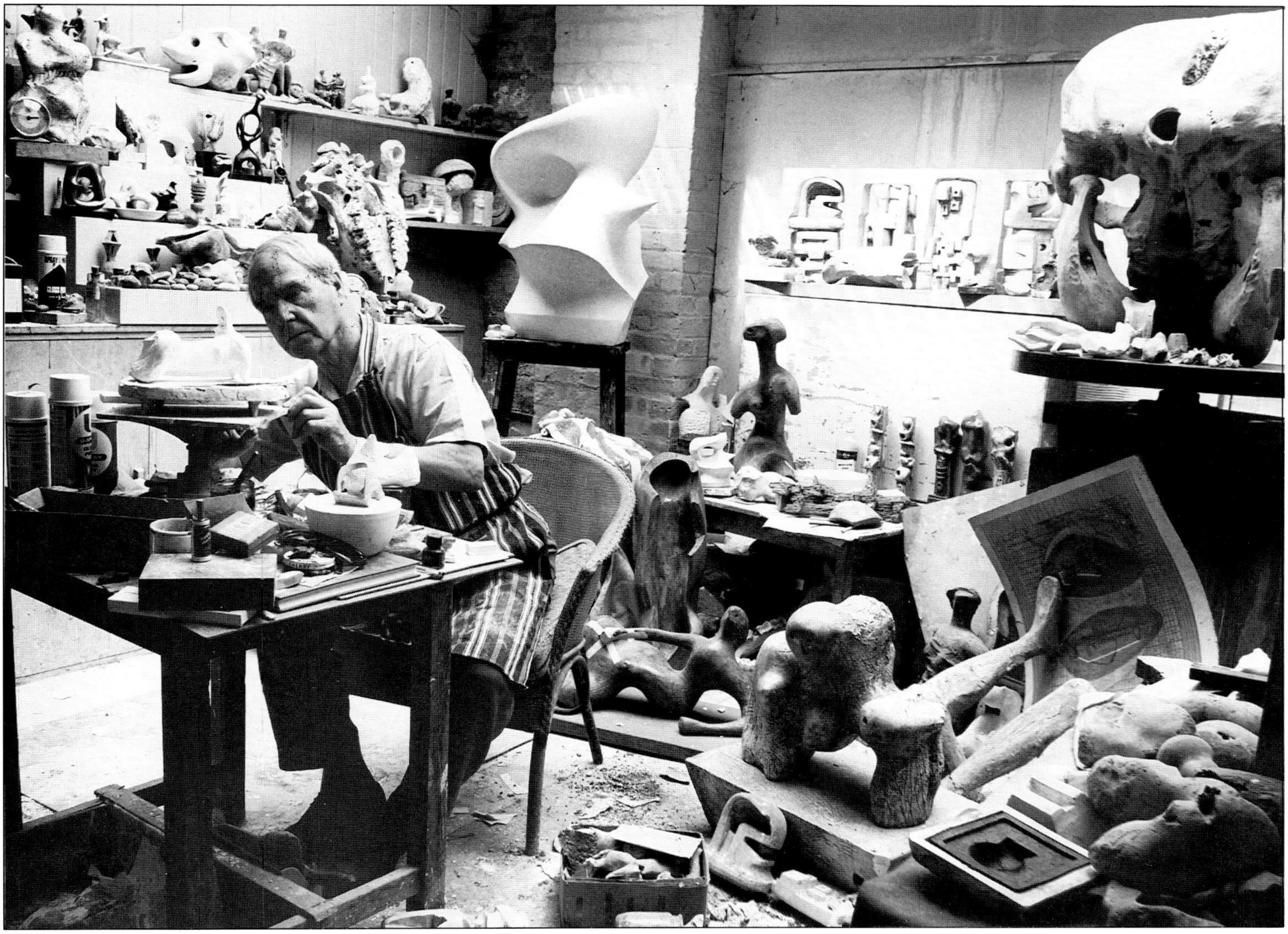

Henry Moore in his maquette studio at Perry Green, *c.*1968. Several of the works in this exhibition may be seen, as maquettes or working models. Note, for example (left to right), **Maquette for Oval with Points** 1968 (LH 594; see cat.130); **Working Model for Spindle Piece** 1968-69 (LH 592) and its maquette (cat.129) below it on the right; **Working Model for Time/ Life Screen** (cat.100); and the elephant skull from which Moore made the etchings cats.134-7.

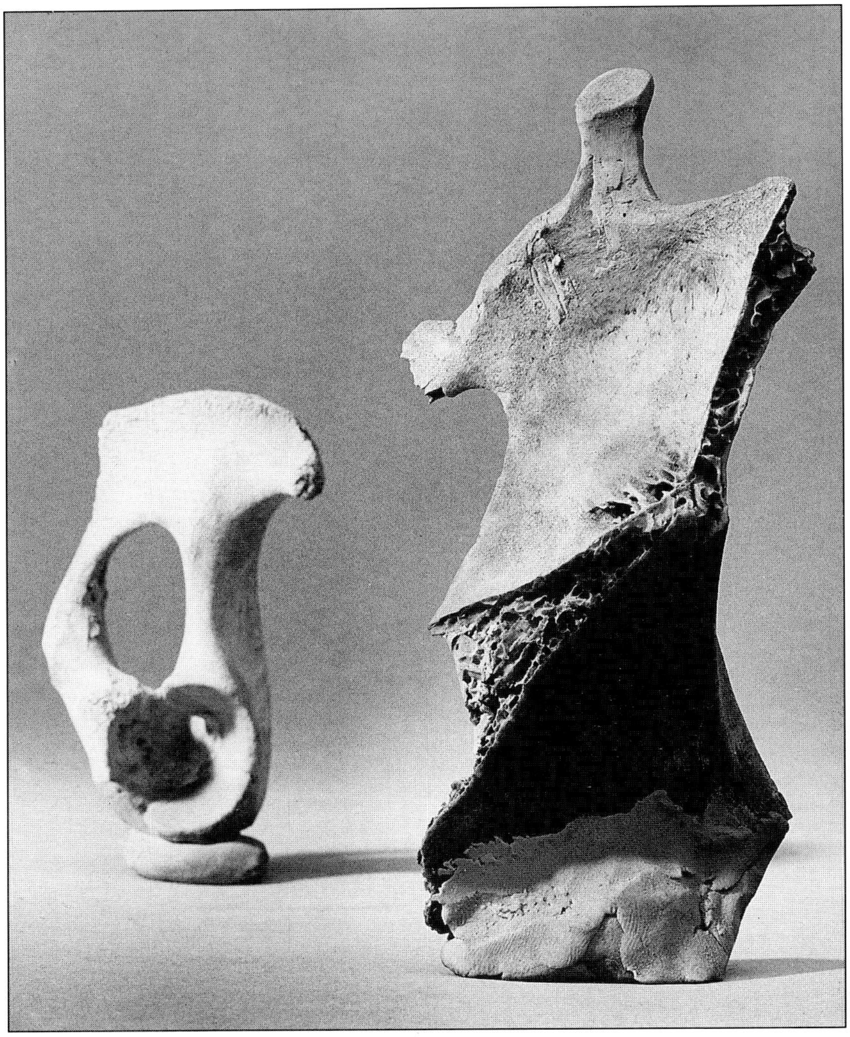

The genesis of **Standing Figure**: **Knife Edge** can clearly be seen here.

Mother and Child (cat.95) that he based on a 'found object' – the design incised on a Peruvian pot in a book of photographs that he owned.[12] He excused his unlikely transformation of the original design (a bird-headed man holding out a bird-headed stick to a fish with a large, devouring mouth) into a voracious child attacking a breast by saying that he was conditioned to seeing the Mother and Child in everything; this image may be so untypical of his work because it was in some sense filtered through contemporary paintings by Picasso. In another search for a new way forward he named one of his Reclining Figures (cat.104) after the sixteenth-century French sculptor Jean Goujon, as though trying to discover whether Renaissance sculpture could, after all, be revitalised in the twentieth century.

The final victor was natural form, the stones and bones that had proved such an inspiration in the 1930s. At the very end of the decade Moore made the dramatic discovery that his Reclining Figures could truly become a part of Nature if he allowed them more closely to resemble the natural weathered forms of the rocky coastline. On at least one occasion in the 1930s Moore had used barely altered pebbles to suggest two small figures (LH 146) but in the 1960s he allowed unaltered flints to give forms for casting into maquettes (cats.110, 113) from which he made enlargements. In his small maquette studio, with shelves round the walls to hold his sculptures, there were collections of 'raw material', especially flints, whose complex shape is very different from the smooth stones of the shoreline that Moore had preferred in the 1930s. He liked to use flints complete: he would hold them in his hands and study them from all angles and then – barely altering them – arrange them in twos or threes to form a new kind of Reclining Figure. The final sculpture thus came directly from Nature – the artist serving as an alchemist to effect the all-important change of scale as well as the change from stone to bronze. In a decade when Feminism was making new headway Moore's rock-like figures were a reminder that the idea of a 'Mother Earth' underlies our culture; in the decade of Marilyn Monroe and Pop Art his work remained timeless, unaffected by fashion.

He discovered that he could bypass the intermediate stage of making drawings to record the transition to human form and work directly with the material itself. The most dramatic transformation is the *Standing Figure: Knife Edge* (LH 482a; see cat.114) which derives from a small piece of shoulder-blade bone to which Moore added only enough material to make a base to keep it upright and to form a head. The resulting enlargement is so effective that his sculpture has been compared to the ancient *Winged Victory* that stands in Paris on the grand staircase of the Louvre. His transformations remained poetic: Moore had been a poet before he became an artist (though none of his poetry has survived); in the 'modern Odyssey' that he had illustrated in 1945, the role of the Poet is described by Sackville-West as 'a mysterious timelessness, the knife edge balance between being and not being, which only the poetic imagination seems able to achieve.'[13] Moore's choice of 'Knife Edge' in the title of his Standing Figure gives us a clue to understanding the metamorphosis of a piece of bone into a figure: it is the artist-poet's imagination that reveals a 'balance between being and not being' with a 'mysterious timelessness' and permits us to find an analogy between his sculpture based on bone and the *Winged Victory*.

Other sculptures from the 1960s are unrelated to the human figure and these serve more directly as a

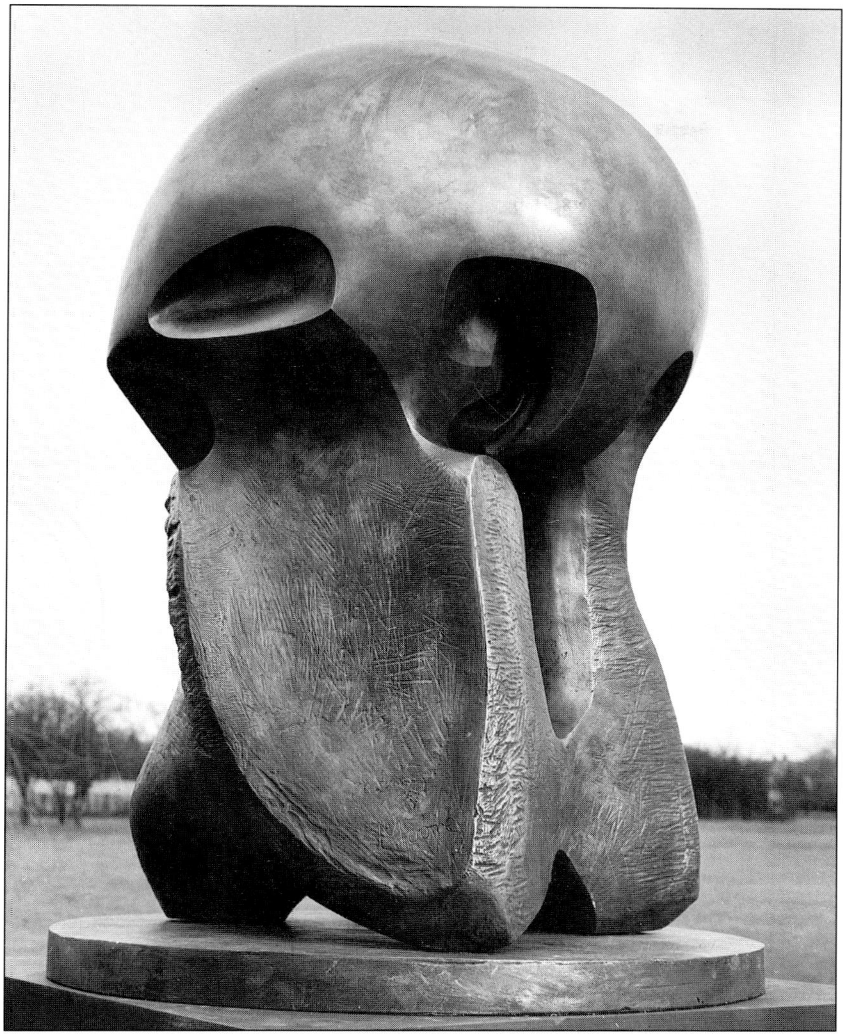

Atom Piece (Working Model for Nuclear Energy) 1964-65 (LH 525).

comment on the age. Moore's choice of sculpture as a calling reflected his own background in manual work – he came from a family of farmers and miners, occupations that in the past required harmony of the human body with its work. *Locking Piece* (cat.125) was inspired by two bones that naturally locked together, and, as Moore progressively enlarged them, they took on an analogy with precision engineering. Underlying his *Spindle Piece* (cat.129) and *Oval with Points* (cat.130) are natural forms, of flint, bone, or even shell, but the artist took such simple shapes, subtly altered them, enlarged them, and made them resonate with echoes of our twentieth-century lives. Consciously or unconsciously he enlarges our awareness of the essential unity between humans and what they make and Nature herself, and this gives universal meaning to his sculptures, wherever they are placed throughout the world. One of the most powerful is *Nuclear Energy* 1964-66 (see above), made as a memorial to the first self-sustaining nuclear chain reaction at the University of Chicago. Moore brought together forms derived from his study of an elephant's skull (cats.134, 135, 136, 137) in which he found an echo of the mushroom-cloud of the atomic explosions that had devastated Hiroshima and Nagasaki. Today, aware that we are destroying the habitat of the elephants and living under the shadow of the destruction of Nature by means of nuclear accident or warfare, we can appreciate the totality of Moore's vision.

As well as condensed sculptural ideas Moore developed complex relationships between his forms: in cat.127 the two figures observe a subtle distance, but *Sheep Piece* (cat.138) celebrates proximity – whether of the sexual act, or of the urgent nuzzling of lamb to its mother. Moore enjoyed a closer contact with Nature in his last years. He drew the sheep which fed in the pasture outside his studio windows (cats.142, 143, 144), and nearby trees – which sometimes took on a near-human form (cats.158, 159, 160). In *Sculptor Looking at Rock Formation* (cat.172) he identified Man with Nature, making an interesting (and probably intended) comment on Picasso's late series of Artist and Model. For Moore, the age-old rocks provided an enduring metaphor for Woman, who, none the less, attained a degree of naturalism in his late sculptures.

His Woman became closer to the elusive mix of head and heart that is familiar to us all, when, after re-establishing the role of drapery in the Reclining Figure (cats.163, 167), he combined more life-like arms and torso with an equivalent for the lower body that remains a symbol of fertility (cats.180, 182). In the Mother and Child groups his children – especially those of cats.166, 171, 181– seem at first glance to pander to our sentimental ideas, but, in each case, the artist reminds us of the complexity of the relationship. Woman must attend to the needs of the child before her own: when she becomes a mother, she becomes the supporting, succouring figure that he shaped so convincingly here. Perhaps because they are less representational, cats.169, 170 reflect the ambiguity of the intense closeness and constant separation of the pair. Although Moore rejected sculpture as a means of story-telling, his creations have the power to evoke emotions: in times of anxiety his figures share our unease; in times of fear, they reflect our terror; when we find joy or horror in Nature, Moore makes permanent our feelings in stone or bronze. This miracle takes place because Moore – as artist and teacher – combined a penetrating observation of natural forms with a unique gift of communication.

Henry Moore Worldwide

Sculpture by Henry Moore can be seen in public collections, museums, municipalities and outside institutions throughout the world in more than two hundred cities spread across thirty-five countries. Some of the larger works in permanent sites are illustrated on the following pages.

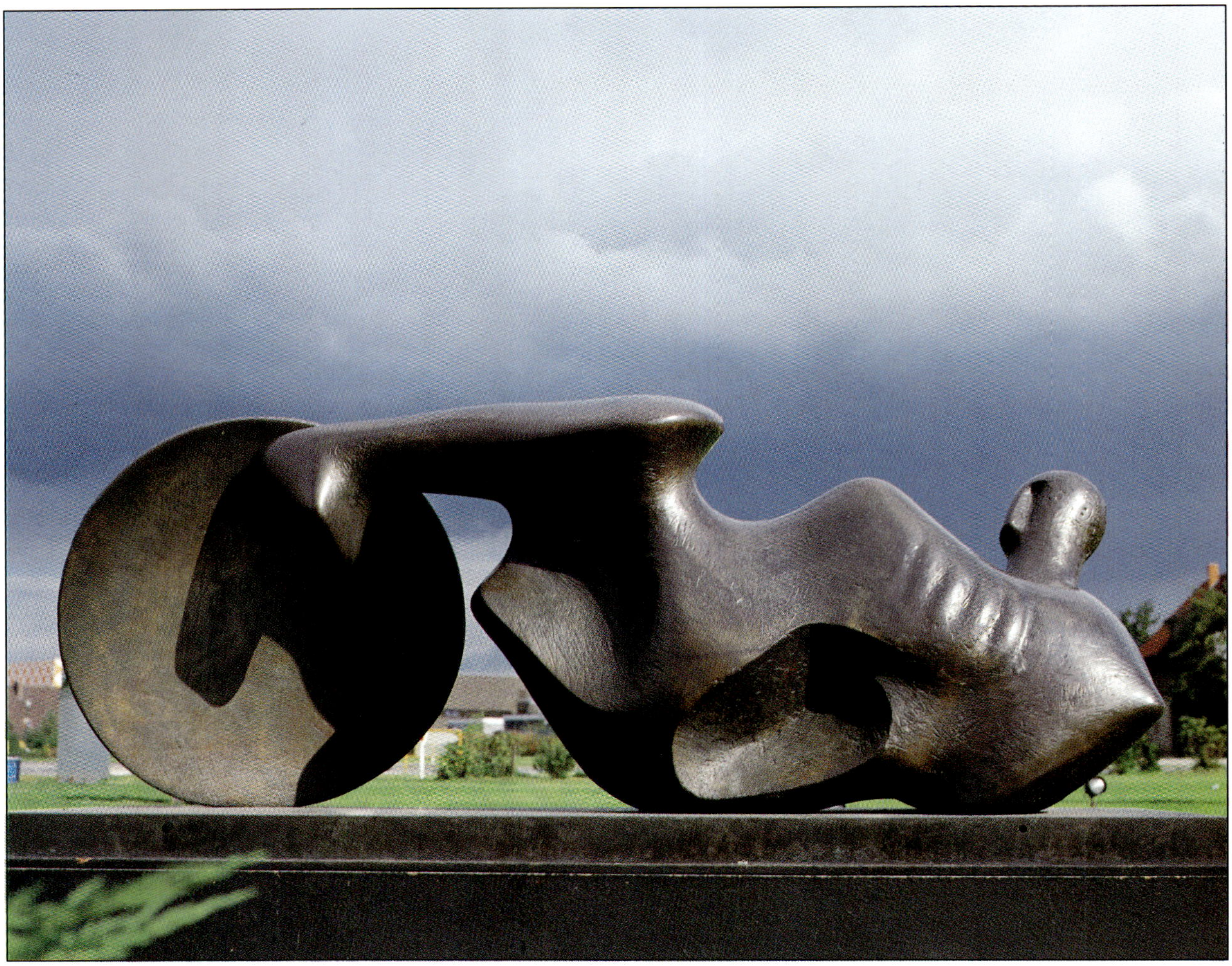

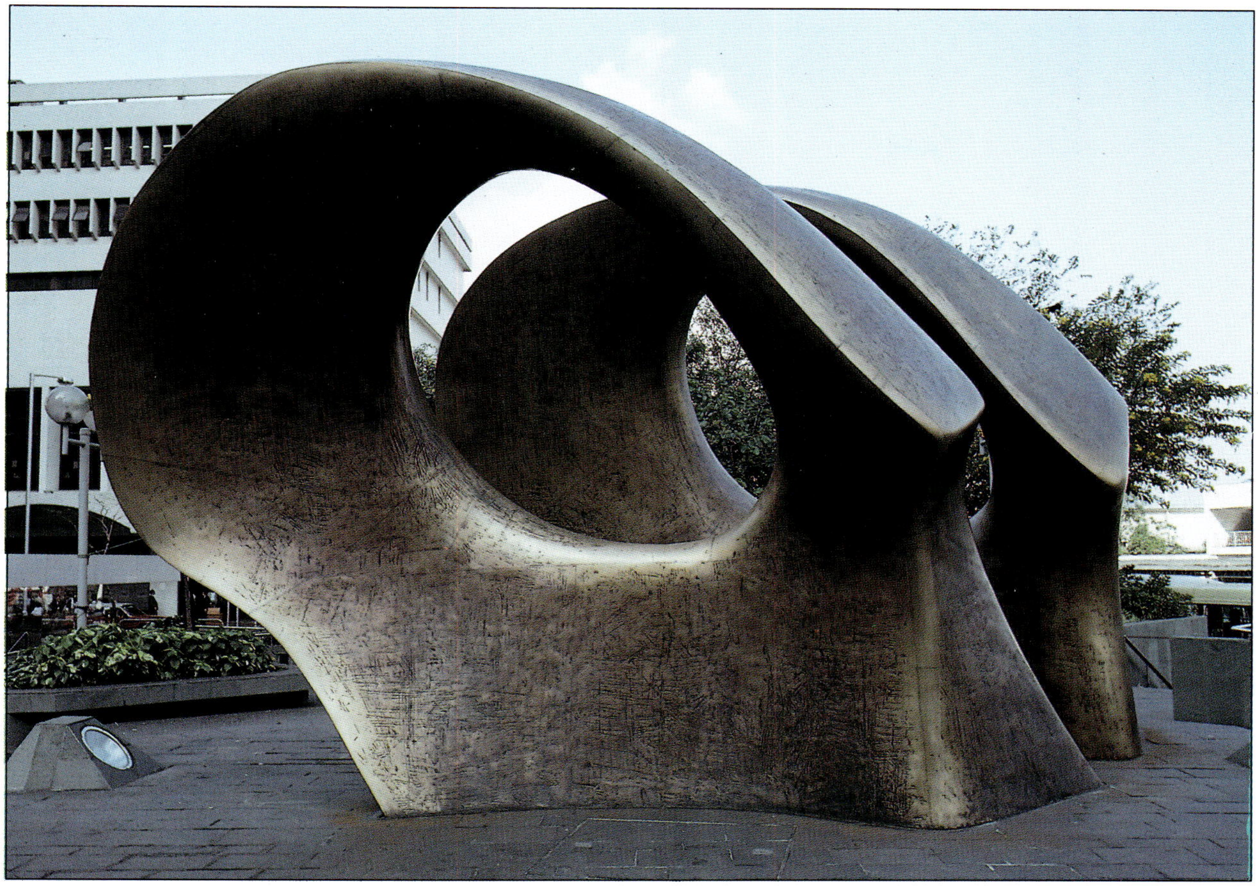

Goslar Warrior 1973-74
L 249cm bronze
City of Goslar,
Germany
LH 641

Double Oval 1966
H approx. 550cm bronze
Hong Kong Land Estates,
Hong Kong
LH 560

Large Two Forms 1966-69
L approx. 610cm bronze
Art Gallery of Ontario,
Toronto, Canada
LH 556

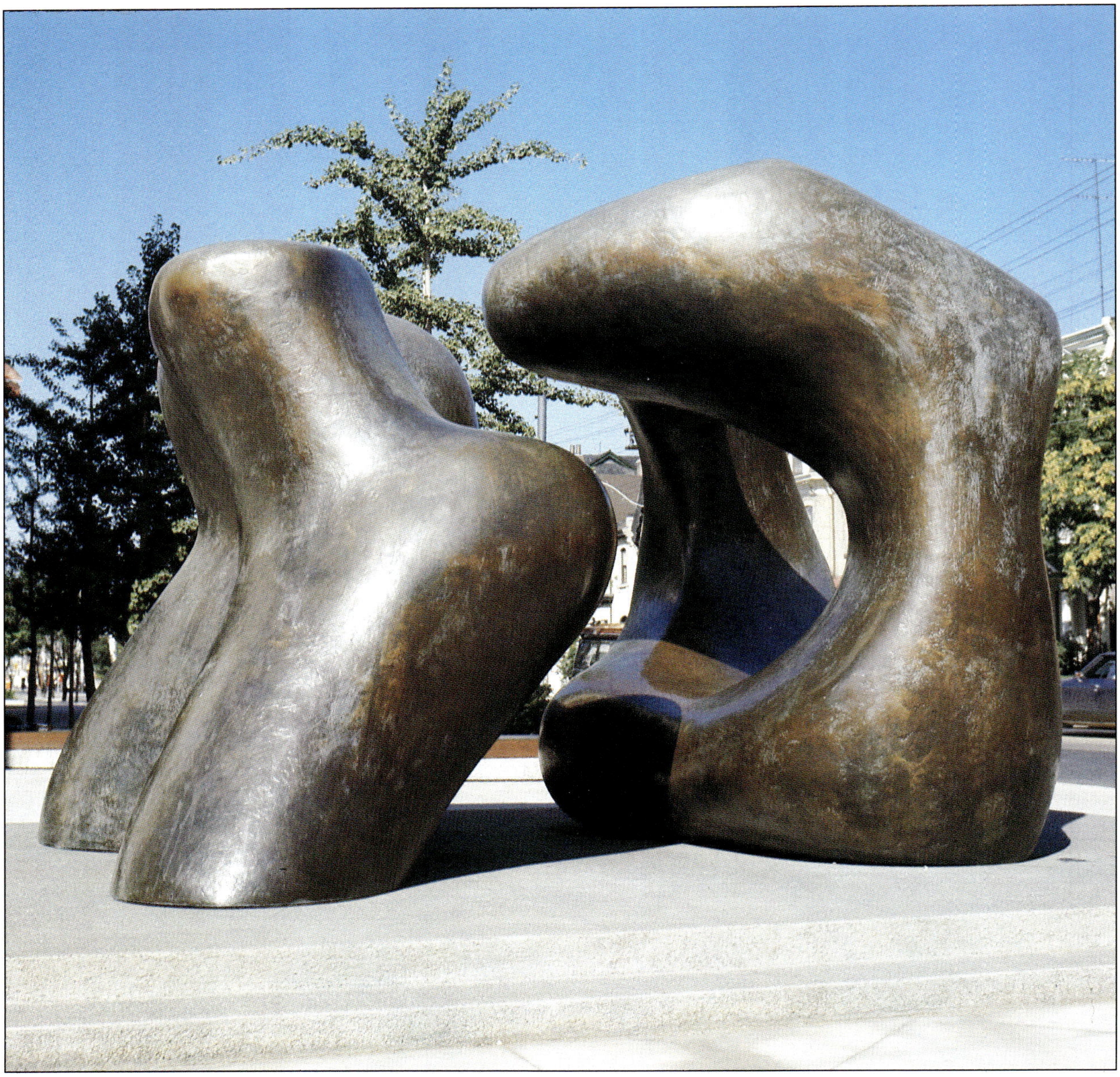

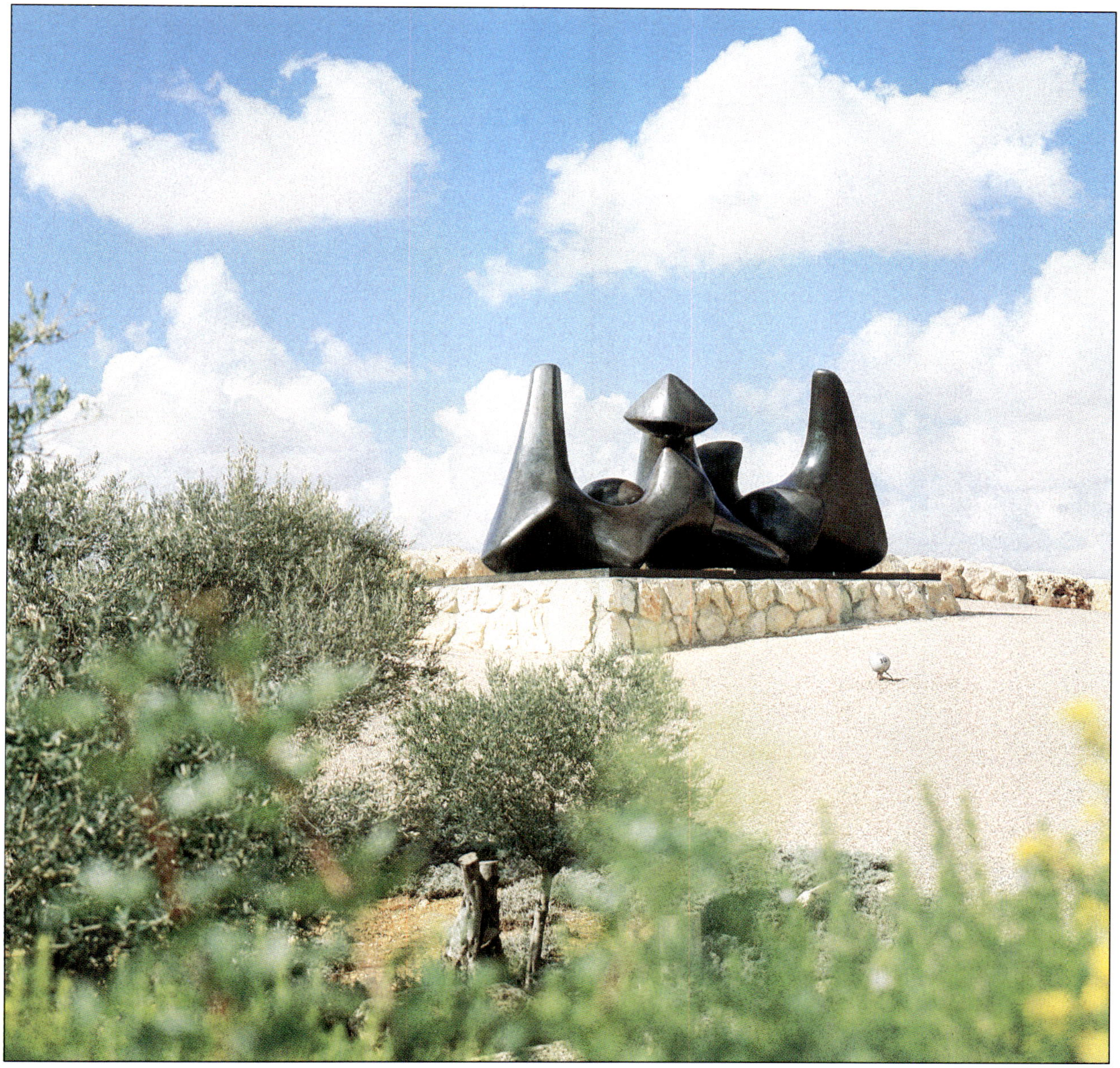

Three Piece Sculpture: Vertebrae 1968-69
L 710cm bronze
Israel Museum,
Jerusalem, Israel
LH 580

Interlocking
Two Piece Sculpture 1968-70
L 325cm white marble
F. Hoffmann-La Roche,
Basel, Switzerland
LH 584

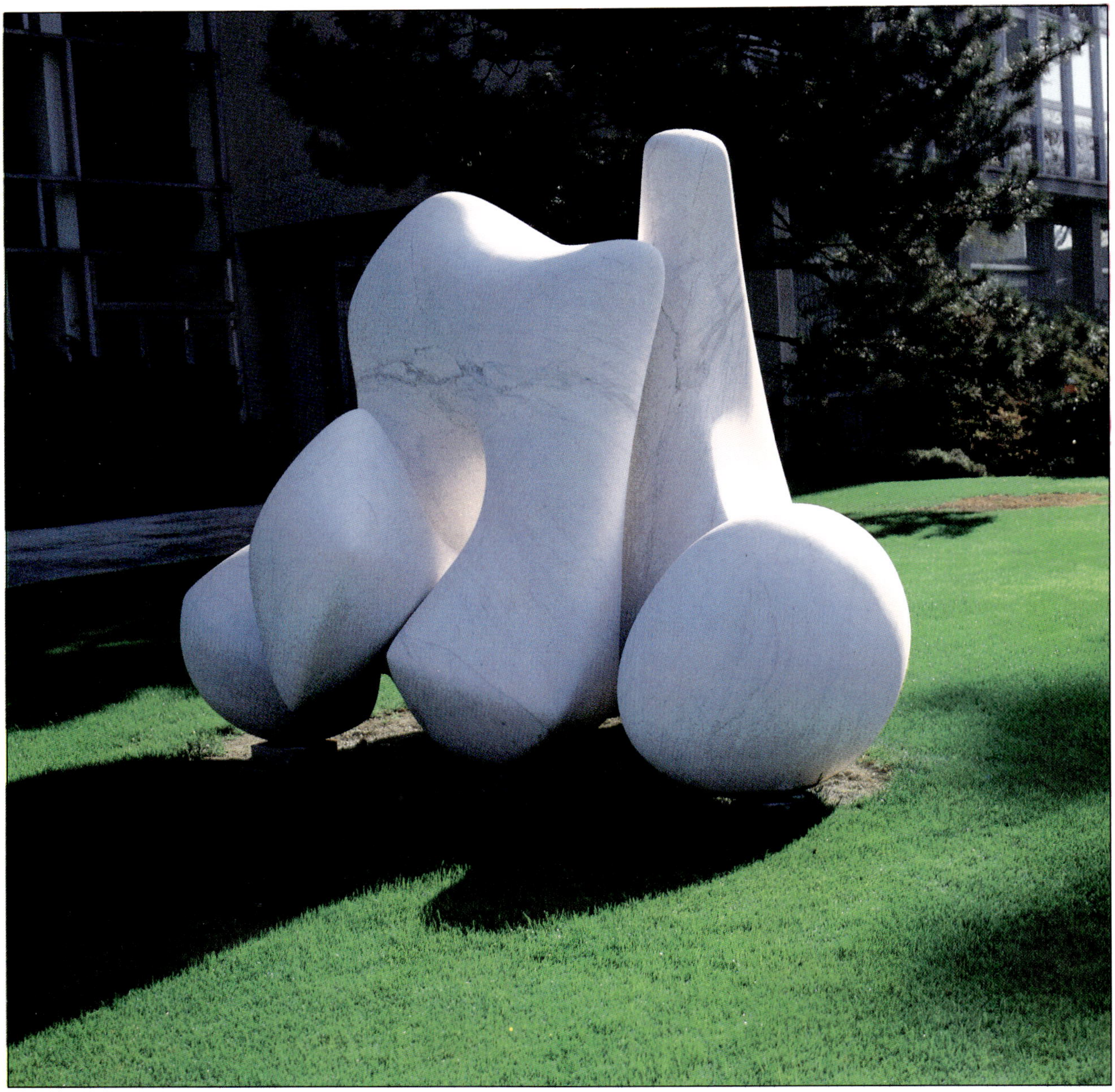

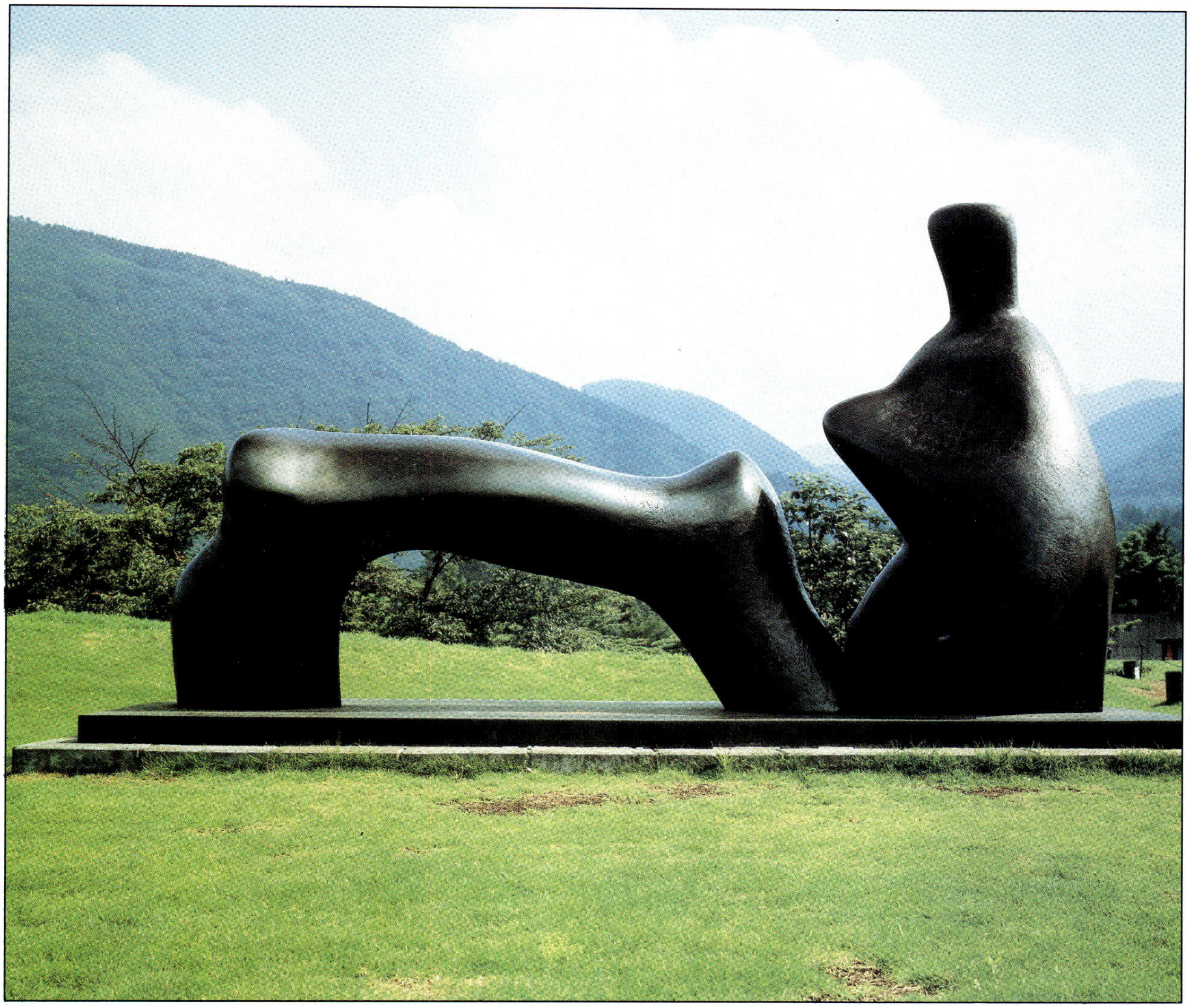

Reclining Figure:
Arch Leg 1969-70
L 442cm bronze
Hakone Open Air Museum,
Japan
LH 610

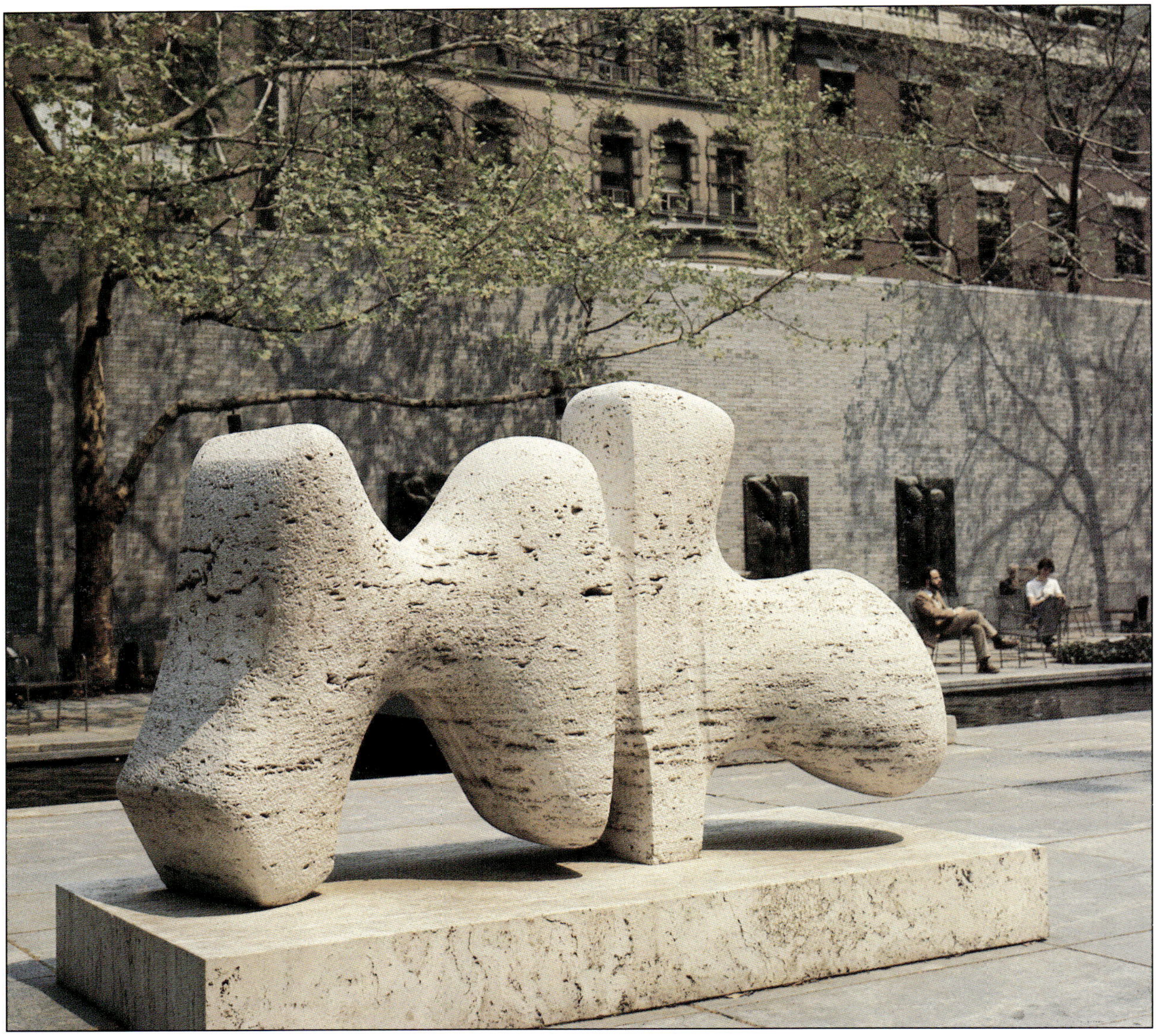

Large Animal Form 1969-70
L 274cm Travertine marble
Museum of Modern Art,
New York
LH 617

Mirror Knife Edge 1977
L 762cm bronze
National Gallery of Art,
Washington DC, USA
LH 714

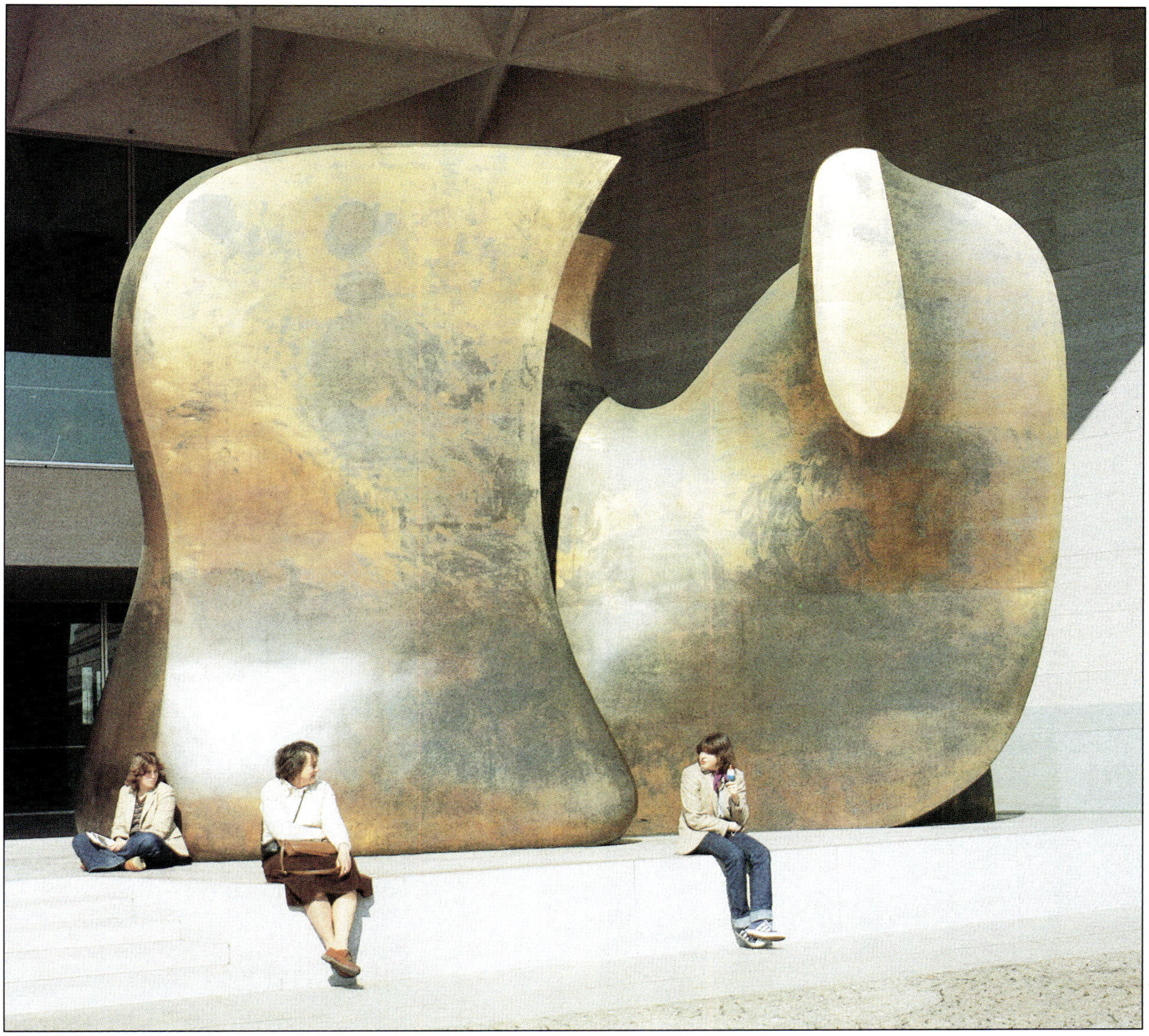

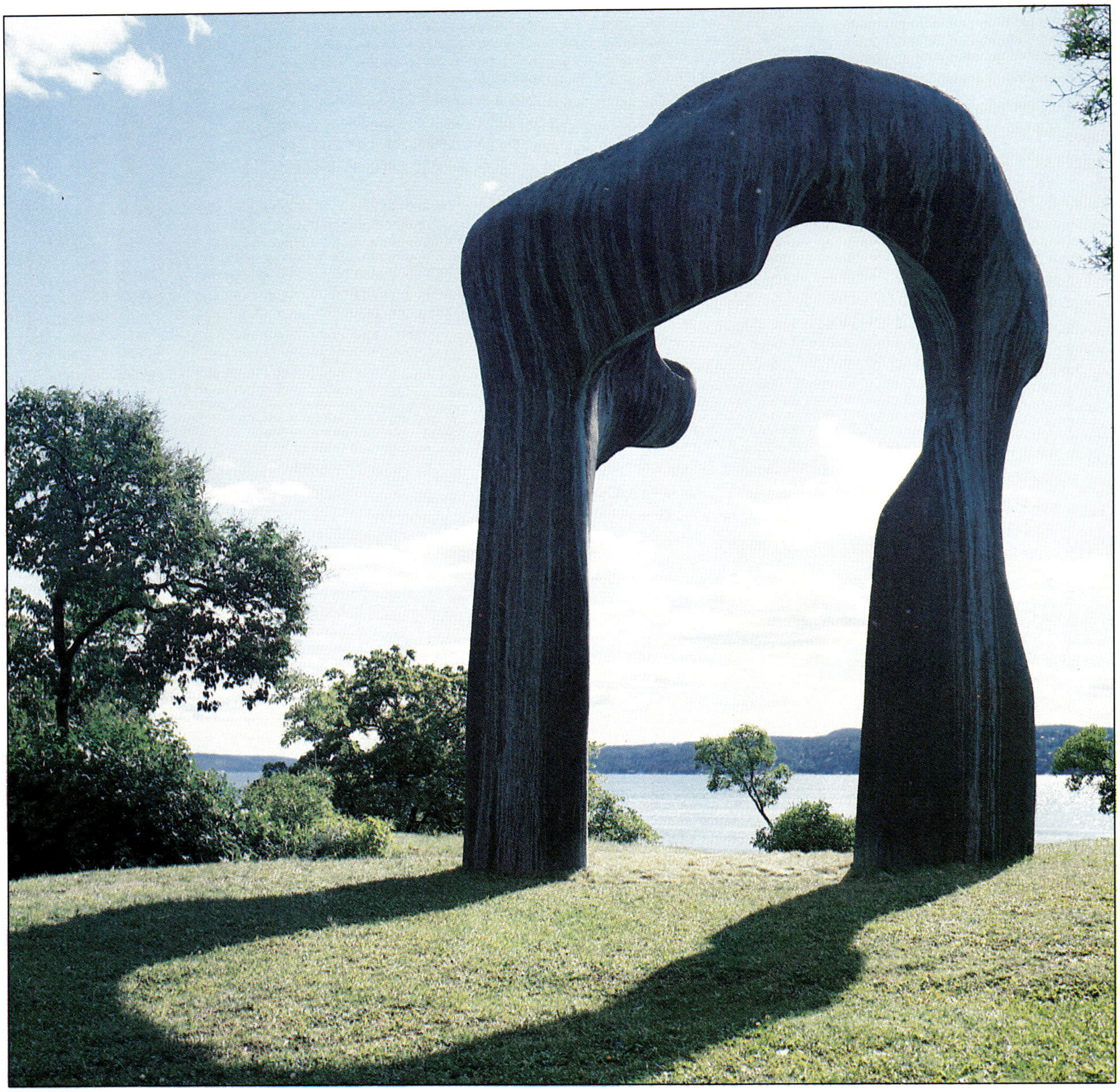

The Arch 1979-80
H approx. 610cm bronze
Sonja Henies-Niels Onstads Kunstsenter,
Hovikodden, Norway
LH 503b

Catalogue

All works in the exhibition are from the collection of the Henry Moore Foundation except where otherwise stated.

All quotations in the following pages are those of the artist.

LH numbers for the sculptures refer to the catalogue raisonné of sculpture published by Lund Humphries; HMF numbers for the drawings refer to the Henry Moore Foundation archive; CGM numbers for the prints refer to the catalogue raisonné of graphic work edited by Cramer, Grant and Mitchinson (see Bibliography for publication details).

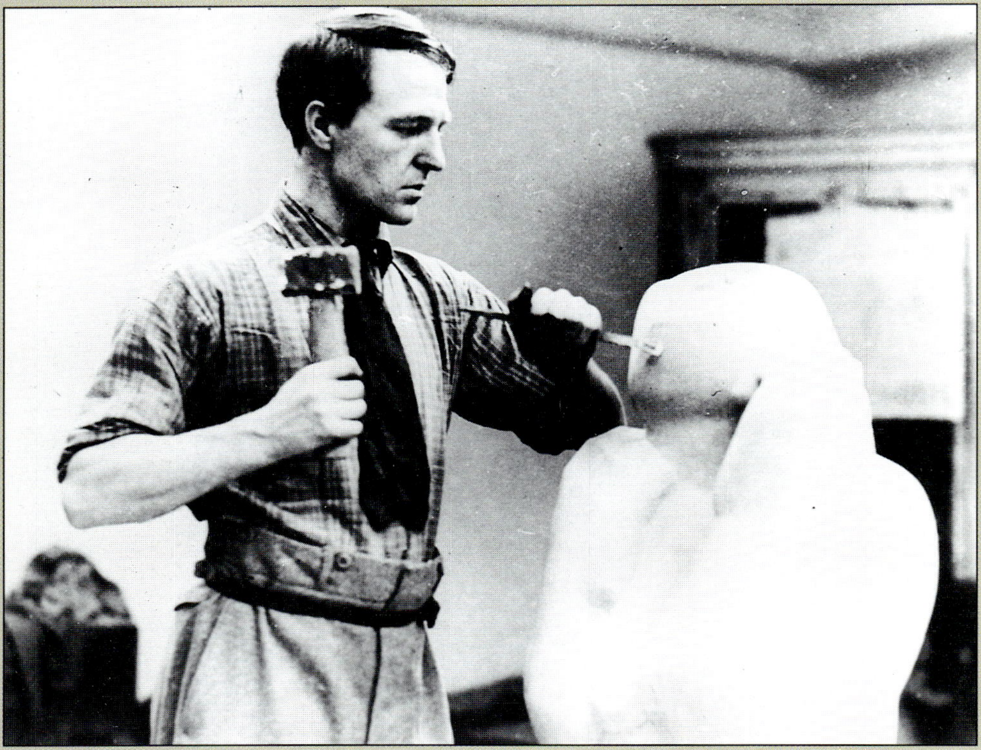

Henry Moore at Grove Studios, Hammersmith, London, *c.*1926, working on a sculpture that he never finished.

1920s

Henry Moore carved *Dog* (cat.3) and *Head of the Virgin* (cat.4) at art college. He was a mature student. He had already served in the Army during the First World War and his father had insisted that he qualify as a school teacher before following his chosen career as a sculptor; his preliminary years of study were at the Leeds School of Art, near his home in Yorkshire. By 1922, when Moore reached the Royal College of Art in London and made these sculptures, he had a very clear idea of what he wanted to do. His priority was carving. He determined to make sculpture by cutting straight into the block of stone, instead of making a preliminary clay model and transferring the image to stone by measuring, which was the usual method taught at the time.

Moore's discovery of non-Western sculpture in the British Museum gave him an alternative to Classical and Renaissance models for his art: the traditional style of the Virgin and Child – copied from an Italian relief as an exercise and preserved because he gave it to fellow students as their wedding present – gave way to the archaic style of the half-length figures cats.18 and 20, which show Moore's fascination for ancient Mexican art as well as Mesopotamian and Sumerian sculpture. He cast the first in concrete because he felt it was the right material to use for sculpture associated with modern architecture. He gouged out a hollow in the body, a mysterious forerunner of the cavities and penetrations so typical of his later figures.

Like most Western sculptors before him, Moore found drawing from life a necessary preparation for working in three dimensions and continued to recommend the practice to his own students. During the 1920s he carefully investigated the figure, using many types of shading to convey three-dimensionality. He often added simple green or brown washes – close to the colours of bronze sculpture. He drew portraits rarely but those of his mother (cat.12) and sister (cat.11) are particularly monumental. Cats.14 and 15 introduce Moore's most characteristic themes – the Reclining Figure, and Mother and Child.

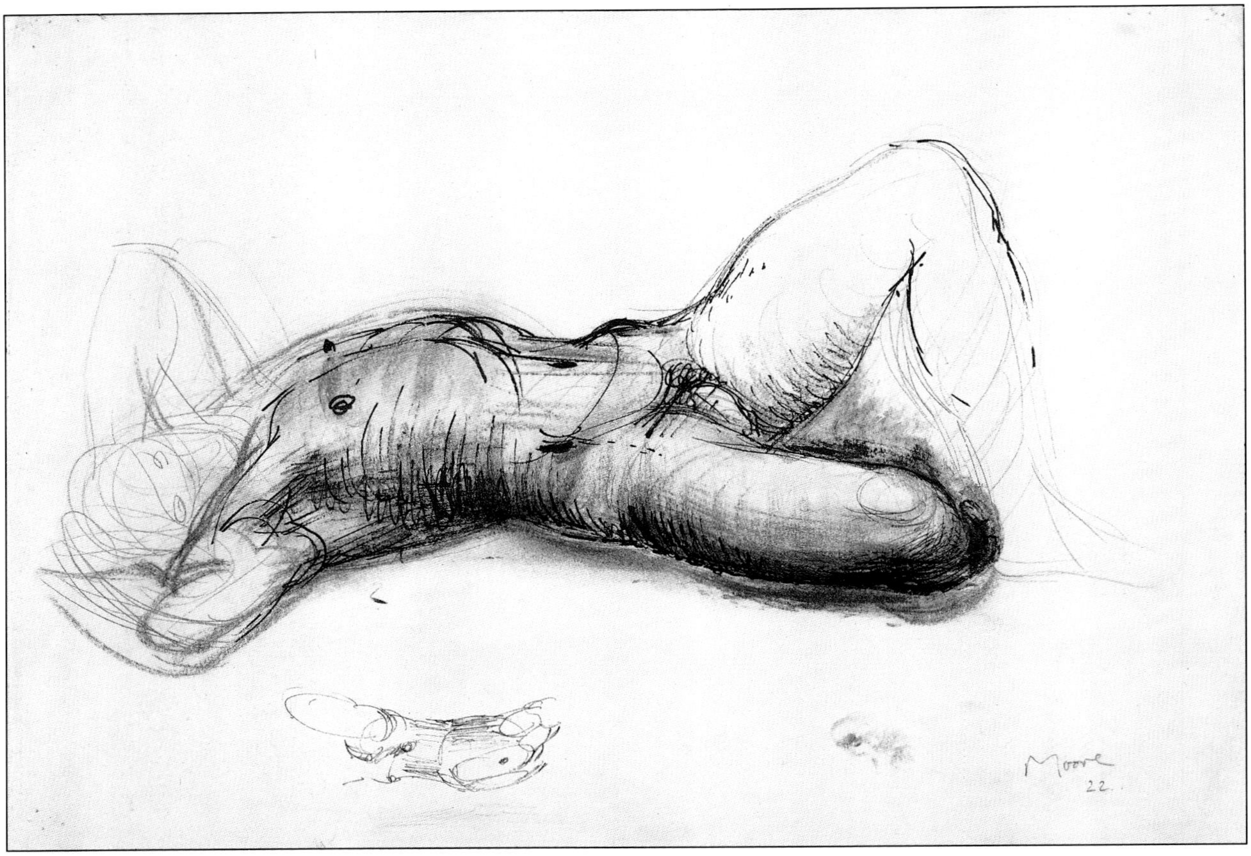

For me, life-drawing has been a continual struggle to understand the complete three-dimensional form of the model and to express it on the flat surface of the paper.

1
Reclining Male Nude 1922
pencil, charcoal, green crayon, pen and Indian ink, ink wash
382 x 555mm
HMF 72

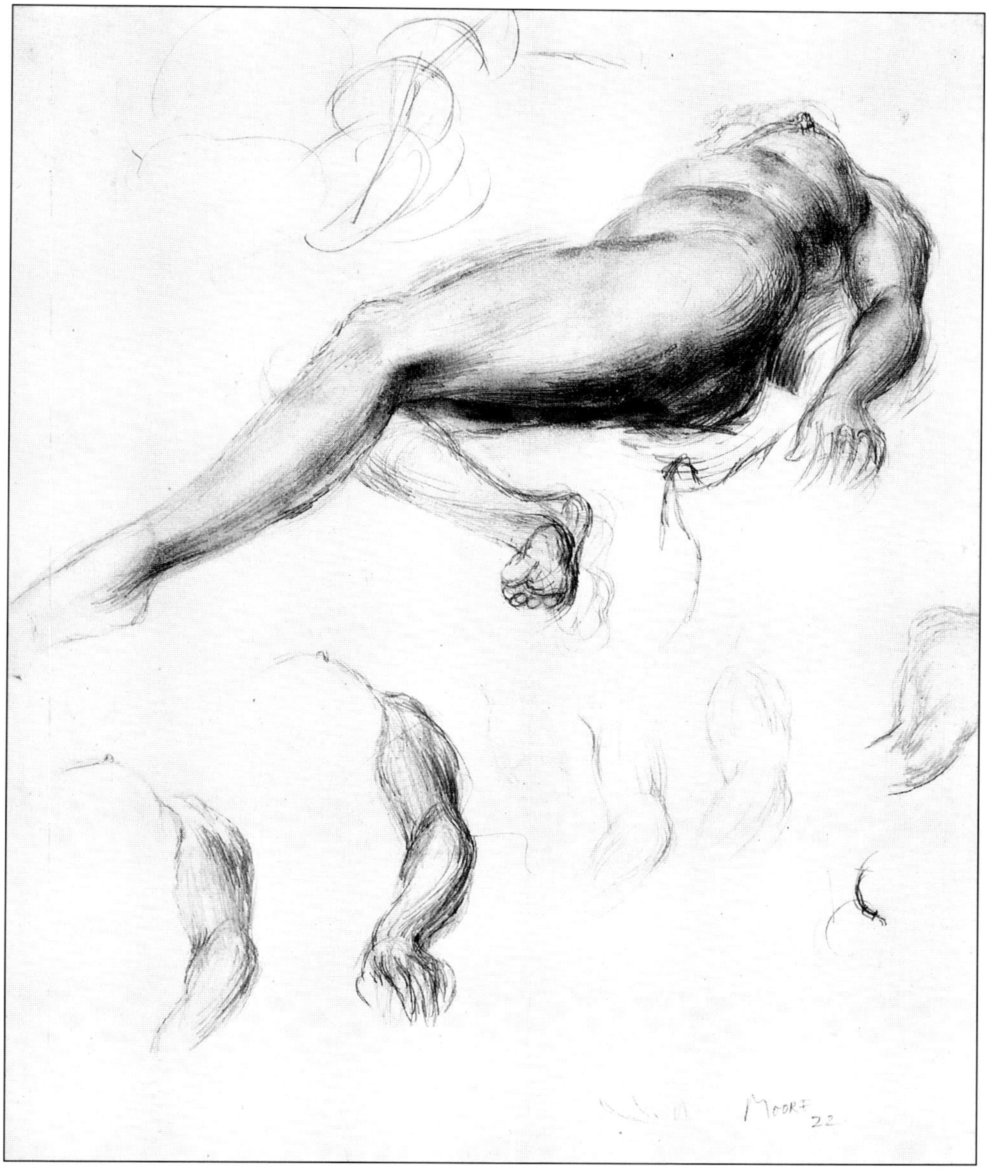

2

Reclining Nude and
Five Studies of an Arm 1922
pencil, crayon, watercolour
437 x 362mm
HMF 81

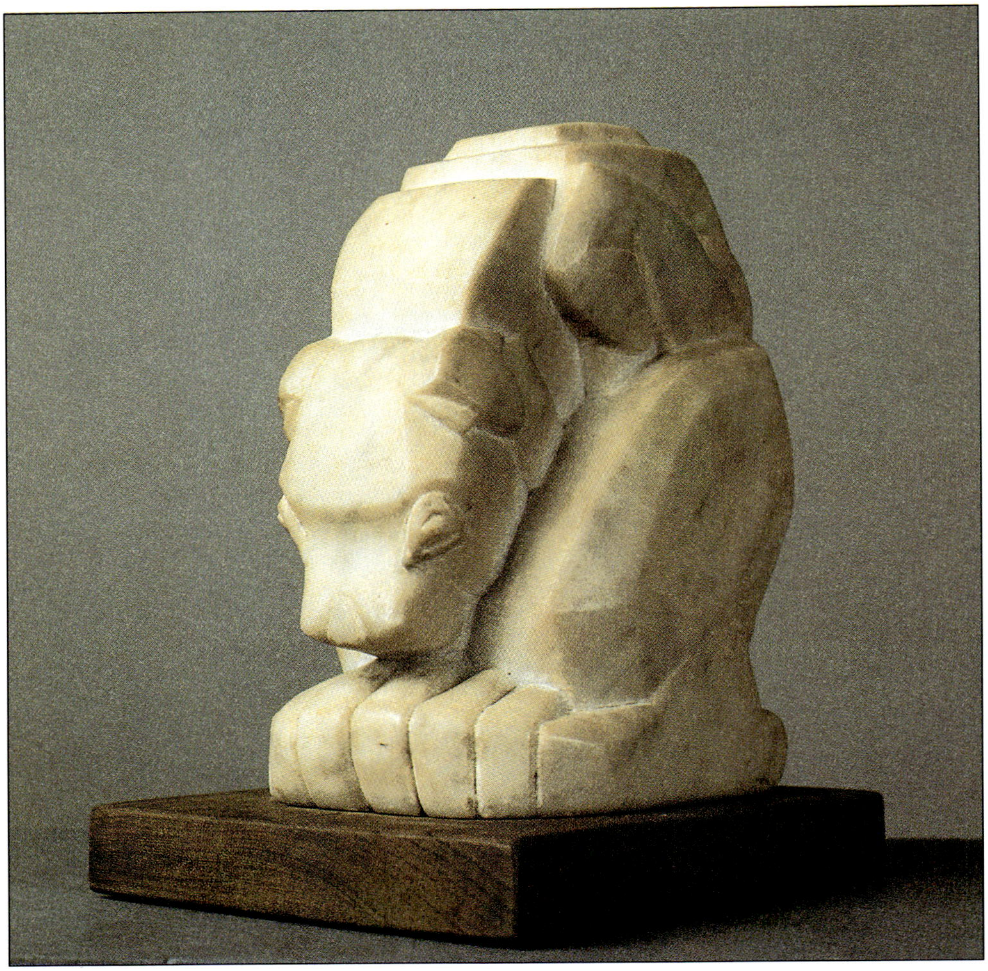

3
Dog 1922
H 17.8cm marble
LH 2

4
Head of the Virgin 1922
H 53.2cm marble
LH 6

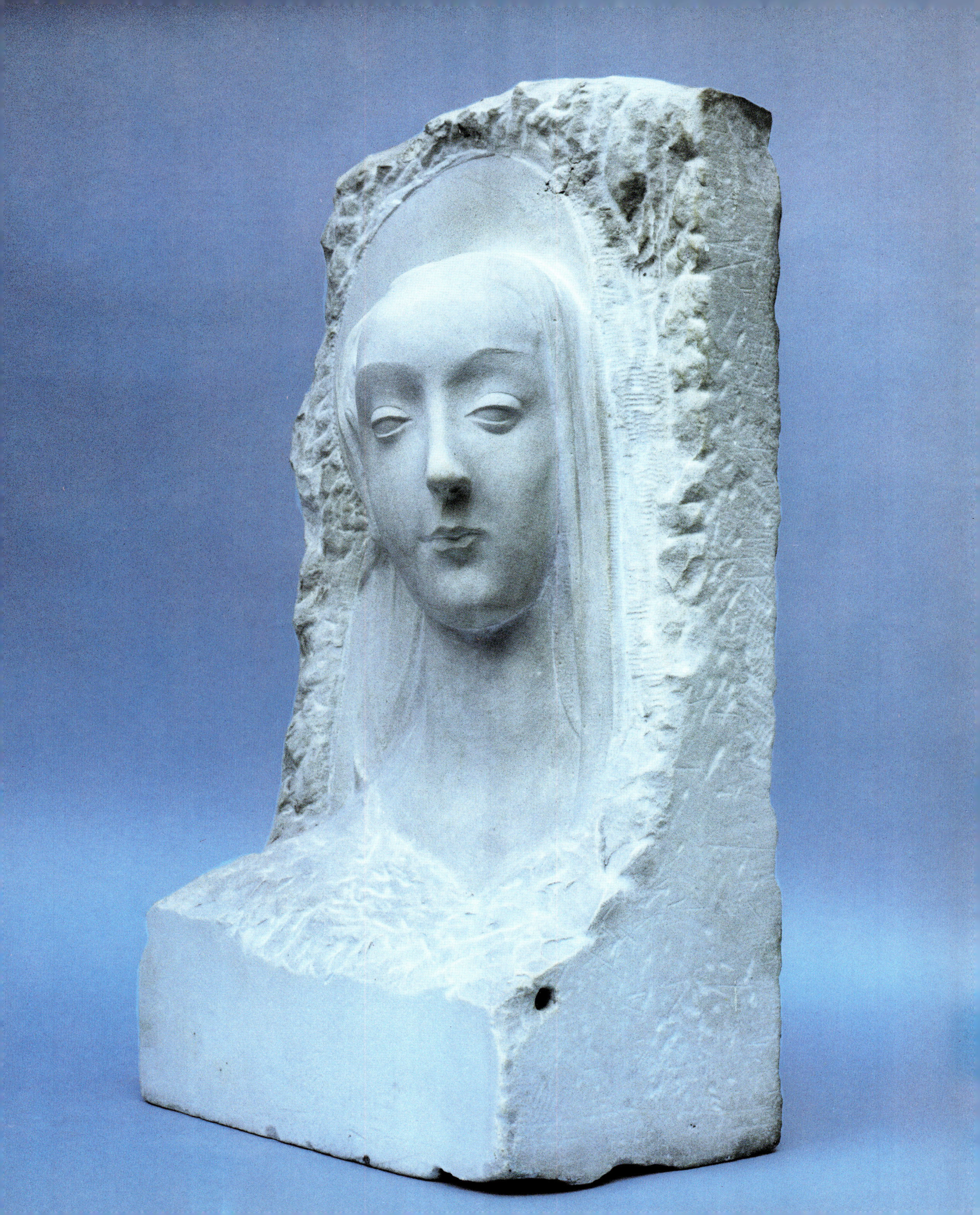

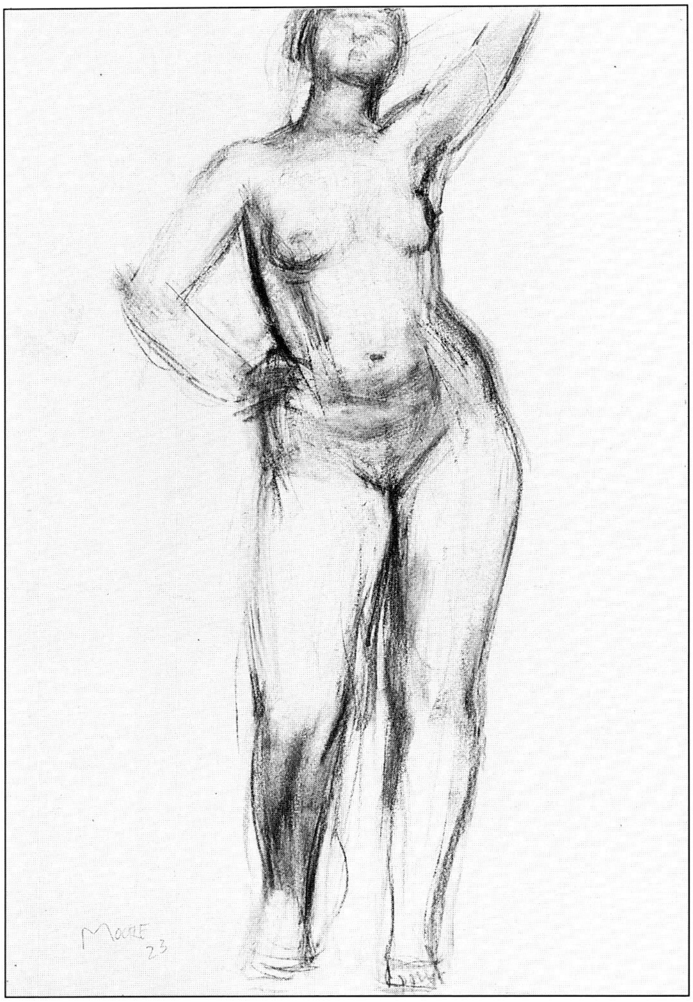

5
Standing Woman 1923
black crayon, charcoal,
ink wash, pencil
483 x 335mm
HMF 180

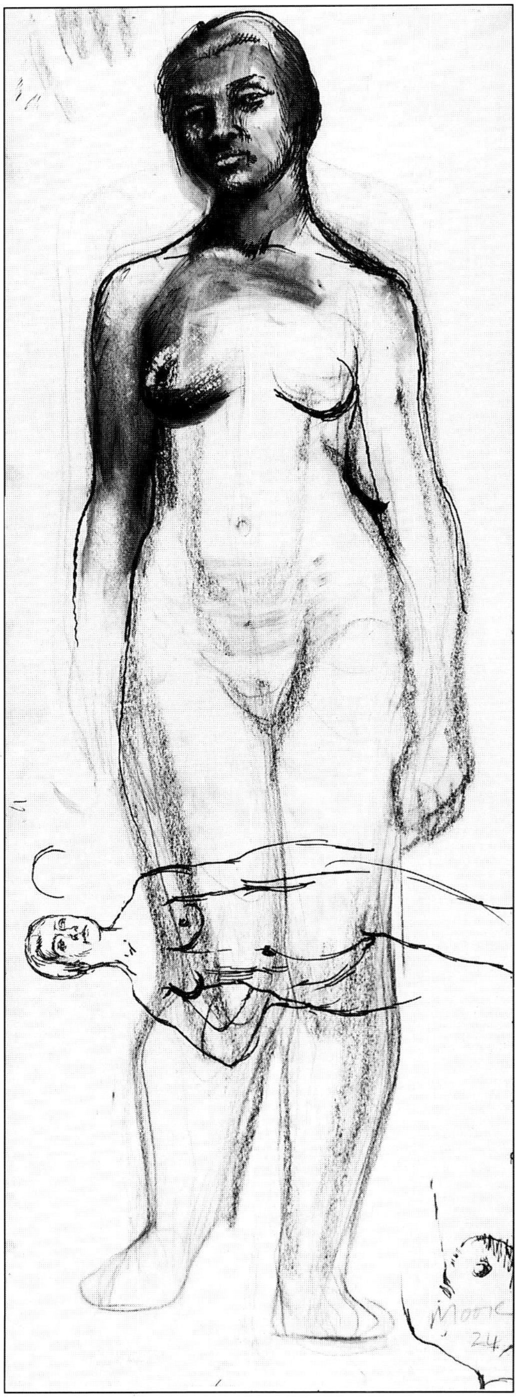

6
Standing Girl 1924
black crayon,
black ink wash,
pen and ink
509 x 195mm
HMF 214

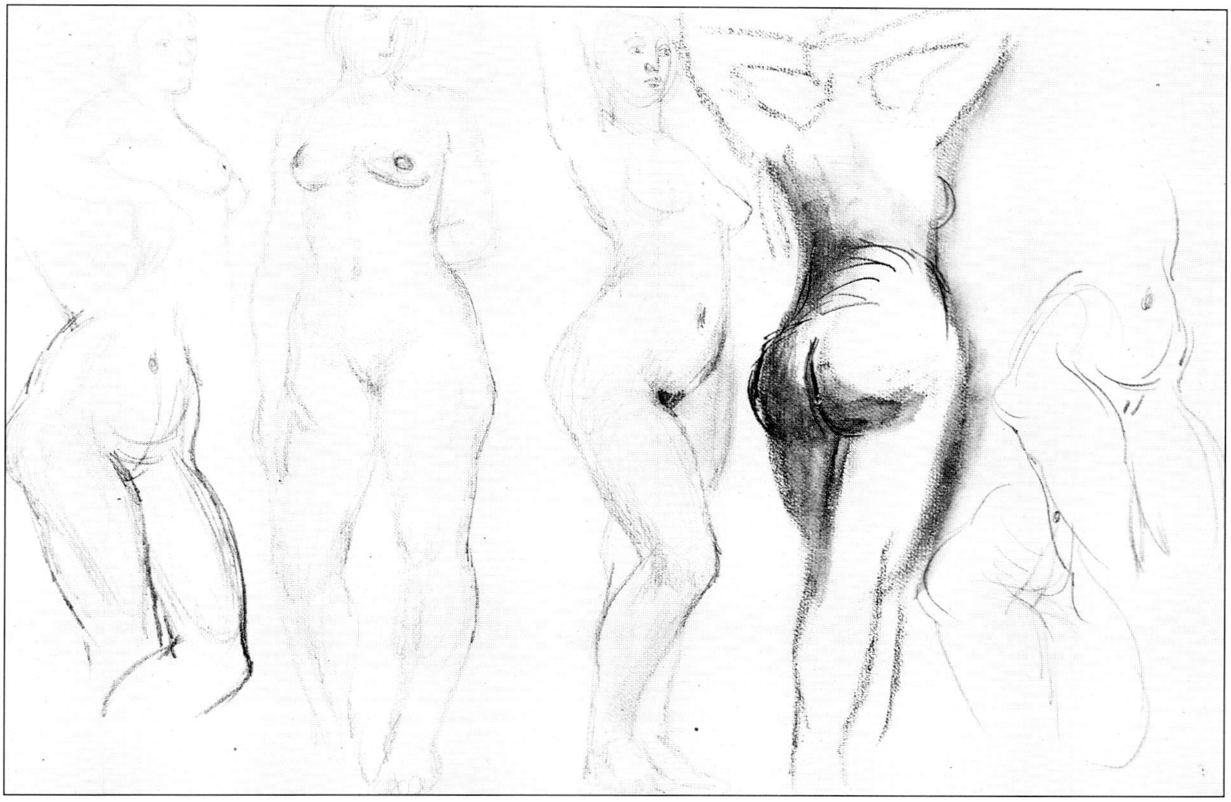

The great value and purpose of drawing from life, from nature, is to intensify one's observations, to concentrate on looking and so increase one's knowledge, understanding and appreciation of the object.

7
Seven Studies of Female Nude 1924
pencil, black chalk or crayon,
diluted black ink wash
316 x 481mm
HMF 240

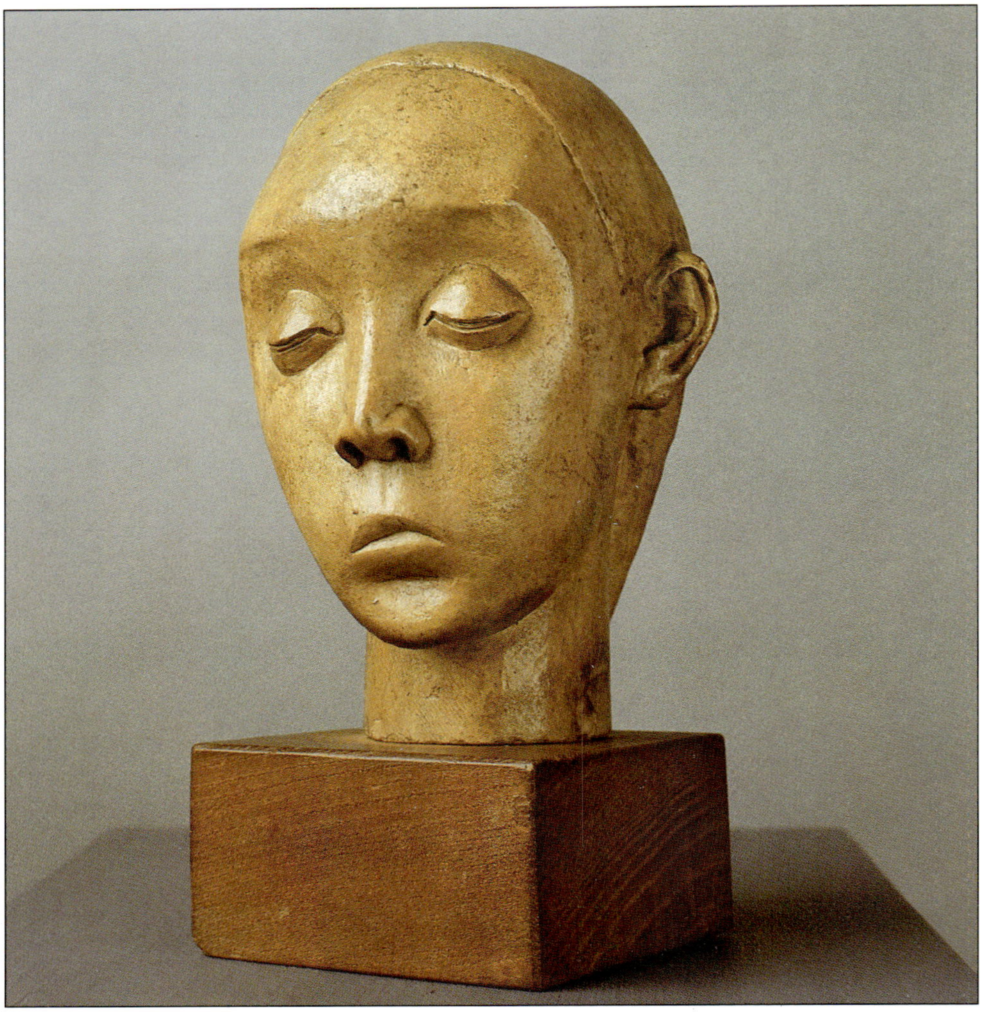

8

Head of a Girl 1923

H 17.5cm terracotta

LH 15

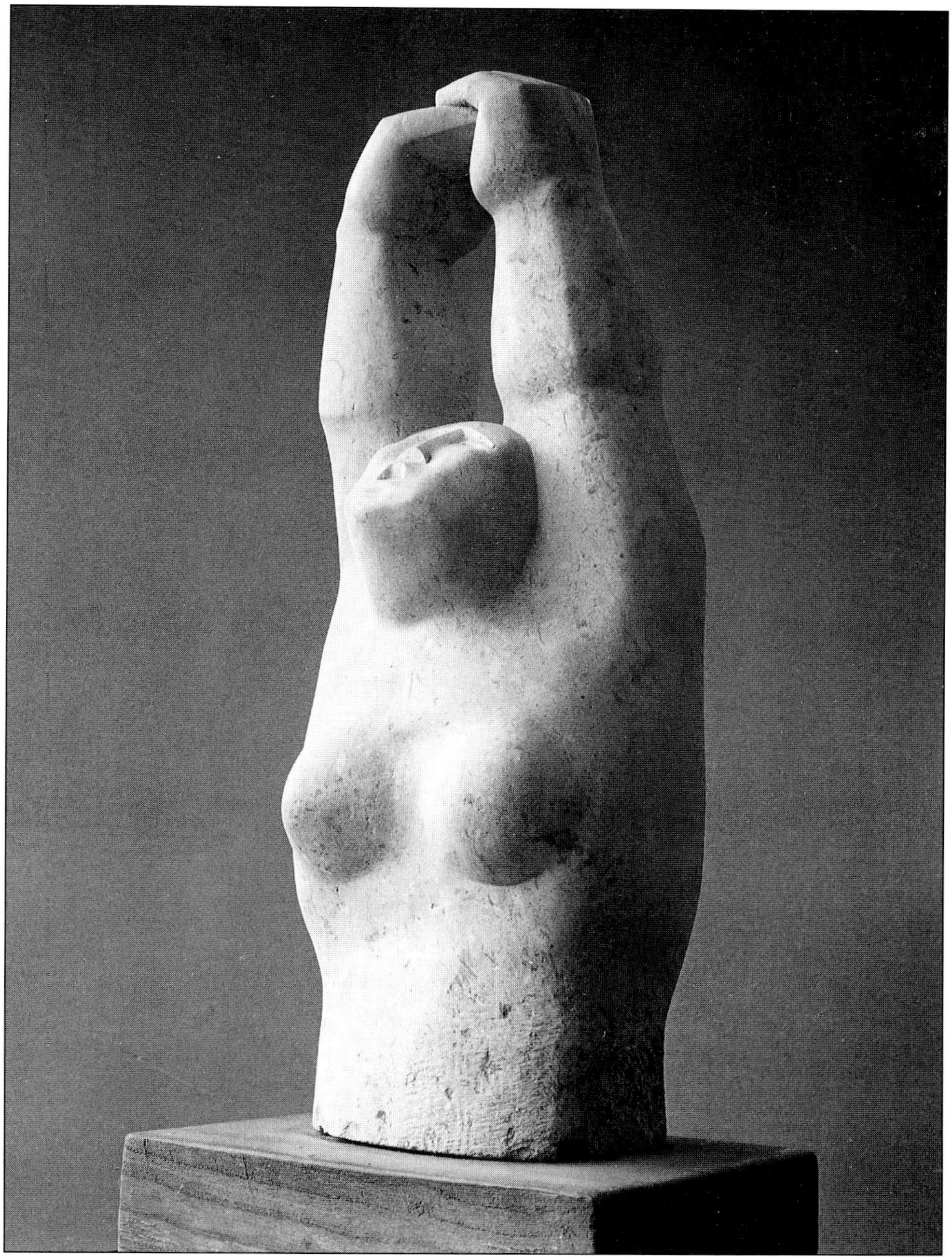

9

Woman with Upraised Arms 1924-25

H 43.2cm Hopton Wood stone

LH 23

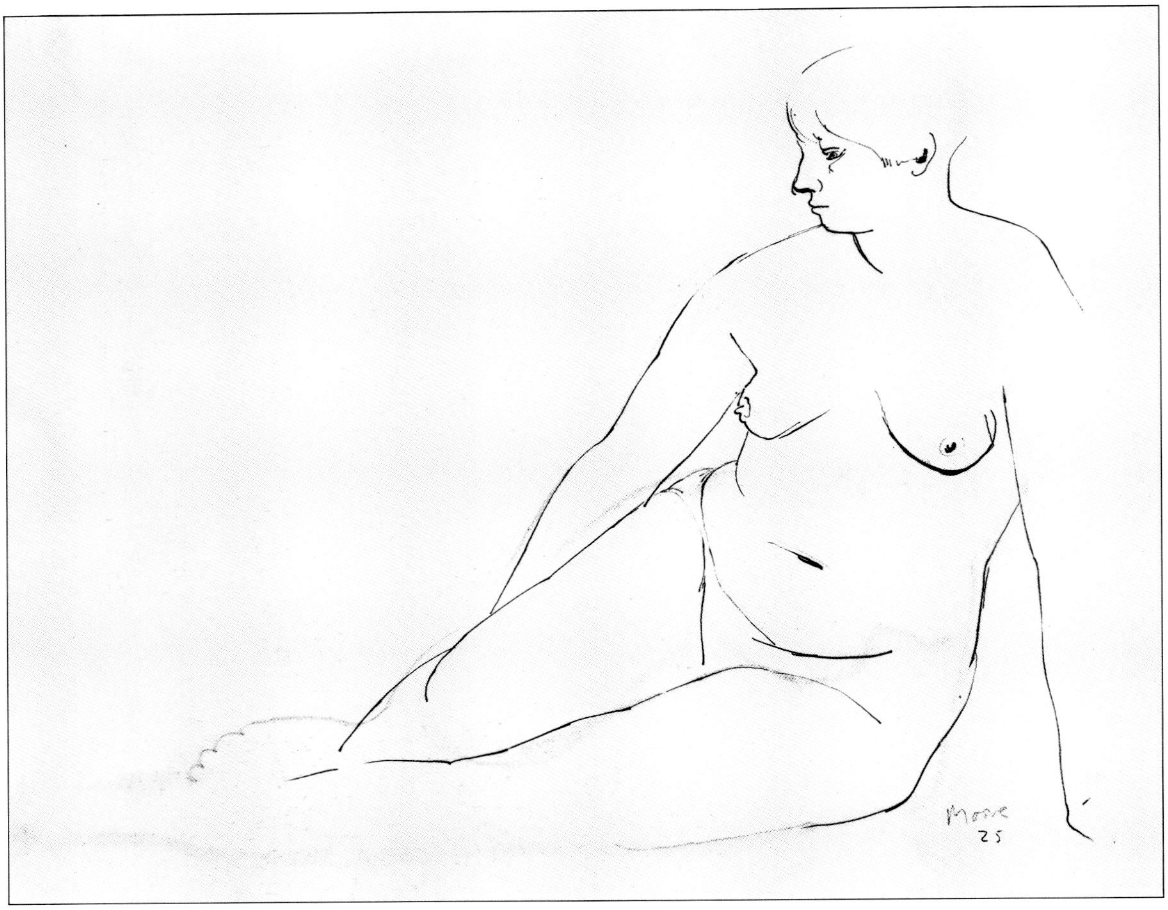

10
Recumbent Figure 1925
pen and ink, chalk
384 x 492mm
HMF 336

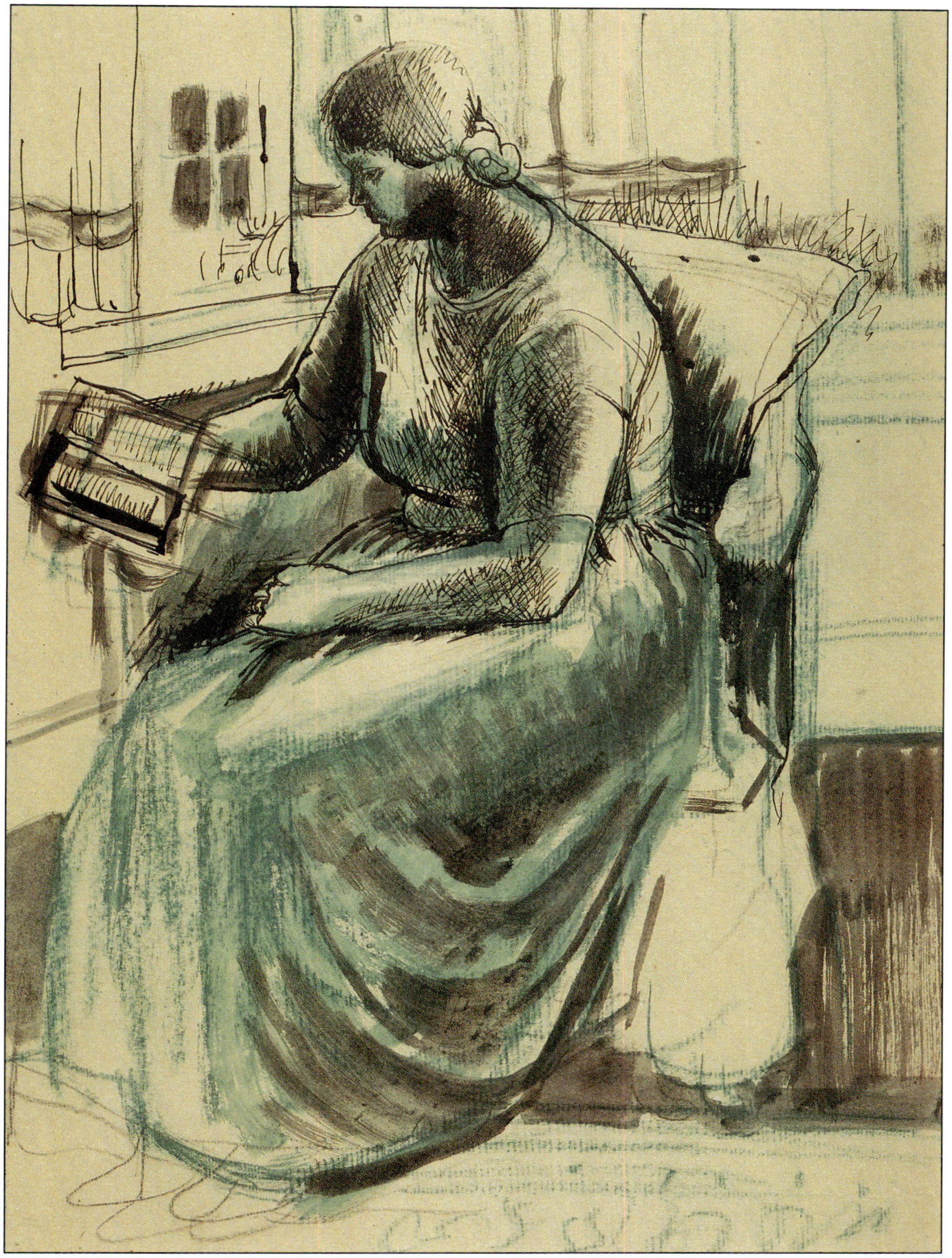

11
Woman Seated Reading
(The Artist's Sister) 1925
ink, wash, watercolour, chalk
445 x 335mm
The British Council, London
HMF 470

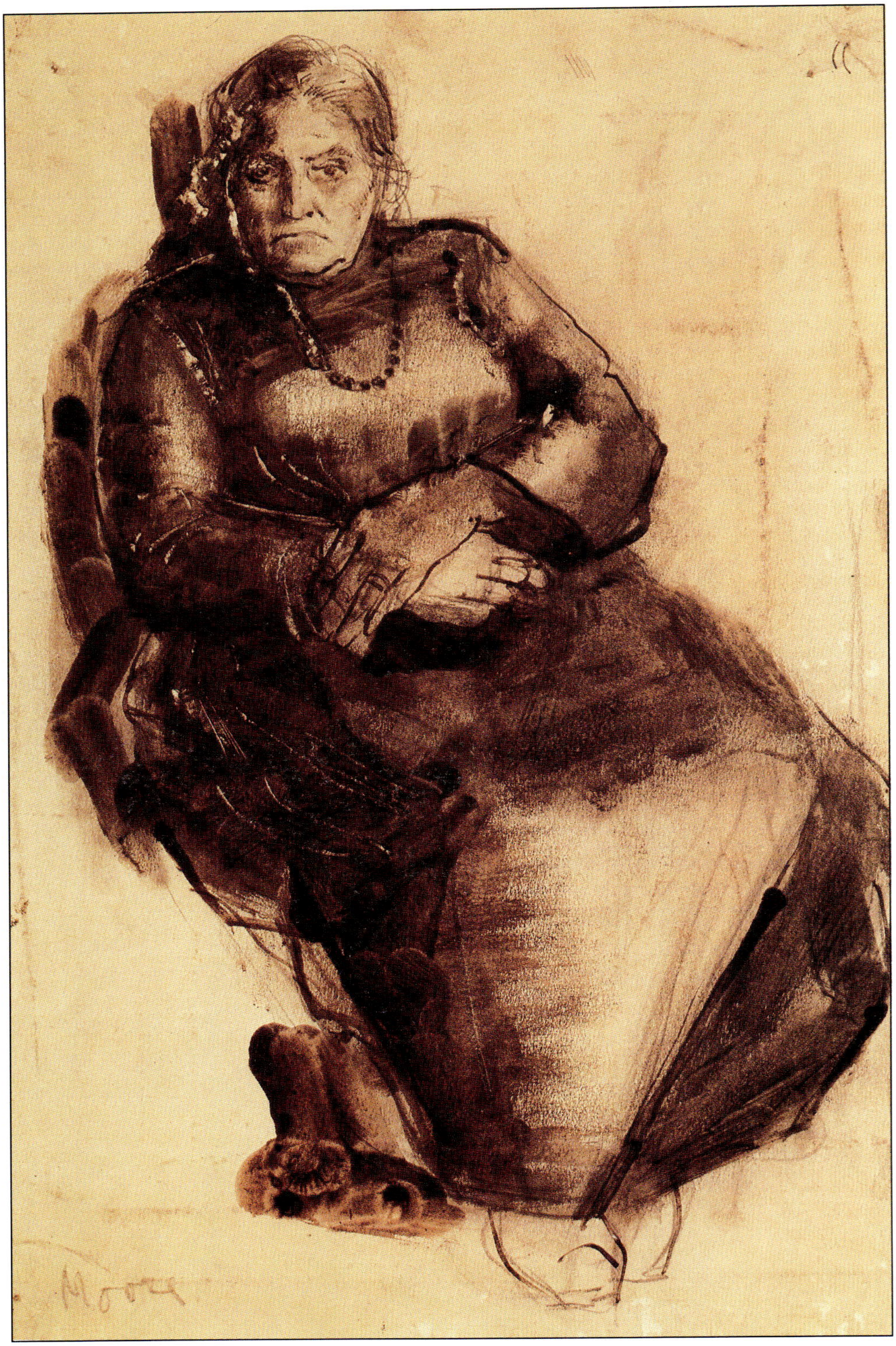

12
The Artist's Mother 1927
pencil, pen and ink,
with finger rub and scraping
277 x 191mm
HMF 488

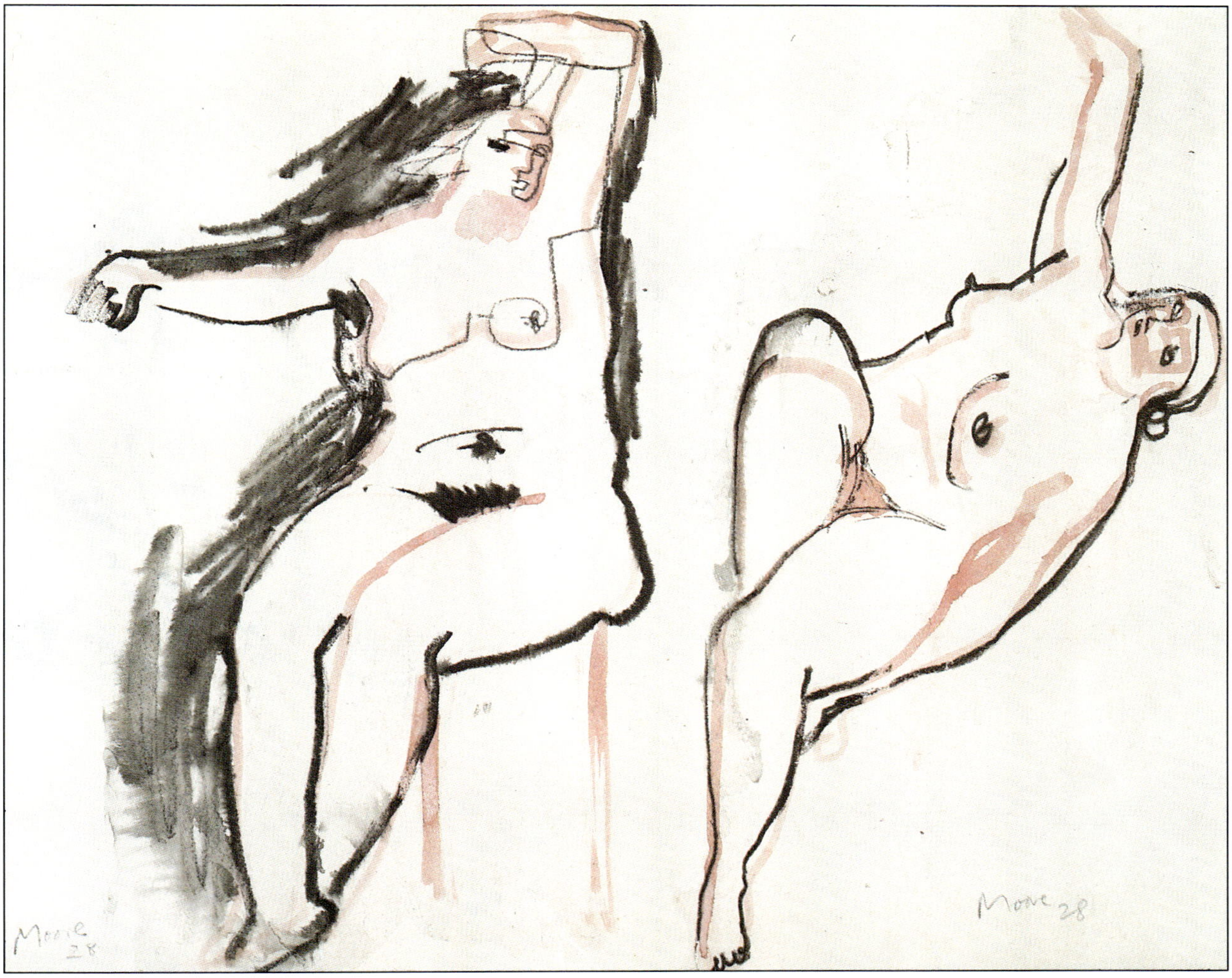

13

Two Studies of Female Nude 1928
brush and ink (black and diluted red),
black chalk, traces of blue and grey
wash, areas of washed charcoal
342 x 428mm
HMF 649a

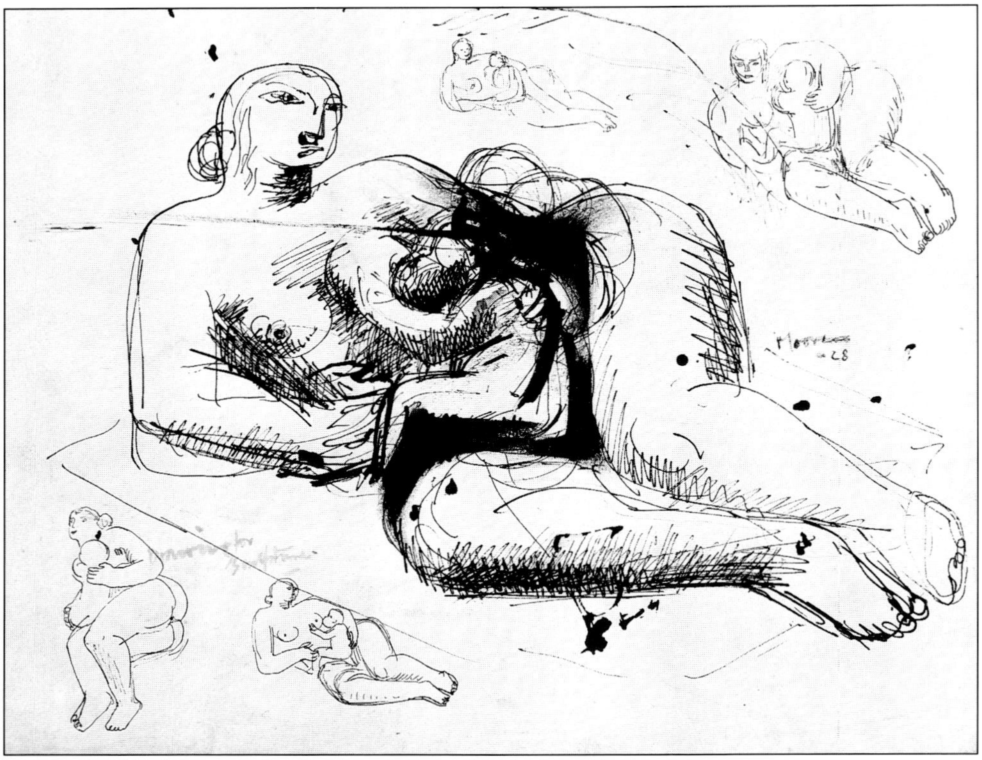

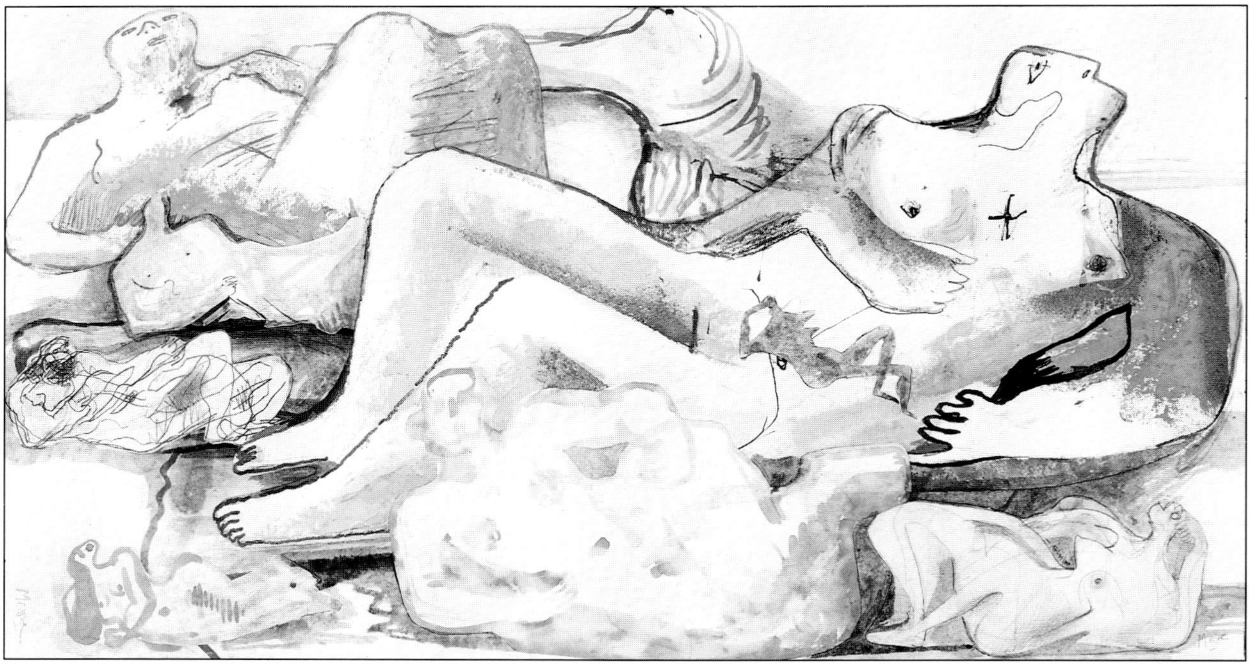

14
Studies for Reclining Figure with Child 1928
pen and Indian ink, rubbed or washed
327 x 424mm
HMF 682

15
Montage of Reclining Figures *c.*1928
collage, pencil, black chalk, watercolour wash, brush and ink, green oil paint, brush and red ink
303 x 567mm
HMF 689

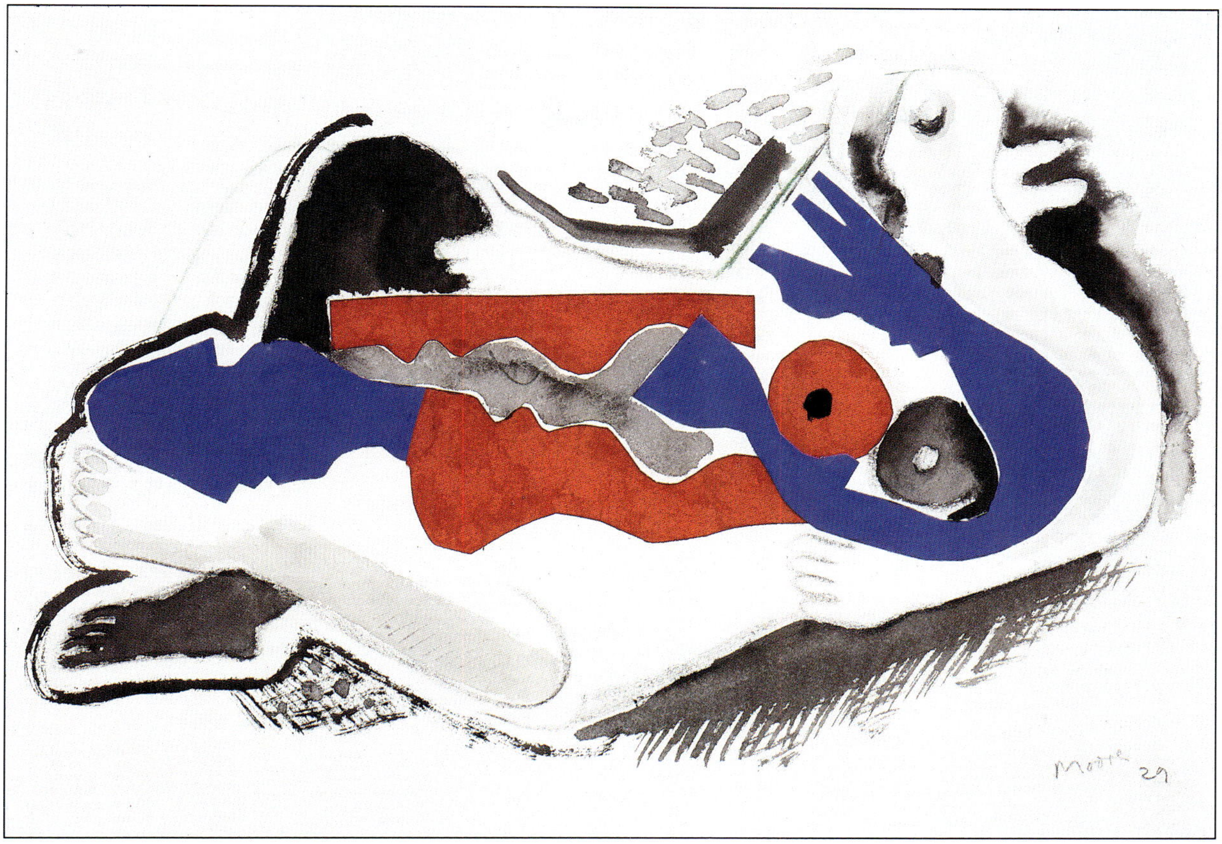

16
Reclining Figure 1929
charcoal, chalk, brush and Indian ink,
collaged blue and red paper
285 x 402/405mm
HMF 730

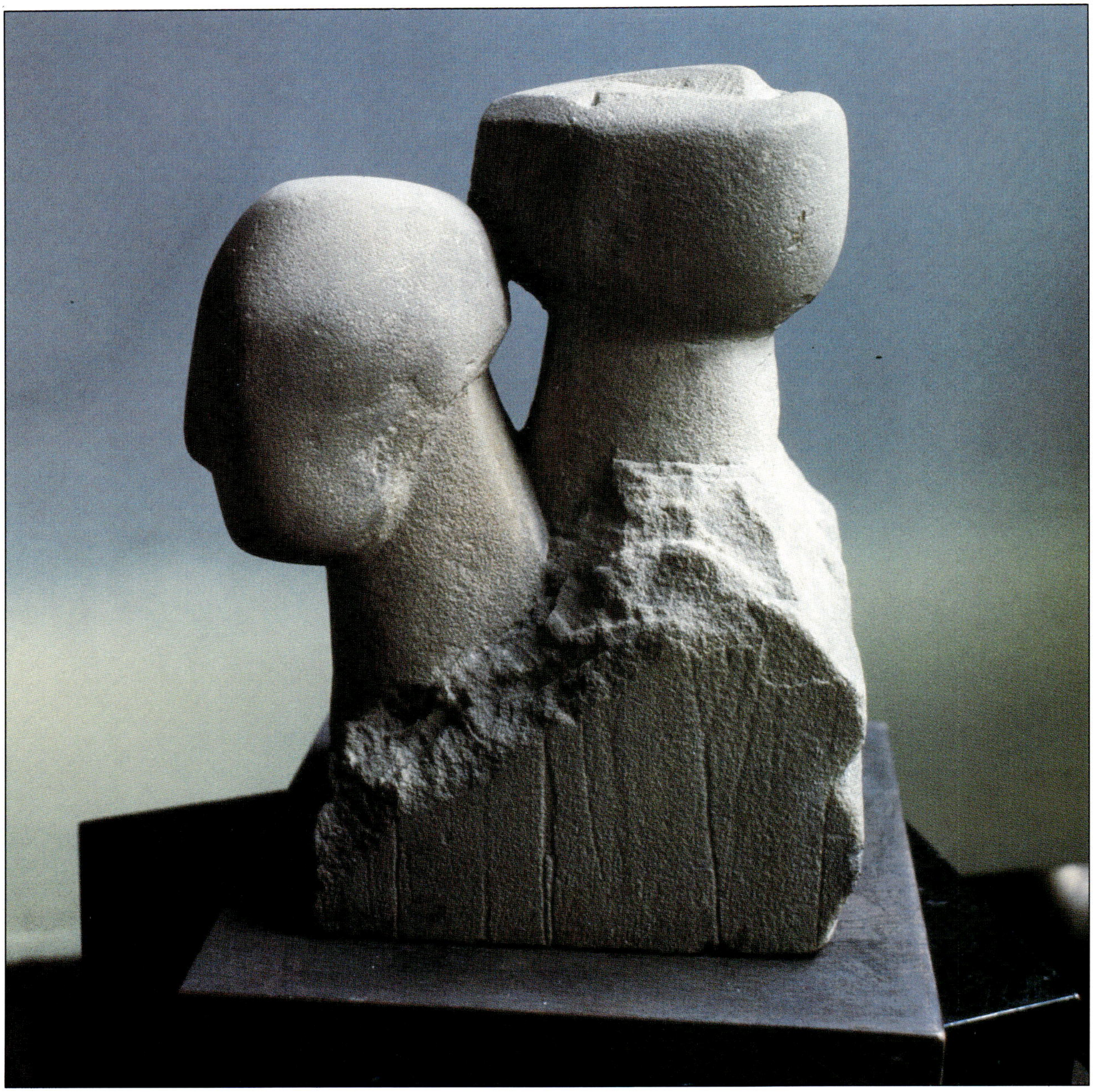

17

Two Heads 1924-25

H 31.7cm Mansfield stone

LH 25

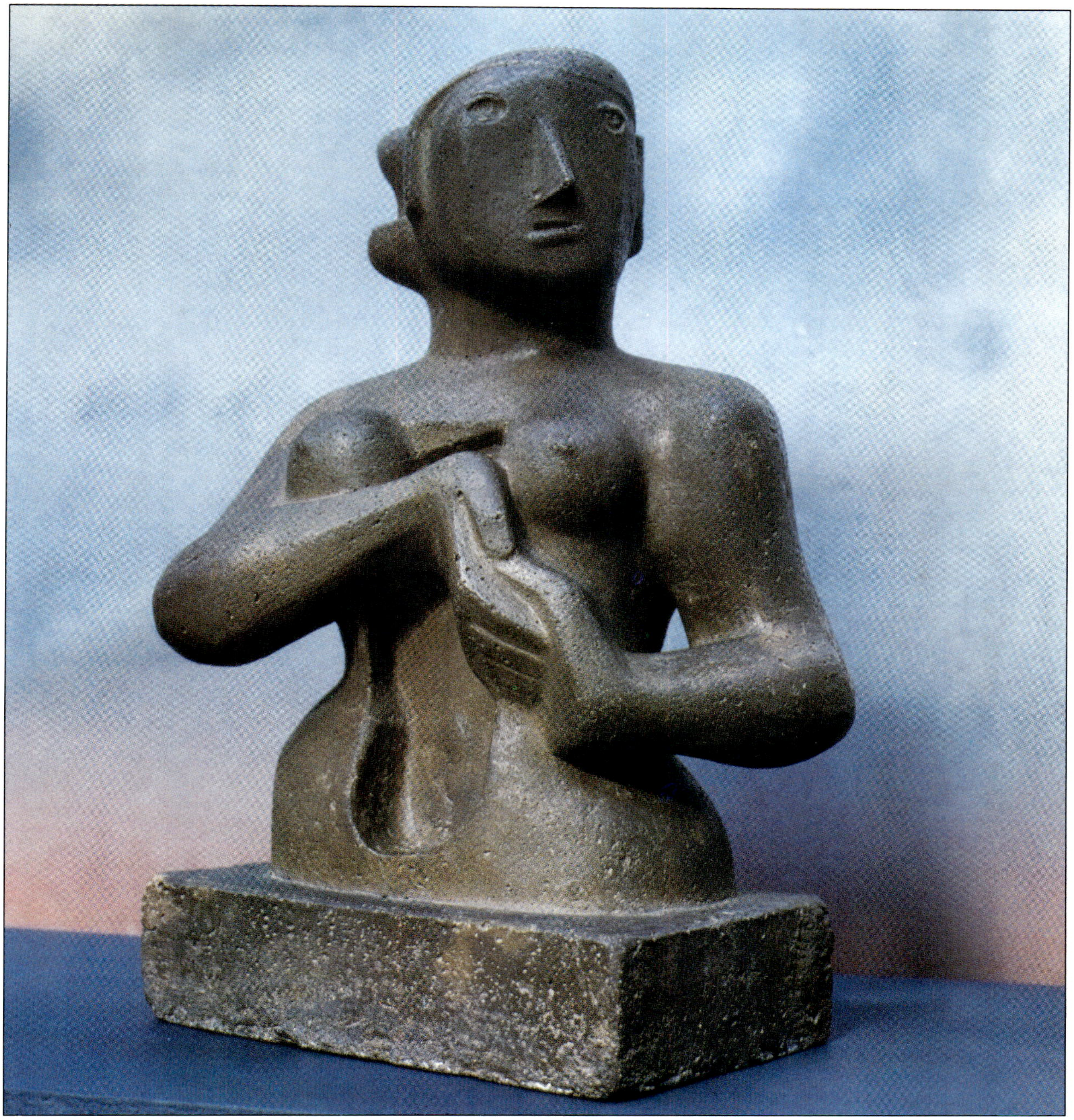

18
Half-Figure 1929
H 36.8cm cast concrete
The British Council, London
LH 67

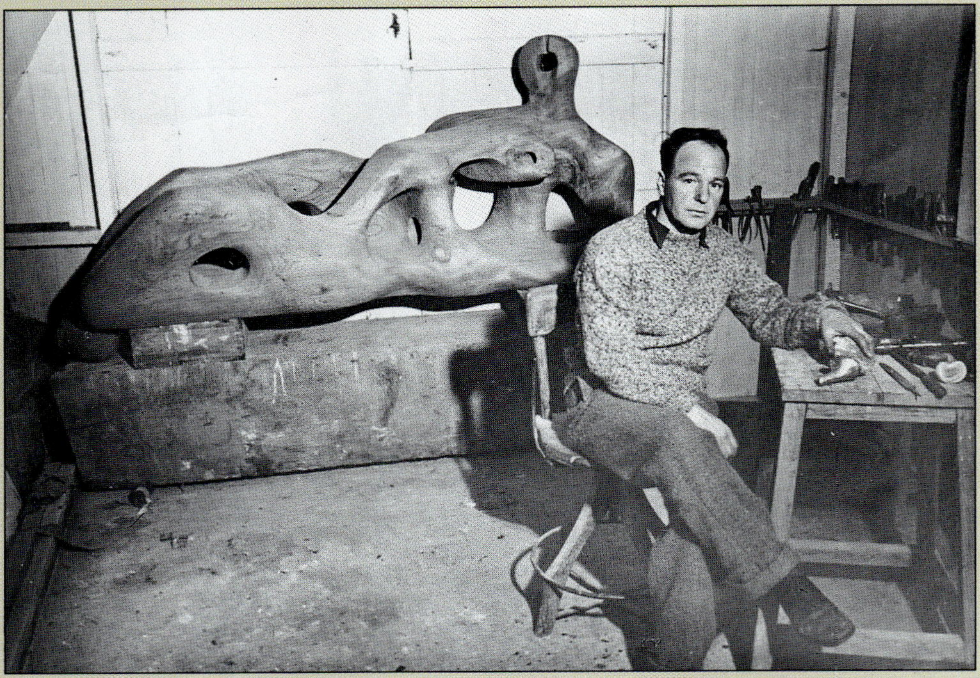

Henry Moore at Burcroft, Kent,
in 1939 with the carved elmwood
Reclining Figure 1939 (LH 210),
now in Detroit Institute of Arts.

1930s

Moore developed a still more personal style after he left the teaching post at the Royal College of Art which he held from 1925 to 1931. He felt free to invent sculptural forms rather than developing them from preconceived ideas of what, say, a figure or a mother and child group should look like. He described the radical cat.31 as a head and torso related to the base; in such works he felt the viewer must explore the separate forms without losing a sense of the whole figure composition.

Throughout this decade Moore's inspiration came primarily from natural forms, rarely the human figure (cat.34). His starting point was found objects such as pebbles and bones which he built up and modified until they became heads and bodies. The transformation from bone to figure is especially clear in cat.26. He was inspired by Surrealists, who used surprising substitutions and juxtapositions in order to conjure up material from the unconscious mind. Moore, none the less, remained attached to the 'real' world; his *Mother and Child* (cat.36) touches the viewer on many levels: it embodies the intimate bonding that we expect of the relationship, without describing a particular case.

Moore remained true to a personal vision while borrowing ideas from Constructivism as well as Surrealism. His stringed figures were inspired by models in the Science Museum in London, where one could see geometric figures joined by coloured strings to demonstrate the complex surfaces between them. Moore gave his solid forms the curves of nature rather than mathematics, so the *Stringed Ball* (cat.53) suggests a bird's nest as well as a sphere and cat.54 may be related to a mother and child.

The fertility of his invention can be seen in drawings for sculpture, such as cats.34 and 39. Both drawings show ideas for carving blocks of stone – horizontal and vertical – with the greatest respect for the material. During the 1930s, however, Moore explored opened-up forms in reclining figures (cats.47, 48), while the solid block was predominant in his vertical figures and square head-forms, such as cats.33 and 35. He also took up the theme of enclosing one form inside another, which he returned to in the 1950s; his first *Helmet* (cat.56) of 1939-40 matches the impending doom of war.

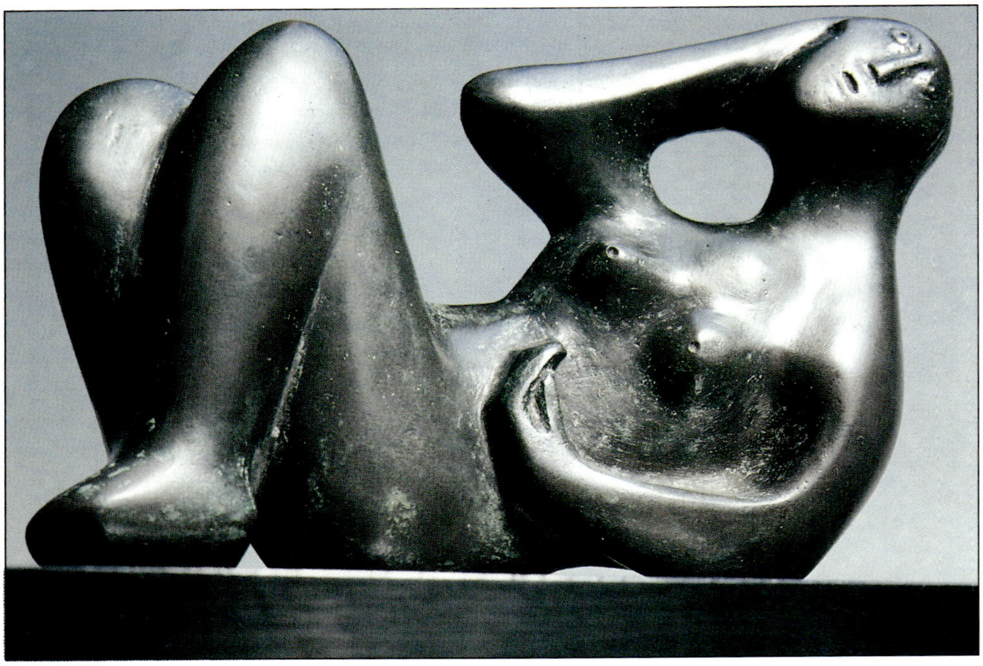

. . . if a work of sculpture has its own life and form, it will be alive and expansive, seeming larger than the stone or wood from which it is carved. It should always give the impression, whether carved or modelled, of having grown organically, created by pressure from within.

19
Reclining Figure 1930
L 17.1cm bronze
edition of 6
LH 85

20
Girl with Clasped Hands 1930
H 41.5cm
Cumberland alabaster
The British Council, London
LH 93

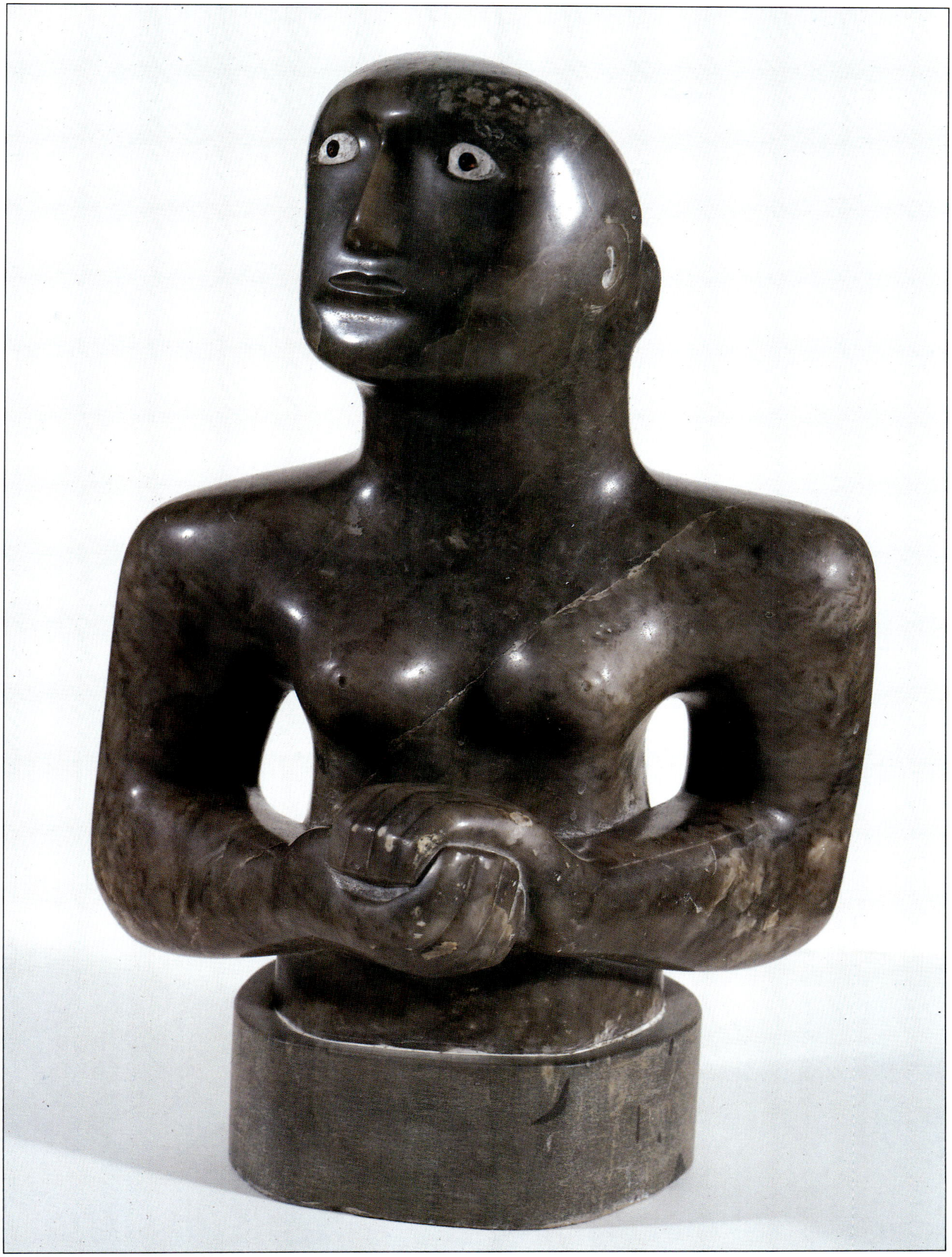

21

Reclining Figure 1931, cast 1963

L 43.2cm bronze edition of 6

LH 101

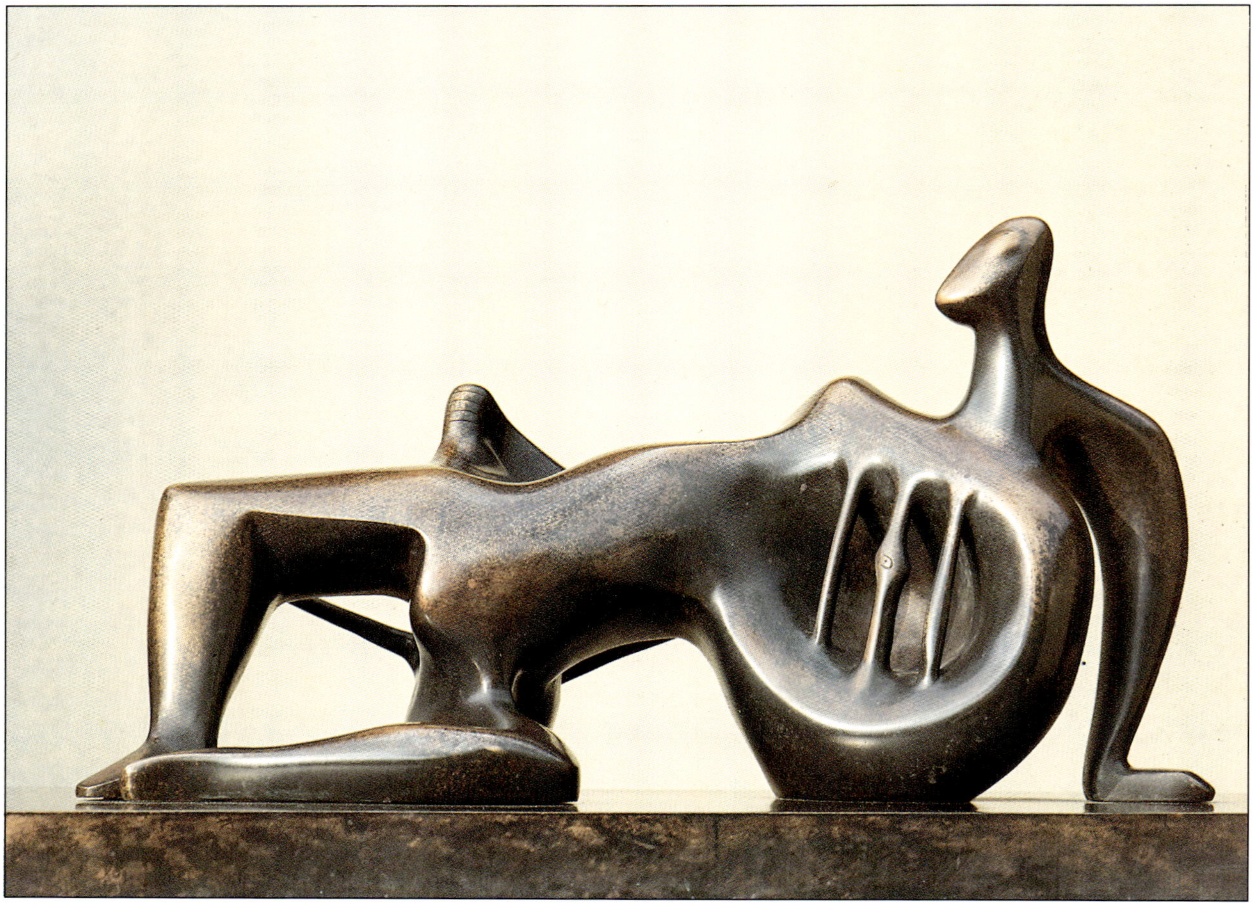

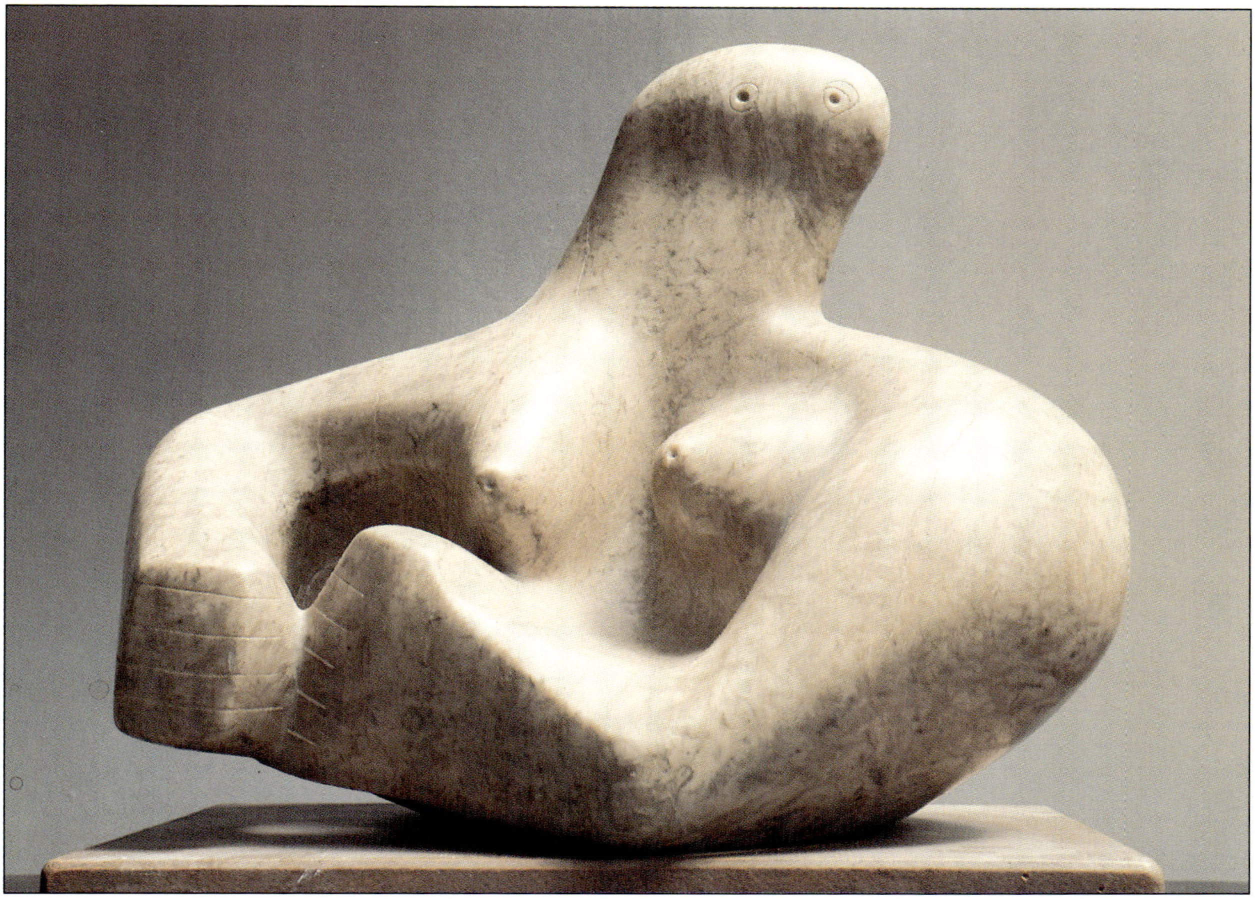

A sculpture must have its own life. Rather than give the impression of a smaller object carved out of a bigger block, it should make the observer feel that what he is seeing contains within itself its own organic energy thrusting outwards.

22
Composition 1931
L 41.5cm Cumberland alabaster
LH 102

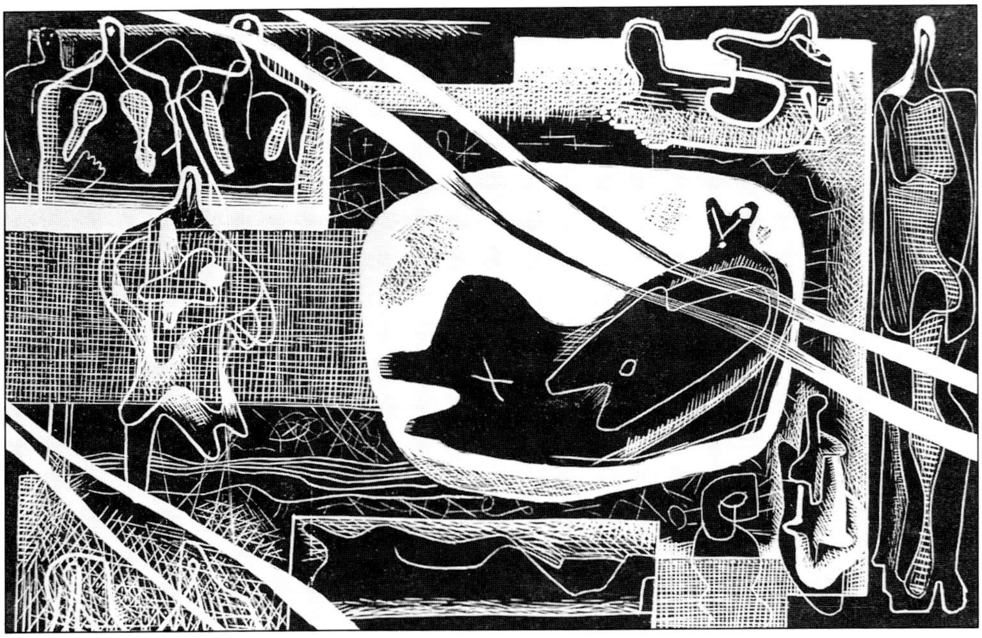

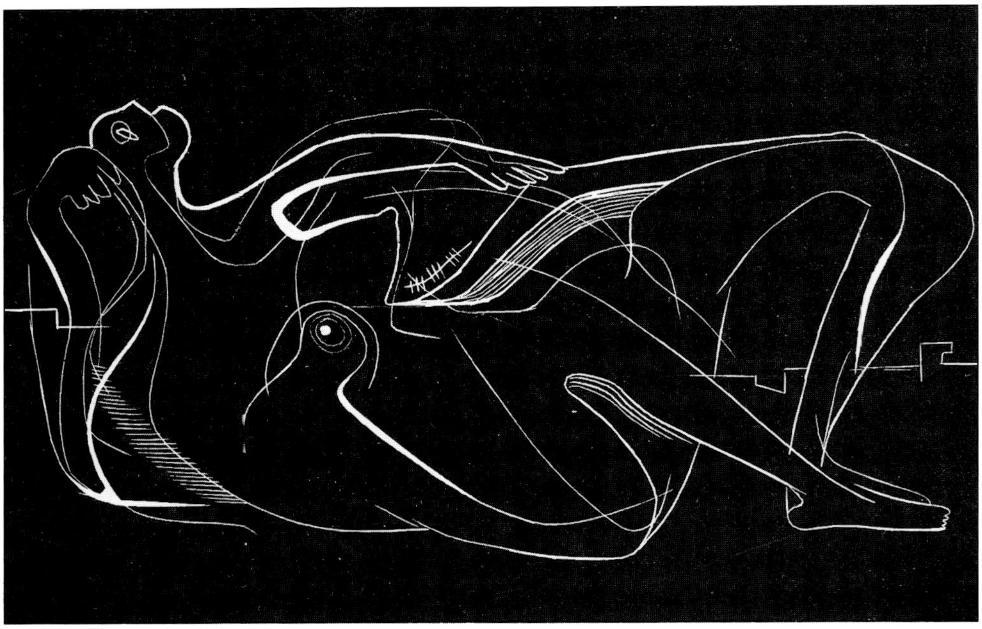

23

Figures, Sculptures 1931

Woodcut

127 x 197mm

CGM 1

24

Reclining Nude 1931

Woodcut

102 x 162mm

CGM 2

25
Page from Sketchbook
Ideas for Sculpture:
Transformation of Bones 1932
pencil
241 x 180mm
HMF 943

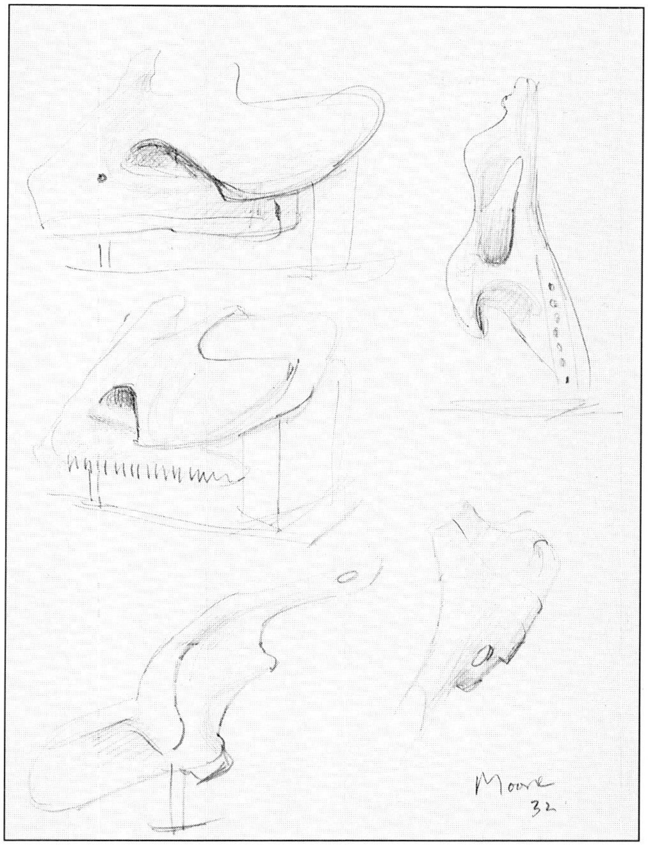

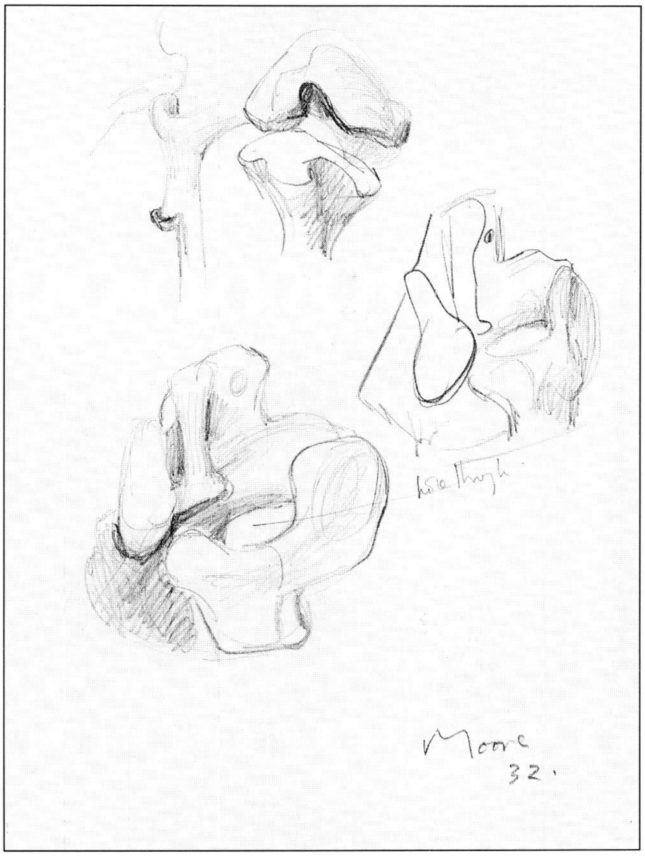

26
Page from Sketchbook
Ideas for Sculpture:
Transformation of Bones 1932
pencil
241 x 180mm
HMF 944

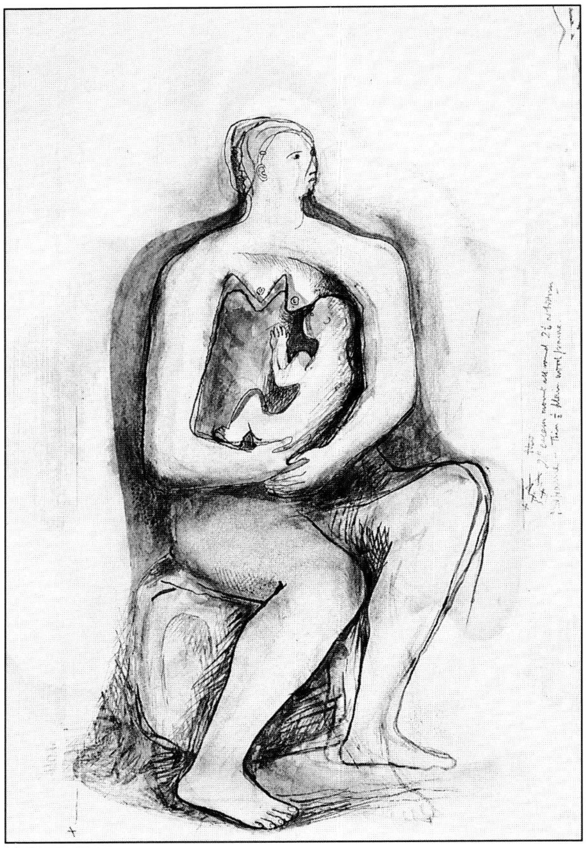

27

Seated Mother and Child 1933
charcoal, washed pastel, pen and
black ink, brush and black ink
556 x 374mm
HMF 1001

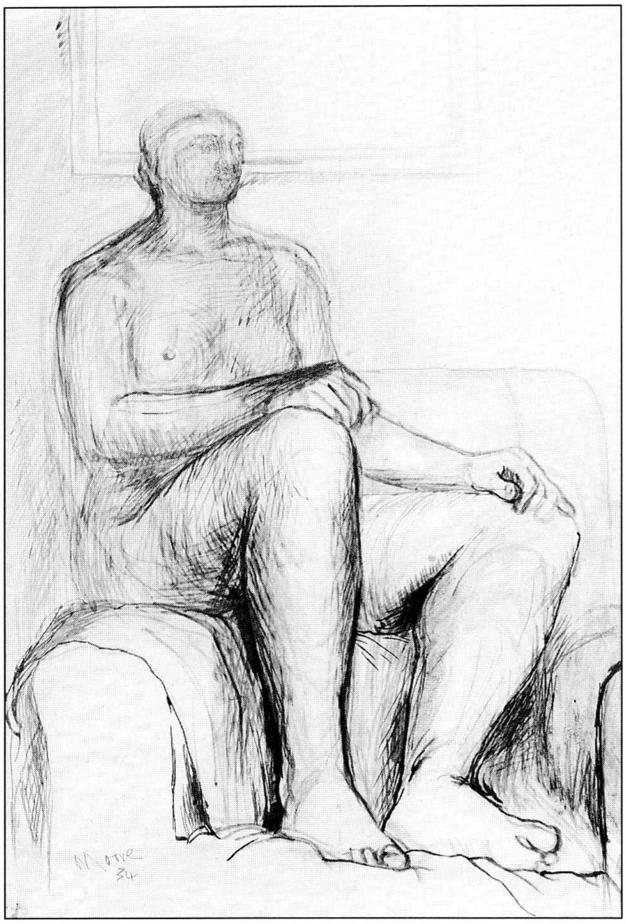

28

Seated Figure 1934
pencil, ink, wash
555 x 380mm
Arts Council of Great Britain,
The South Bank Centre
HMF 1047

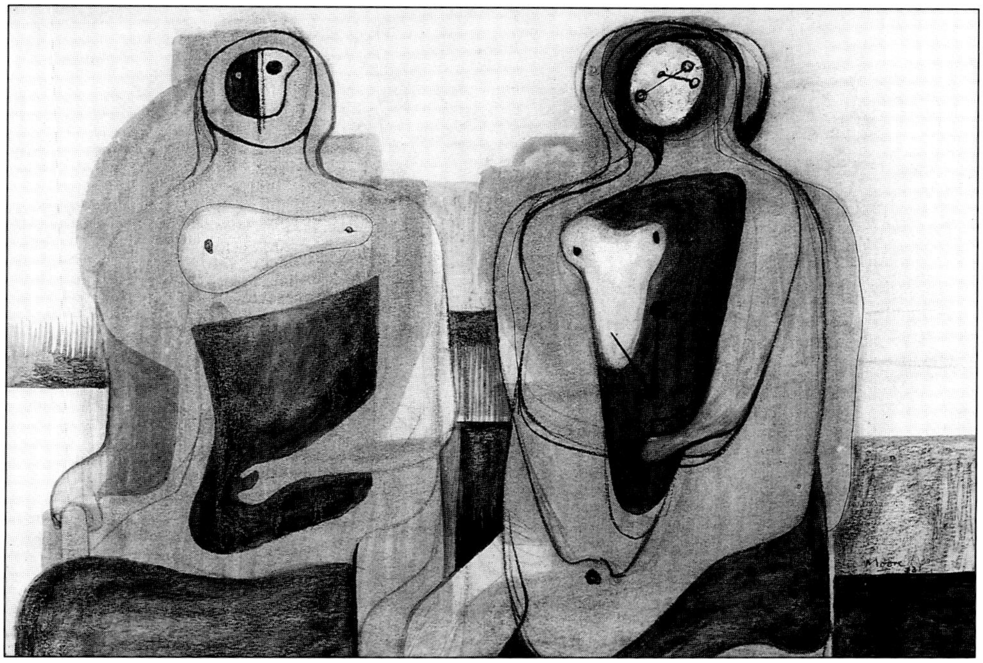

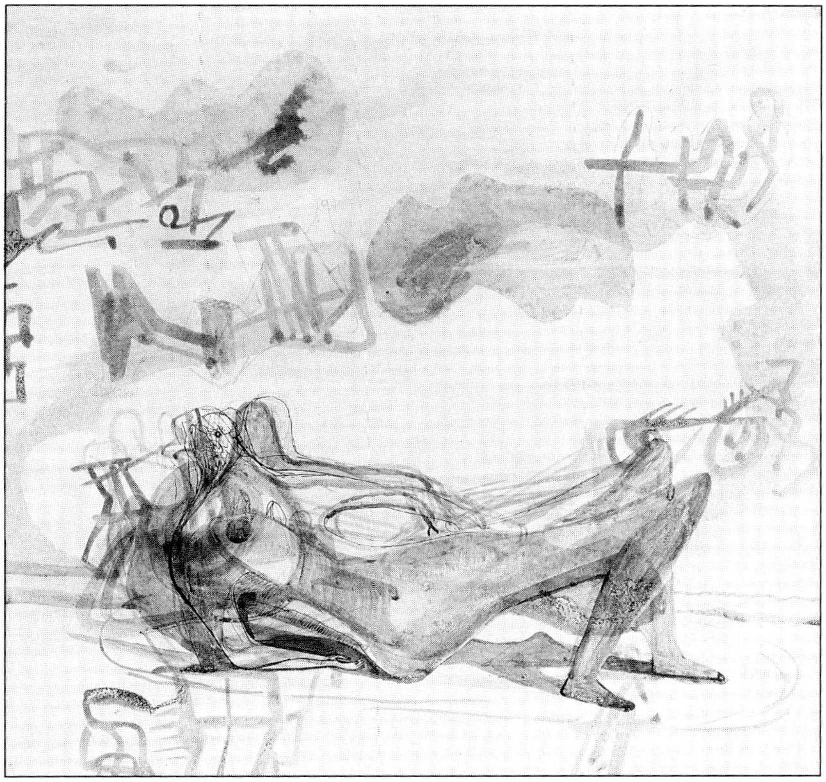

29
Two Seated Women *c.*1934
charcoal (rubbed and washed),
watercolour wash, pen and
Indian ink, black crayon
370 x 553mm
HMF 1077

30
Reclining Figure:
Drawing for Sculpture 1933
pencil, pen and ink,
brush and ink, wash
364 x 380mm
Art Gallery of New South Wales,
Sydney
HMF 992

31

Composition 1934

L 44.5cm cast concrete

LH 140

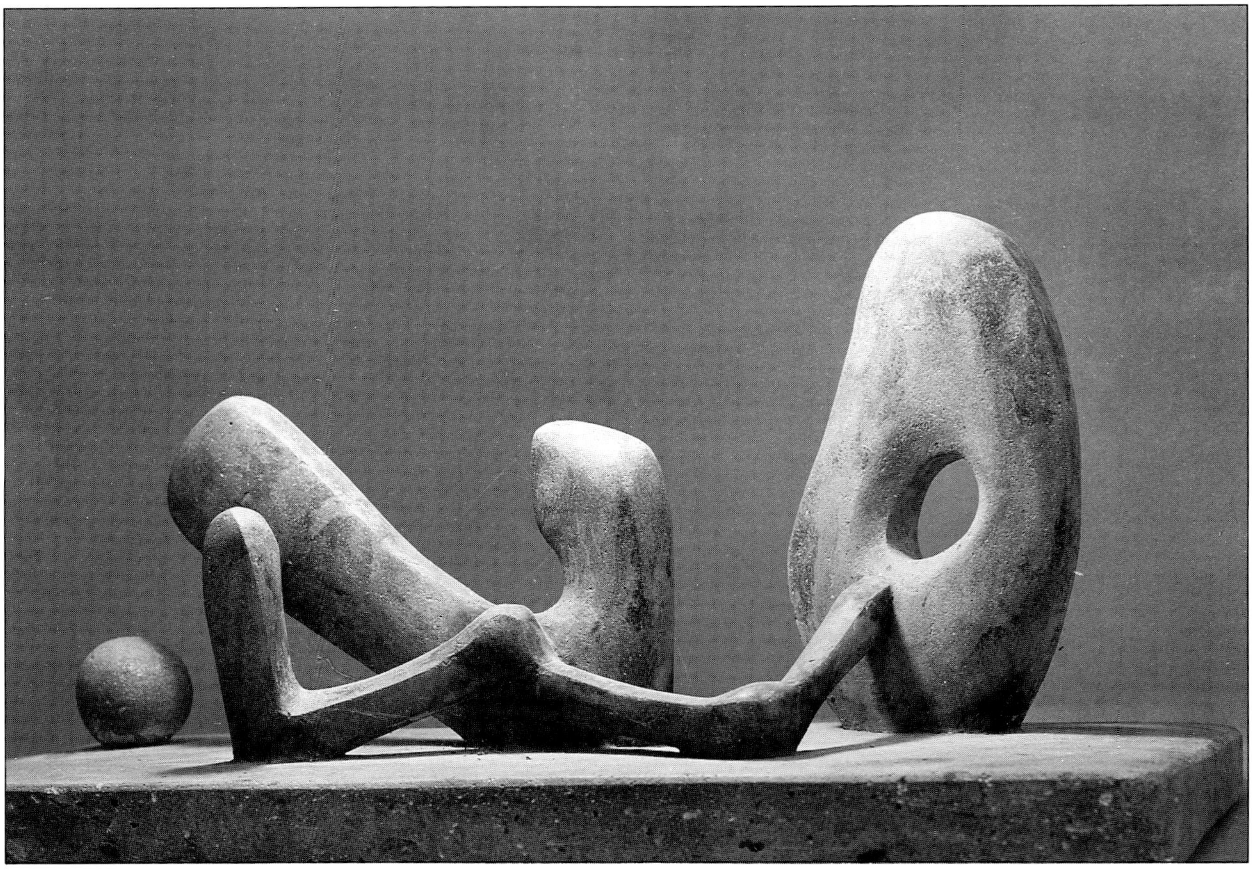

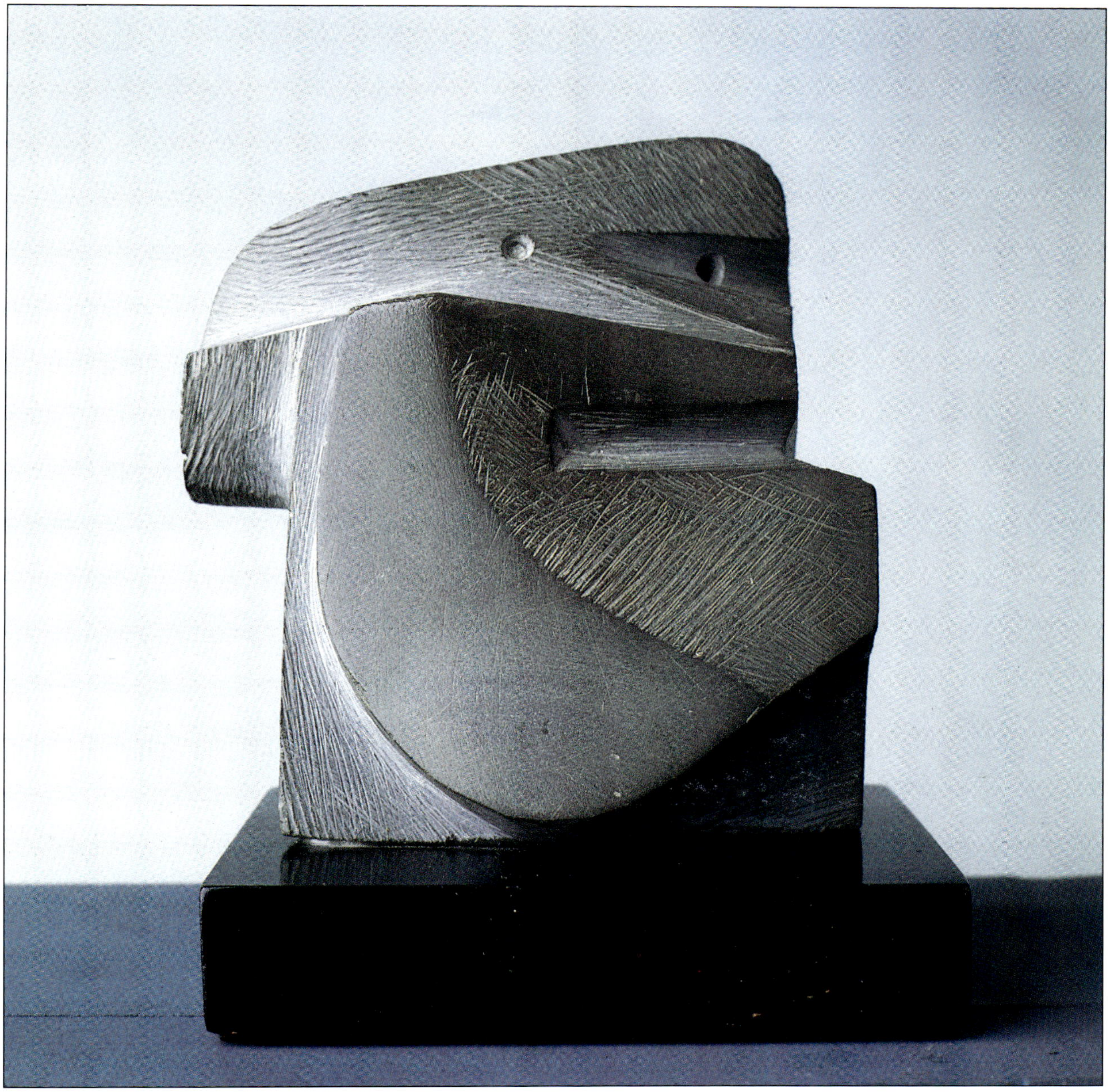

32
Carving 1934
H 9.8cm African wonderstone
LH 142

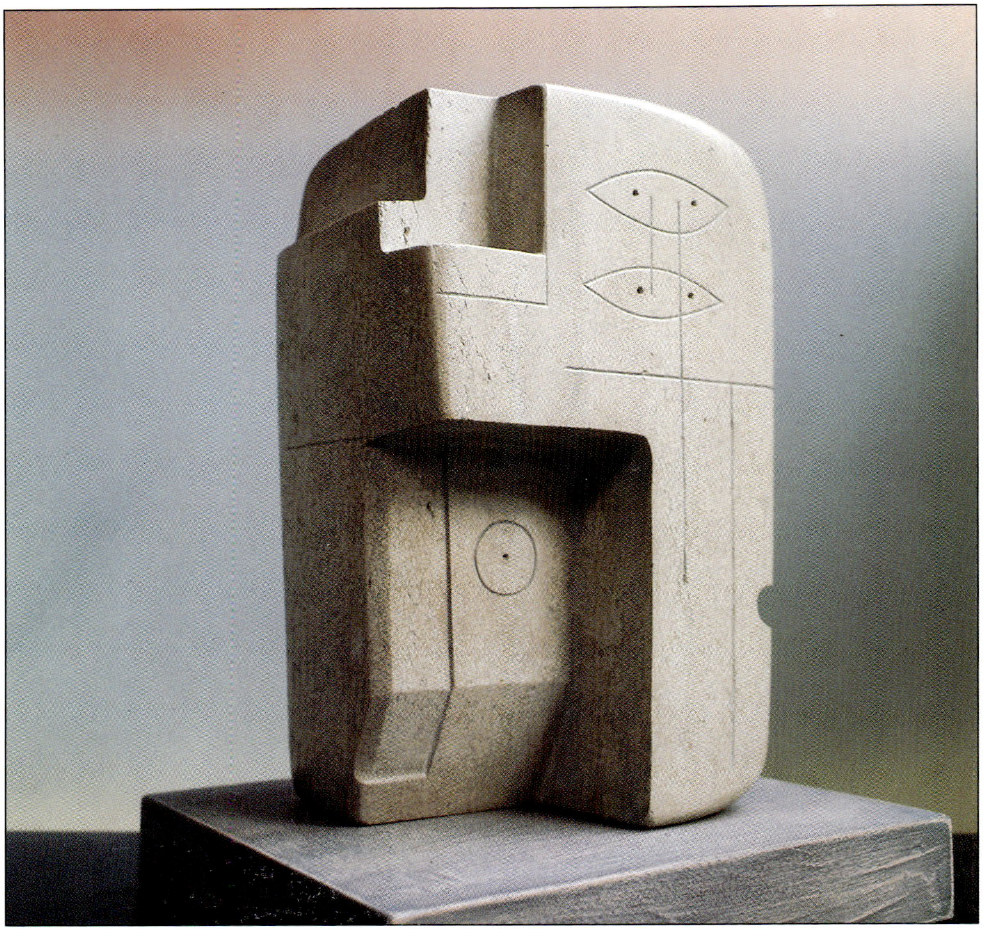

33
Square Form 1934
H 31.7cm Burgundy stone
LH 154b

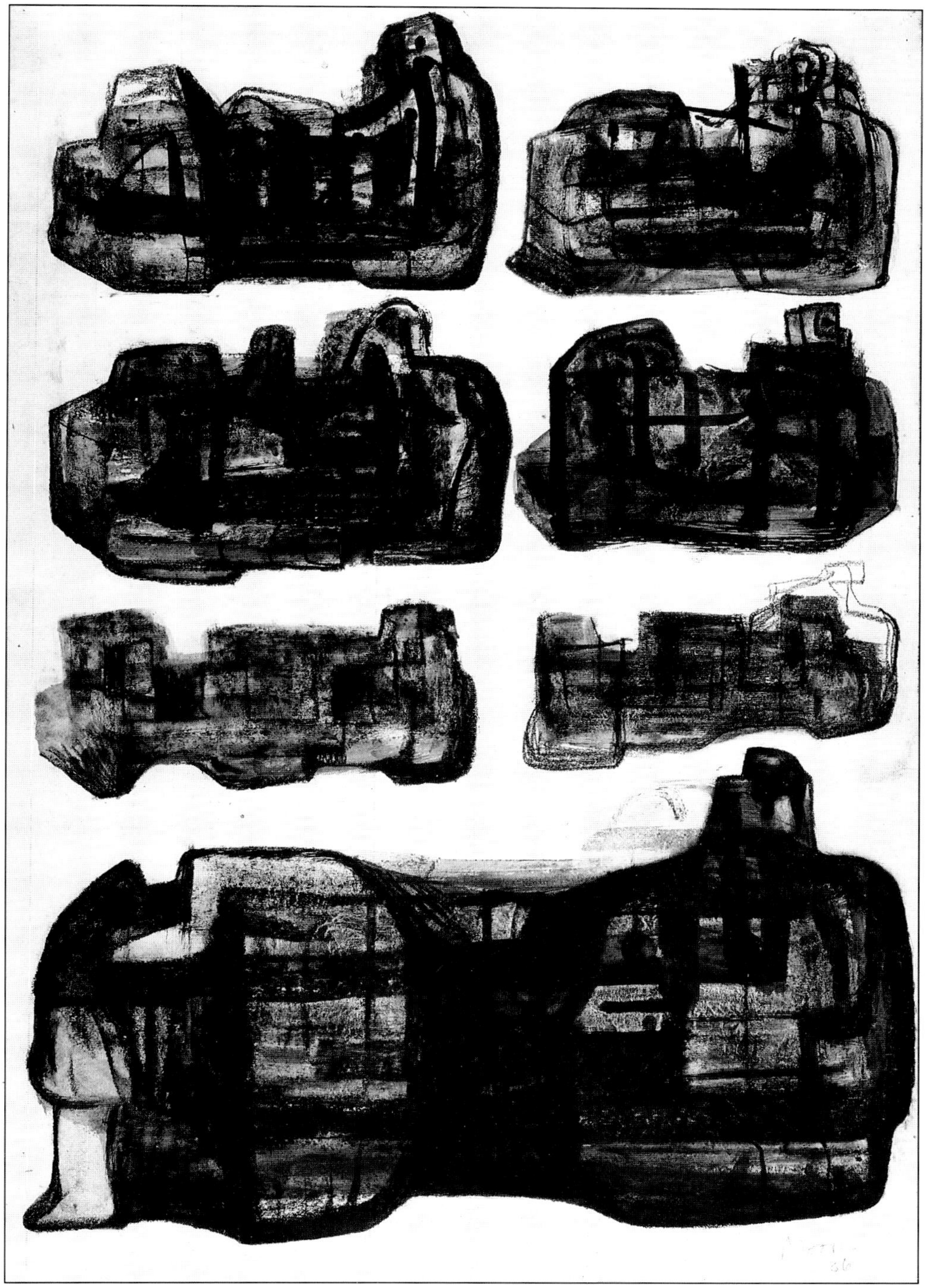

34

Square Form Reclining Figure 1936
black chalk, black ink wash
555 x 392mm
HMF 1242

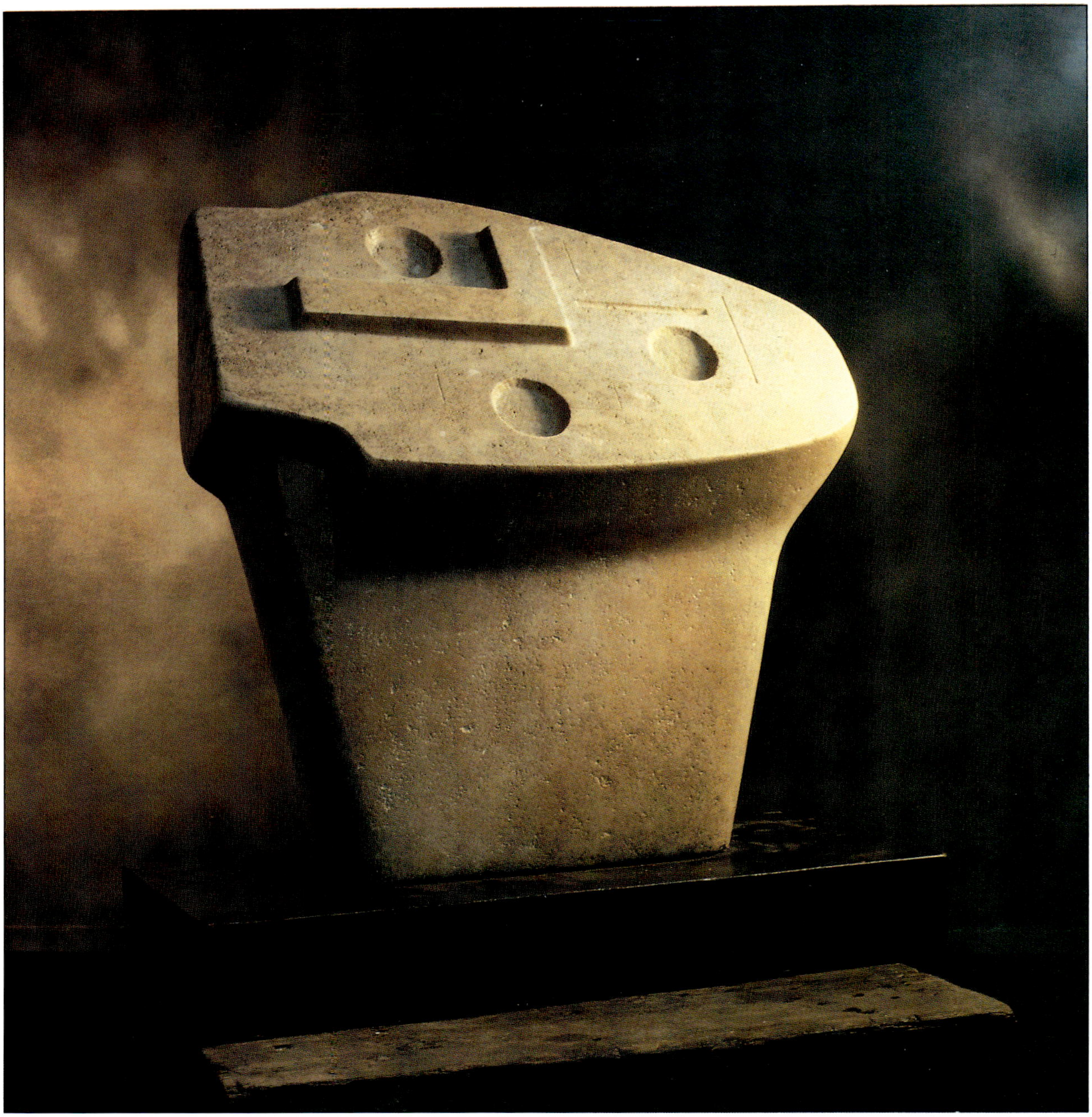

35

Carving 1936

H 45.7cm Travertine marble

LH 164

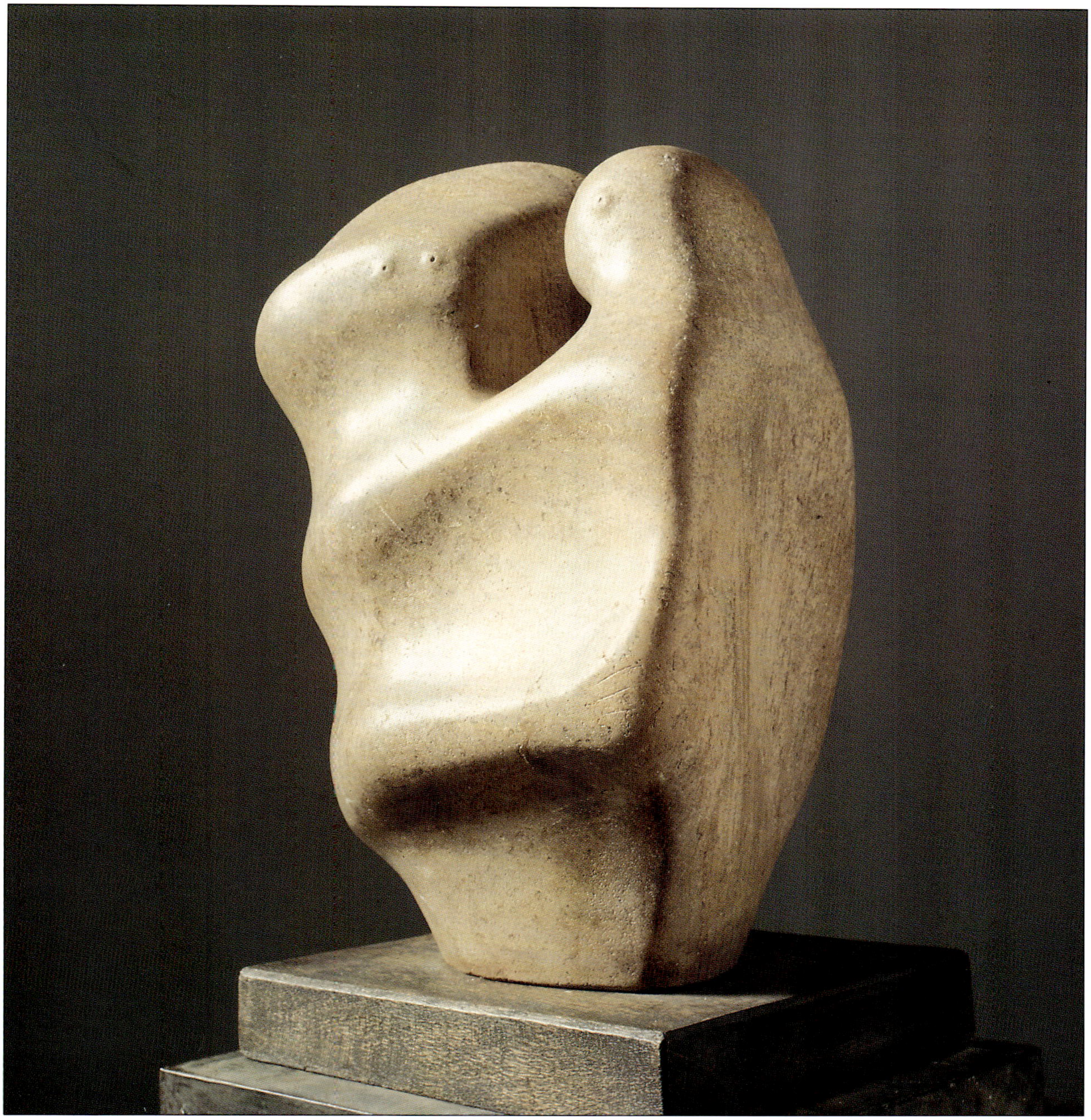

36
Mother and Child 1936
H 51cm Ancaster stone
The British Council, London
LH 165

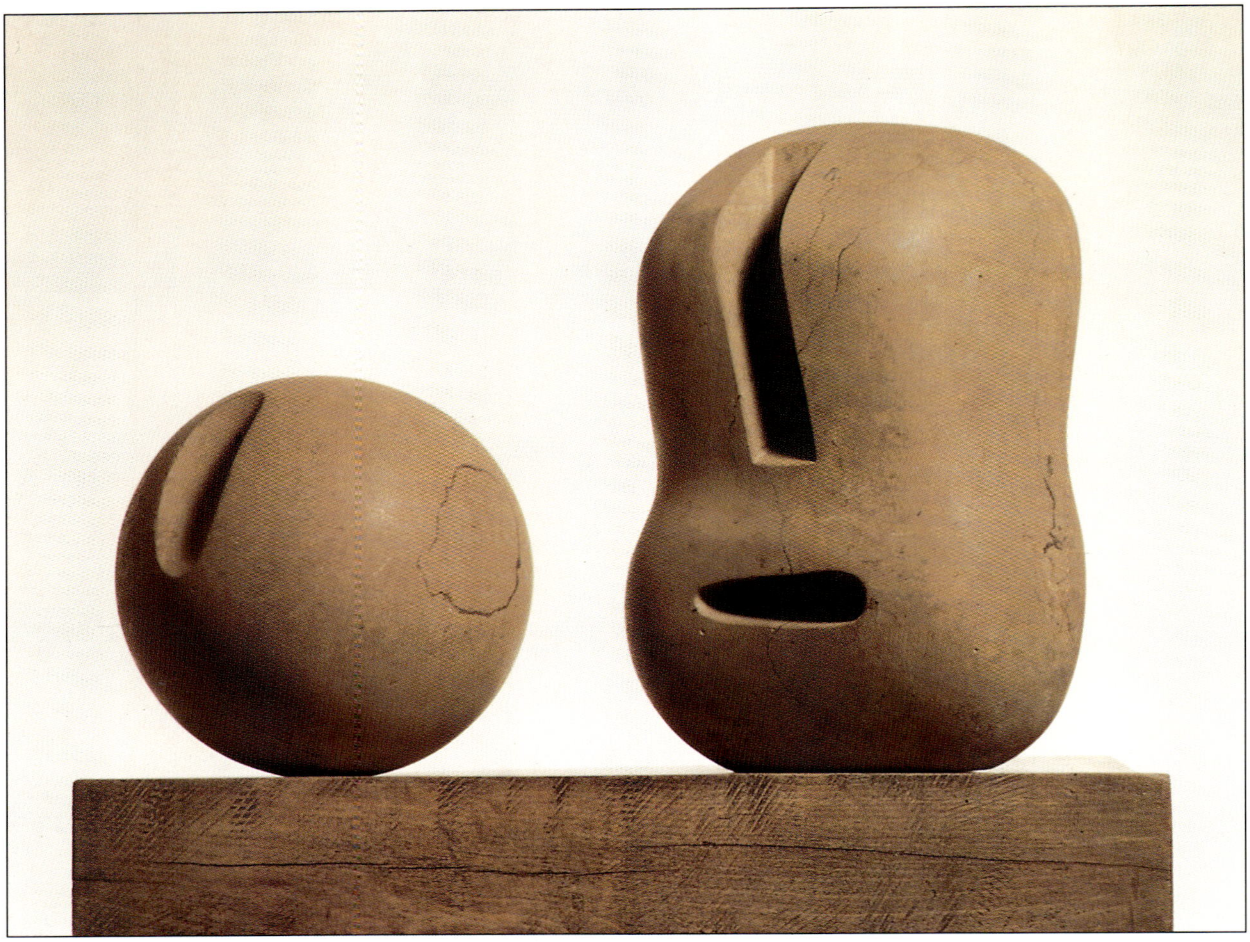

Sculpture fully in the round has no two points of view alike. The desire for form completely realised is connected with asymmetry. For a symmetrical mass being the same from both sides cannot have more than half the number of different points of view possessed by a non-symmetrical mass.

37
Two Forms 1936
L 64cm brown Hornton stone
LH 166

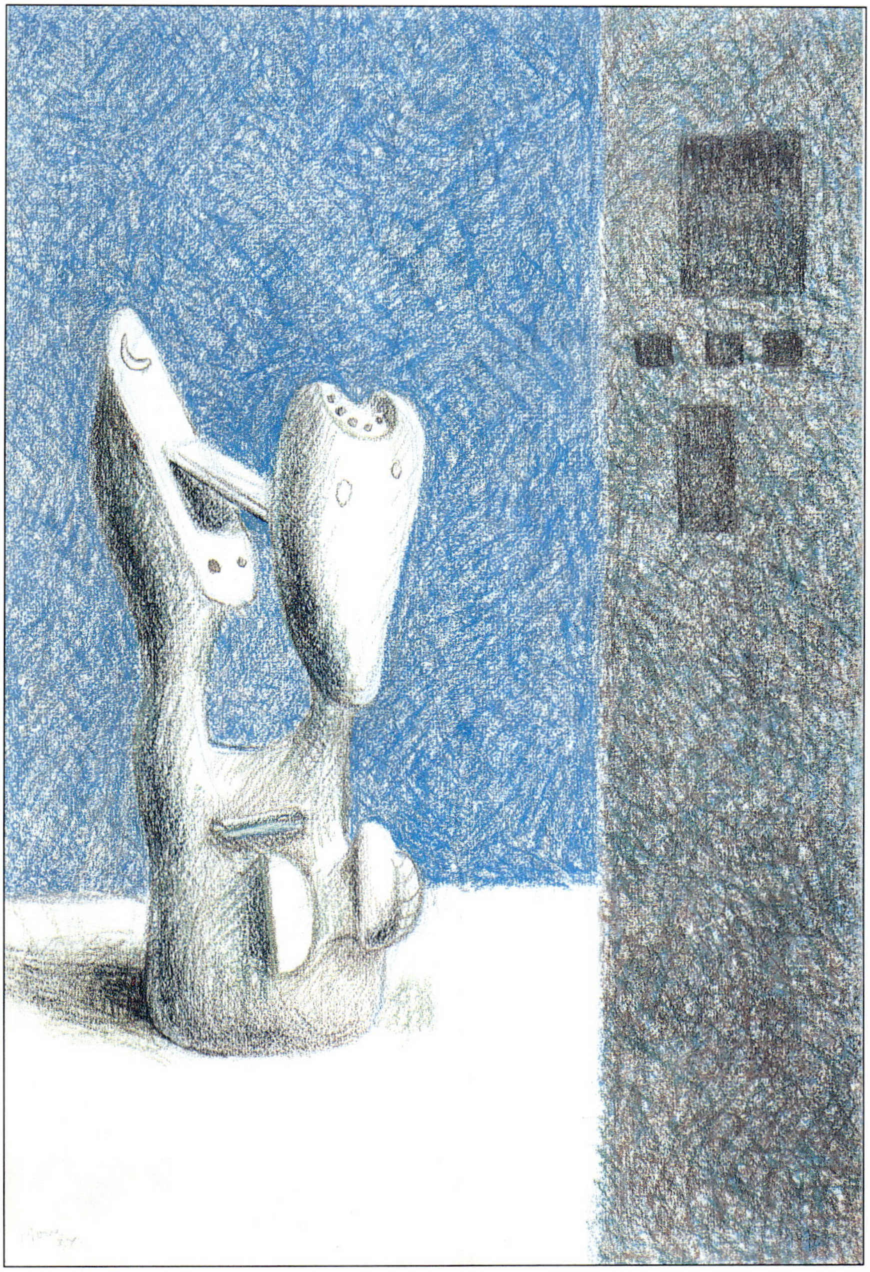

38
Sculpture in a Setting 1937
coloured chalk
569 x 380mm
HMF 1318

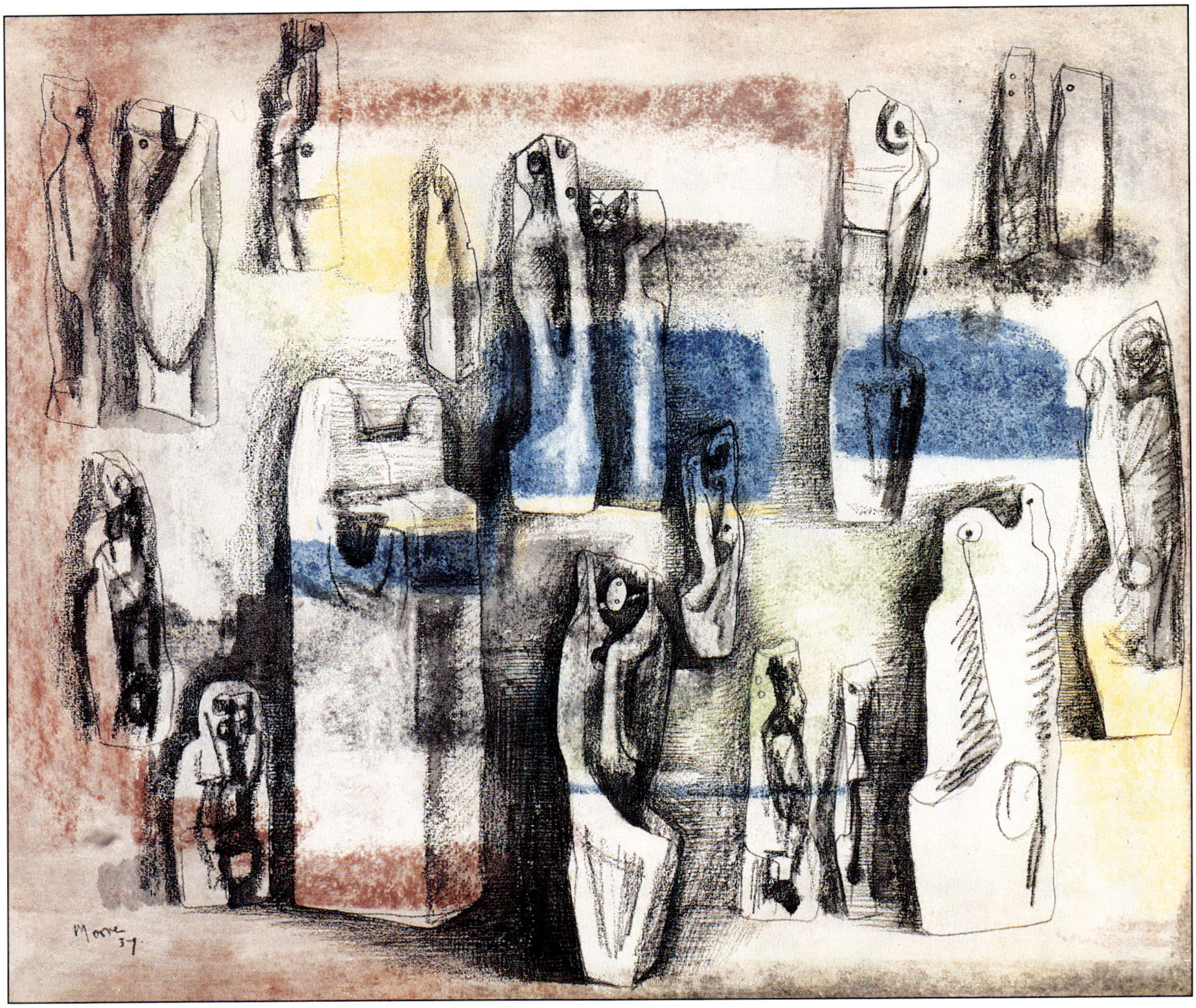

39
Drawing for Stone Sculpture 1937
watercolour, coloured chalk, pencil, ink wash
407 x 535mm
HMF 1320

40
Seventeen Ideas for Metal Sculpture 1937
pencil, washed pastel, watercolour, pen and black ink, gouache
666 x 517mm
HMF 1321

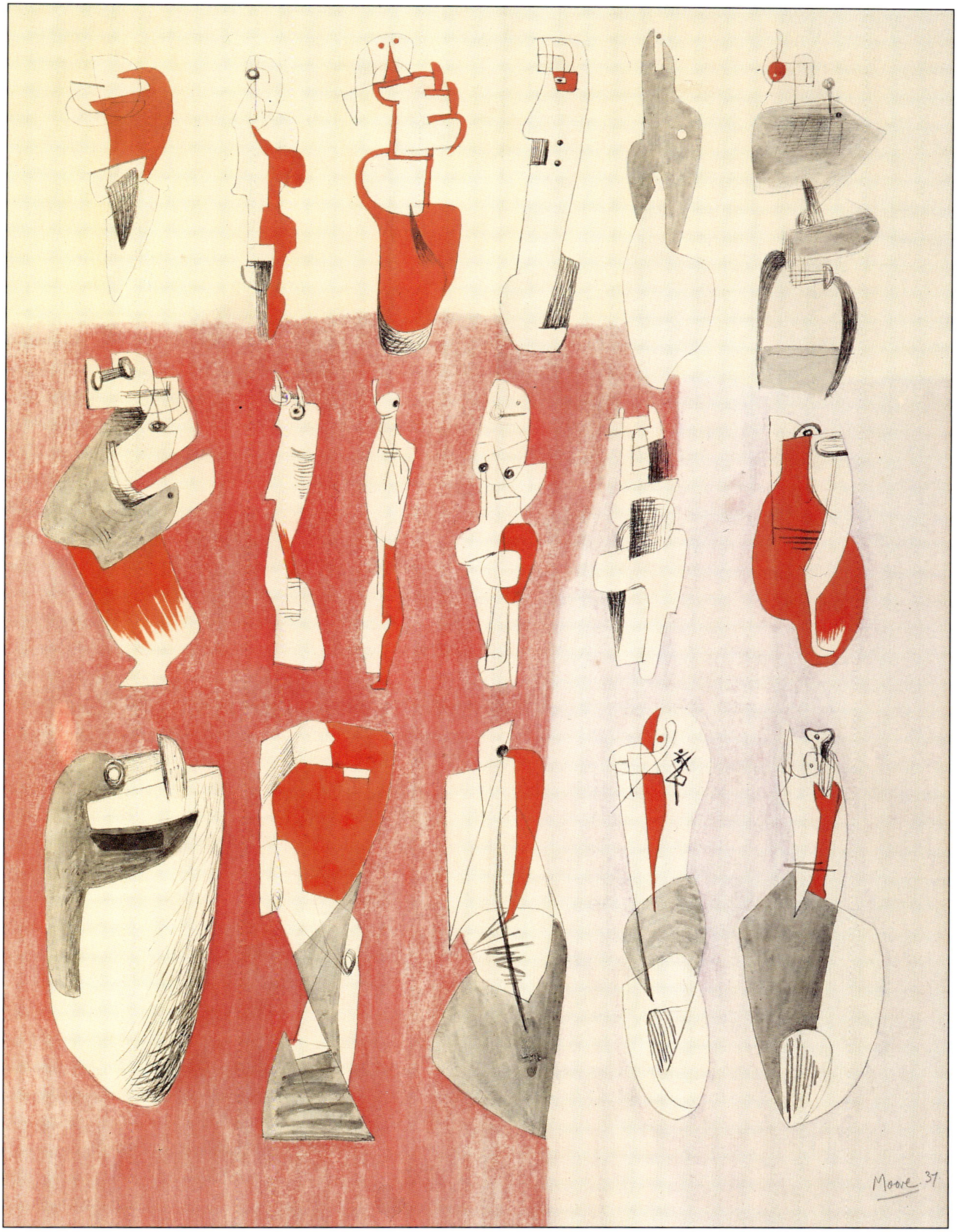
Moore 37

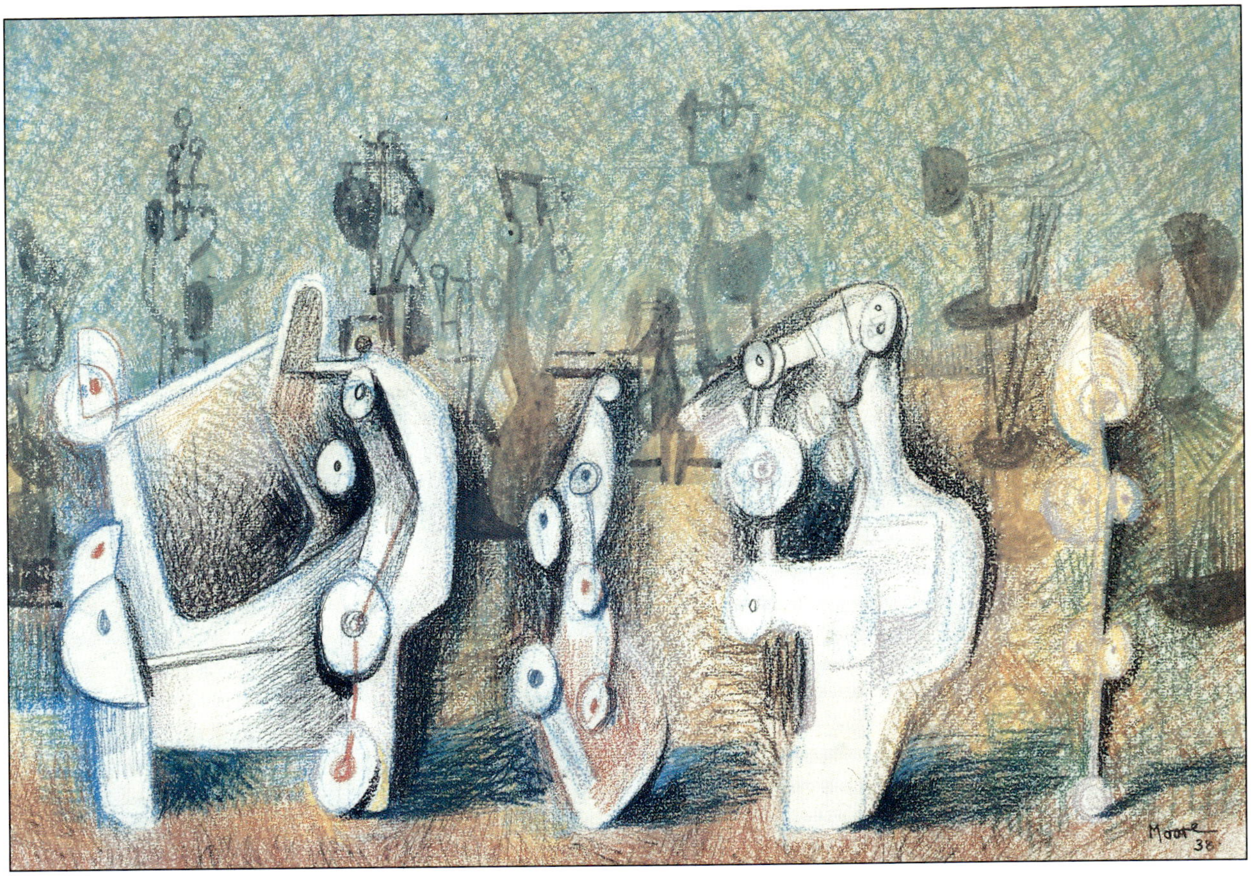
Moore
38

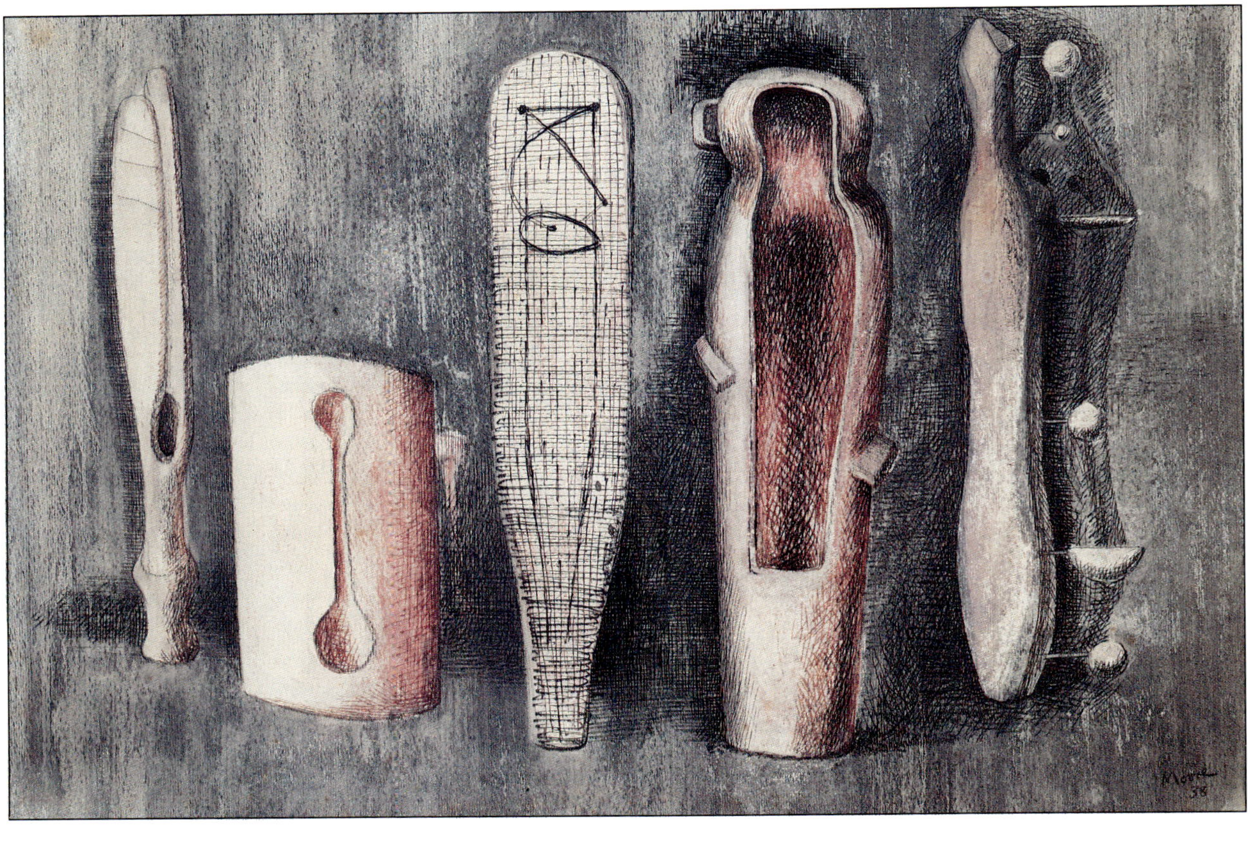
Moore
38

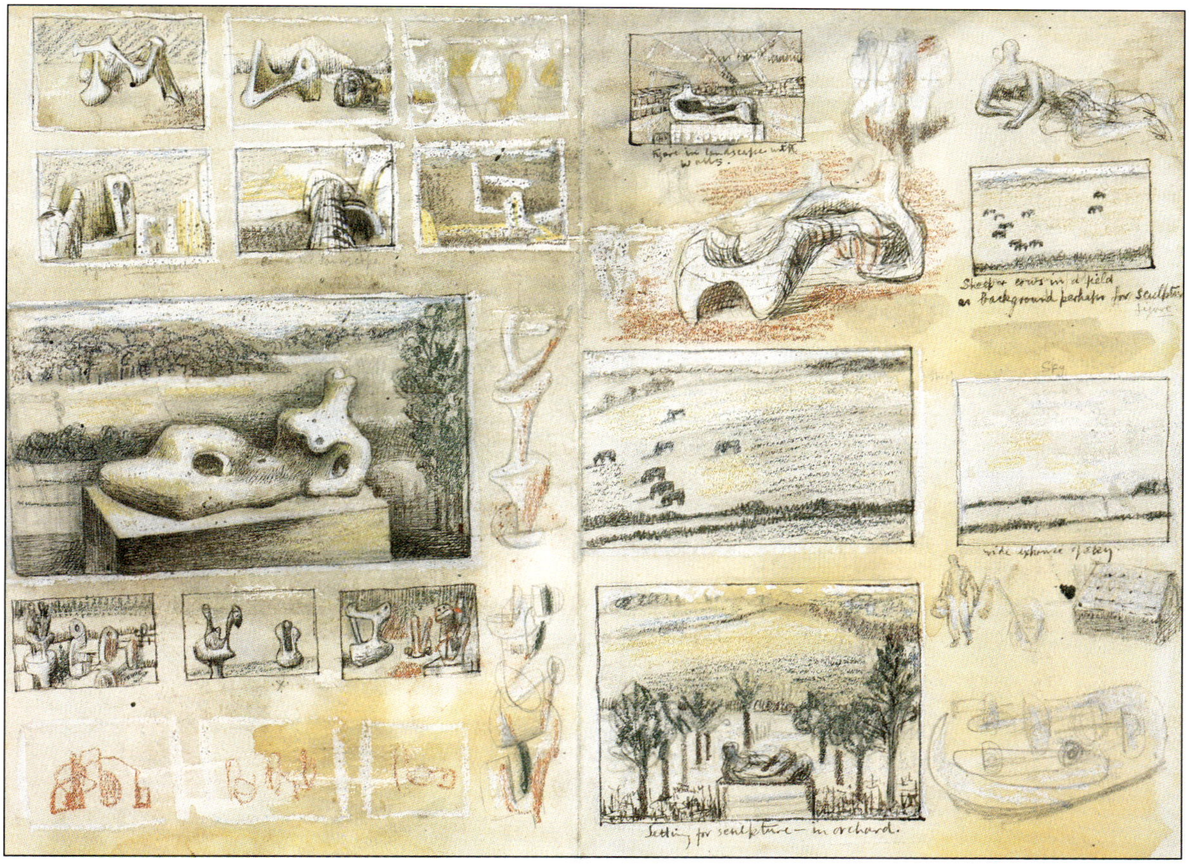

41

Mechanisms 1938

coloured chalk, wash

397 x 572mm

HMF 1367

42

Sculptural Ideas:

Hollow Form 1938

pen and red and black inks,
red and grey wash

381 x 559mm

Art Gallery of New South Wales,
Sydney

HMF 1378

43

Page from Sketchbook

Ideas for Sculpture in Landscape c.1938

pencil, white wax, coloured crayon,
watercolour, pen and ink

277 x 381mm

HMF 1391a

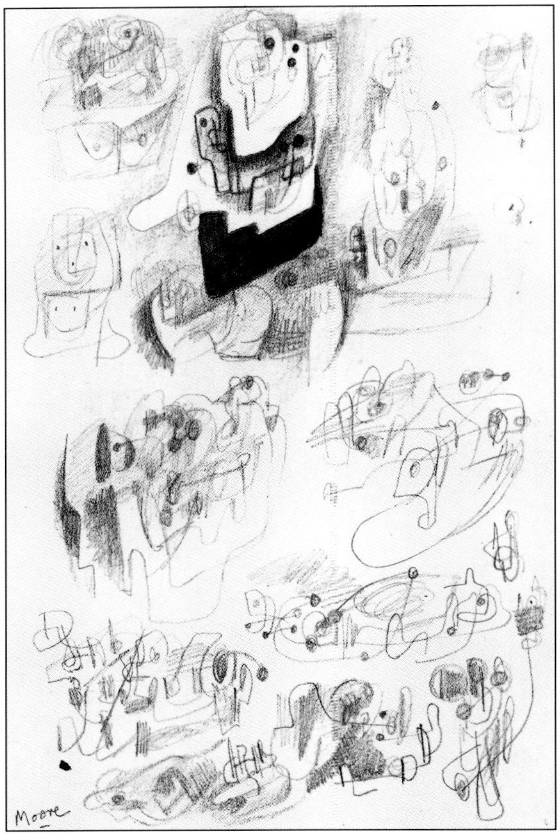

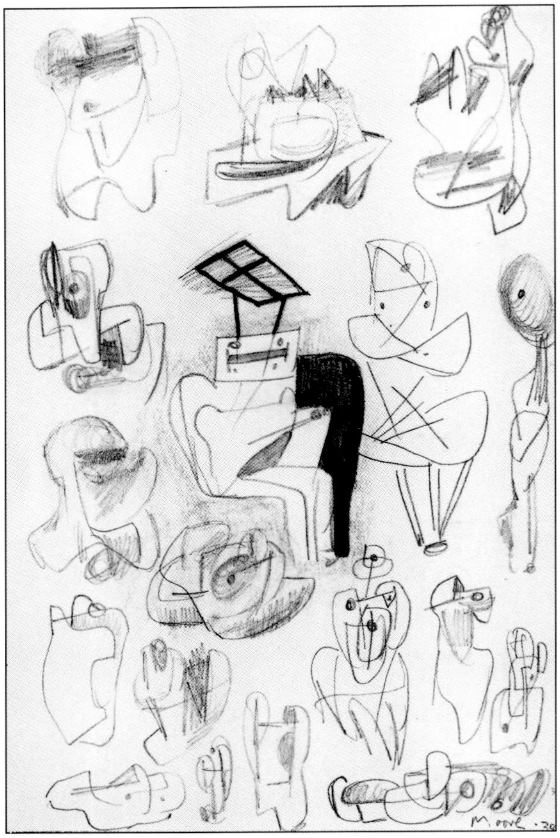

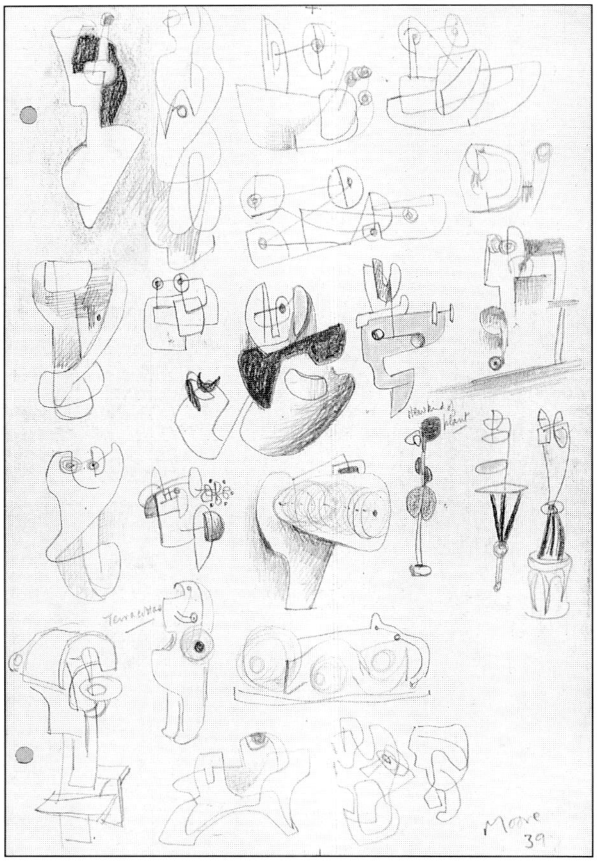

44
Page from Sketchbook
Ideas for Sculpture 1938
pencil, pastel, charcoal, watercolour wash
277 x 183mm
HMF 1410

45
Page from Sketchbook
Ideas for Sculpture 1938
pencil, pastel, crayon
277 x 183mm
HMF 1411

46
Page from Sketchbook
Ideas for Sculpture 1939
pencil, coloured crayon
278 x 190mm
HMF 1412

47
Recumbent Figure 1938
L 14cm lead
private collection
LH 184

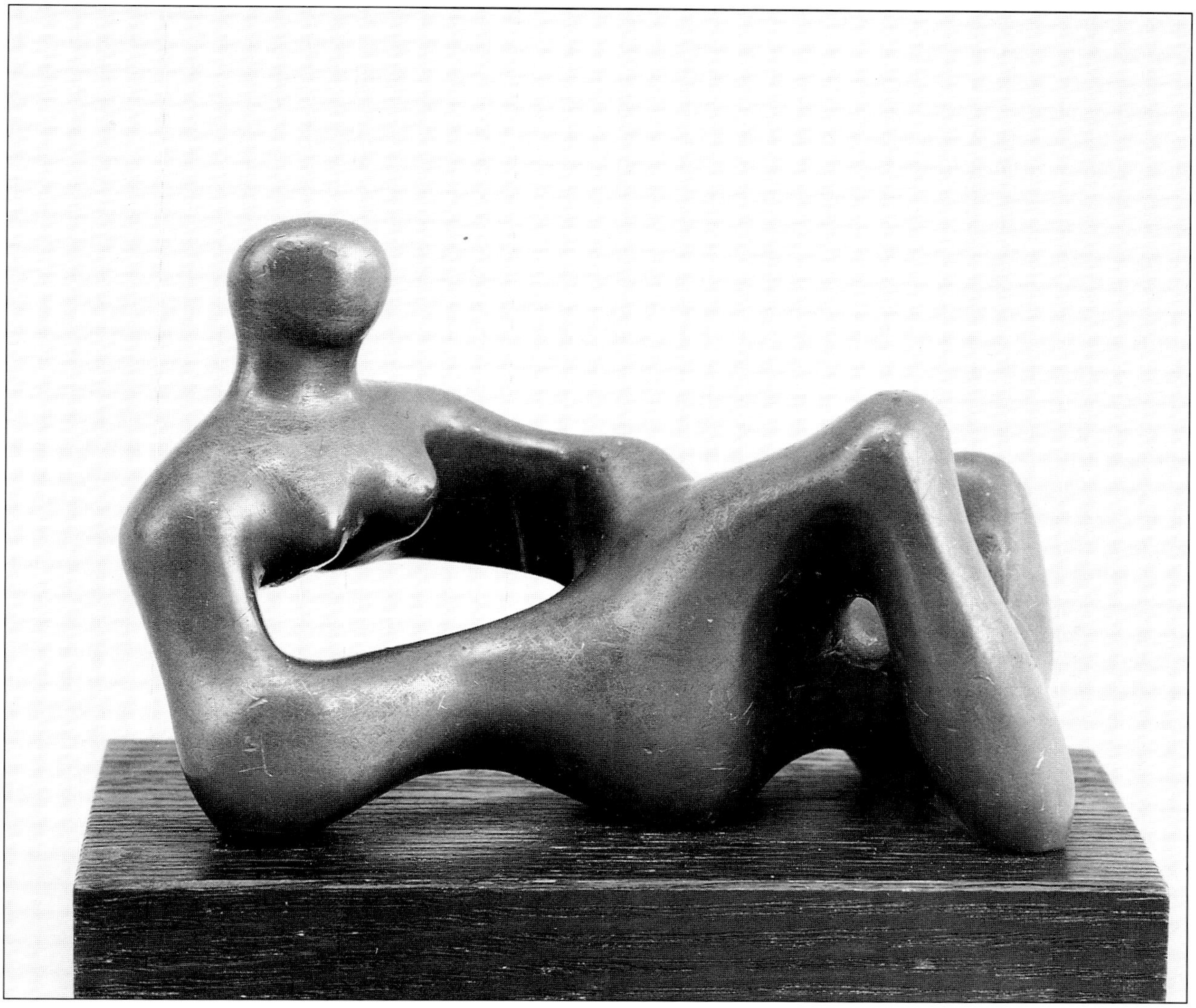

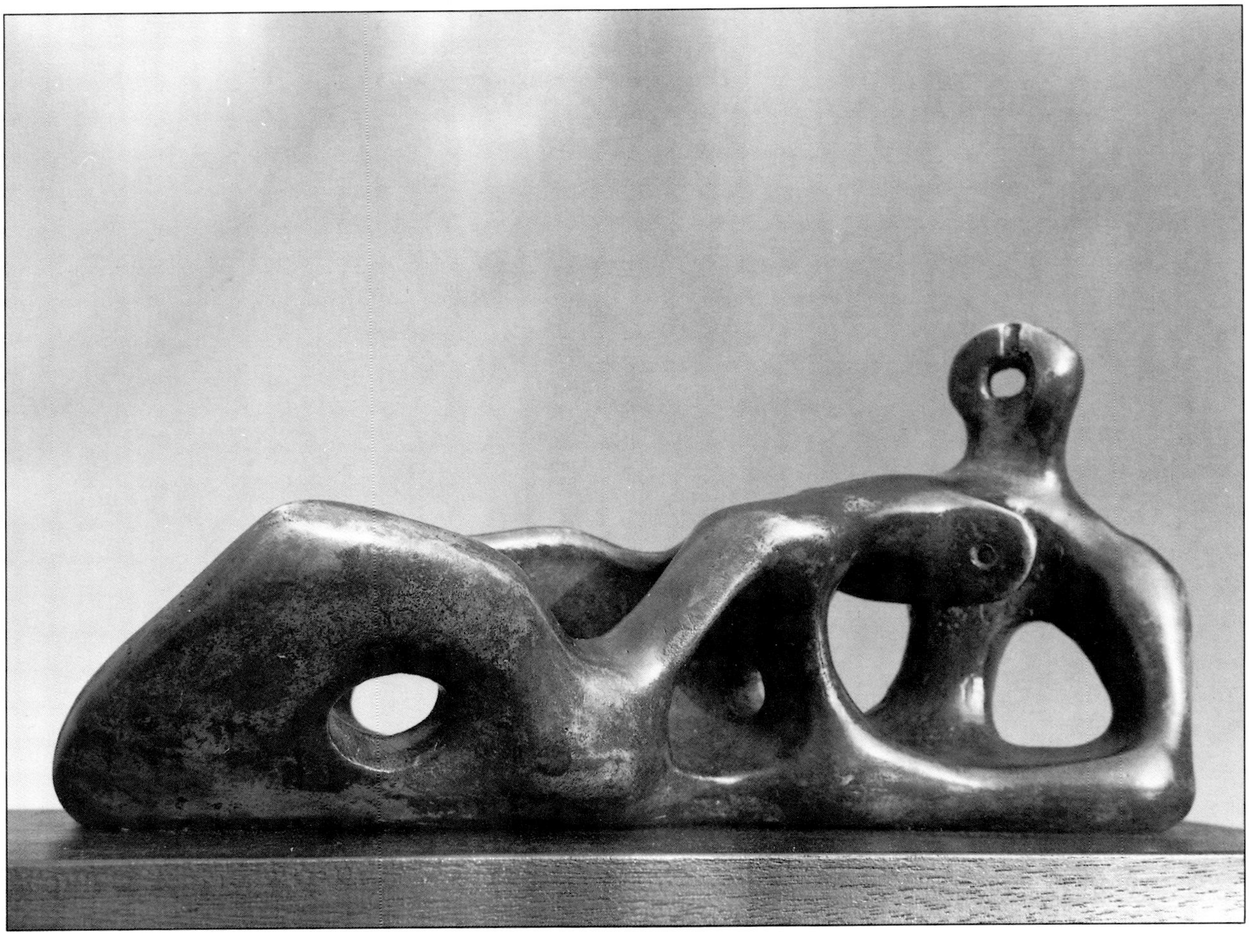

49
Ideas for Sculpture 1939
(misdated 1938)
pencil, white wax crayon,
watercolour wash, pen and
black ink, black crayon
257 x 432mm
HMF 1431

48
Reclining Figure 1938
L 21.6cm bronze
edition of 7
LH 185

50
Studies for Sculpture in Various Materials 1939
pencil, white wax crayon,
yellow crayon, watercolour,
pen and Indian ink,
black crayon
254 x 432mm
HMF 1435

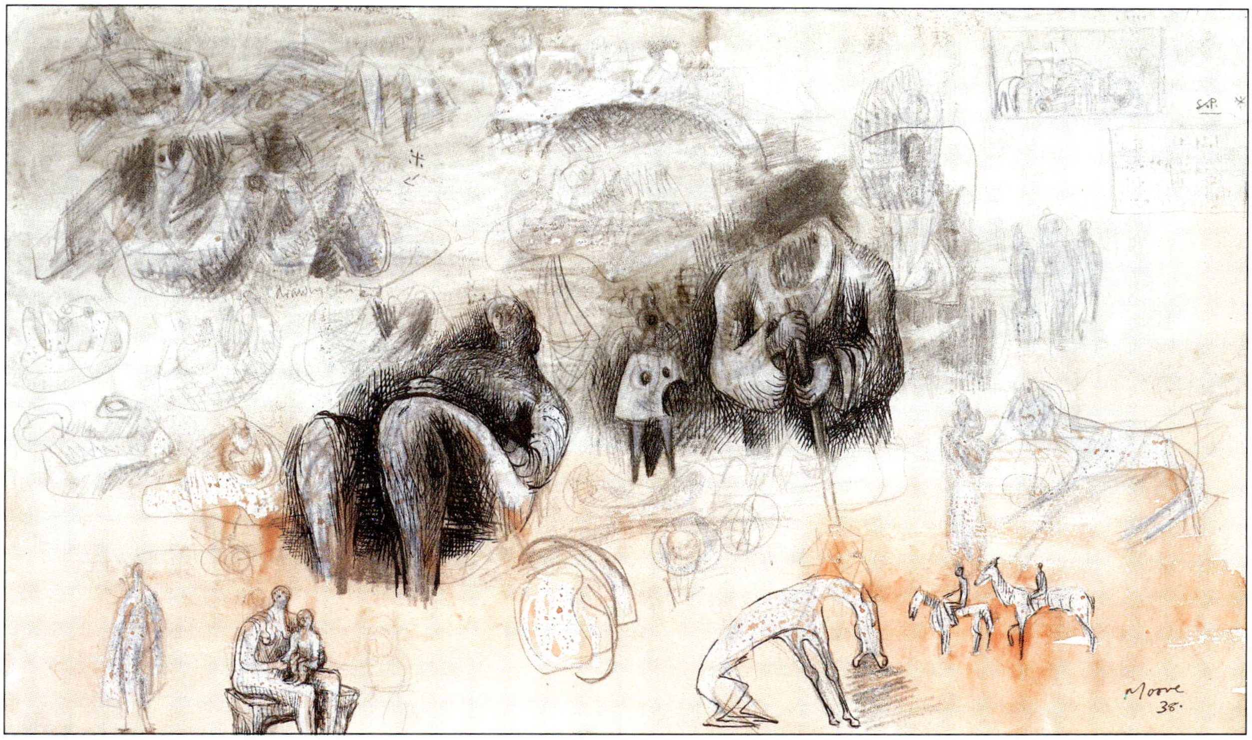
Moore
38.

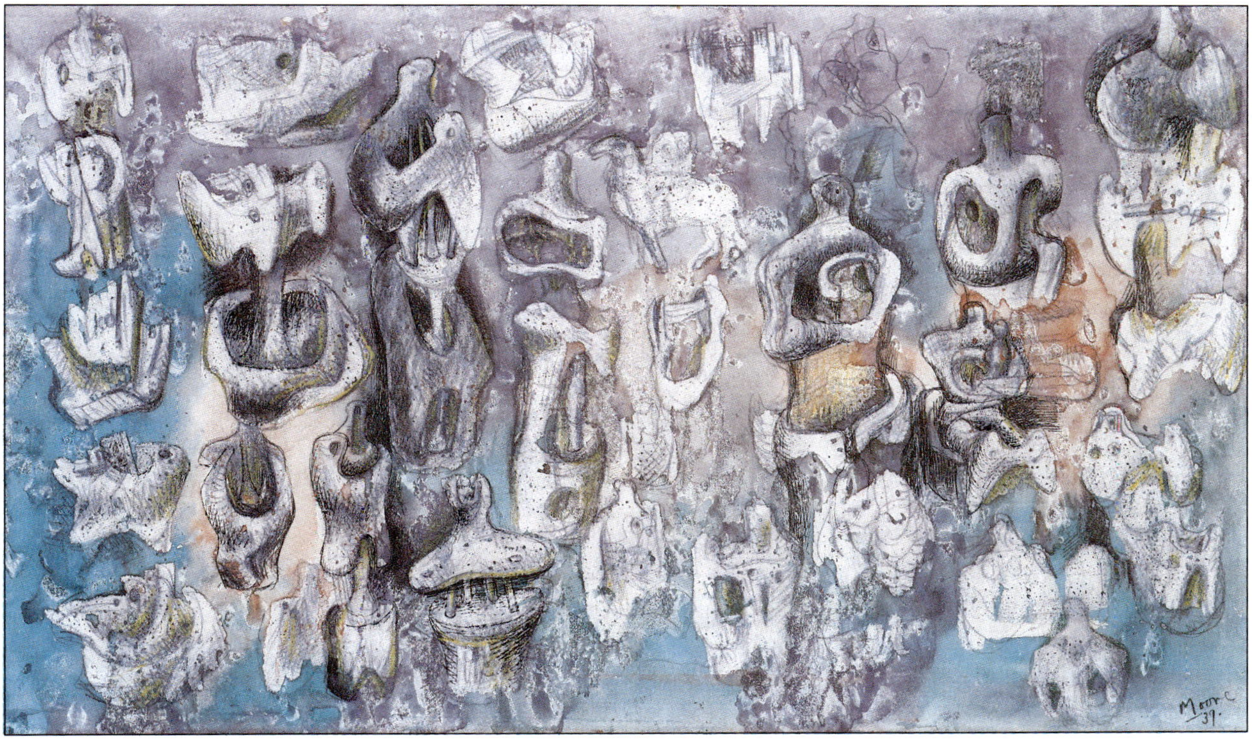
Moore
37.

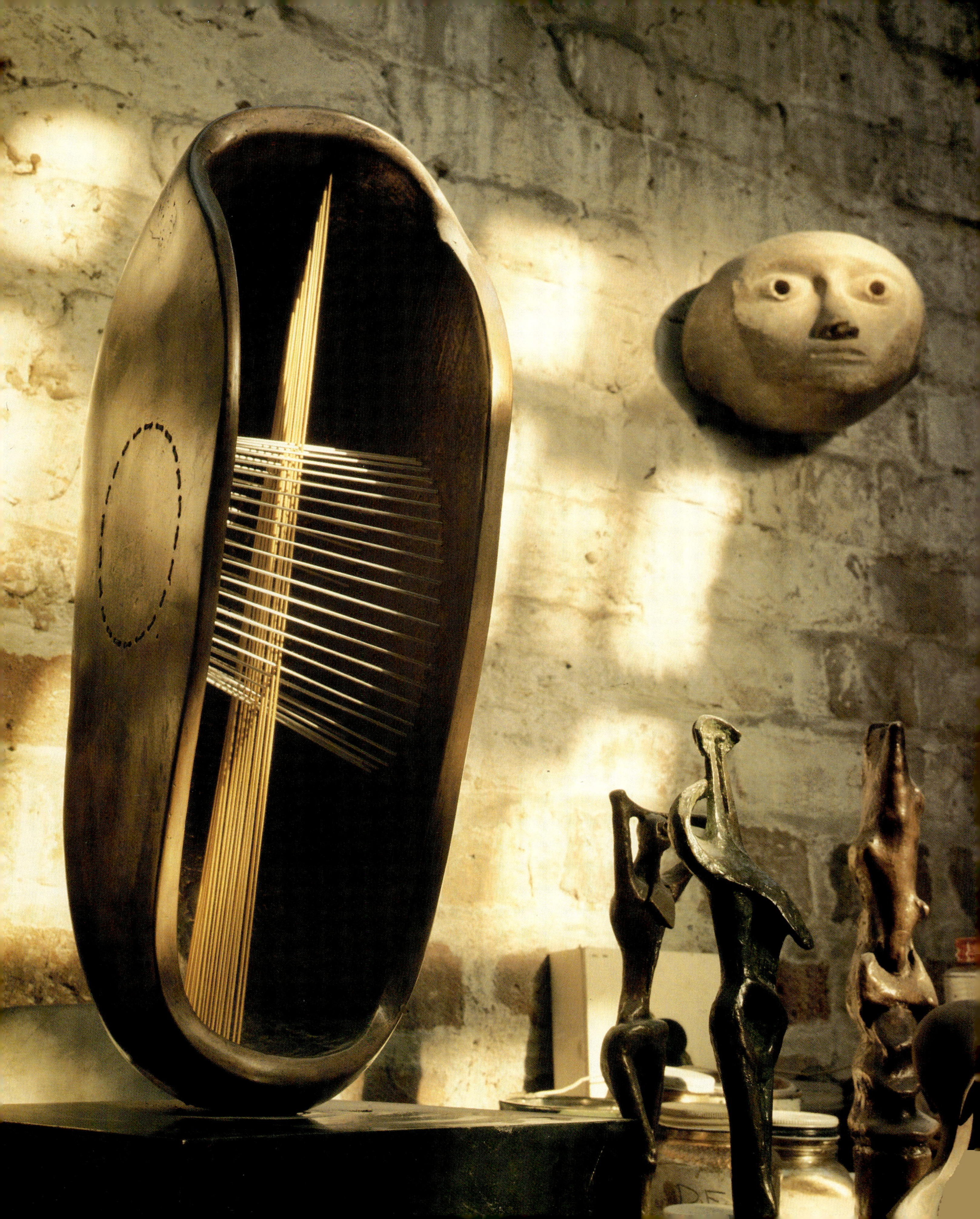

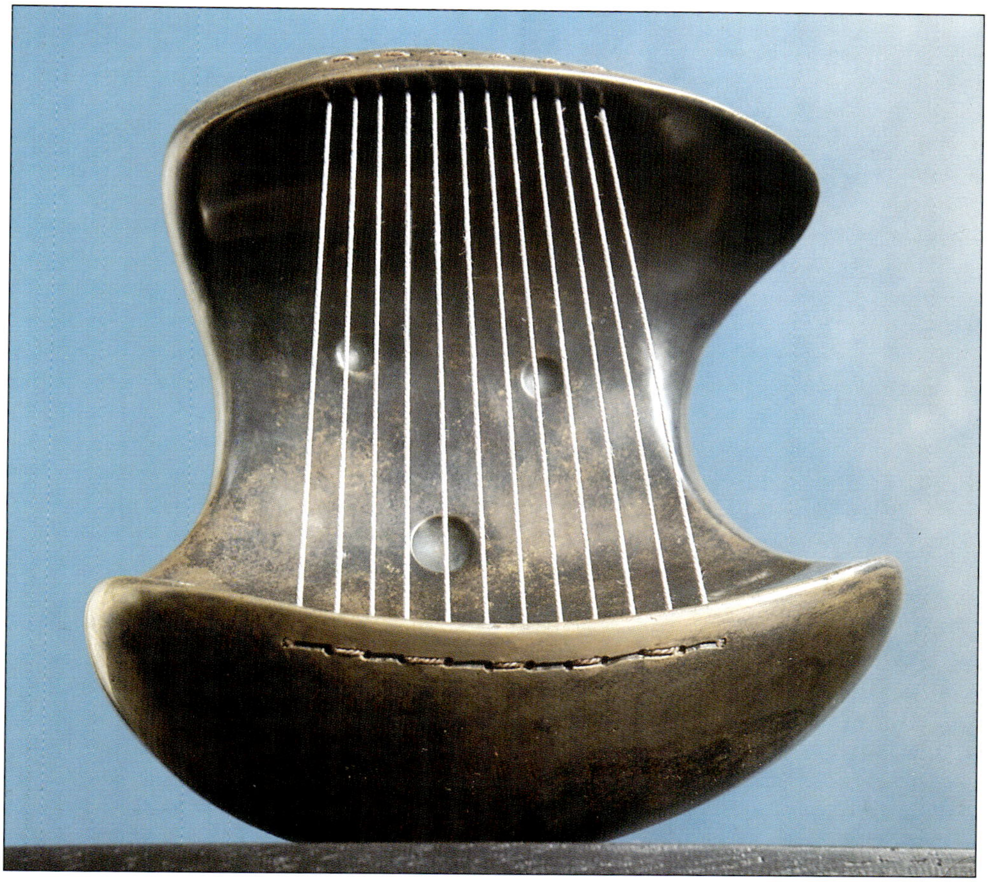

Undoubtedly the source of my stringed figures was the Science Museum . . . I was fascinated by the mathematical models I saw there, which had been made to illustrate the difference of the form that is halfway between a square and a circle. One end could also be twisted to produce forms that would be terribly difficult to draw on a flat surface. It wasn't the scientific study of these models but the ability to look through the strings as with a bird cage and to see one form within another which excited me.

51
Stringed Figure: Bowl 1938
H 54.6cm bronze and string
edition of 9
LH 186c

52
Head 1939
H 13.7cm bronze and string
edition of 6
LH 195

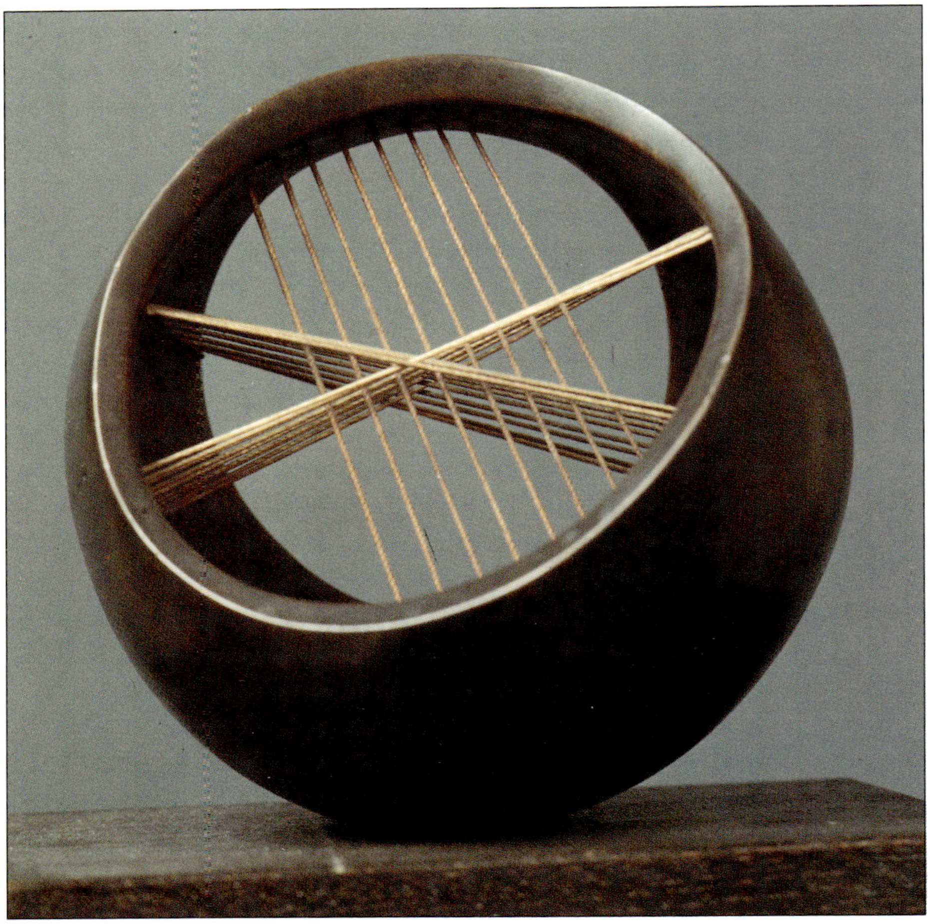

53
Stringed Ball 1939
L 8.9cm bronze and string
edition of 9
LH 198

54

Mother and Child 1939

L 19cm bronze and string

edition of 7

LH 201

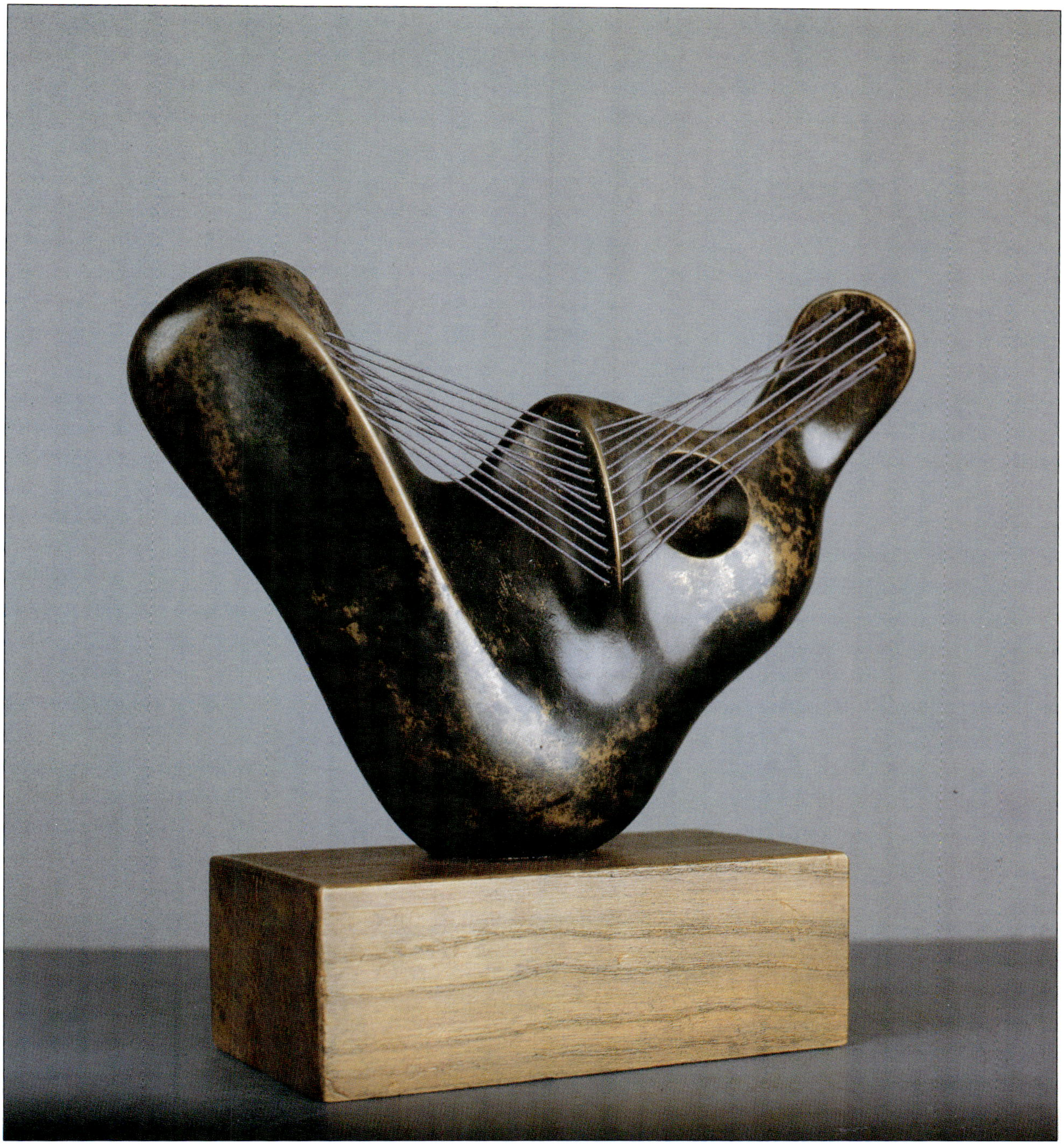

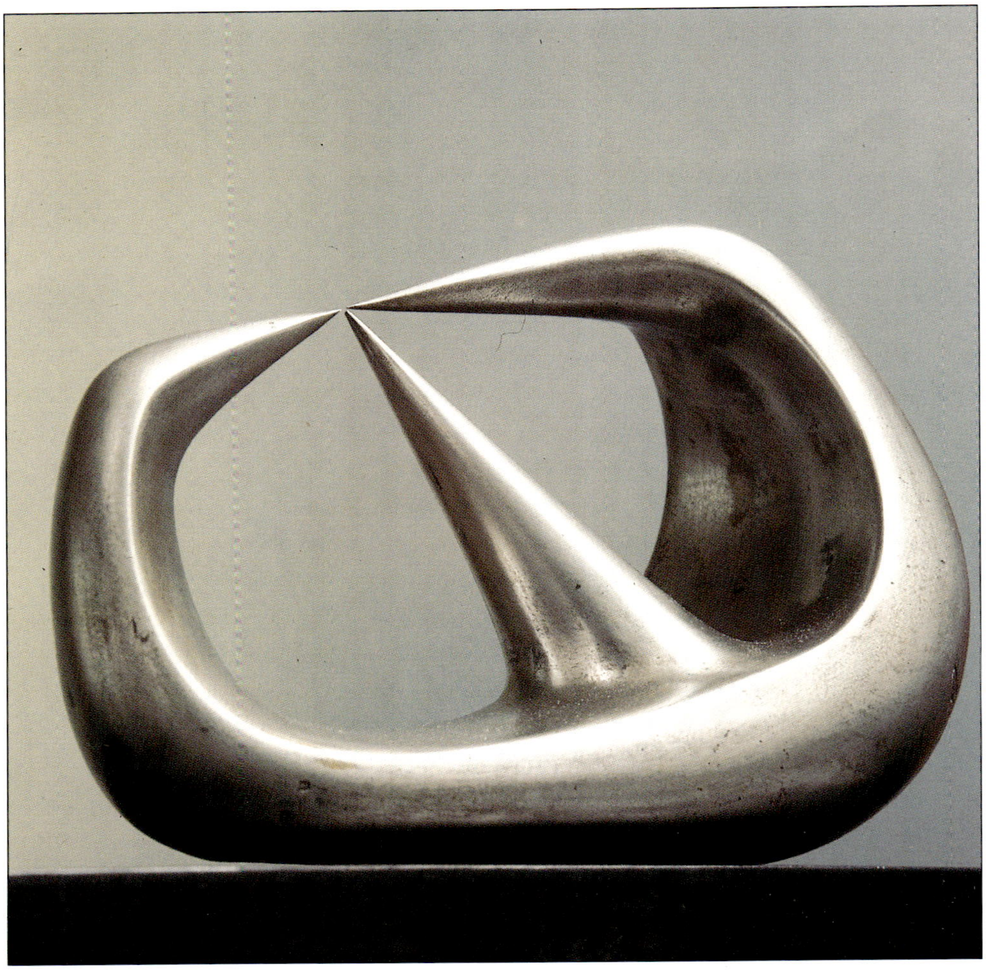

55
Three Points 1939-40
L 20cm cast iron
LH 211

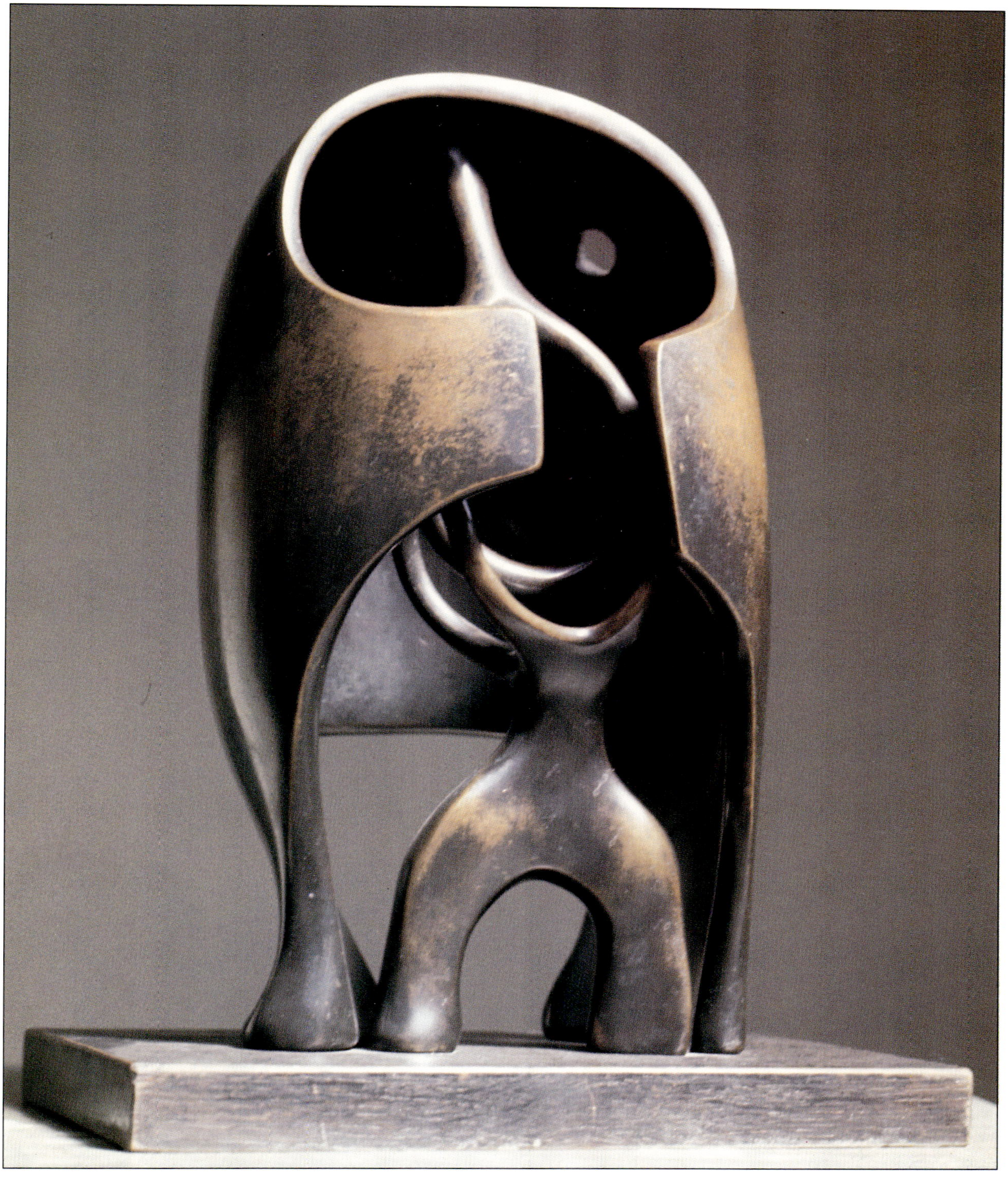

56
The Helmet 1939-40
H 29.2cm bronze
edition of 3
LH 212

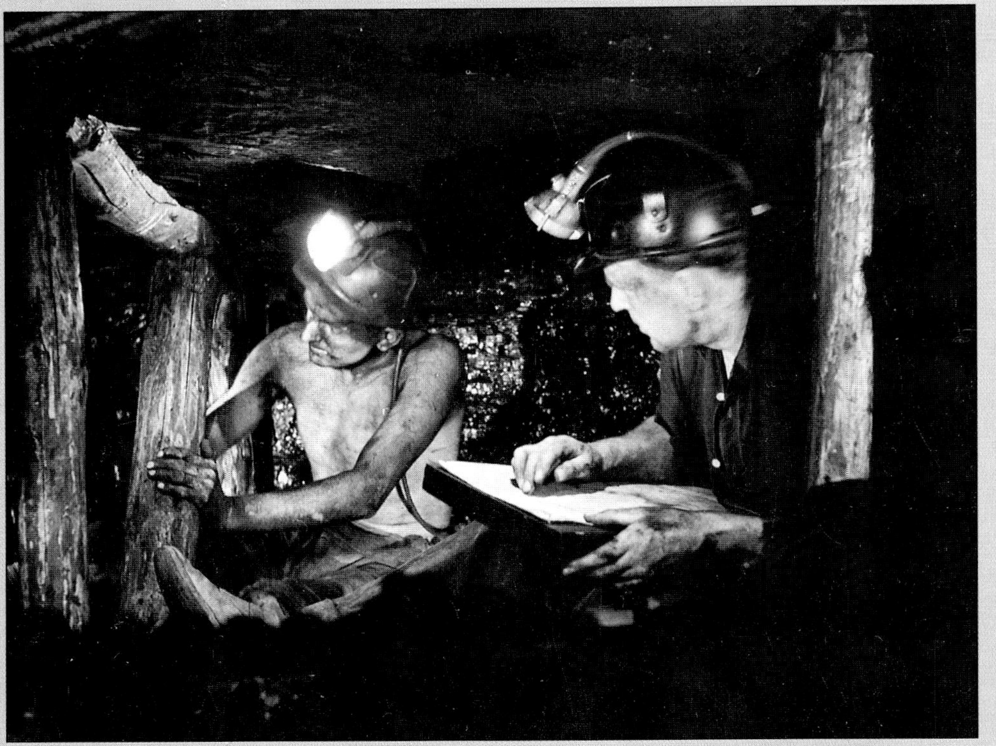

Henry Moore sketching a miner
at the coalface in Wheldale
Colliery, Castleford, Yorkshire.

1940s

Hundreds of what he saw as 'Henry Moore reclining figures' huddled under blankets on the platforms of the London Underground in 1940-41, sheltering from nightly air raids, inspired drawings such as cats.60-66. During the war years Moore drew the human figure in a more recognisable way than he had done in the 1930s: he caught the mood of stoicism in the face of danger as mothers nursed their children and comforted each other. As an Official War Artist, Moore also made his first drawings of men since he had left art school. These were miners at Wheldale Colliery in Yorkshire, where his father had once worked (cat.68).

The sketches and finished drawings that he made as a War Artist are summed up in two commissions for public sculptures: the *Madonna and Child* and *Family Group*. In 1942 Moore was asked to carve a Madonna and Child to celebrate the fiftieth anniversary of St Matthew's church, Northampton; it is represented here by two models, originally made in clay baked as terracotta and later cast in bronze. In the first (cat.74), the mother and child proved too self-contained to symbolise the Christian Madonna and Child; the life-sized carving is based on the second (cat.71), in which the child looks out on the world from the safety of the mother's knee. The *Family Group*, made for a secondary school in Hertfordshire, is represented by a model (cat.74) as well as two preliminary ideas (cats.72, 73). As a teacher himself, Moore responded to this challenge to represent education as an enrichment for parents and children alike; he had hoped to include two children in the group, as in cat.73, but this idea proved too complicated for enlargement as well as threatening to become too much of a 'story'.

Moore's feelings at the birth of his own daughter in 1946 moved him to make a new series of drawings from life (cats.77-81), and also revitalised the theme of one form enclosing another. A sheet of ideas for horizontal and vertical figures of 1949 (cat.88) looks towards the *Working Model for Upright Internal/External Form* (cat.93) made two years later.

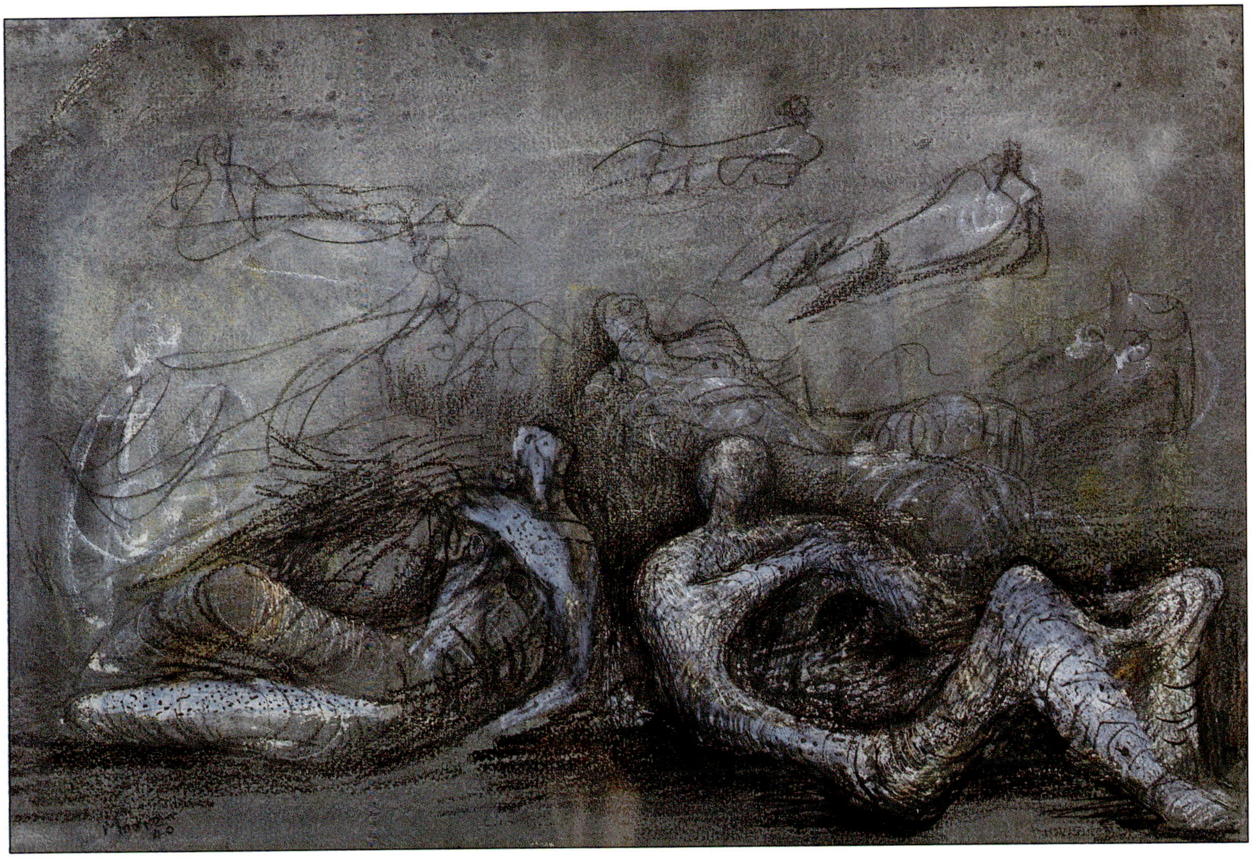

57
Studies of Reclining Figures 1940
pencil, white wax crayon (scraped in places), pastel, watercolour wash, coloured wax crayon, gouache, pen and Indian ink
380 x 560mm
HMF 1478

58
Seated Figures: Ten Studies of Mother and Child 1940
pencil, wax crayon, watercolour,
pen and ink, gouache
276 x 381mm
HMF 1513a

59
Eighteen Ideas for War Drawings 1940
pencil, white wax crayon, watercolour and ink wash, coloured crayons,
pen and black ink
277 x 376mm
HMF 1553

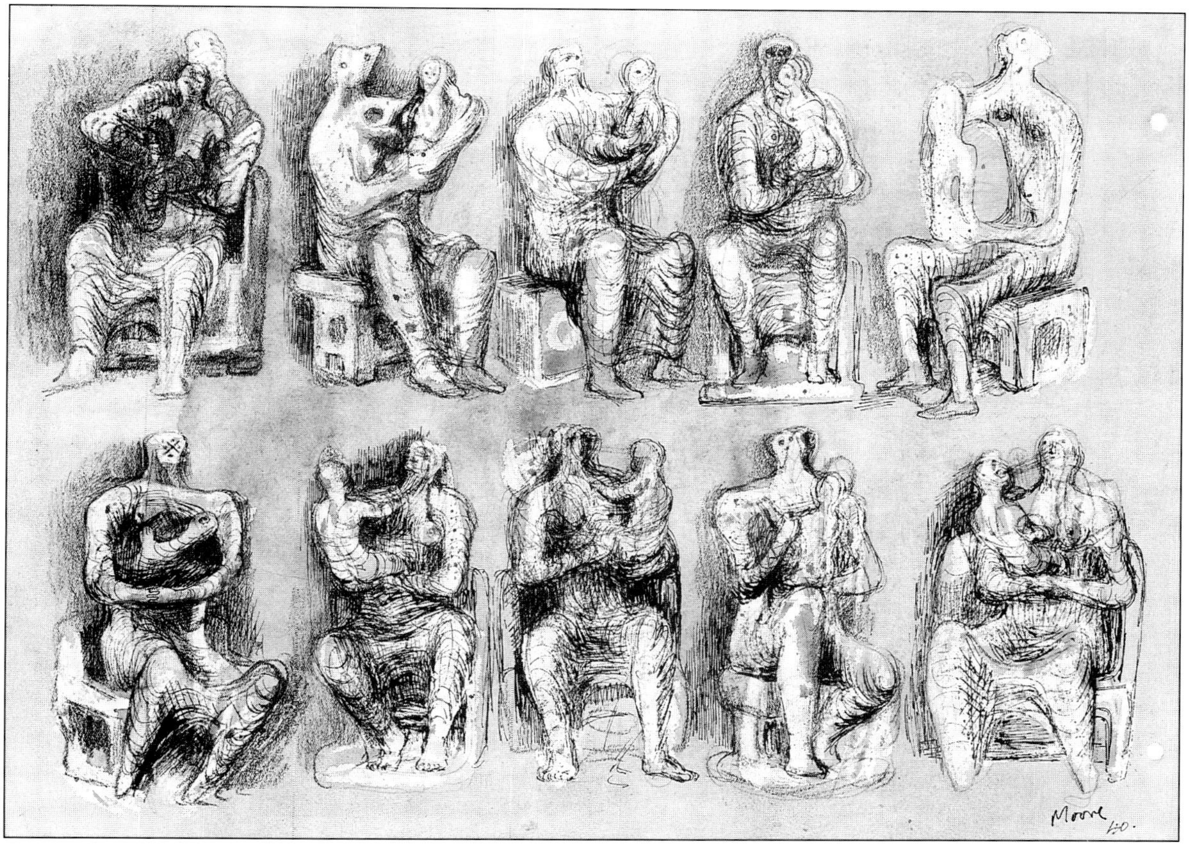
Moore 40.

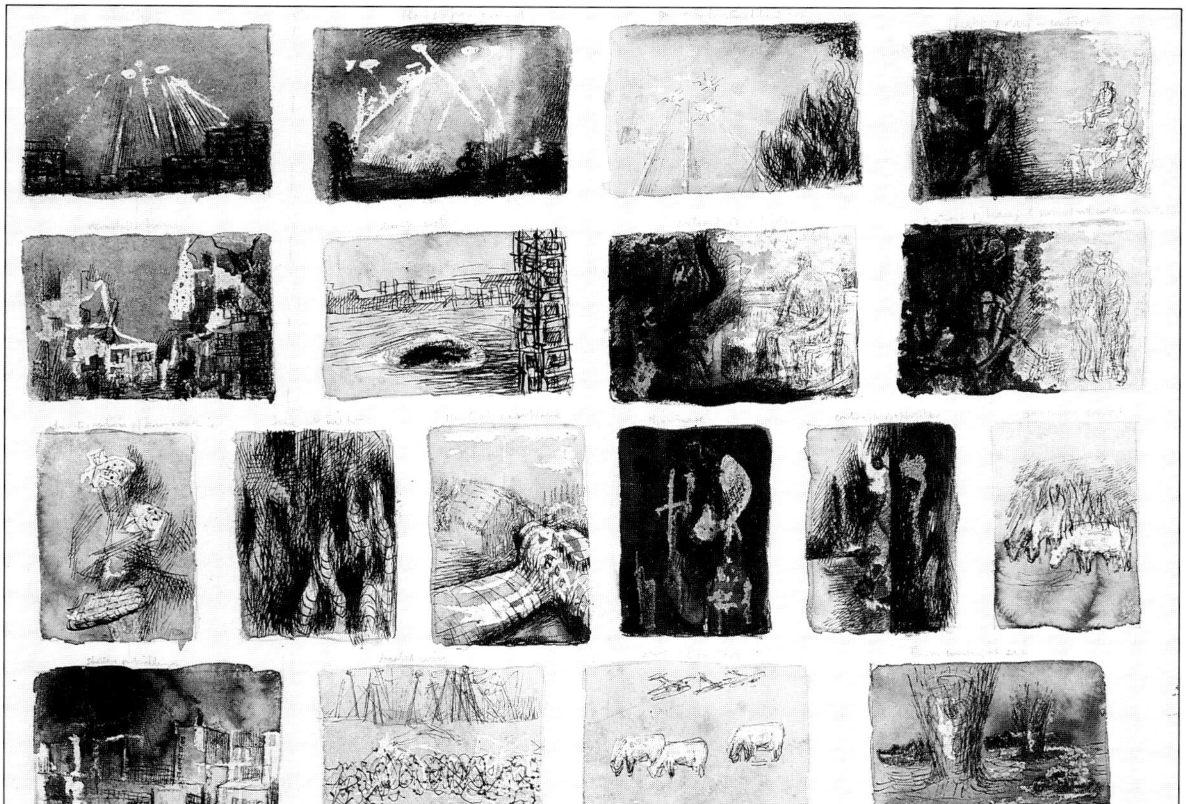
Moore 40.

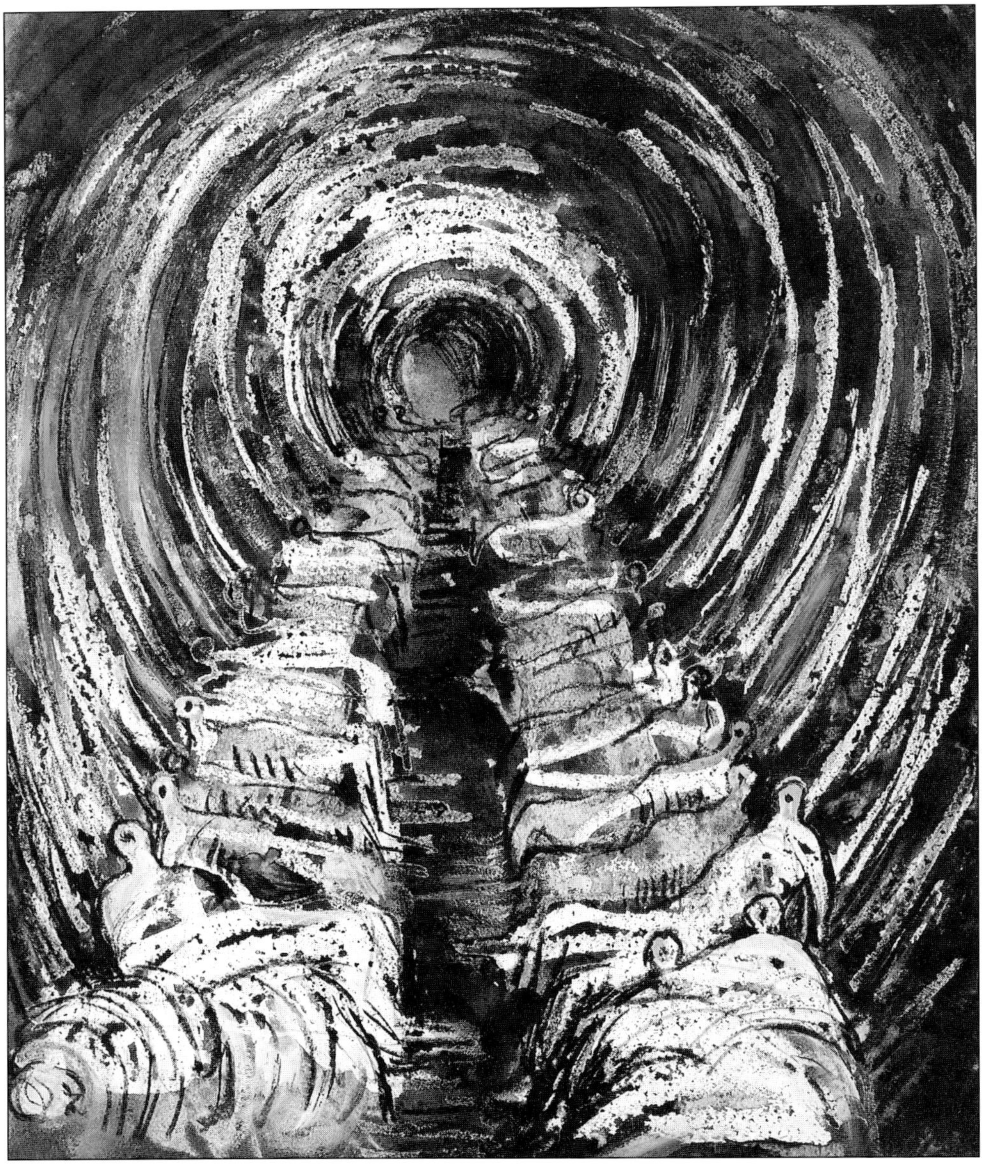

60

Tube Shelter Perspective 1941

pencil, coloured wax crayon,
watercolour wash,
green poster colour
292 x 242mm
HMF 1773

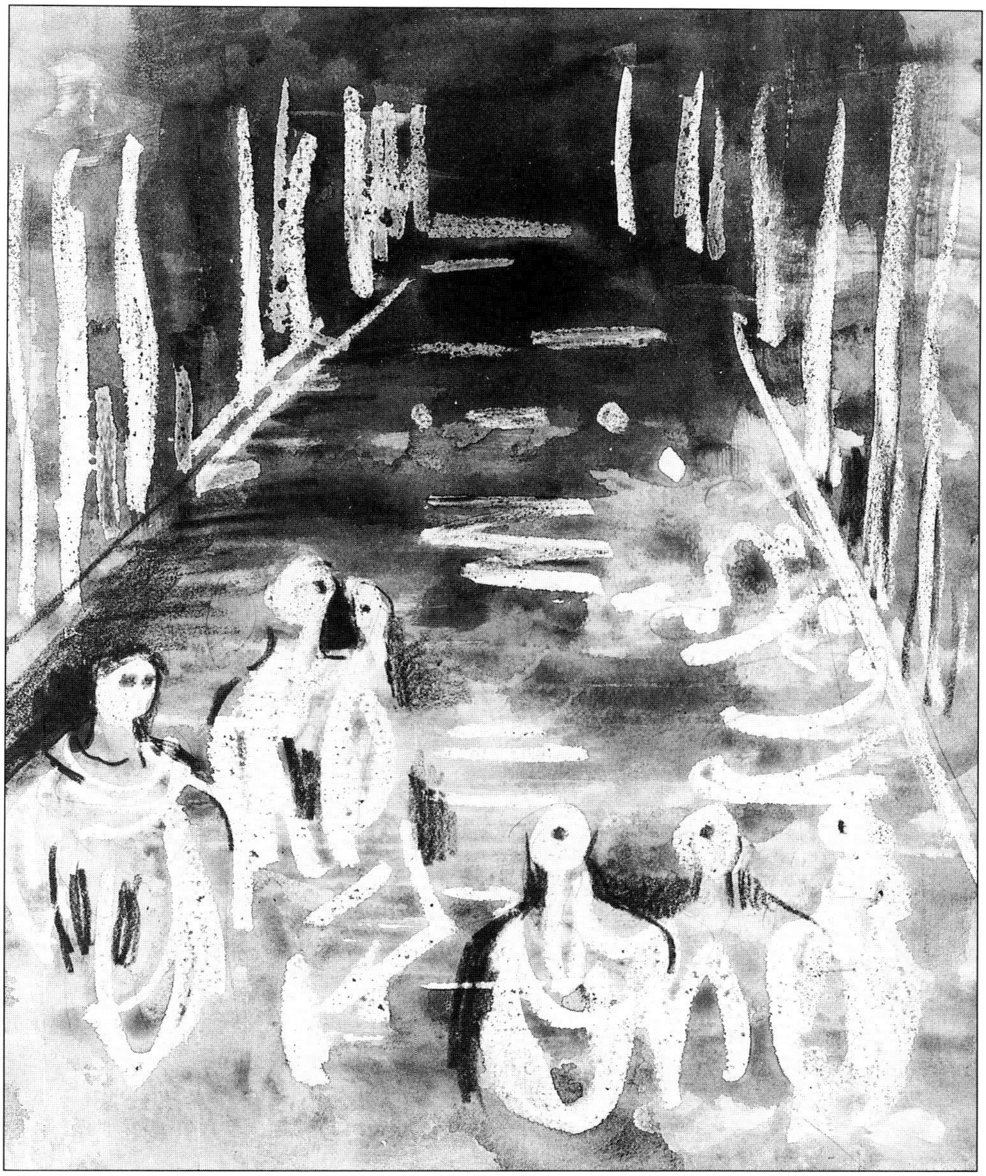

61
Shelter Drawing 1941
pencil, coloured wax crayon,
watercolour
290 x 238mm
HMF 1779

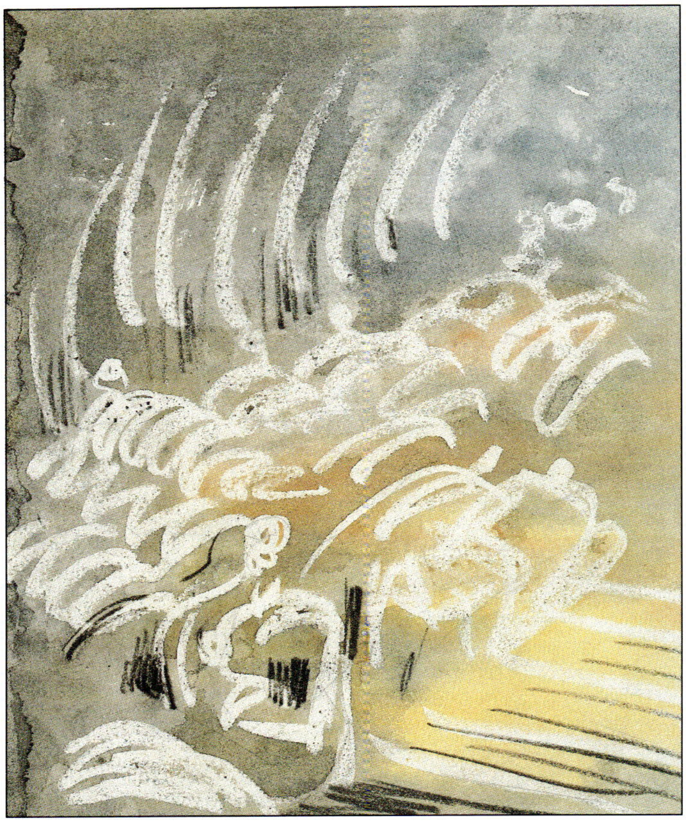

62
Shelter Drawing:
Tube Shelter Perspective 1941
pencil, white wax crayon,
watercolour wash, black crayon
288 x 236mm
HMF 1780

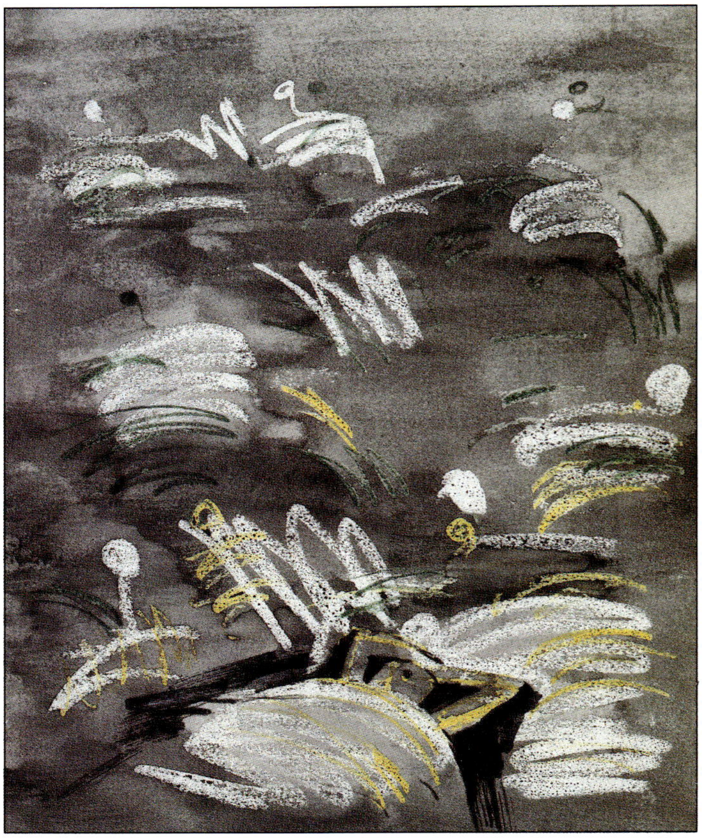

63
Sleeping Figures 1941
white wax crayon, watercolour
and ink wash, coloured crayons
290 x 238mm
HMF 1782

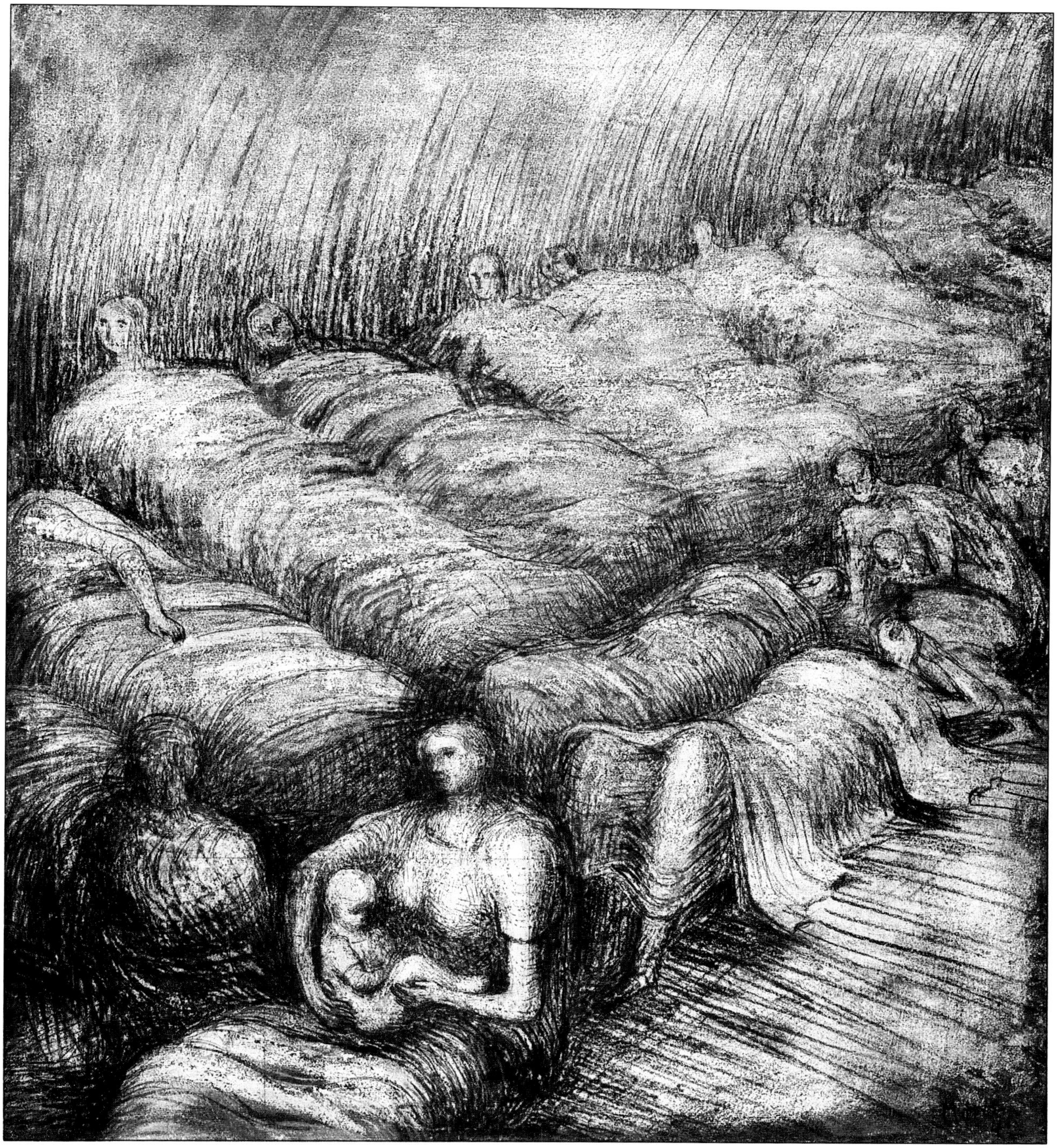

64

Mother and Child among

Underground Sleepers 1941

pencil, wax crayon, watercolour wash,

pen and black ink, gouache

485 x 439mm

HMF 1798

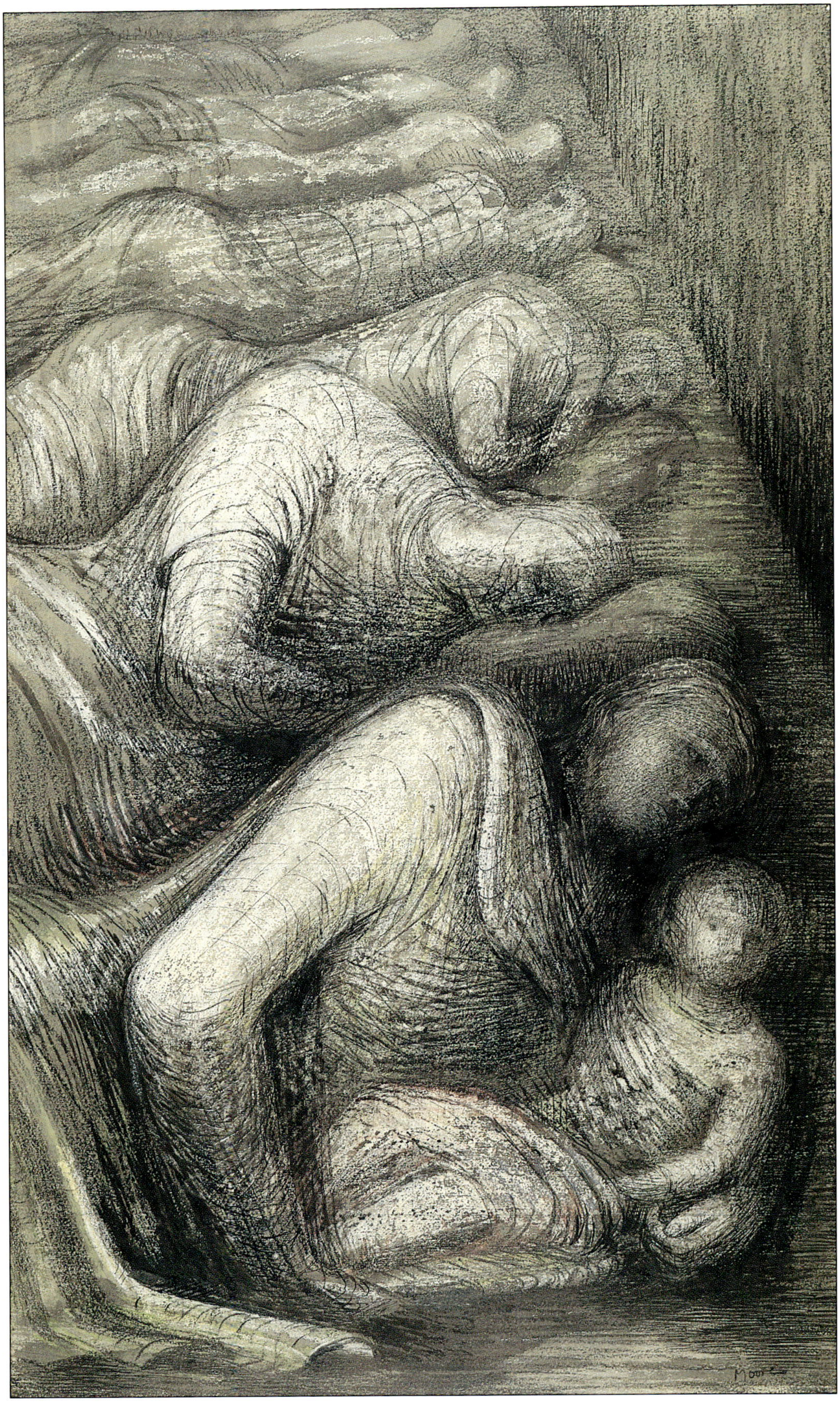

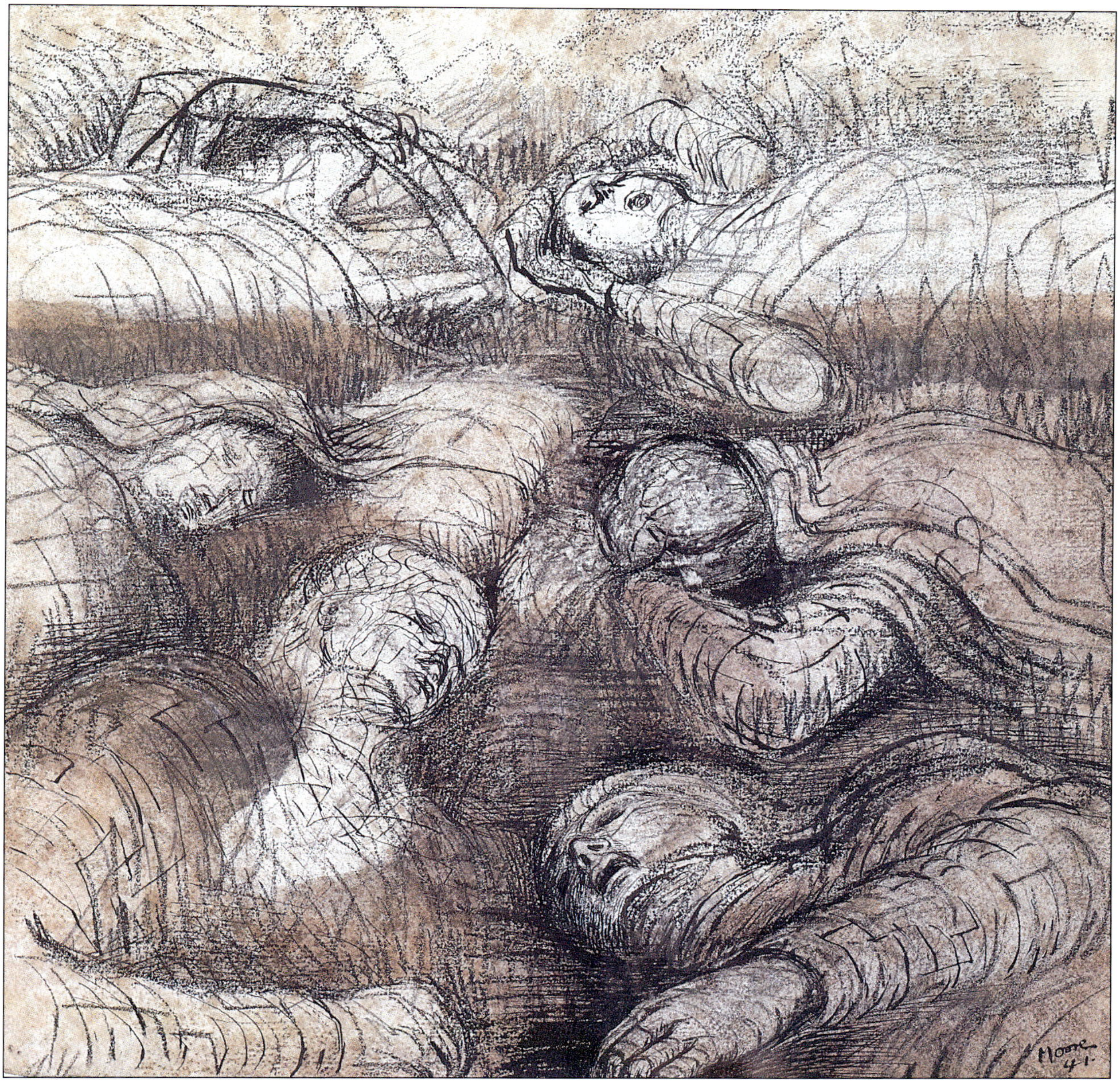

65

Row of Sleepers 1941

pen and ink, chalk, wax crayon, watercolour, wash

545 x 320mm

The British Council, London

HMF 1799

66

Shelter Drawing: Sleeping Figures 1941

pencil, watercolour wash,
black wax crayon, pen and Indian ink

303 x 308mm

HMF 1816

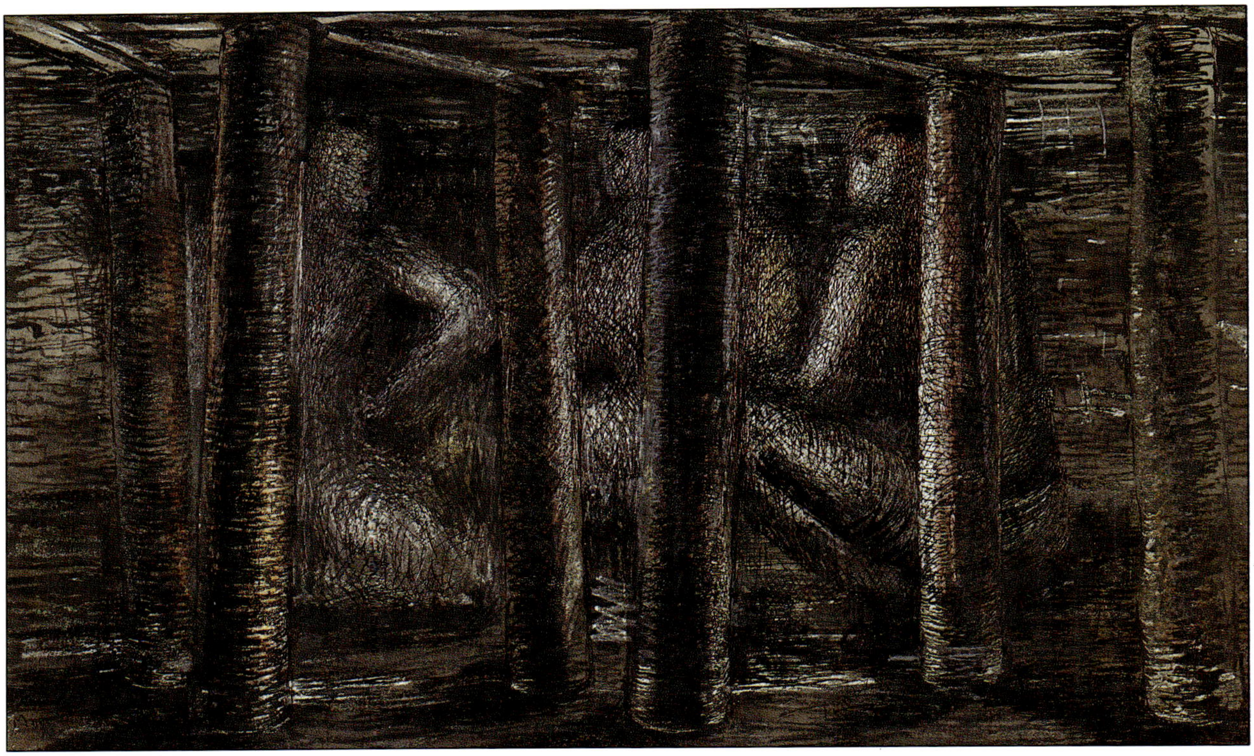

. . . for about two weeks I went every day down Wheldale Colliery at Castleford and sketched the miners at their various tasks, especially those working at the coal face. . . . To record in drawing what I felt and saw was a new and very difficult struggle. There was first the difficulty of seeing forms emerging out of deep darkness, then the problem of conveying the claustrophobic effect of countless wooden pit-props, 2 or 3 feet apart, receding into blackness, and of expressing the gritty, grubby smears of black coal-dust on the miners' bodies and faces at the same time as the anatomy underneath.

67
Miners Resting during Stoppage of Conveyor Belt 1942
pen and ink, chalk, crayon, wash, watercolour
339 x 560mm
Leeds City Art Gallery
HMF 1997

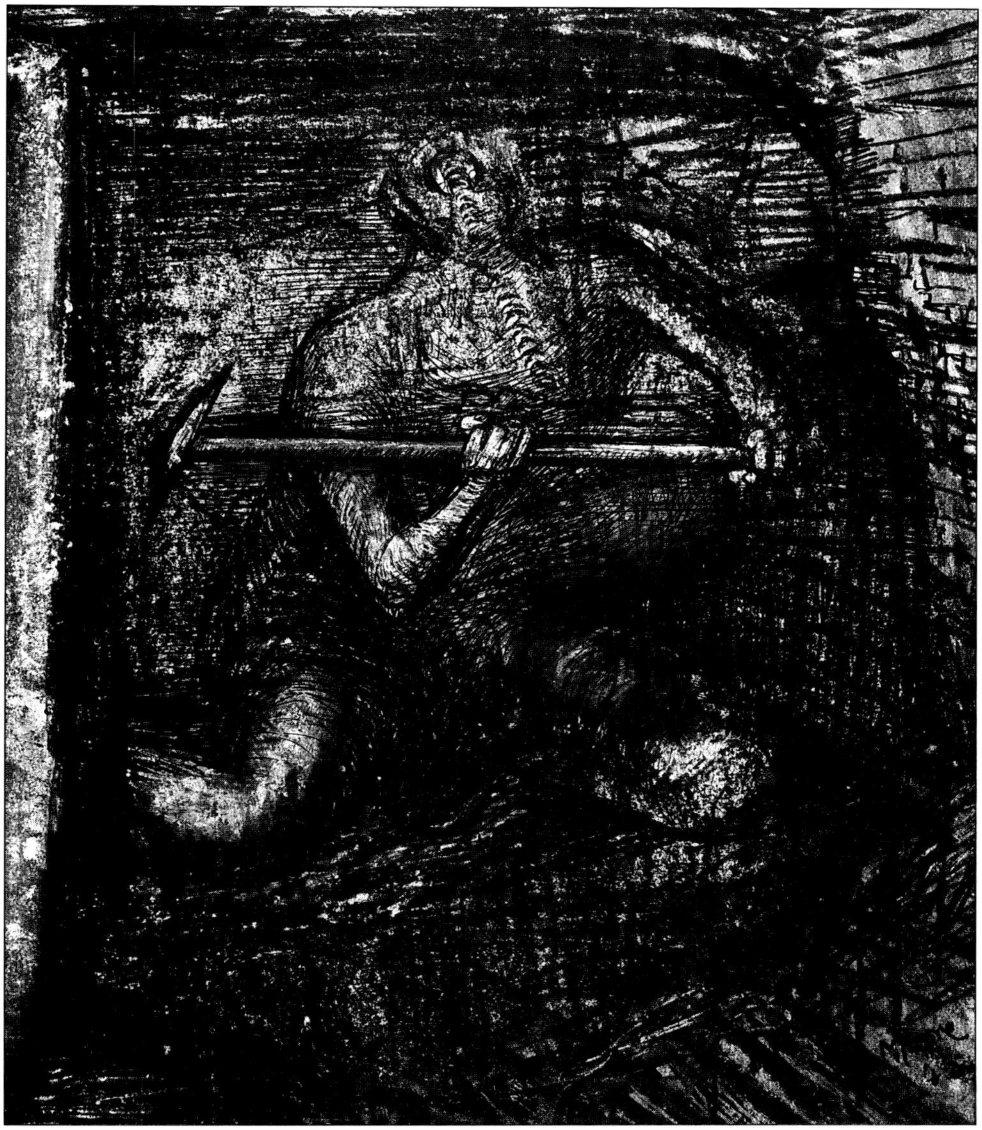

68
Miner at Work 1942
pencil, white wax crayon,
watercolour wash, pen and
Indian ink, coloured crayon
311 x 267mm
HMF 1999

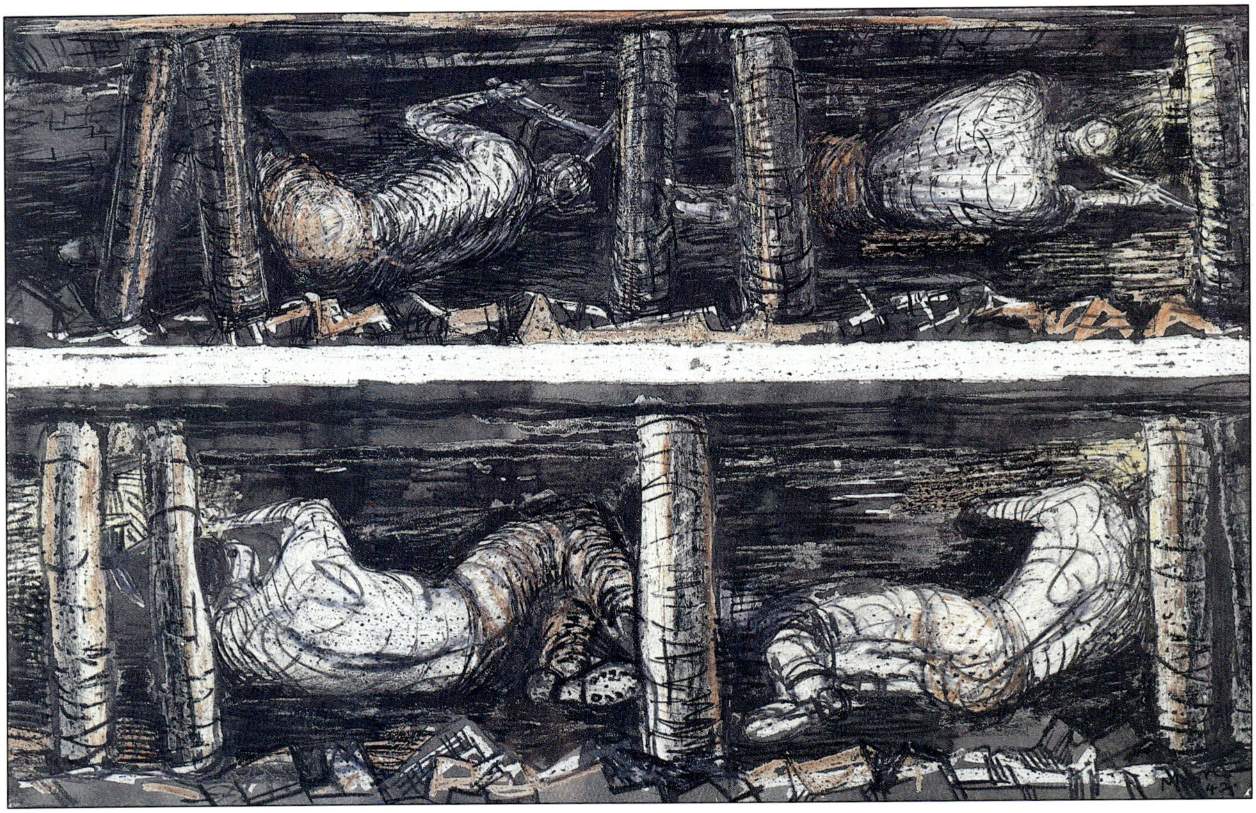

69

Four Studies of Miners at the Coalface 1942

pencil, white wax crayon scraped in some areas, coloured crayon, watercolour wash, gouache, Indian ink wash

365 x 562mm

HMF 2000a

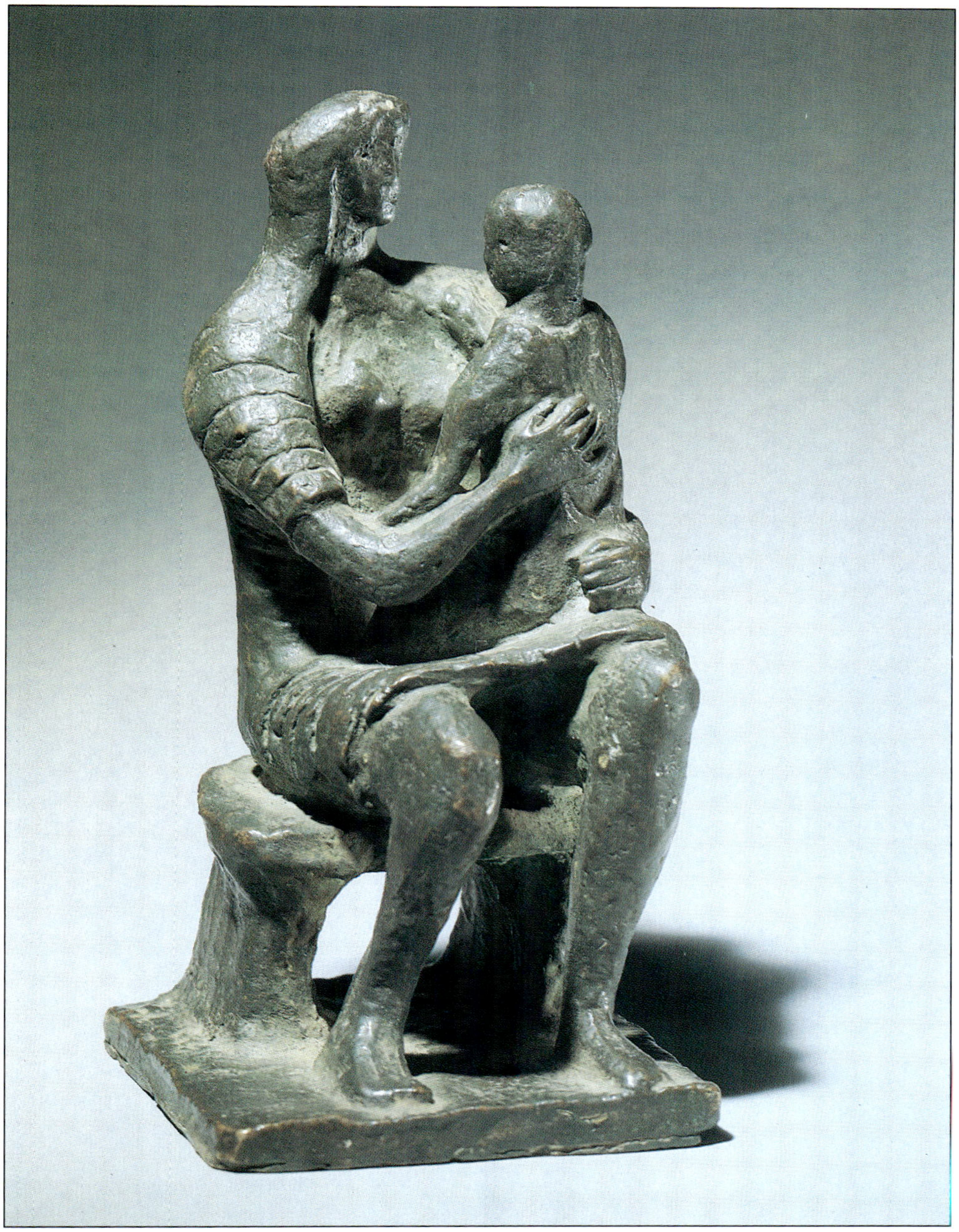

70
Madonna and Child 1943
H 14cm bronze edition of 7
LH 216

71

Madonna and Child 1943

H 15.2cm bronze edition of 7

The British Council, London

LH 224

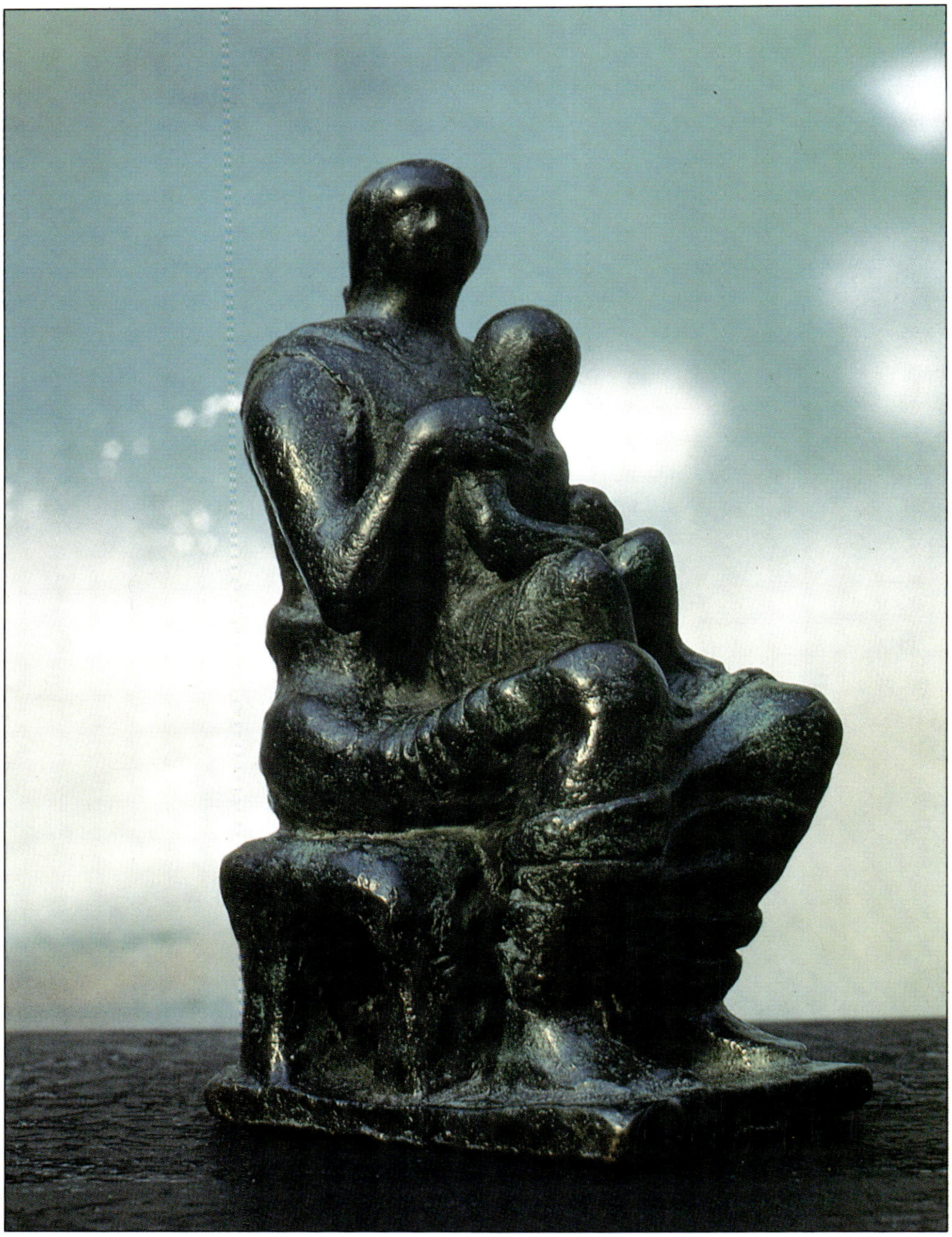

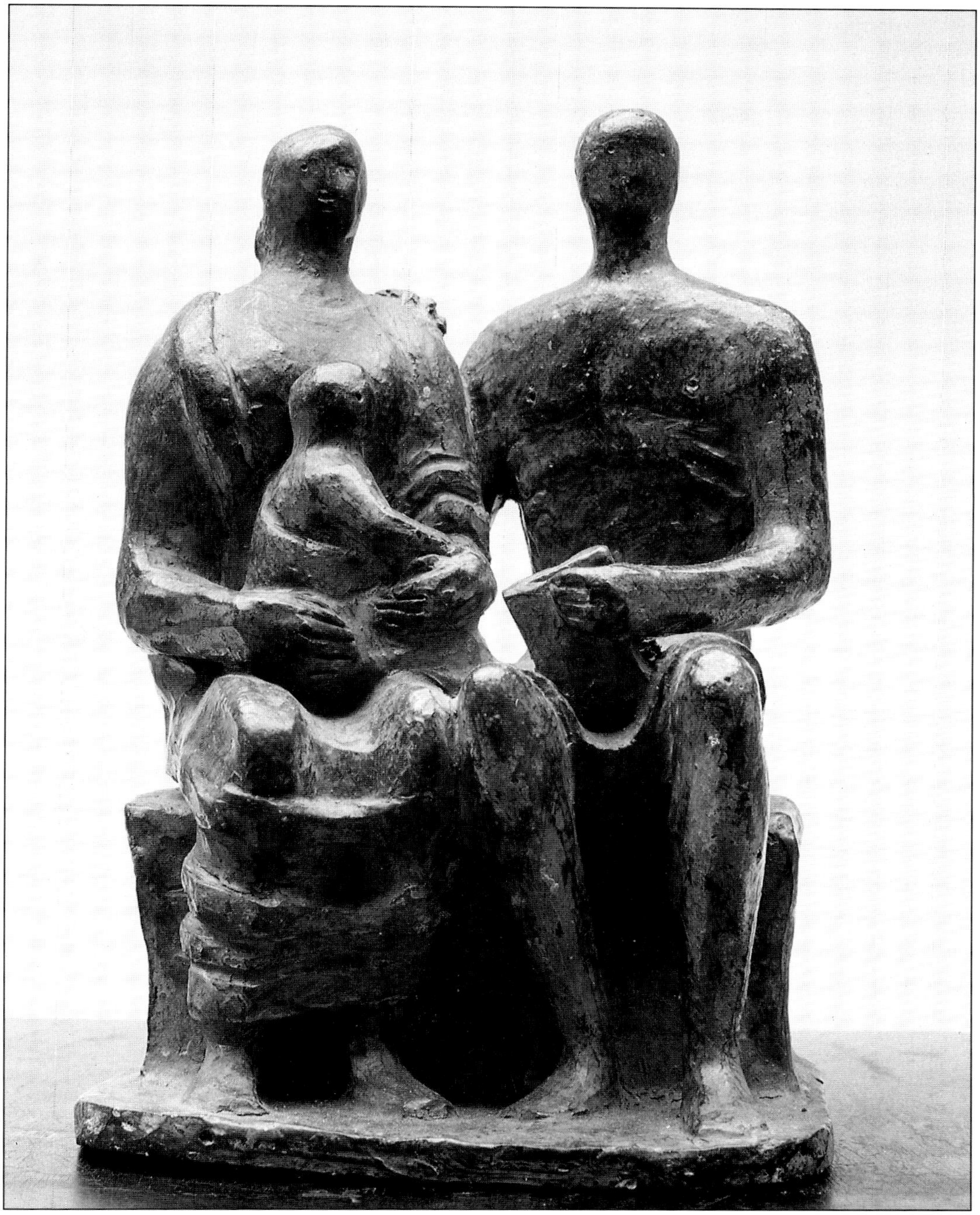

72
Family Group 1944
H 15.6cm terracotta
LH 231

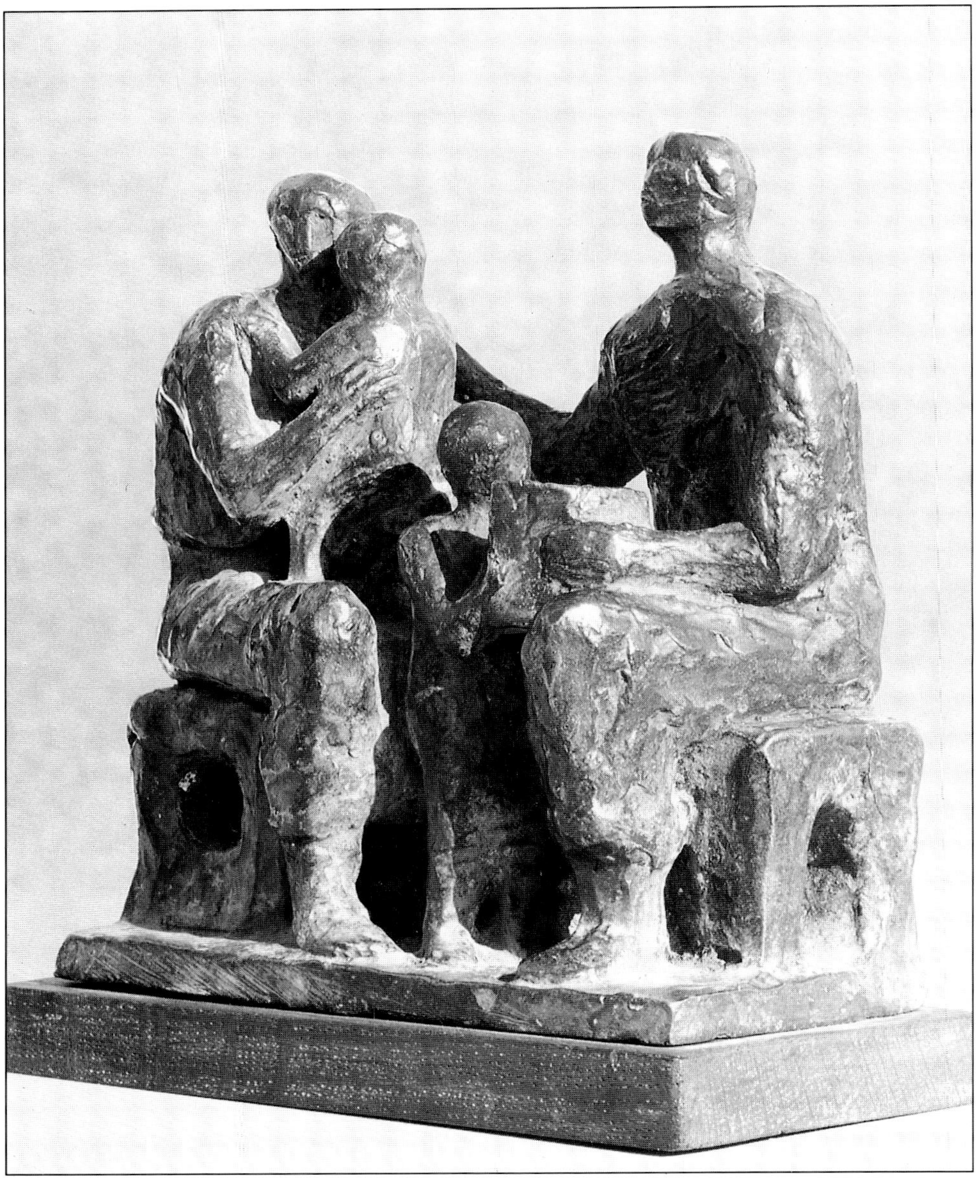

73
Family Group 1944
H 16.2cm terracotta
LH 232

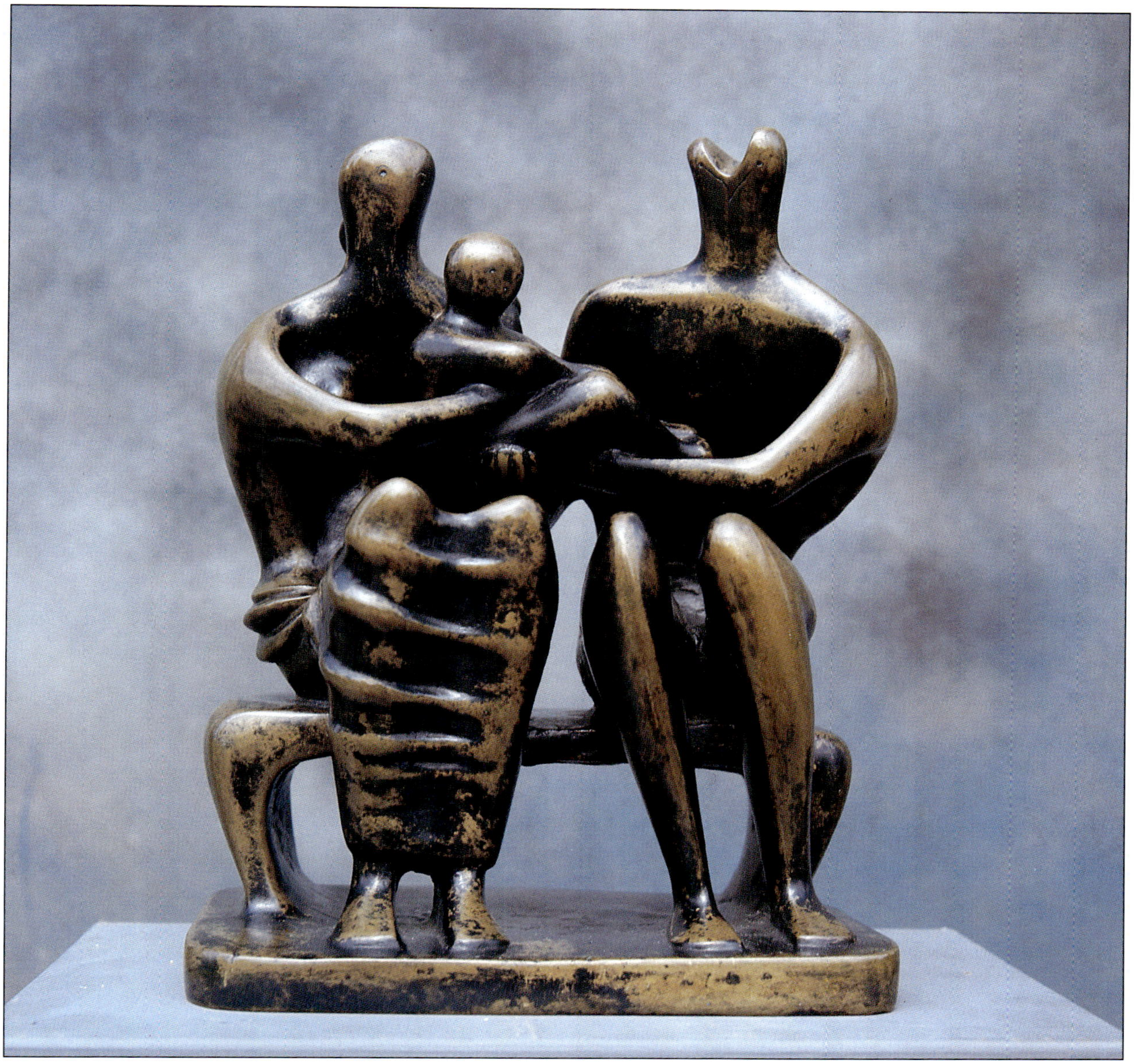

74

Family Group 1945

H 24.1 cm bronze edition of 9

LH 259

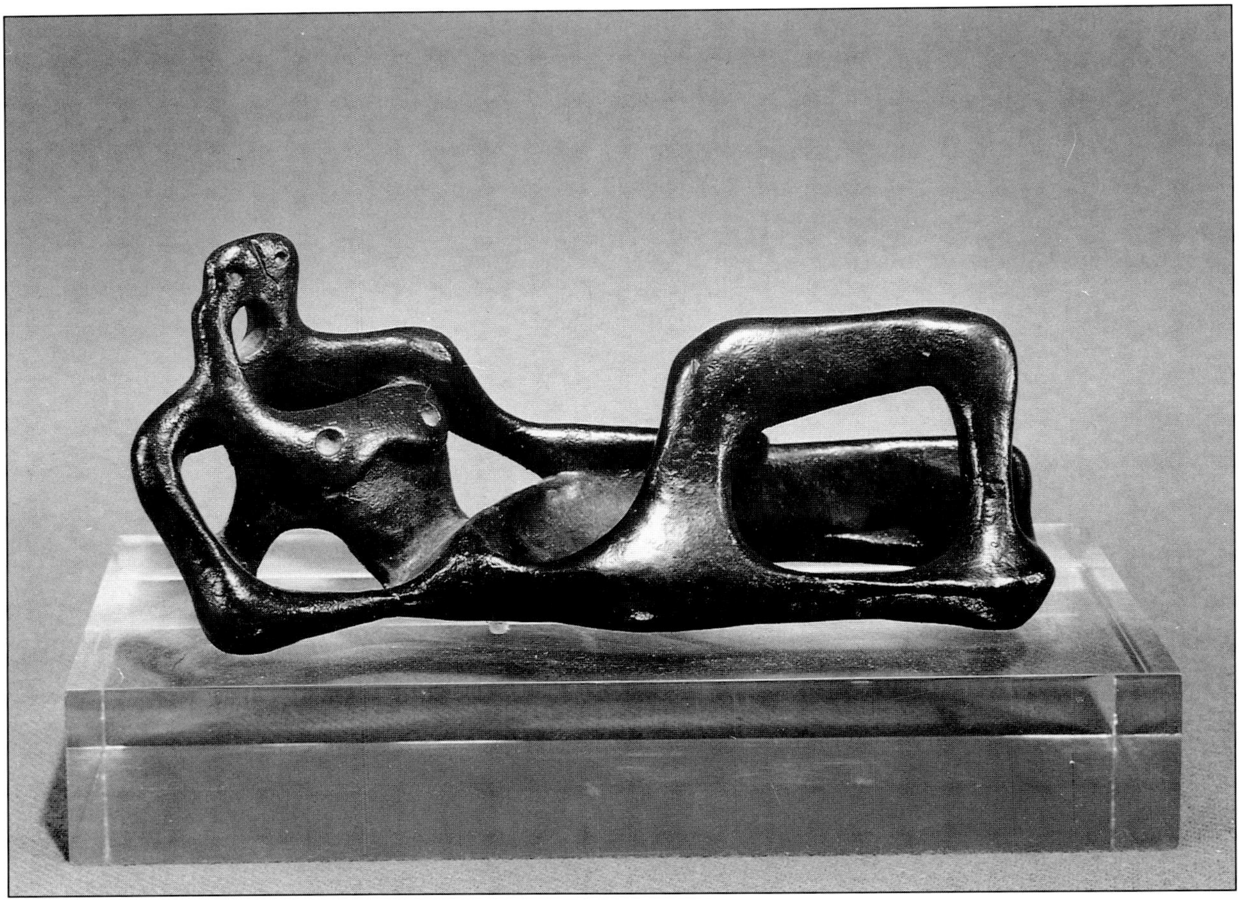

There are three fundamental poses of the human figure. One is standing, the other is seated and the third is lying down . . . of the three poses, the reclining figure gives the most freedom, compositionally and spatially. The seated figure has to have something to sit on. You can't free it from its pedestal. A reclining figure can recline on any surface. It is free and stable at the same time. It fits in with my belief that sculpture should be permanent, should last for eternity.

75
Reclining Figure 1945
L 17.8cm bronze edition of 7
LH 251

76

Reclining Figure 1945

L 18.4cm bronze edition of 10

LH 252

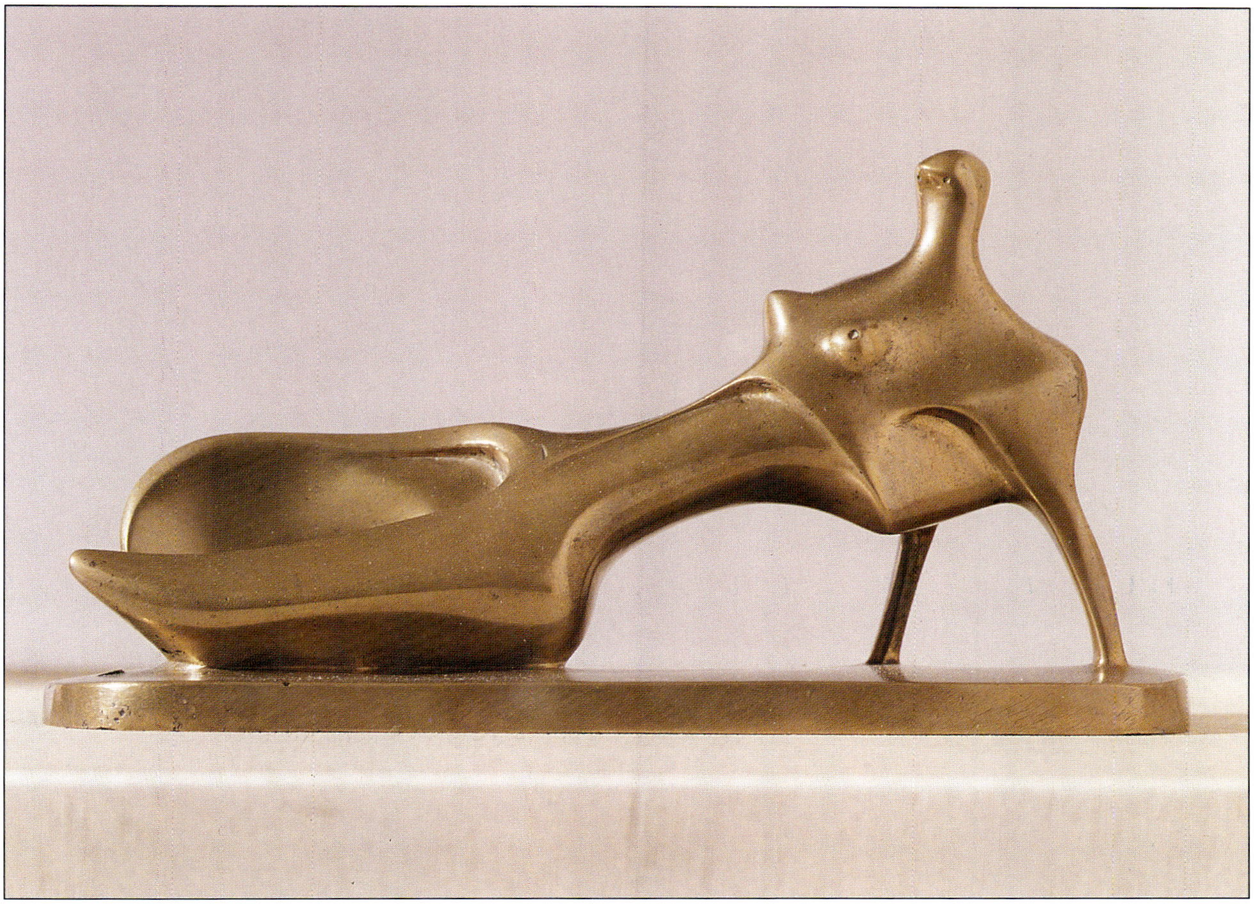

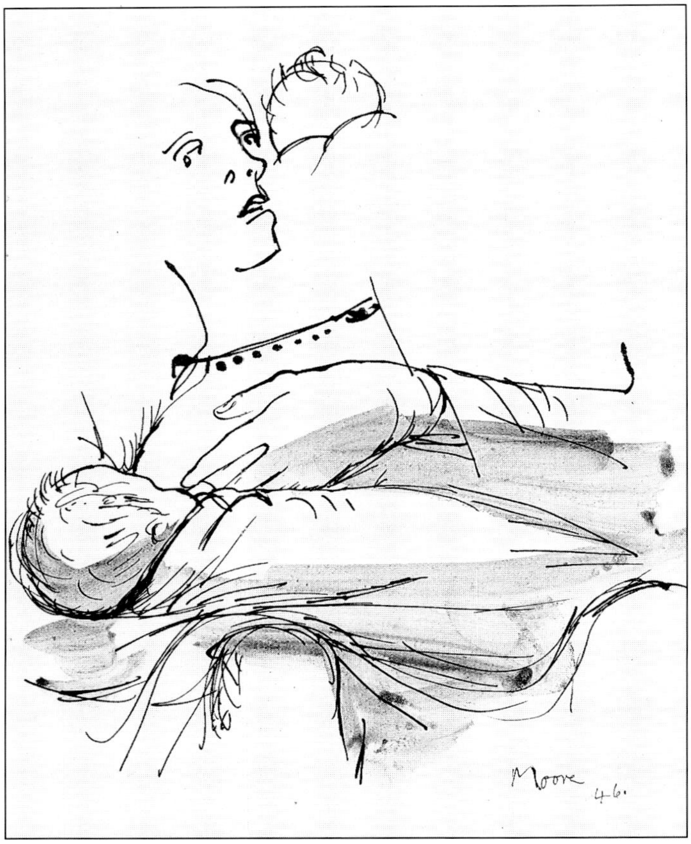

77
Mother Nursing Child 1946
pen and Indian ink, wash
203 x 163mm
HMF 2340

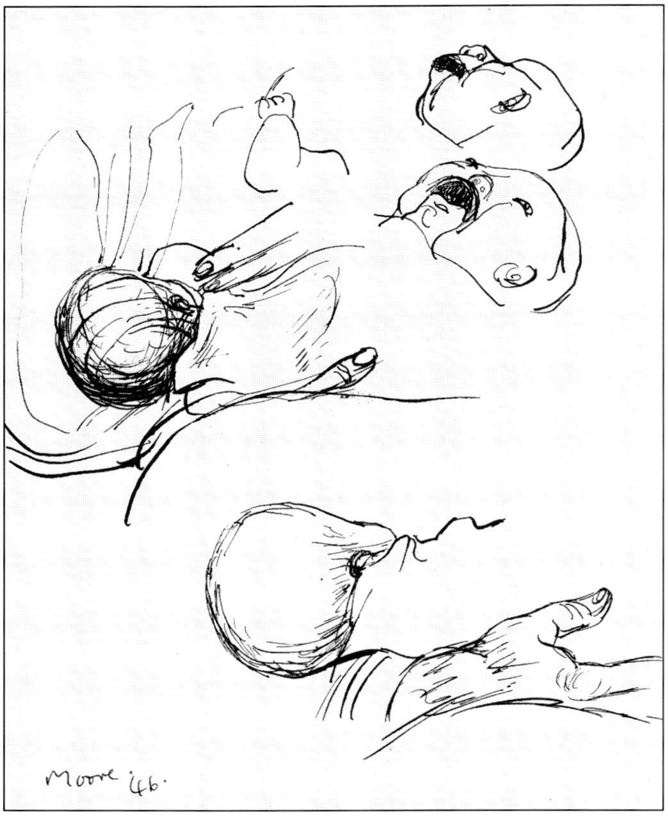

78
Mother and
Child Studies 1946
pen and Indian ink
204 x 264mm
HMF 2353

79
Child Studies 1946
pen and Indian ink
204 x 163mm
HMF 2355

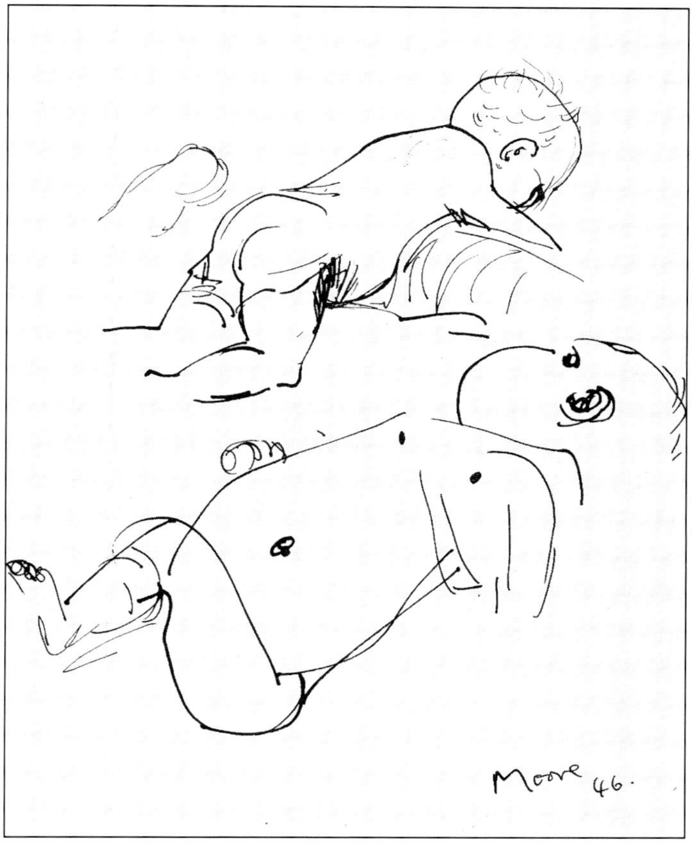

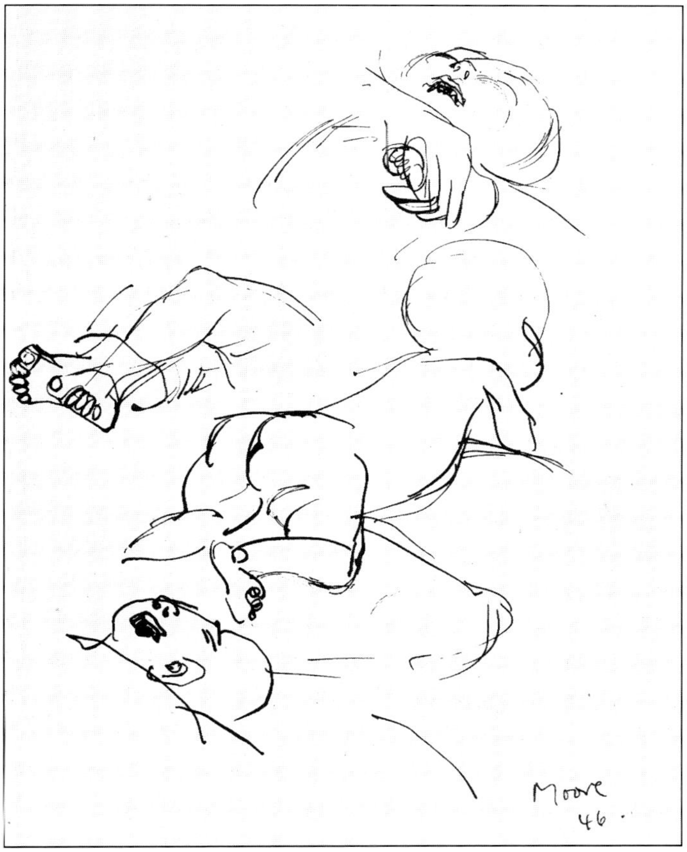

80
Child Studies 1946
pen and Indian ink
204 x 161mm
HMF 2356

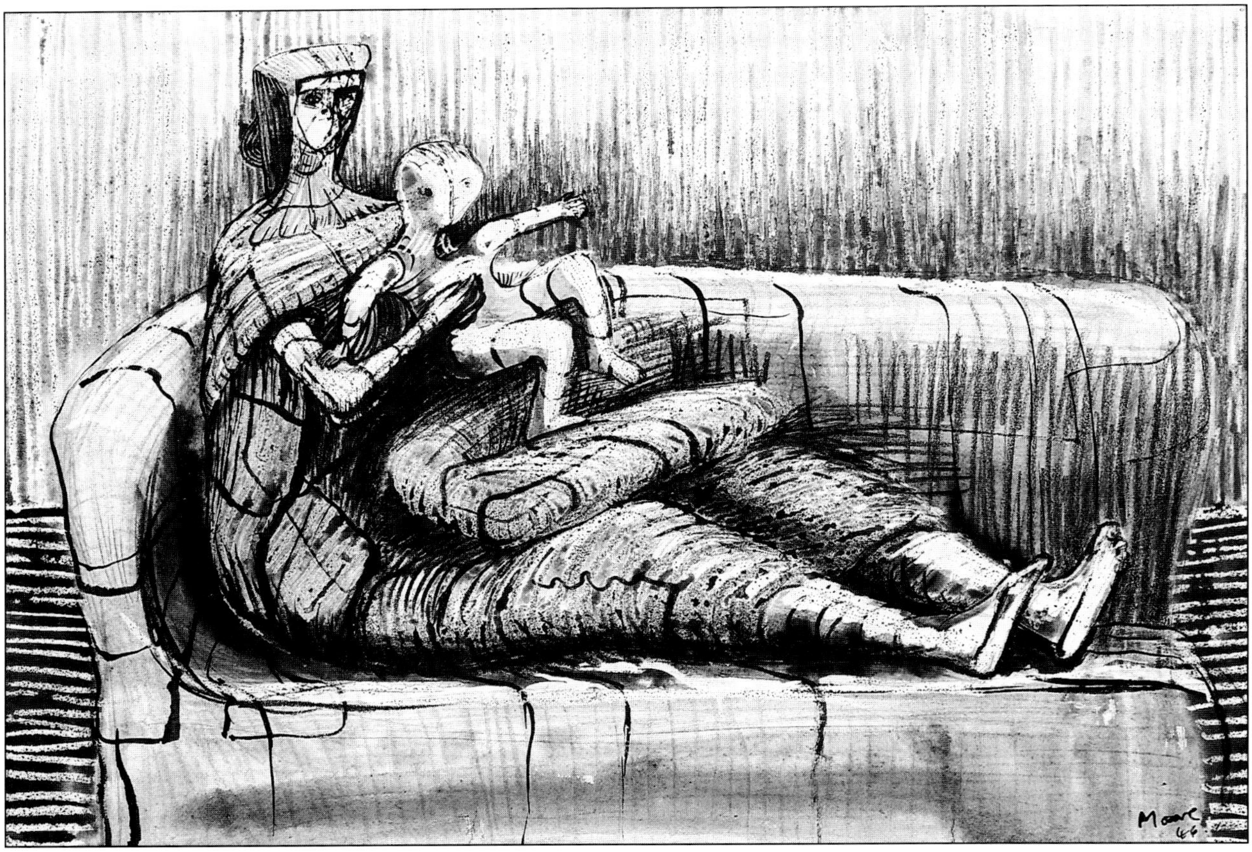

The idea of the climbing child was a new little phase of the mother and child relationship, in which the child is using its mother as a big object that can be played upon.

81
Mother and Child on a Sofa 1946
pen and ink, chalk, crayon, watercolour
378 x 555mm
The British Council, London
HMF 2387

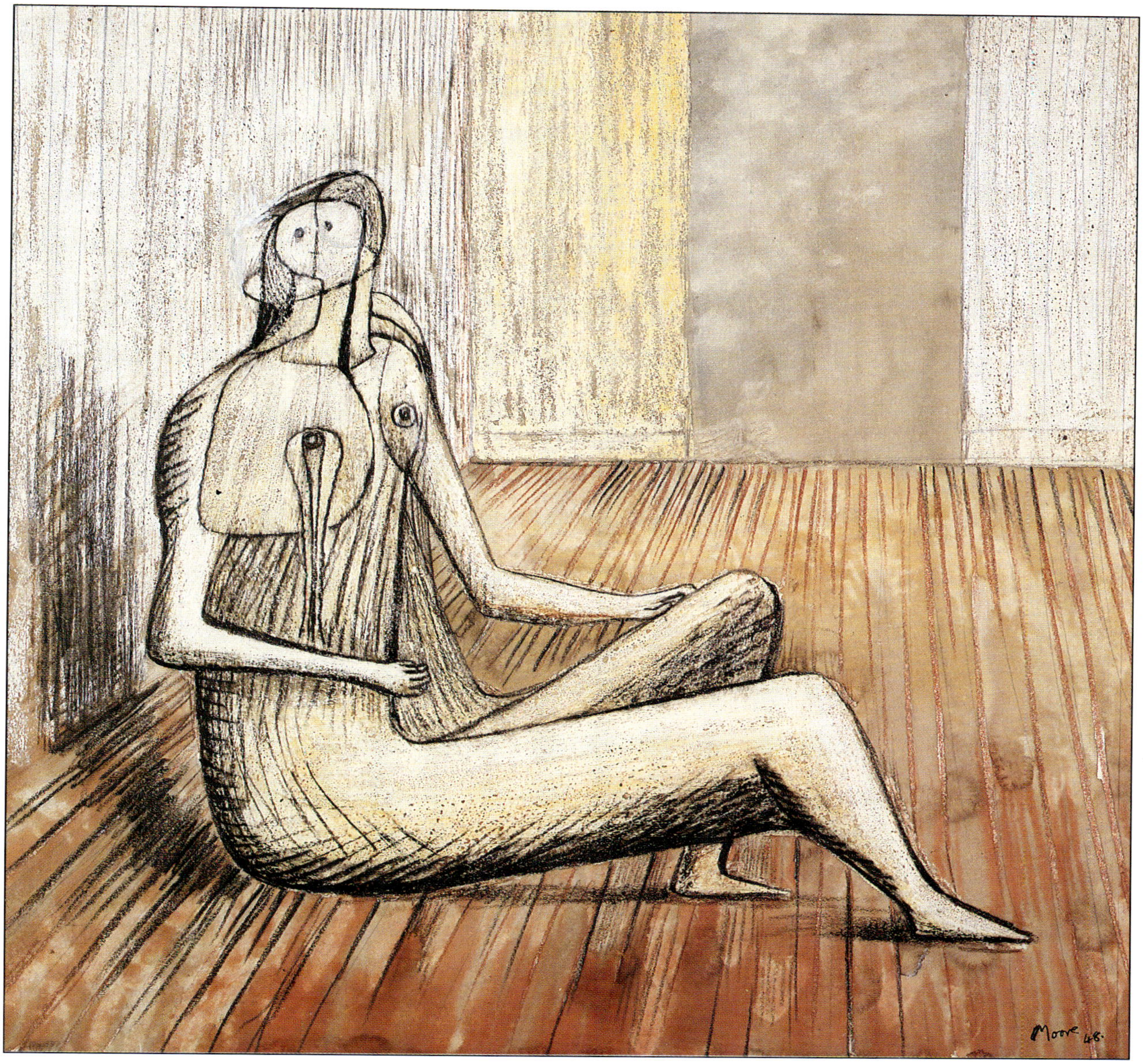

82
Seated Figure 1948
pencil, white wax crayon,
coloured crayon, watercolour wash,
gouache
555 x 587mm
HMF 2488

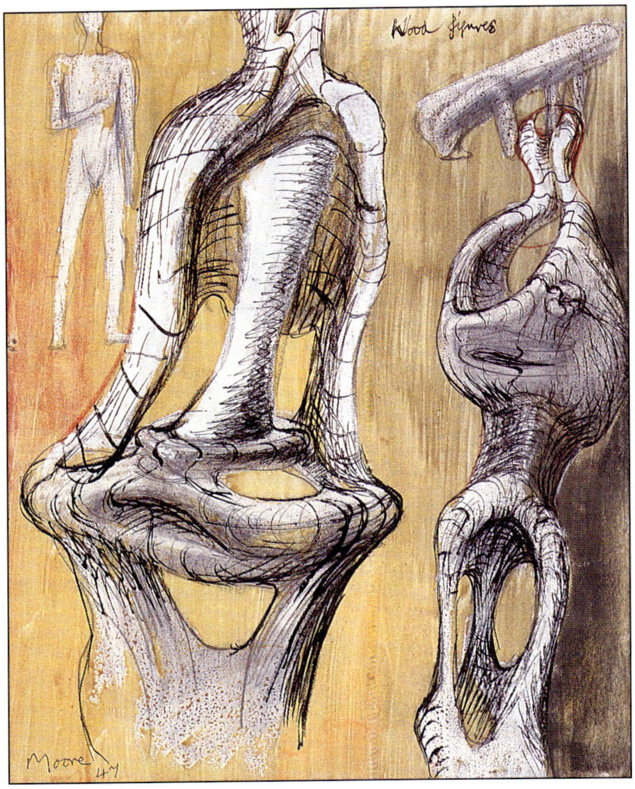

83
Page from Sketchbook 1947-49
Drawing for Wood Sculpture 1947
pencil, white wax crayon, coloured crayon, watercolour wash, pen and black ink, gouache
292 x 242mm
HMF 2403

84
Two Seated Figures 1948
ink, chalk, crayon, watercolour
542 x 568mm
The British Council, London
HMF 2492

85 ▶
Six Studies for Family Group 1948
pencil, white wax crayon, coloured crayon, grey watercolour wash, pen and Indian ink
525 x 384mm
HMF 2501a

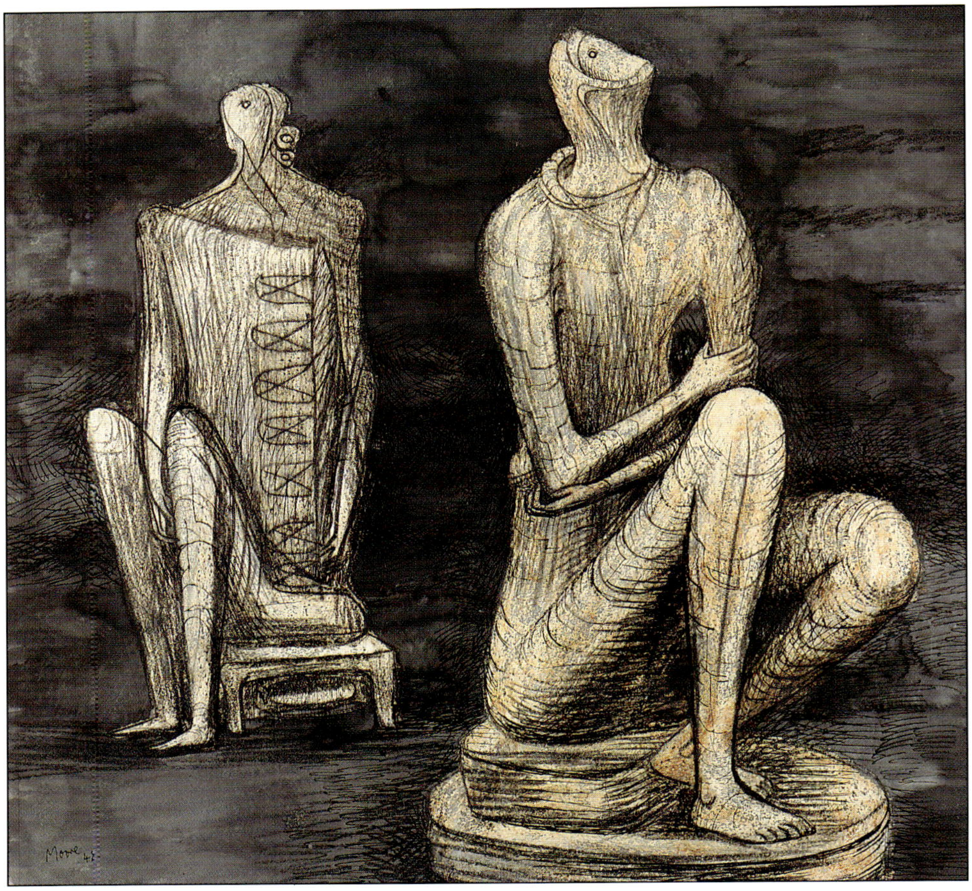

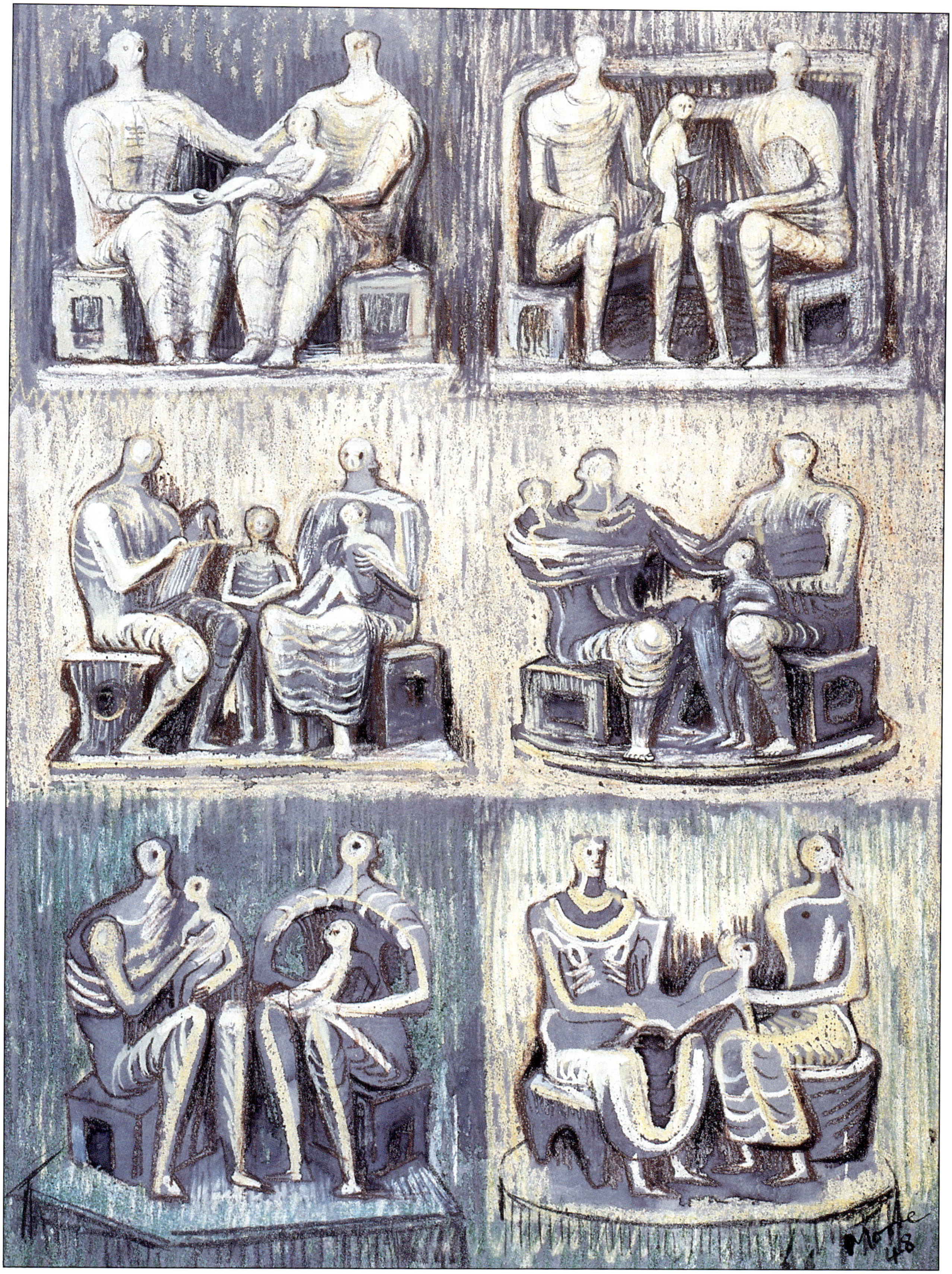

86
Figures in Settings 1949
lithograph in five colours
575 x 400mm
CGM 5

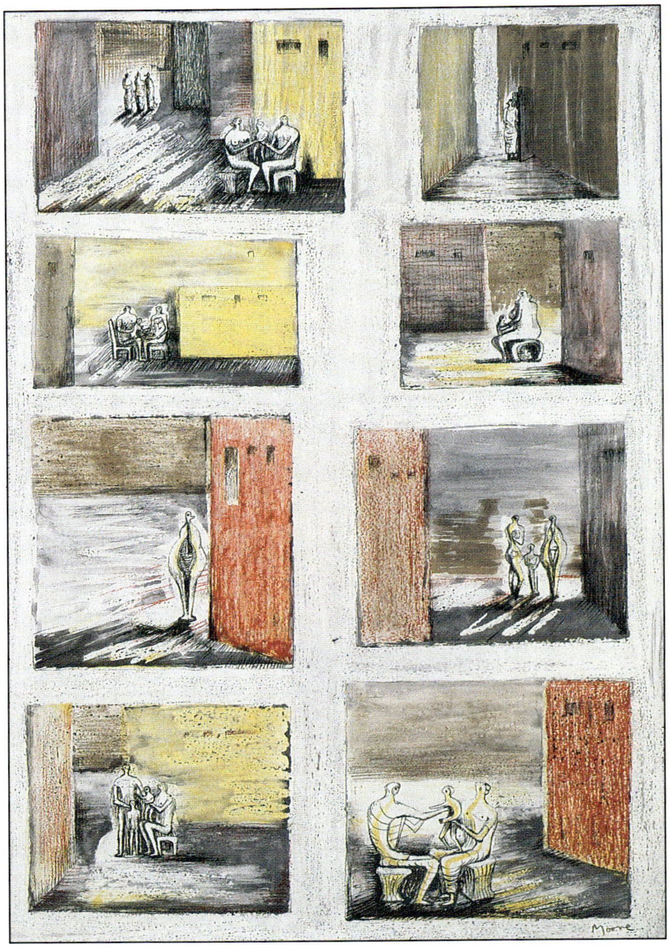

87
Woman Holding Cat 1949
lithograph in four colours
298 x 489mm
CGM 10

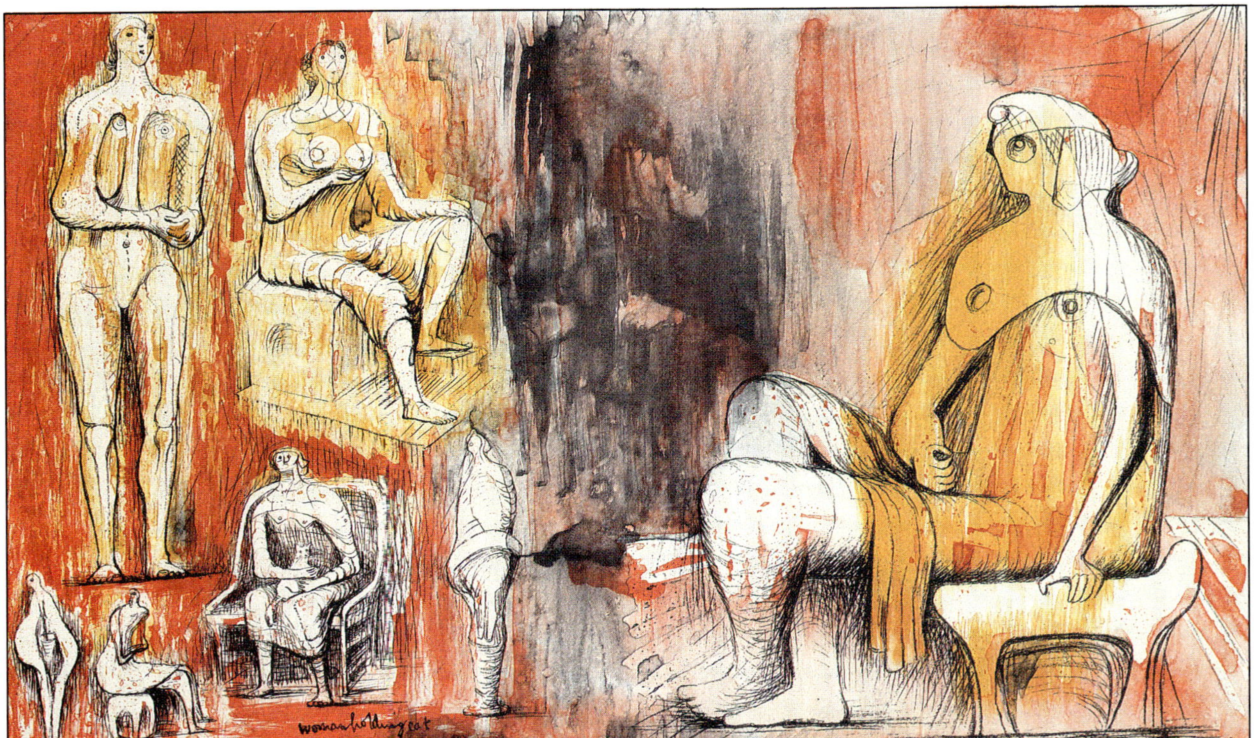

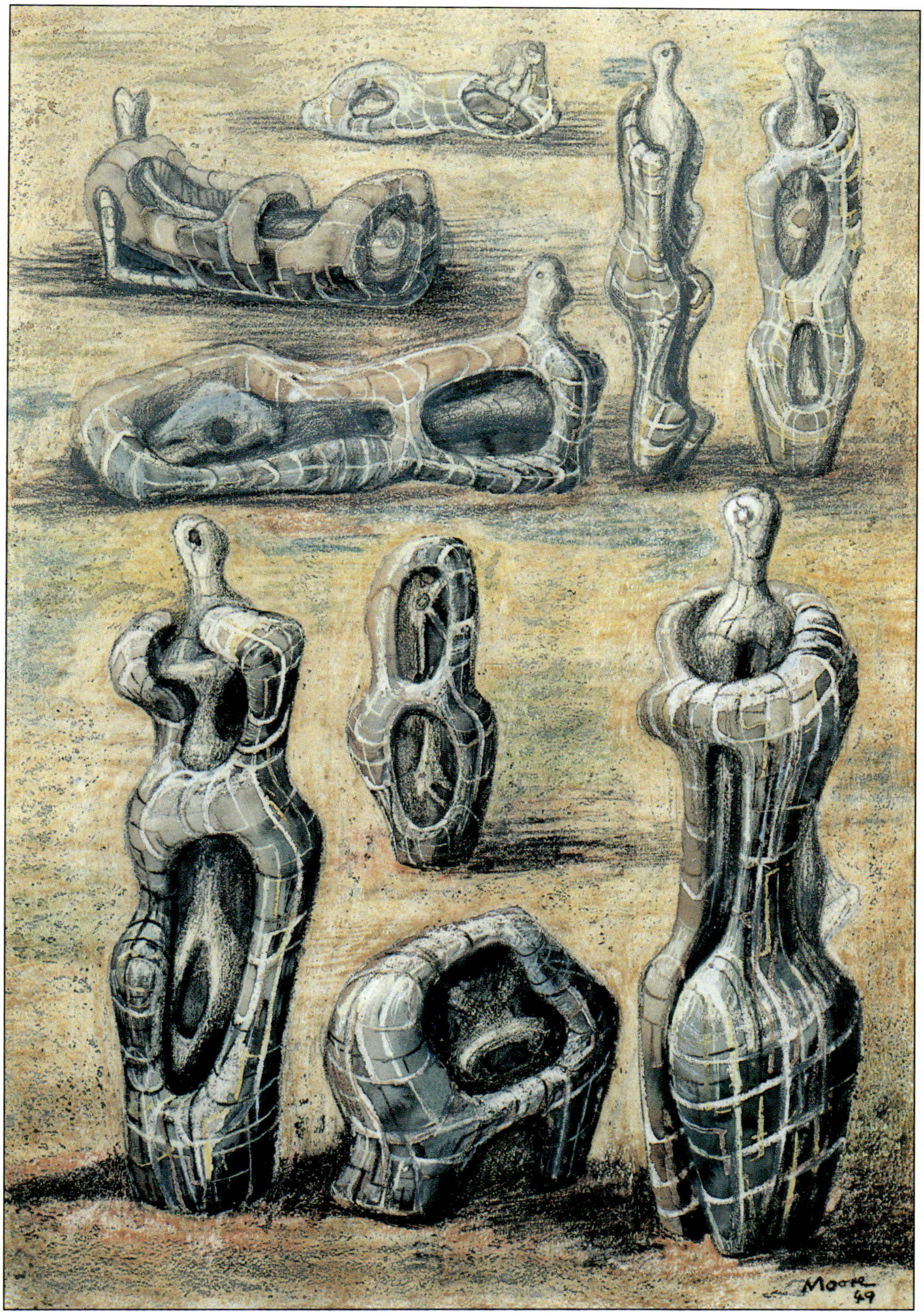

88

Studies for Sculpture: Ideas for Internal/External Forms 1949

pencil, white wax, coloured crayon, watercolour, pen and ink

277 x 381mm

HMF 2540a

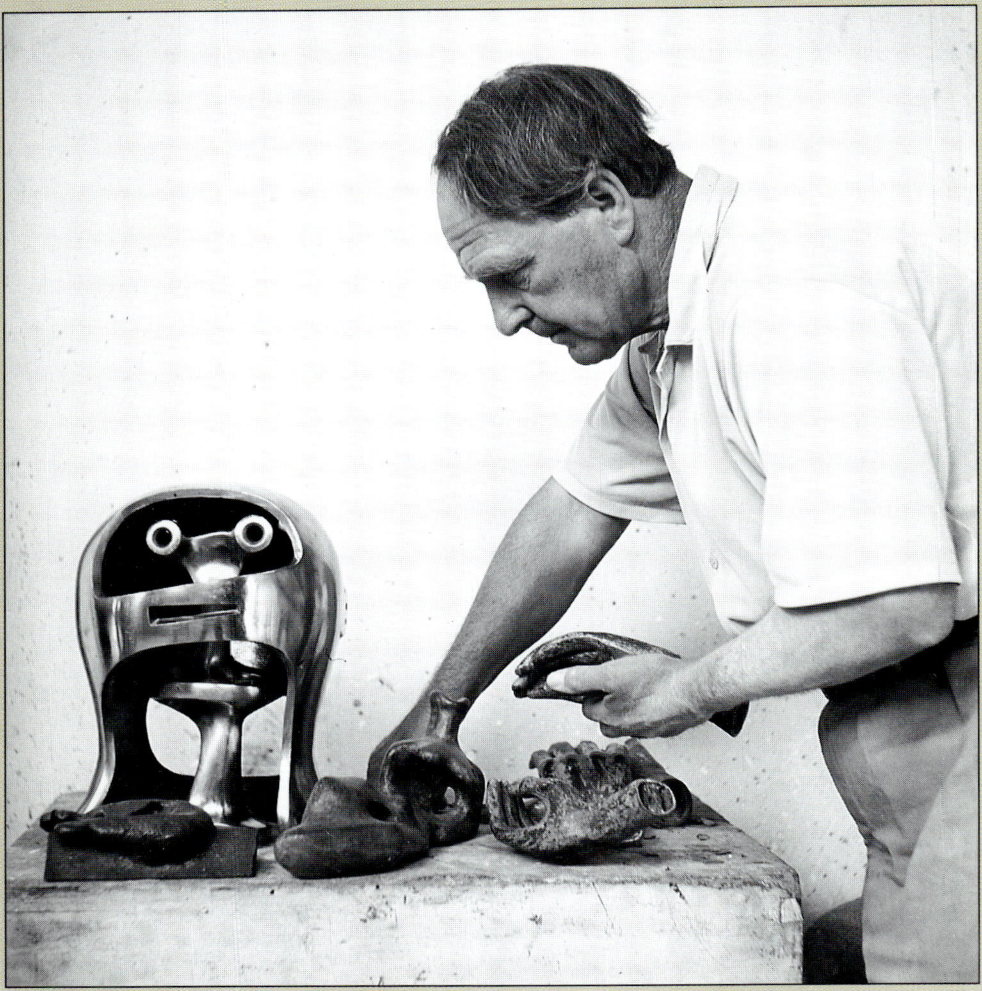

Henry Moore in his studio at Perry Green with **Helmet Head No. 2** (cat.90) in 1955.

1950s

Moore's *Draped Reclining Figure* (cat.98) may be seen as a response to sculptures that he saw on a visit to Greece in 1951. These were often draped in a manner that resembled his own shelter drawings. The visit reconciled him to the beauty of work by the ancient Greeks and, for this figure, he adapted a technique used in the Renaissance, that he had previously resisted. When making the full-size plaster from which the bronze was cast, Moore created the folds of drapery by using real fabric soaked in plaster; this can be seen where the surface has worn away on the original plaster (now in Canada at the Art Gallery of Ontario) from which the bronze was cast. The *Draped Reclining Figure* was planned for the terrace of a London office block and Moore was asked to provide a screen wall to shield the terrace: he designed a double-sided pierced screen, which was carved in stone and differs slightly from the working model shown here (cat.100). The shapes are a reminder of Moore's abstracted stone figures of the 1930s, as well as of his drawings of square forms from the same decade.

In the early 1950s Moore also took up again the theme of helmets, making a series of heads including cats.89 and 90. He explored the male figure on its own: he did not enlarge this *Fallen Warrior* (cat.103) because he preferred instead to depict a Falling Warrior at a moment before death – a subject to which he returned in 1973 (see cat.151).

Archaic and primitive ideas inspired the *King and Queen* (cat.101) – the title was added after the figures were finished. In 1954, when the sculpture was shown at the Curt Valentin Gallery in New York, Moore explained: 'The "King and Queen" group has nothing to do with present-day Kings and Queens . . . The "clue" to the group is perhaps the head of the King which is a head and crown, face and beard combined into one form and in my mind has some slight Pan-like suggestion, almost animal, and yet, I think, something Kingly.'

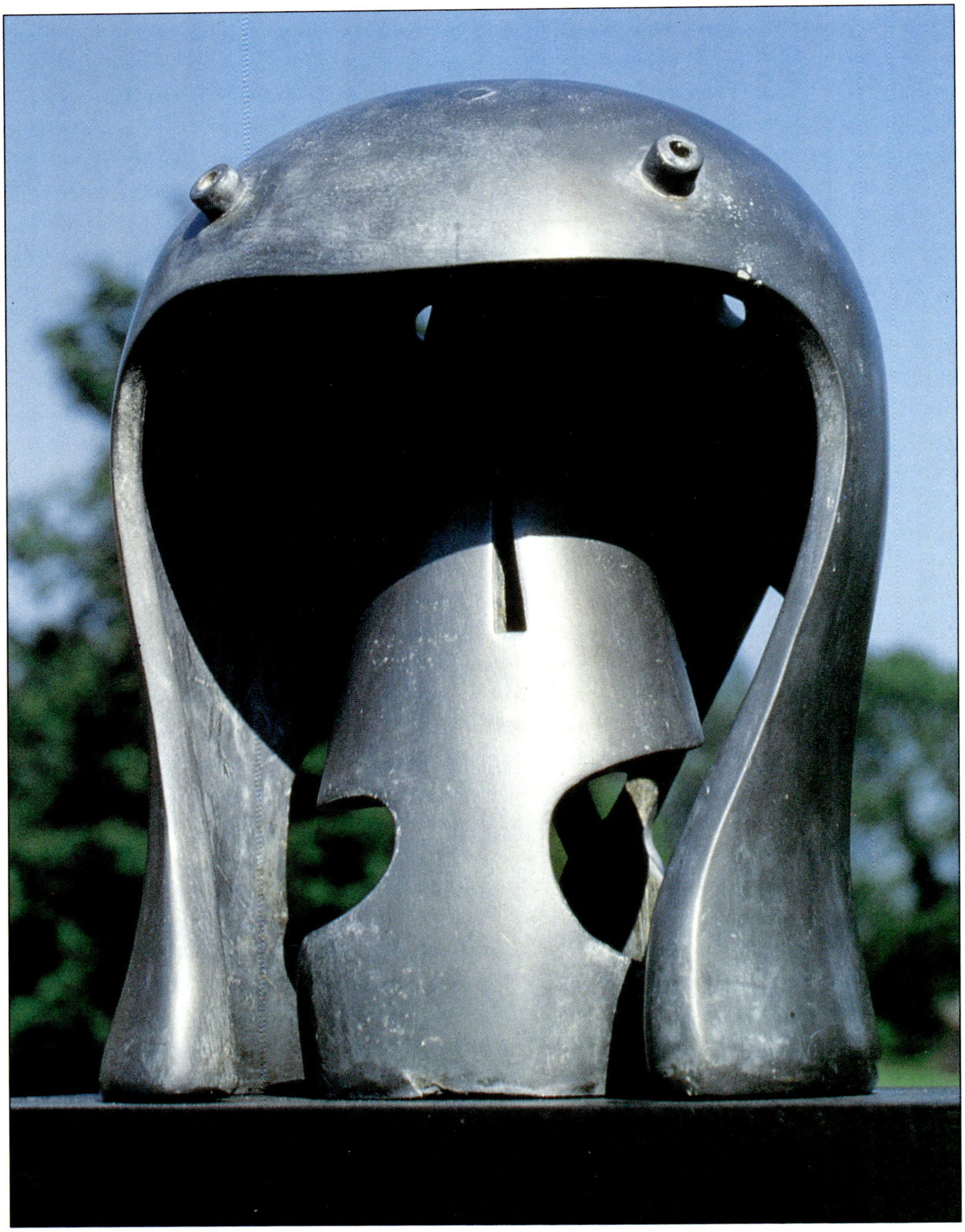

89

Helmet Head No.1 1950

H 34cm lead, unique cast

LH 279

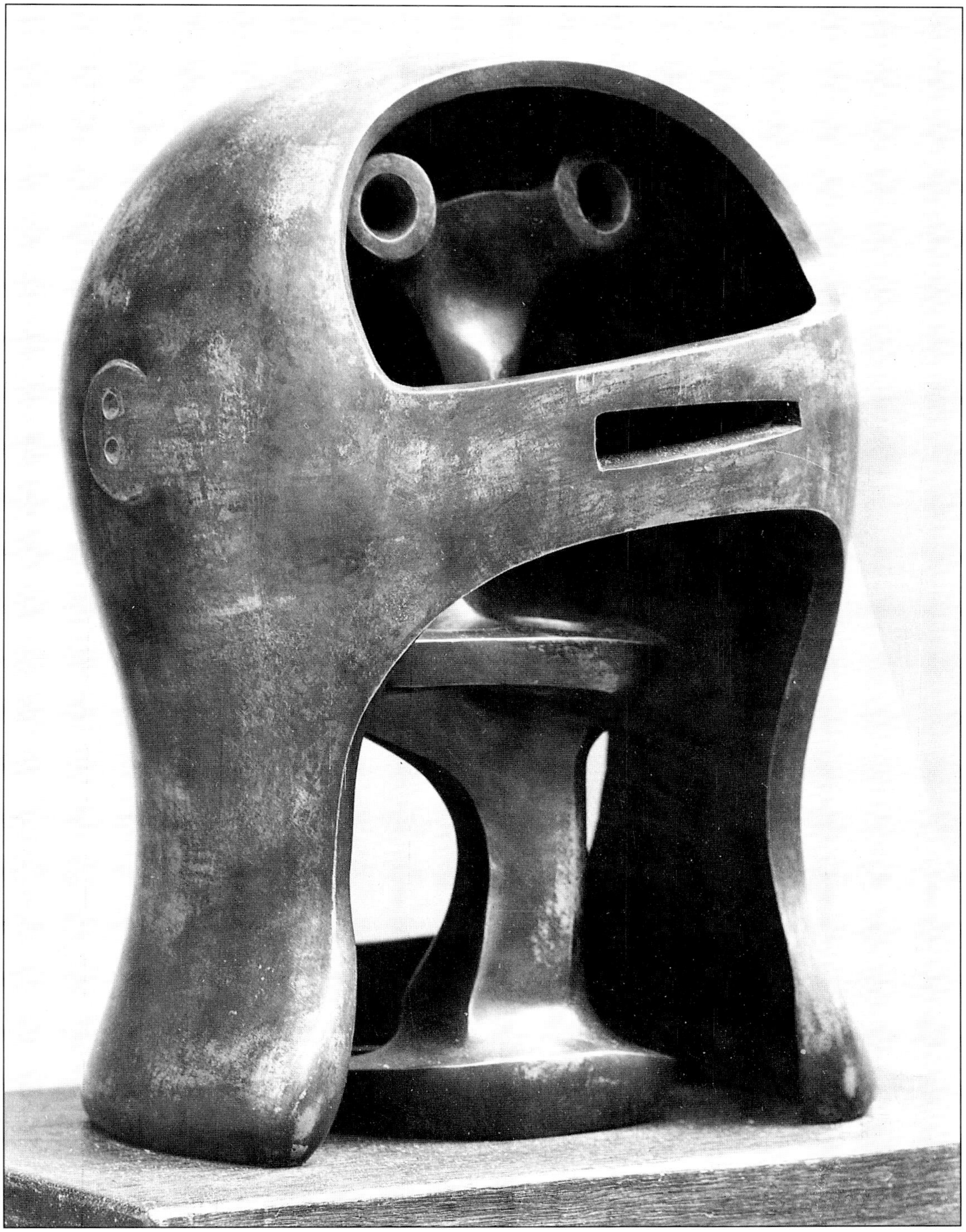

90

Helmet Head No.2 1950, cast 1955
H 34cm bronze edition of 9
Art Gallery of New South Wales, Sydney
LH 281

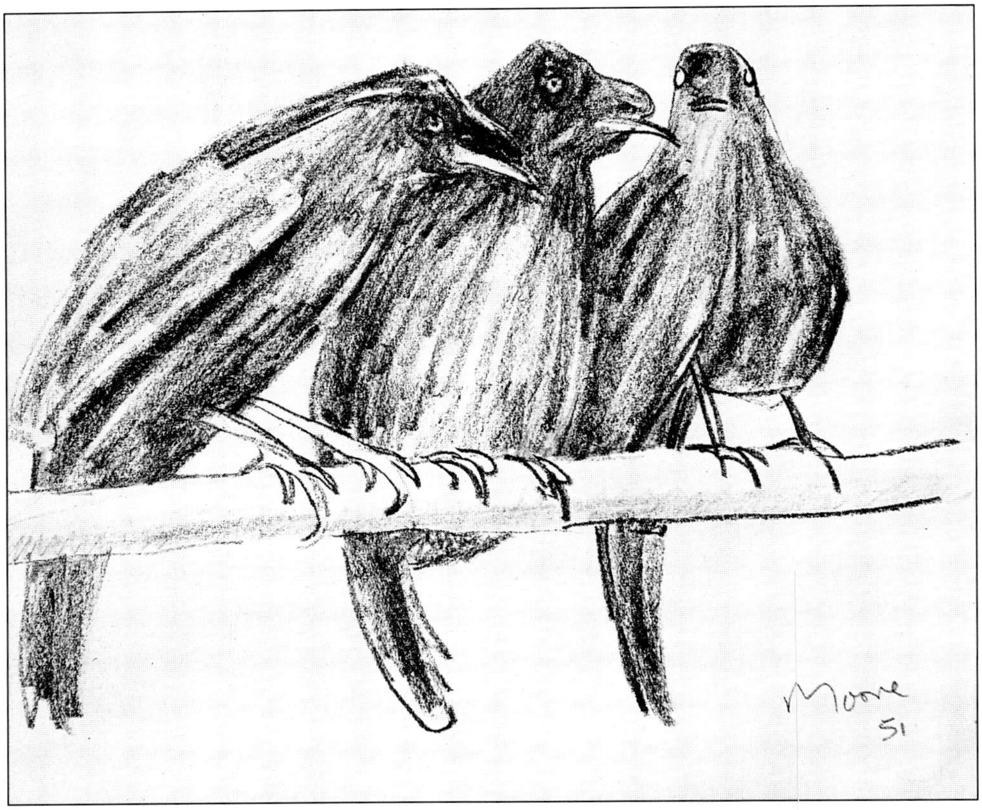

91

Page 63 from Sketchbook 1950-51

Birds: Three Crows 1951

188 x 215mm

black crayon

private collection

HMF 2652

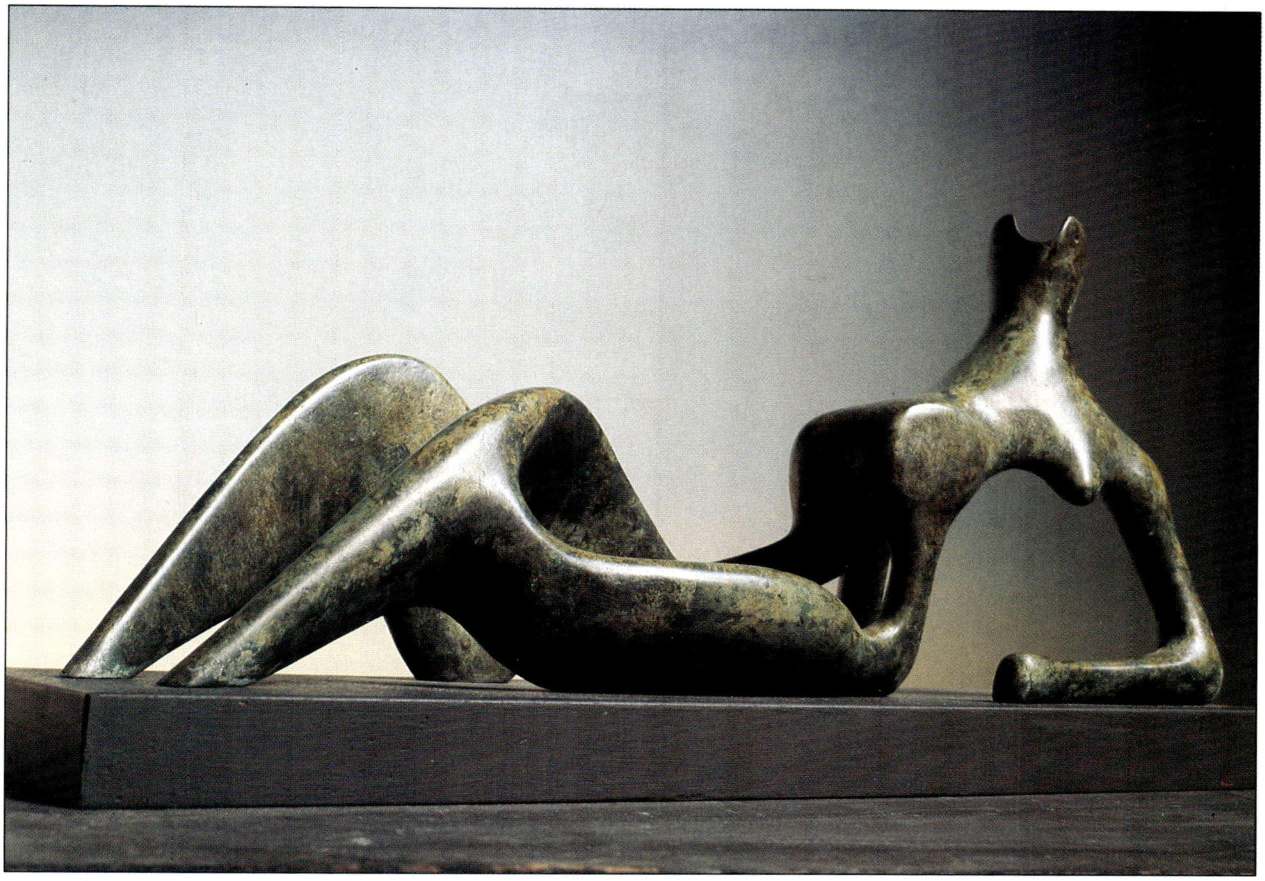

92
Working Model for Reclining Figure: Festival 1950
L 43cm bronze edition of 7
LH 292

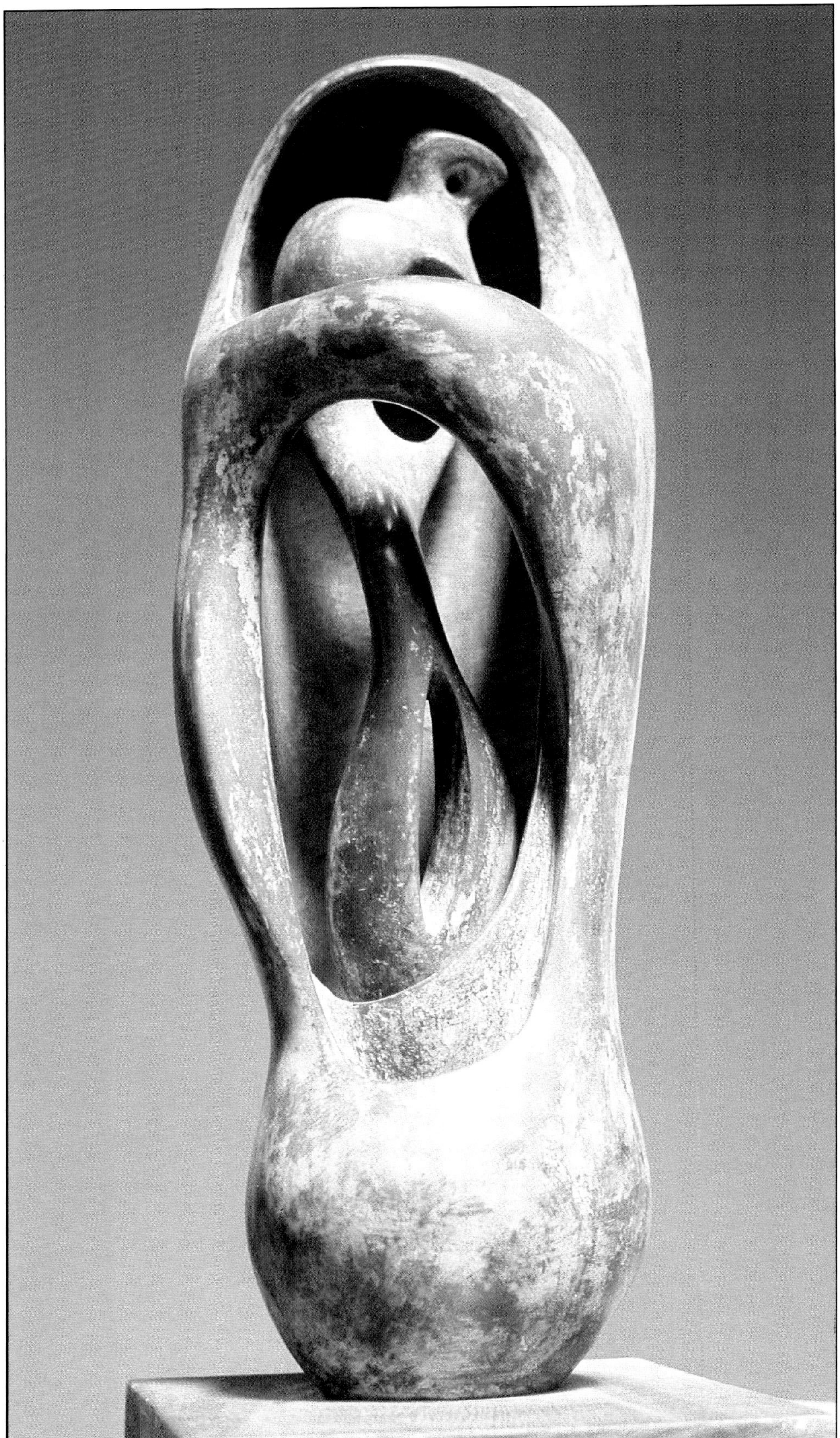

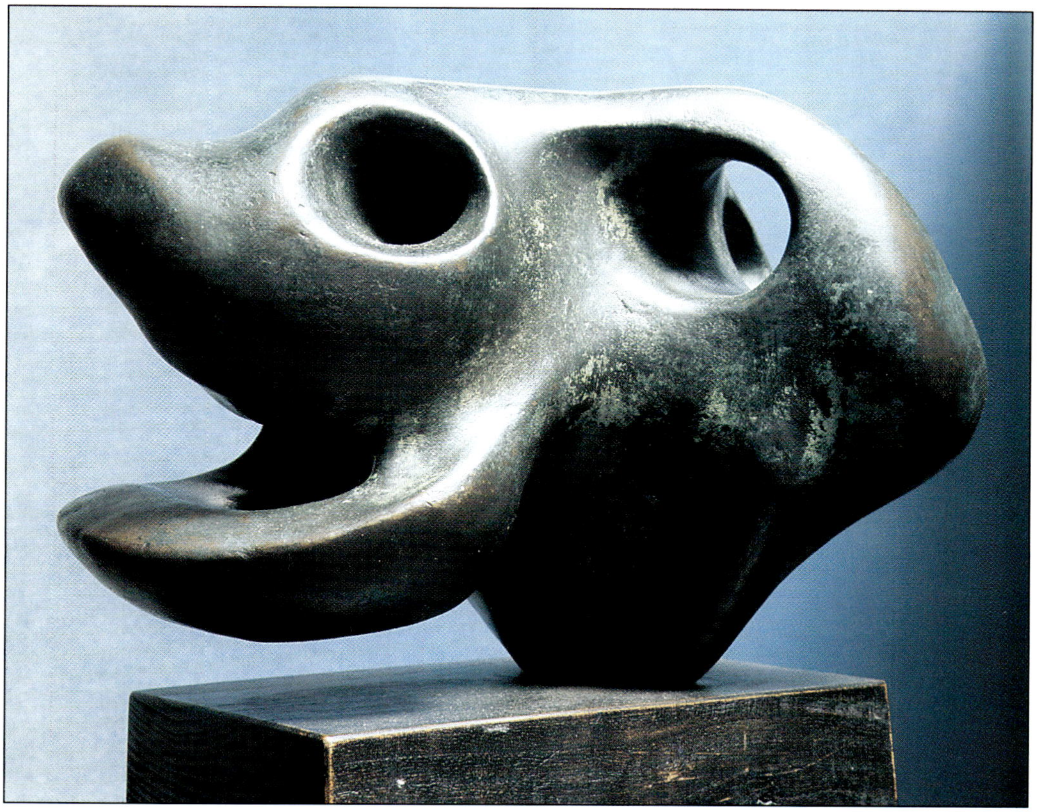

I think the humanist organic element will always be for me of fundamental importance in sculpture, giving sculpture its vitality. Each particular carving I make takes on in my mind a human, or occasionally animal character and personality, and this personality controls its design and formal qualities, and makes me satisfied or dissatisfied with the work as it develops.

93
Working Model for Upright Internal/External Form 1951
H 63.2cm bronze edition of 7
LH 295

94
Animal Head 1951
L 30.5cm bronze edition of 6
LH 301

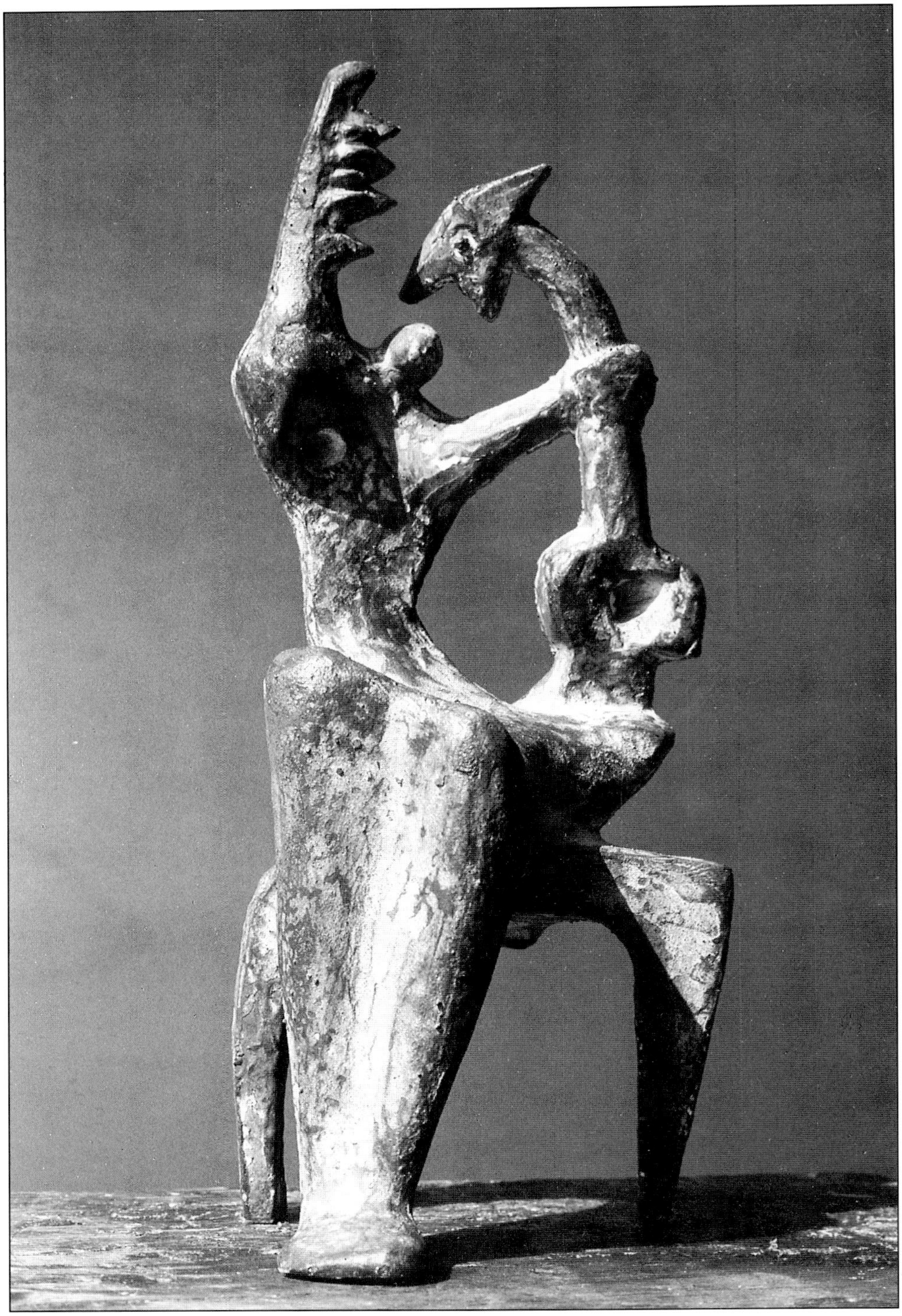

95

Maquette for Mother and Child 1952

H 21.6cm bronze edition of 9

LH 314

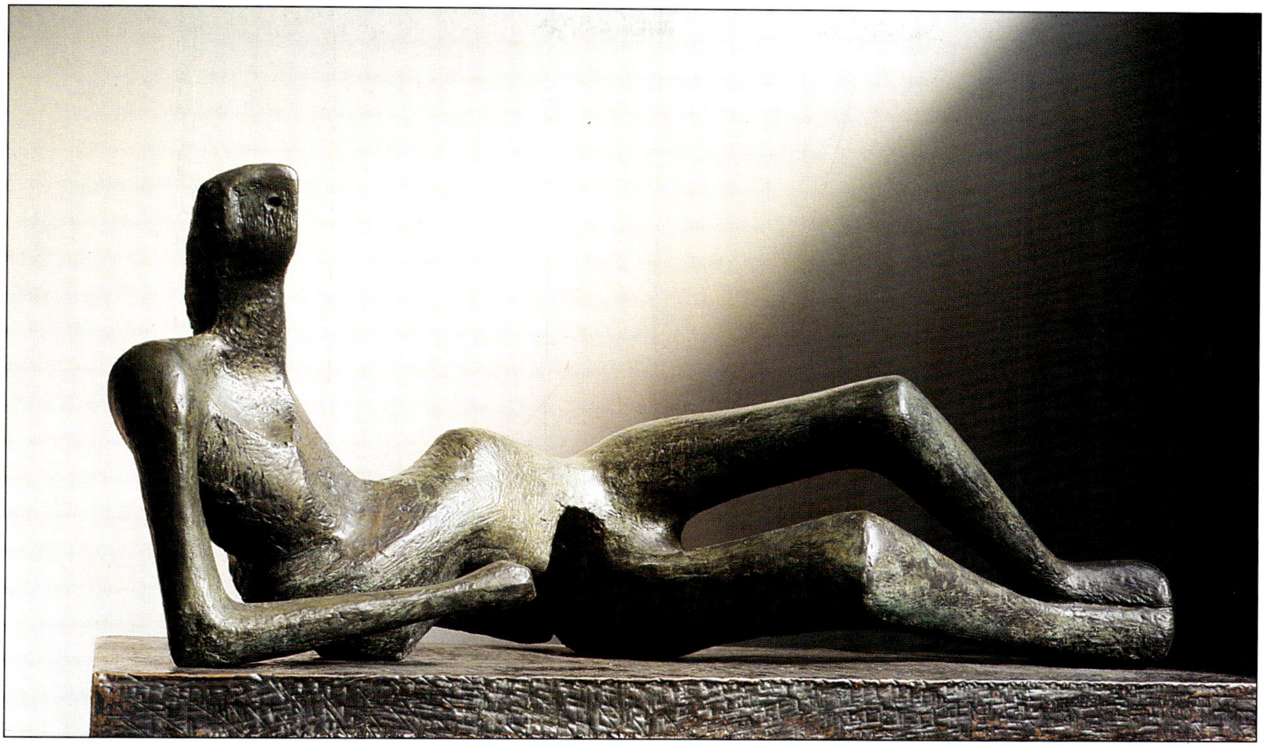

In many of my reclining figures the head and neck part of the sculpture, sometimes the torso part too, is upright, giving contrast to the horizontal direction of the whole sculpture. Also in my reclining figures I have often made a sort of looming leg – the top leg in the sculpture projecting over the lower leg which gives a sense of thrust and power – as a large branch of a tree might move outwards from the main limb – or as a seaside cliff might overhang from below if you are on the beach.

96

Reclining Figure No.2 1953

L 91.5cm bronze edition of 7

private collection

LH 329

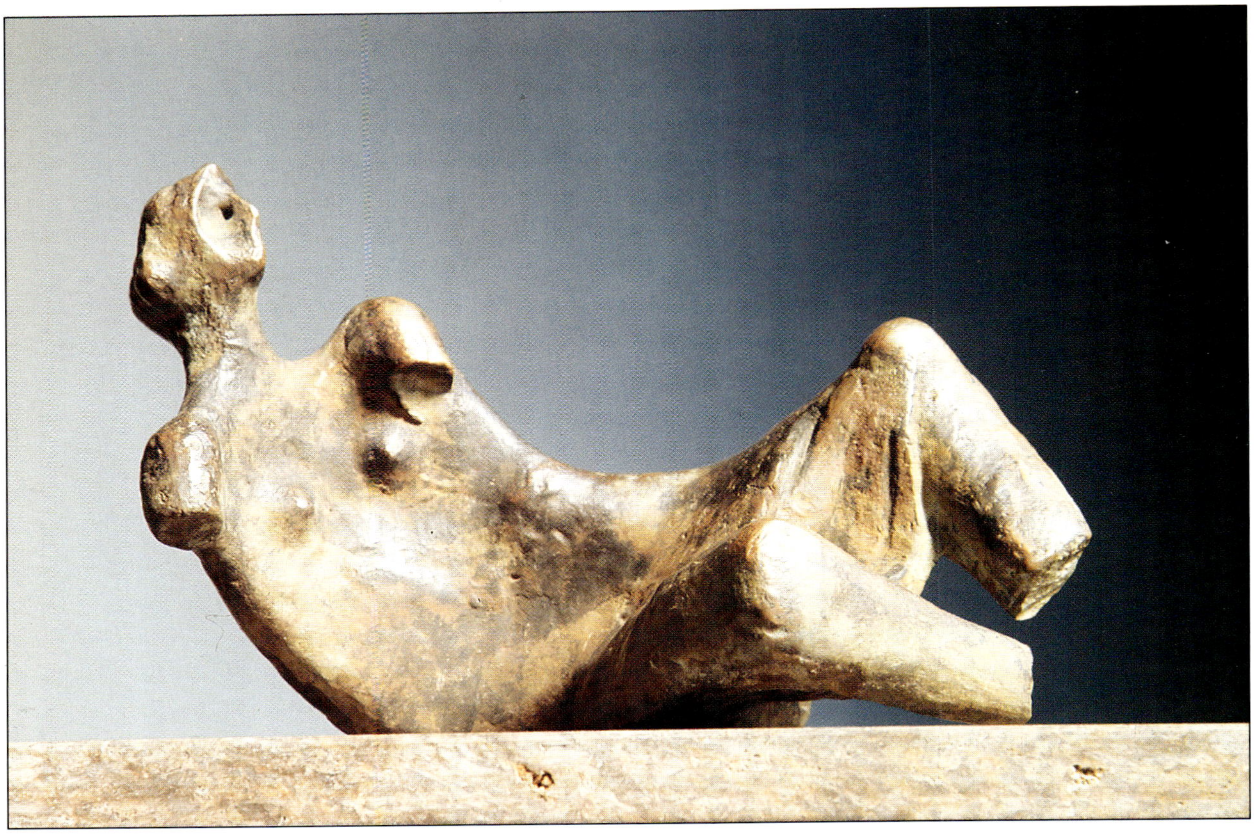

Drapery can emphasise the tension in a figure, for where the form pushes outwards, such as on the shoulders, the thighs, the breasts, etc., it can be pulled tight across the form (almost like a bandage), and by contrast with the crumpled slackness of the drapery which lies between the salient points, the pressure from inside is intensified.

97
Reclining Figure: Fragment 1952, cast 1969
L 14cm bronze
edition of 9
LH 331a

98
Draped Reclining Figure 1952-53
L 157.5cm bronze
edition of 3
LH 336

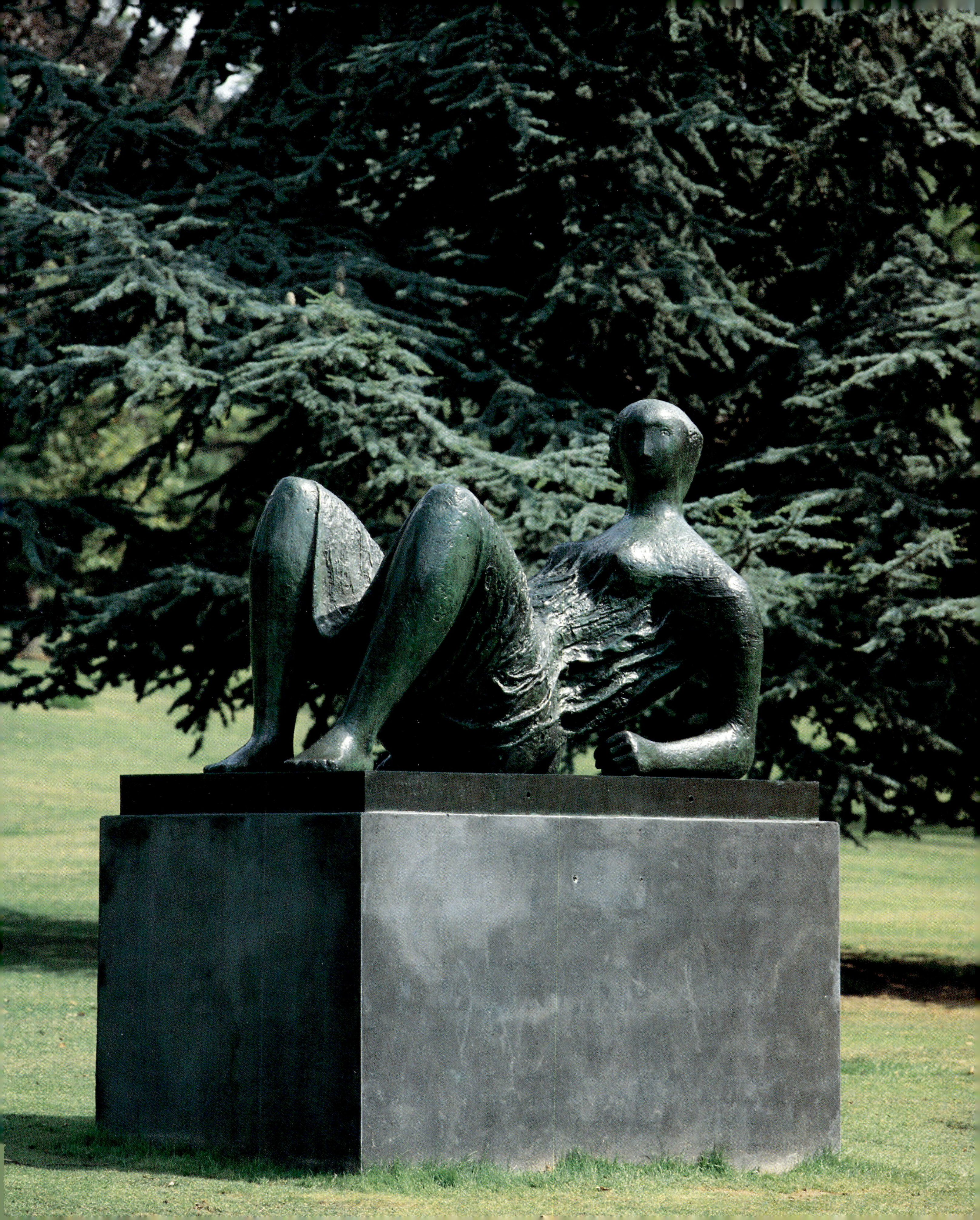

99

Reclining Figure No.6 1954

L 21.6cm bronze edition of 12

LH 337

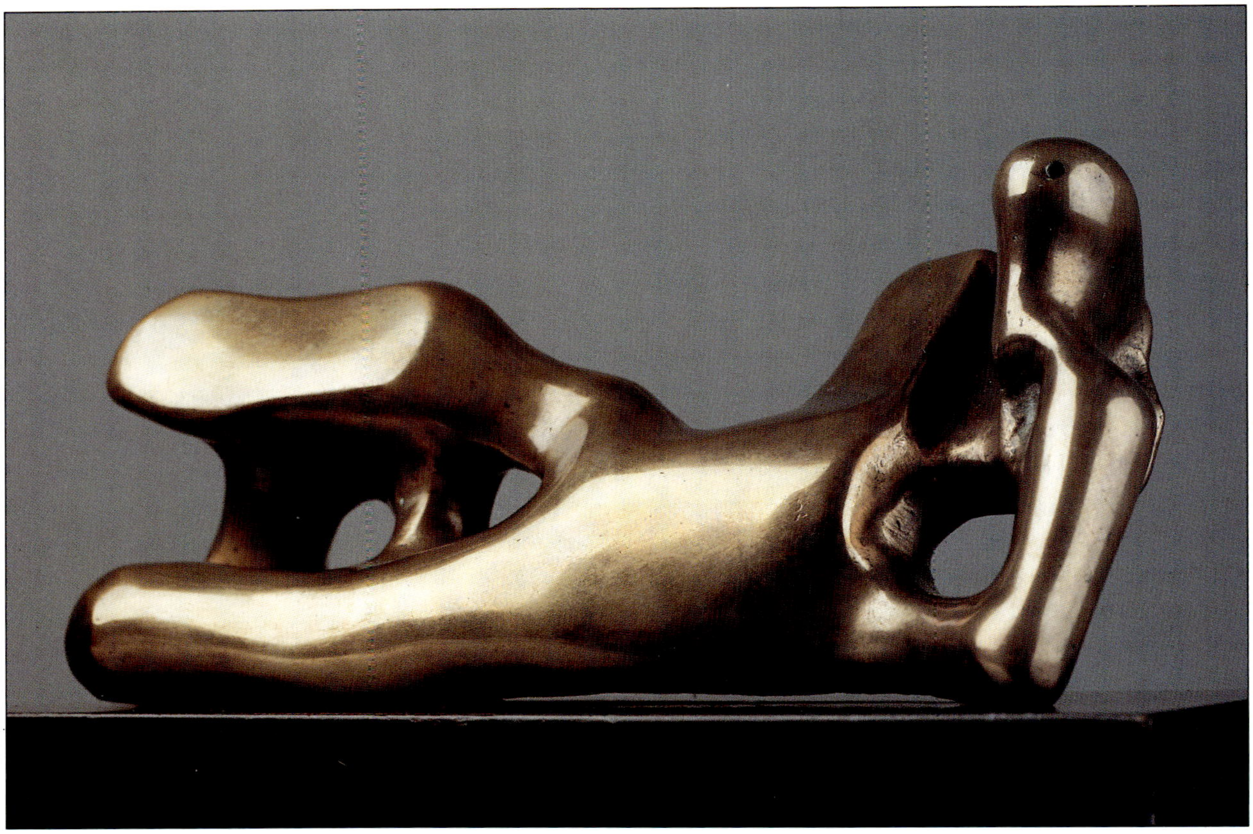

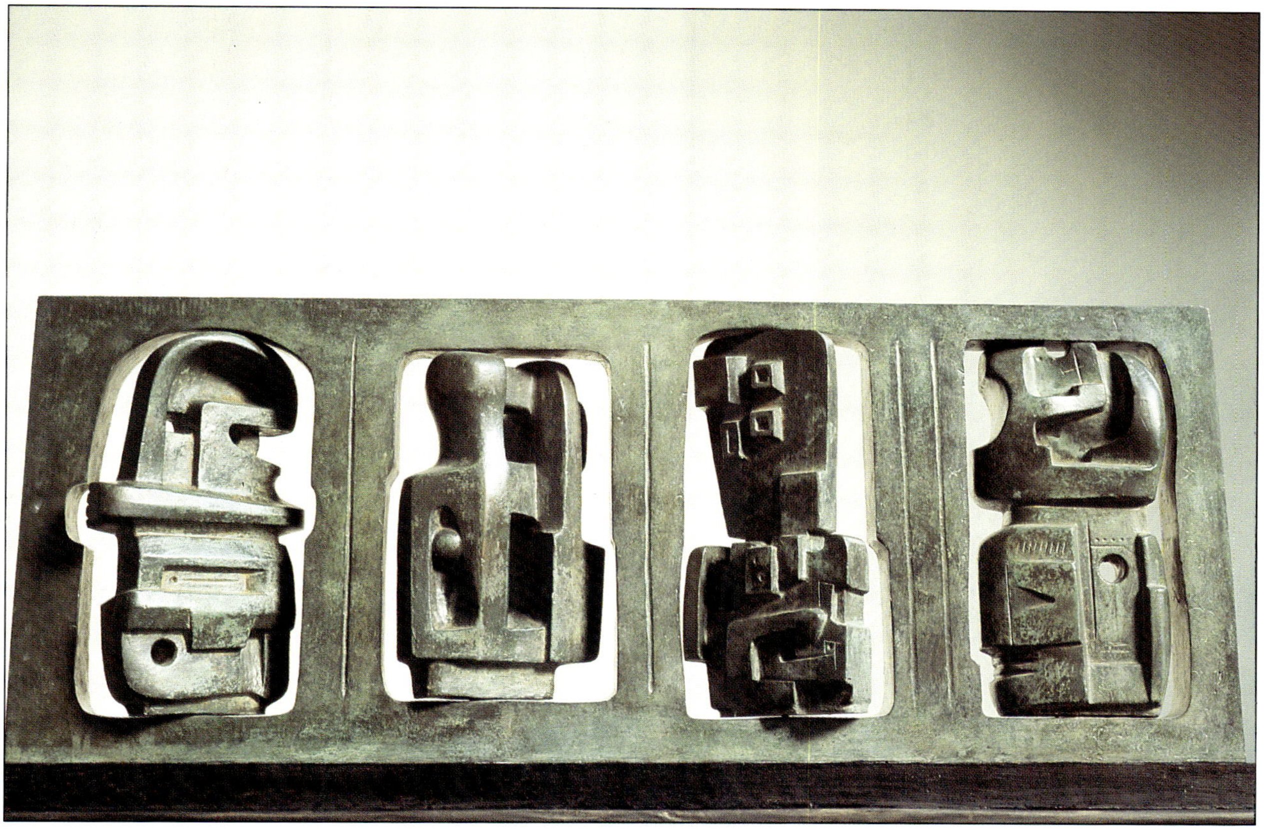

I found too that my project really demanded a turntable for each of the carvings, so that they could be turned, say, on the first of each month, each to a different view, and project from the building like some of those half animals that look as if they are escaping through the walls in Romanesque architecture. I wanted them to be like half-buried pebbles whose form one's eye instinctively completes.

100
Working Model for Time/Life Screen 1952
L 101cm bronze edition of 10
LH 343

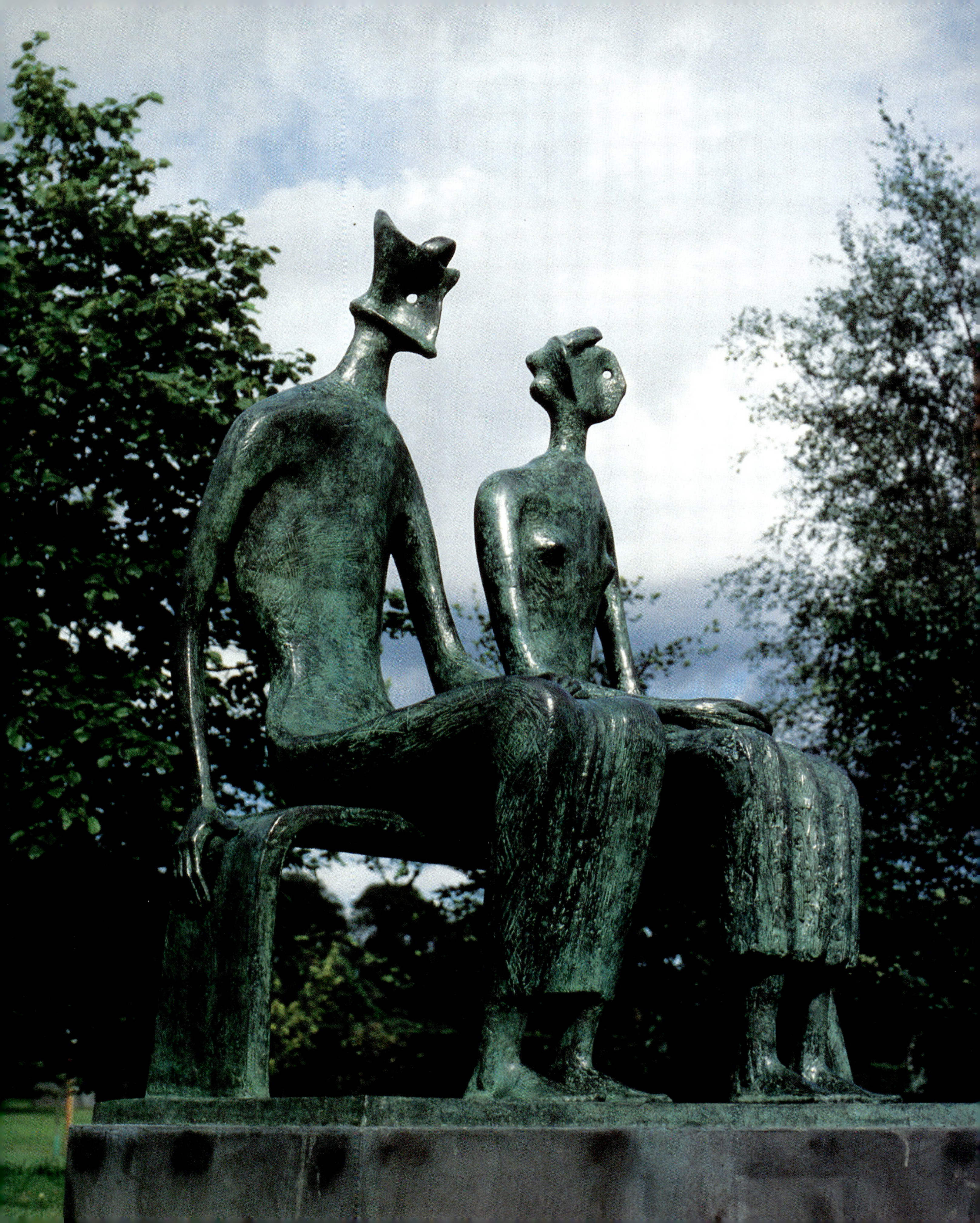

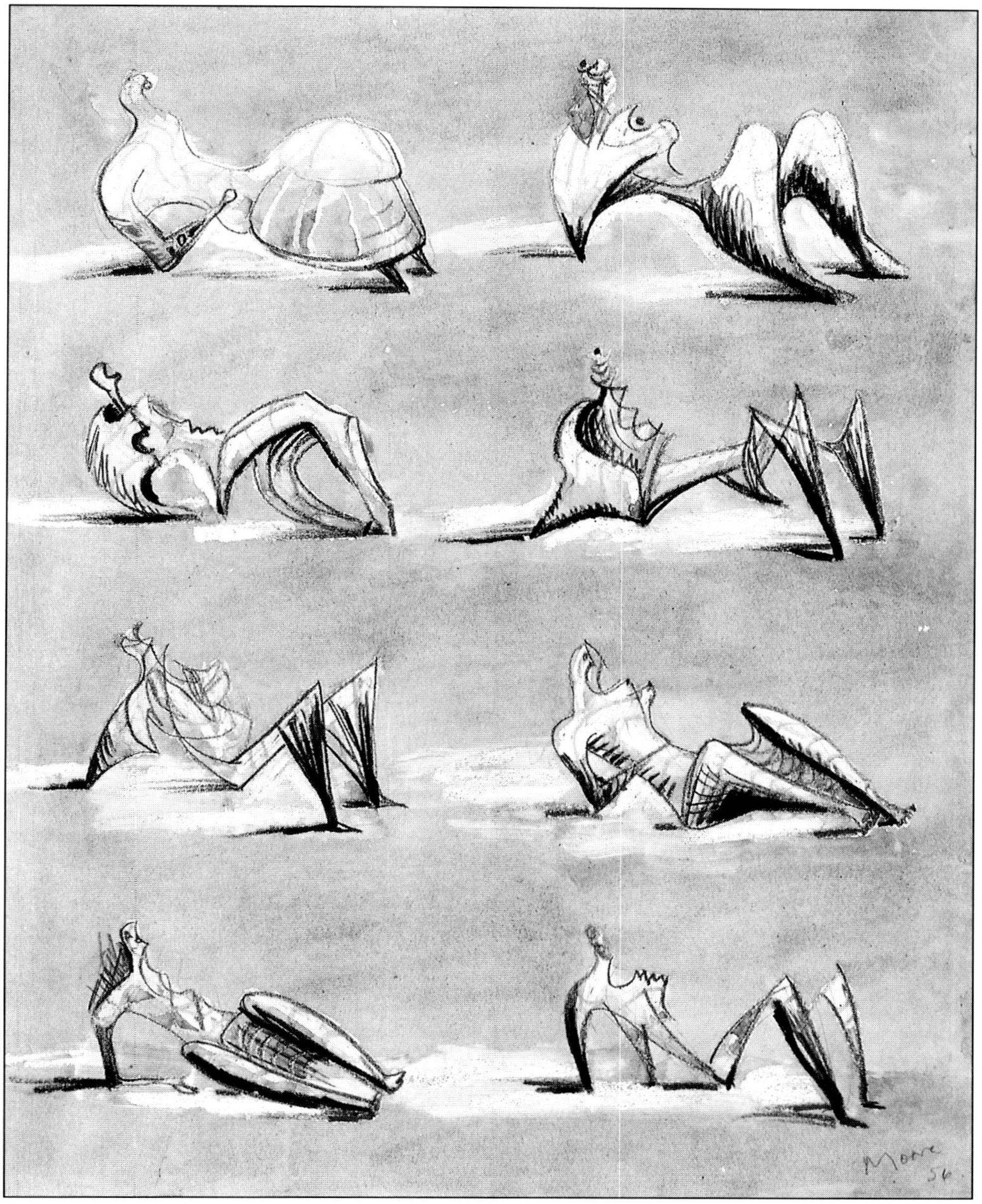

101
King and Queen 1952-53
H 164cm bronze edition of 6
LH 350

102
Eight Reclining Figures for Metal Sculpture 1956
conté crayon, wax crayon, watercolour wash
426 x 341 mm
HMF 2911a

103

Maquette for Fallen Warrior 1956

L 22.9cm bronze edition of 10

LH 404

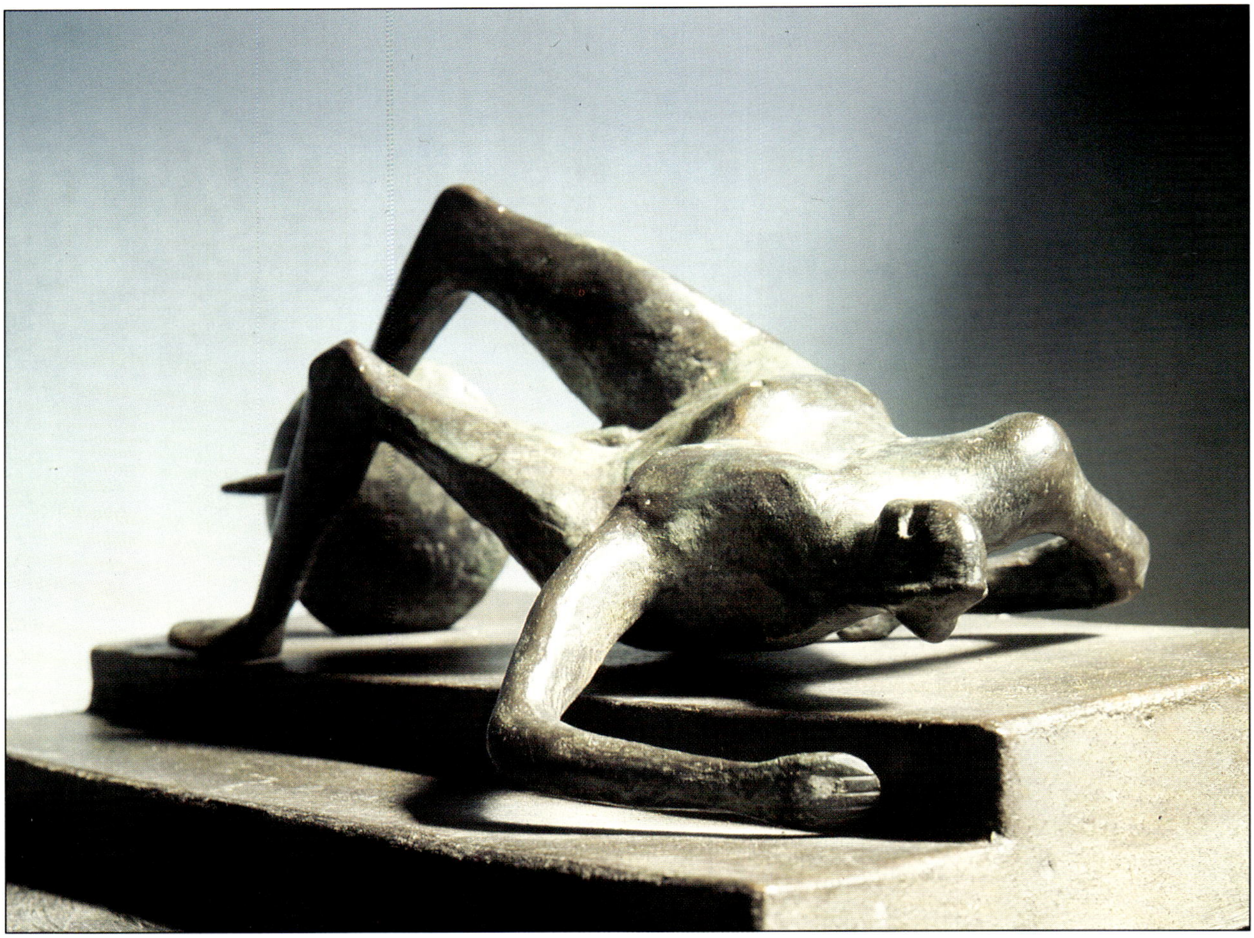

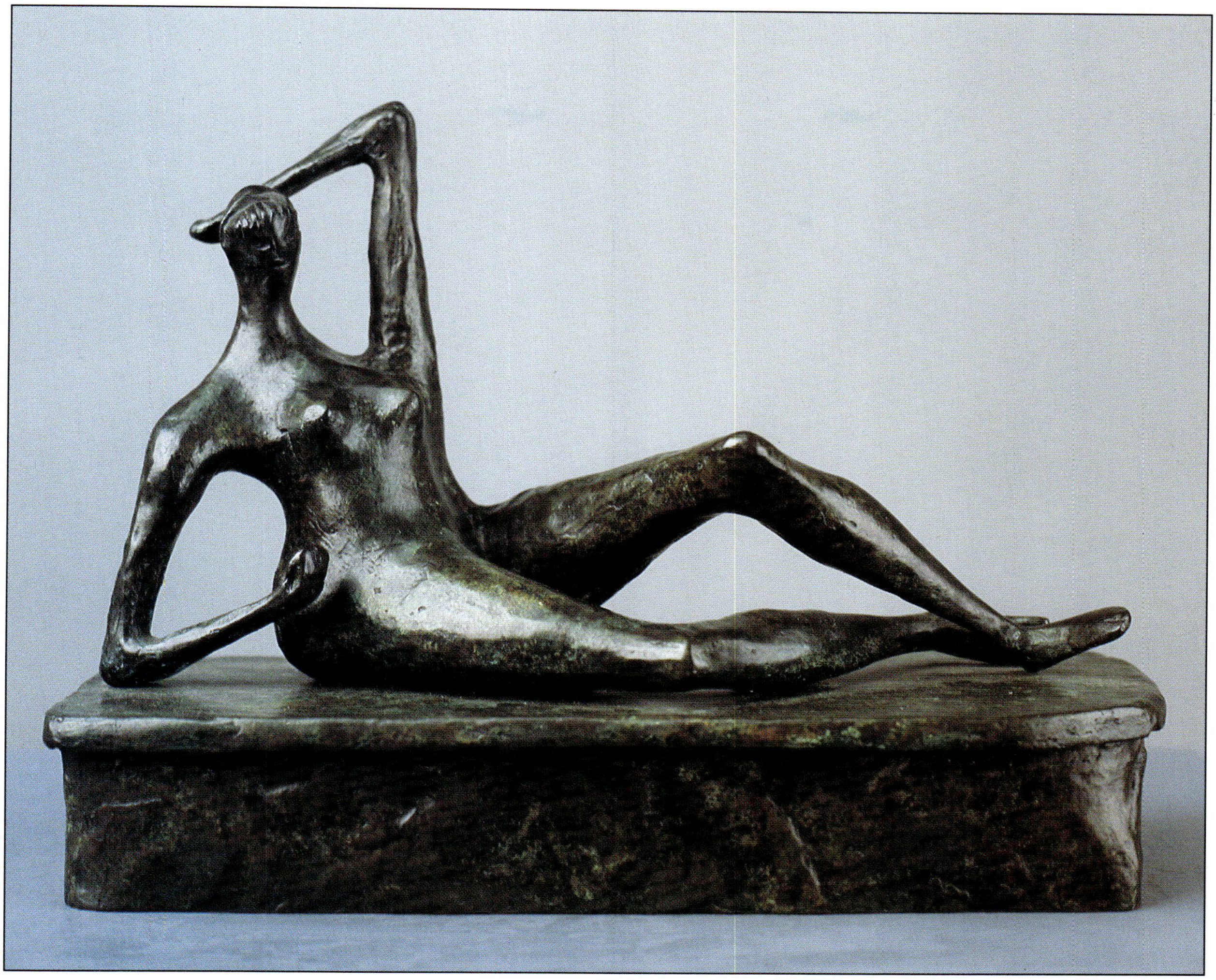

104
Reclining Figure: Goujon 1956, cast 1971
L 24cm bronze edition of 9
LH 411a

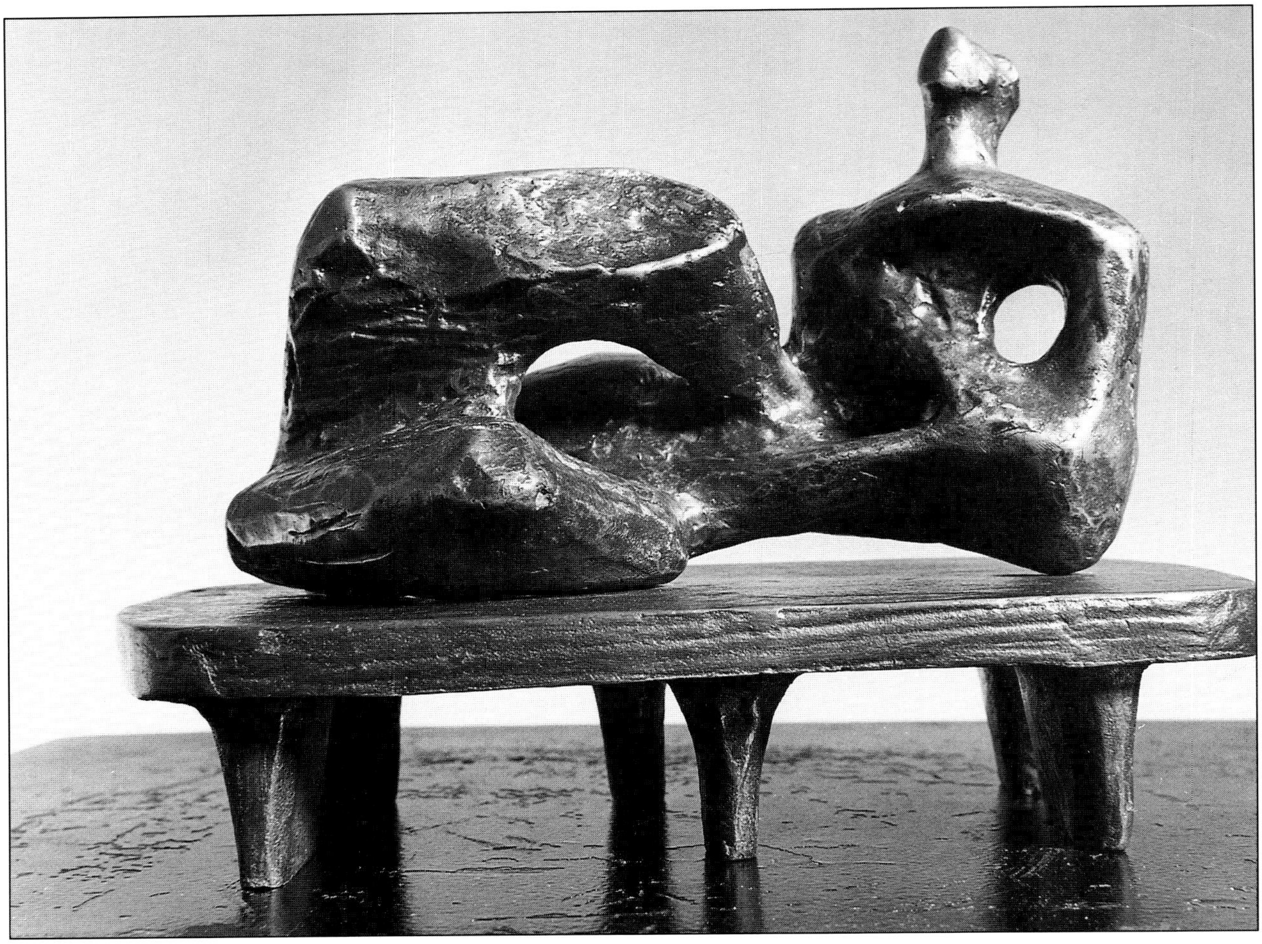

105
Maquette for Unesco Reclining Figure 1956
L 21.6cm bronze
edition of 6
LH 414

106
Seated Figures 1957
lithograph in six colours
533 x 362mm
CGM 37

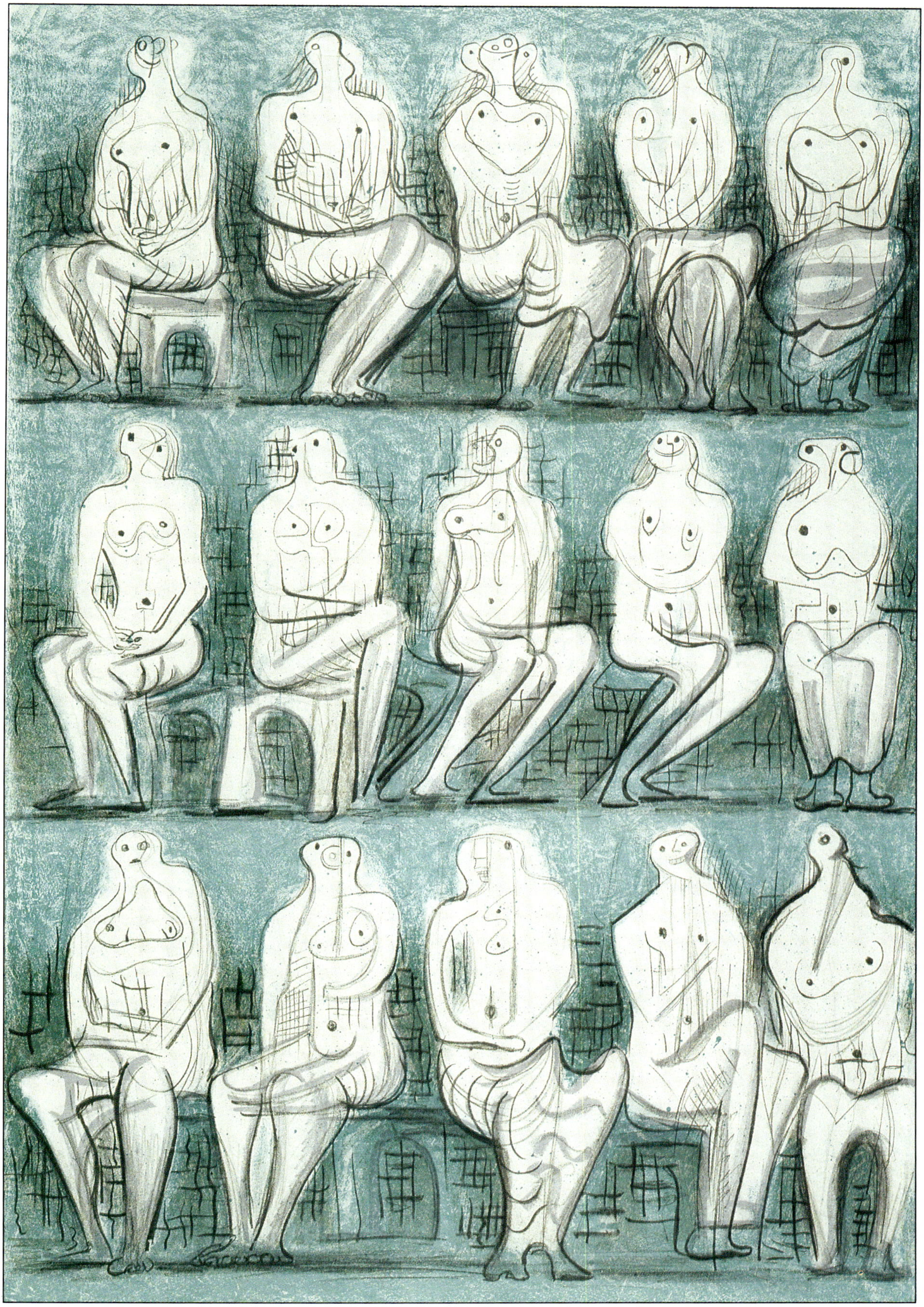

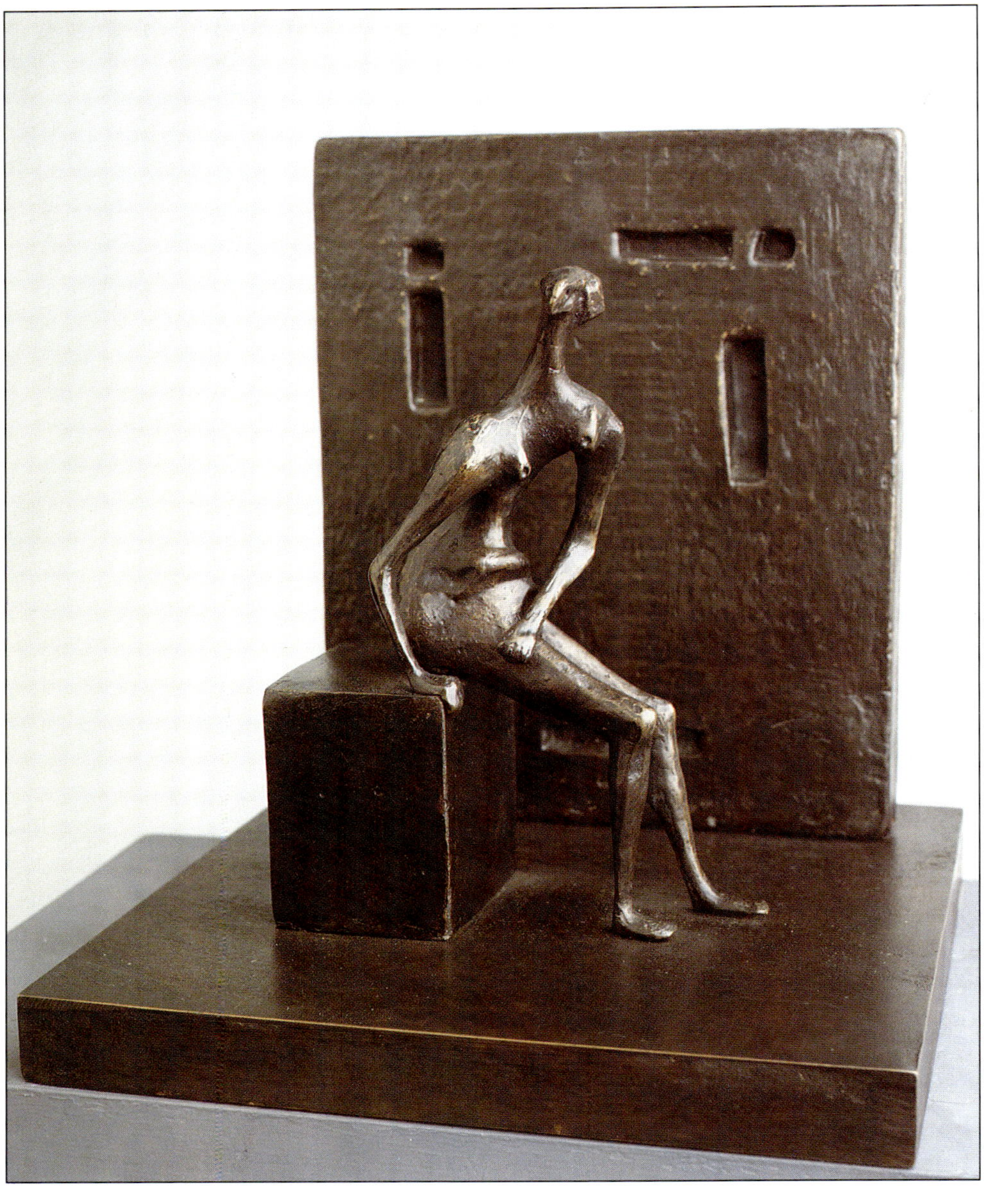

107

Maquette for Girl Seated against Square Wall 1957

H 24cm bronze edition of 12

LH 424

108

Seated Woman with Crossed Feet 1957

H 19cm bronze edition of 6

LH 432

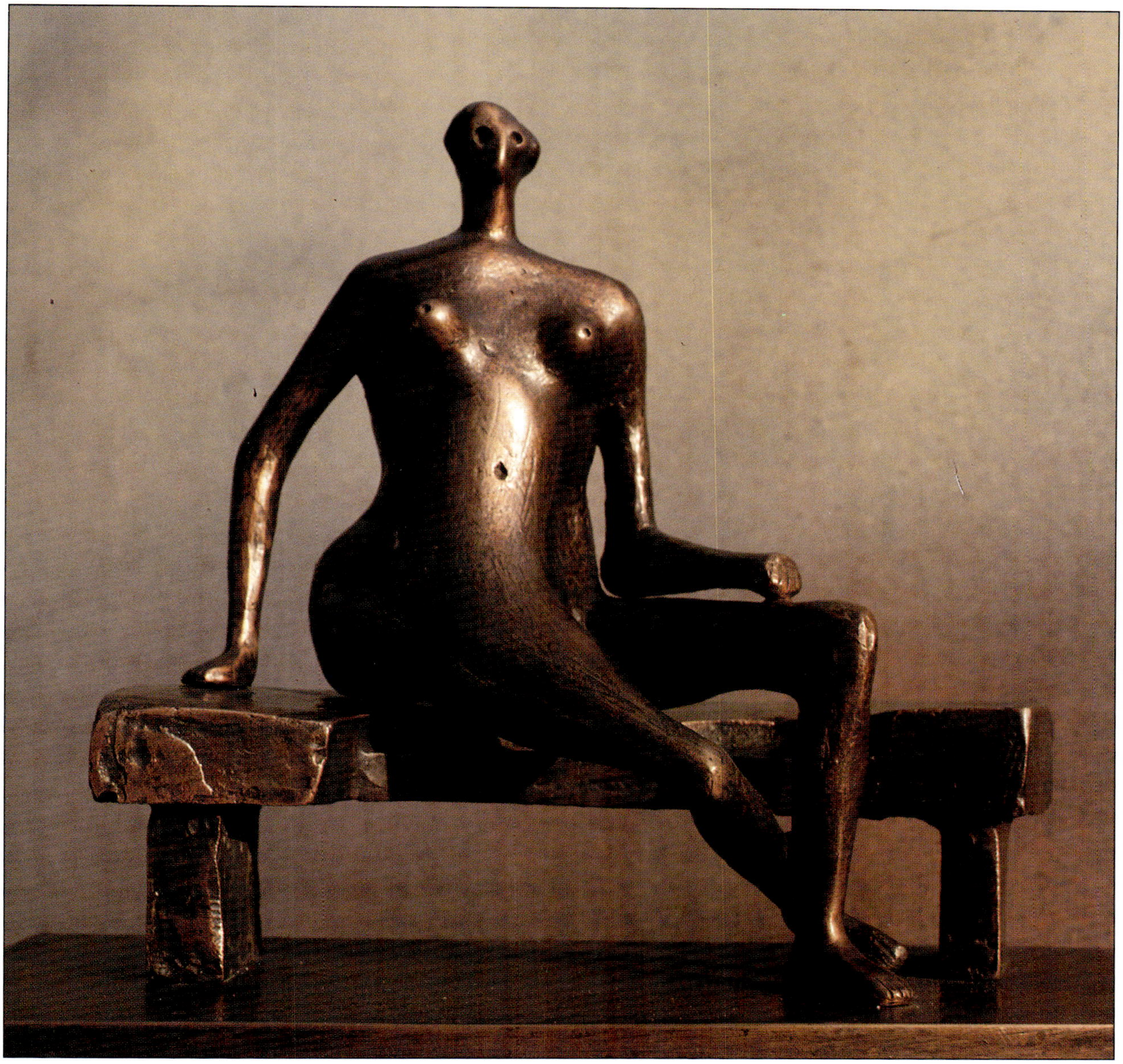

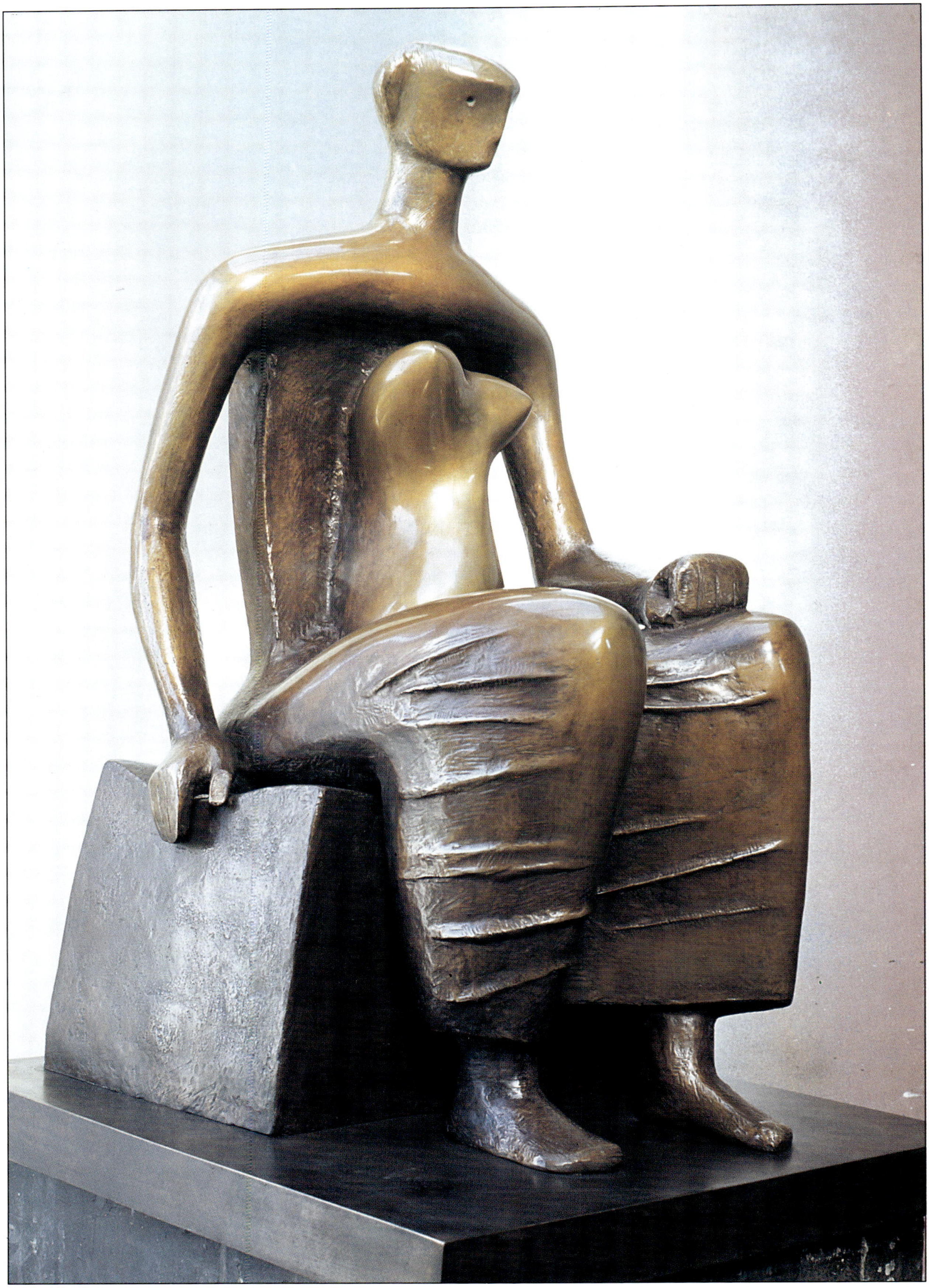

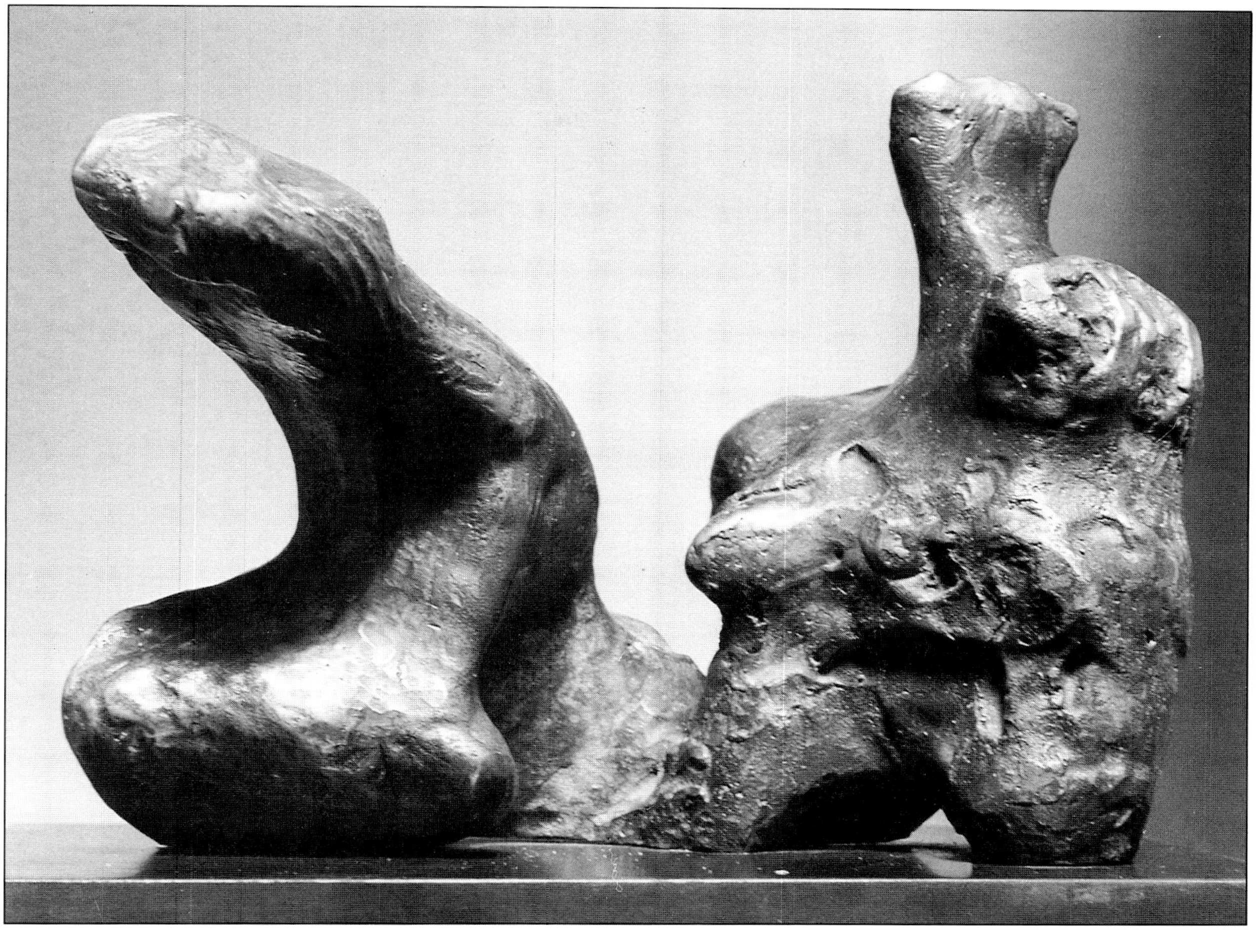

If it is in two pieces, there's bigger surprise, you have more unexpected views; therefore the special advantage over painting – of having the possibility of many different views – is more fully exploited. The front view doesn't enable one to foresee the back view. As you move round it, the two parts overlap or they open up and there's space between. Sculpture is like a journey. You have a different view as you return.

109
Working Model for Seated Woman
cast 1980
H 76cm bronze edition of 9
LH 433b

110
Maquette for Two Piece Reclining Figure No.1 1959, cast 1974
L 15.9cm bronze edition of 7
LH 457a

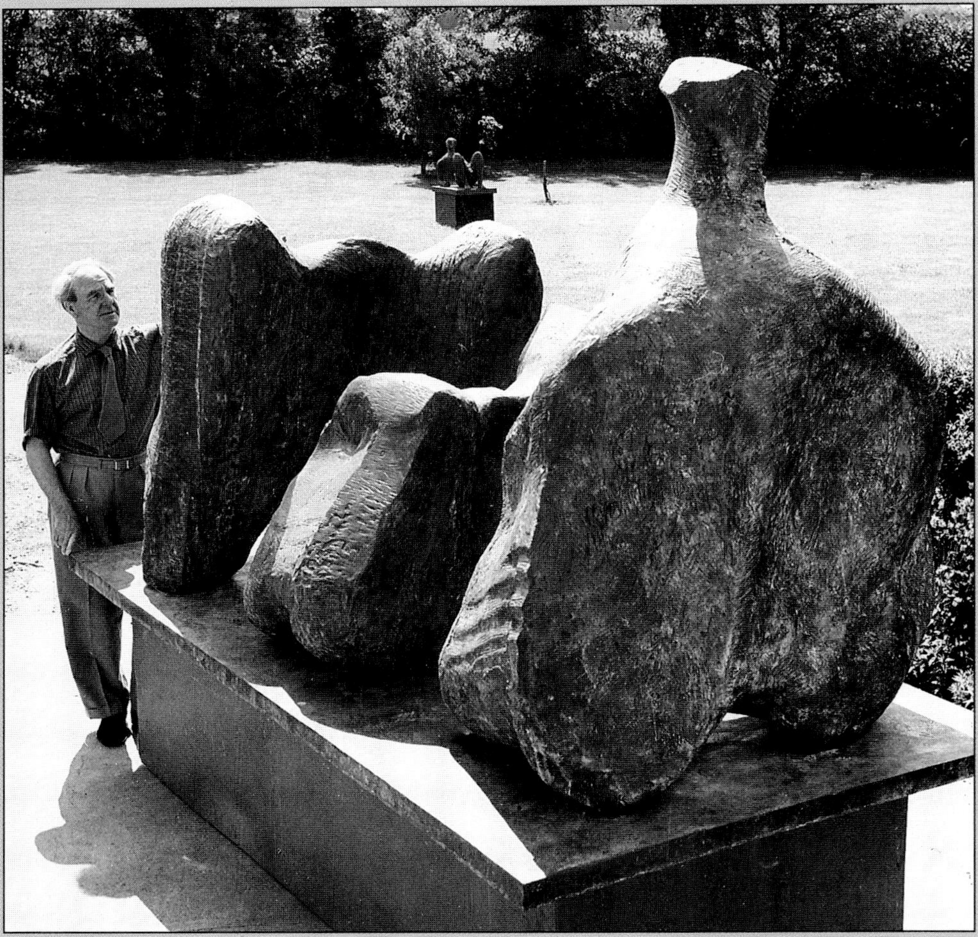

Henry Moore in the garden at
Perry Green in the mid-1960s with
Three Piece Reclining Figure No.1
1961-62 (LH 500).

1960s

Moore's sculptures became larger in response to his undertaking to provide a sculpture for the site in front of the Unesco building in Paris. He gave much thought to the project before finally settling on a monumental *Reclining Figure* (represented here by the maquette, cat.105). Soon afterwards he allowed the parts of a reclining figure to remain separate, taking further his multi-part inventions of the 1930s (cat.31). Characteristic two- and three-piece reclining figures of the early 1960s are represented here by four maquettes (cats.110, 113, 118, 128). By working with plaster rather than clay to create the preliminary models from which the bronzes were to be cast, he could add to the figure or cut it away at will; clay soon dries out and cannot then be worked, whereas plaster can be added to even after it has dried. Plaster dries to the consistency of soft stone and Moore found he could create rock-like surfaces by grinding it with files and even a cheese grater; sometimes he smoothed the surface until it resembled bone. When cast in bronze the resulting surfaces, rock-like or polished, were quite unlike traditional bronze surfaces produced from preliminary models made in clay.

Moore continued to rely for inspiration on found objects, and the *Standing Figure: Knife Edge* (cat.114) was derived from a fragment of bone (see illustration on p.20). He now preferred to begin with a piece of flintstone or bone and add clay, Plasticine or plaster to them to form a new, three-dimensional reality. He found this more useful than making preliminary drawings, because it enabled him to see the nascent sculpture from all angles instead of imagining the other side, as is necessary when working from a two-dimensional drawing, such as cat.115.

At the same time Moore began a series of less representational monumental forms, often with interlocking parts. These, like the figure sculptures, he built up in plaster on wire mesh supports; he went straight from a hand-held maquette to what he called 'working model' size – usually about one metre cubed: an example here is *Working Model for Locking Piece* (cat.125). From this he enlarged again to the full size, represented in the exhibition by a fibreglass cast (cat.126).

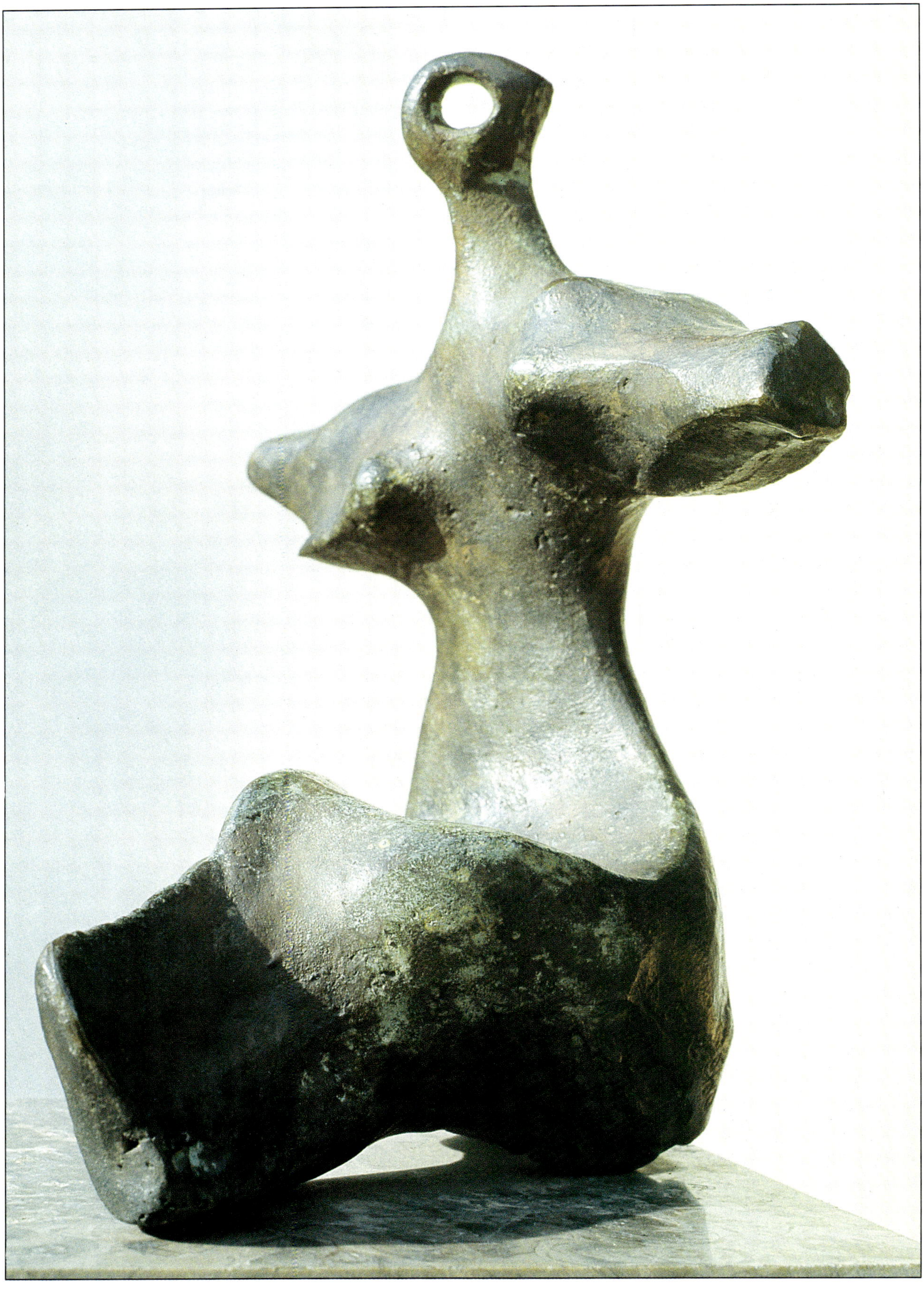

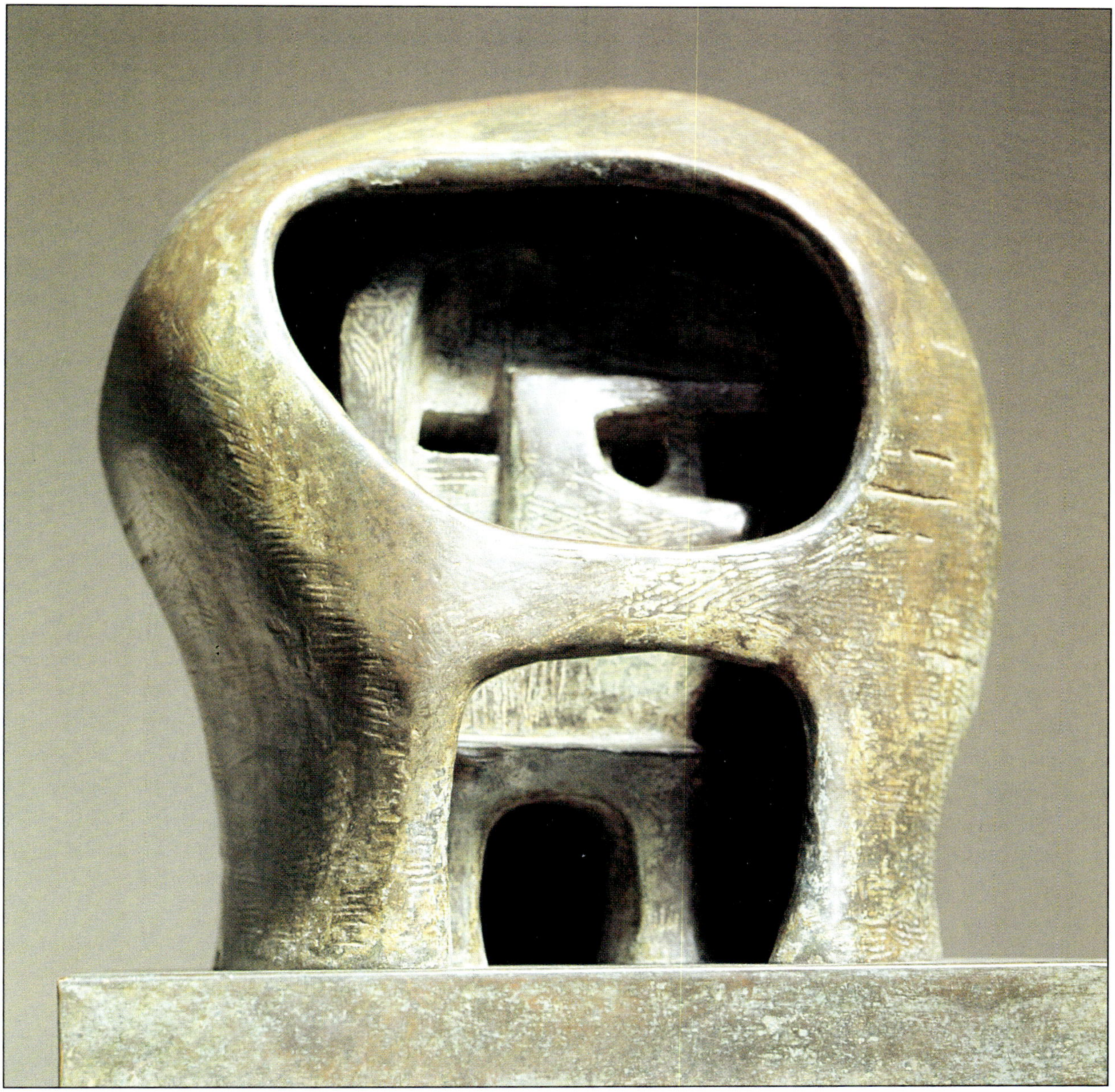

111
Maquette for Seated Figure: Arms Outstretched 1960
H 16.5cm bronze edition of 9
LH 463

112
Helmet Head No.3 1960
H 29.5cm bronze edition of 14
LH 467

113

Two Piece Reclining Figure: Maquette No.3 1961

L 20.5cm bronze edition of 9

LH 475

114

Working Model for Standing Figure: Knife Edge 1961

H 162.5cm fibreglass

LH 481

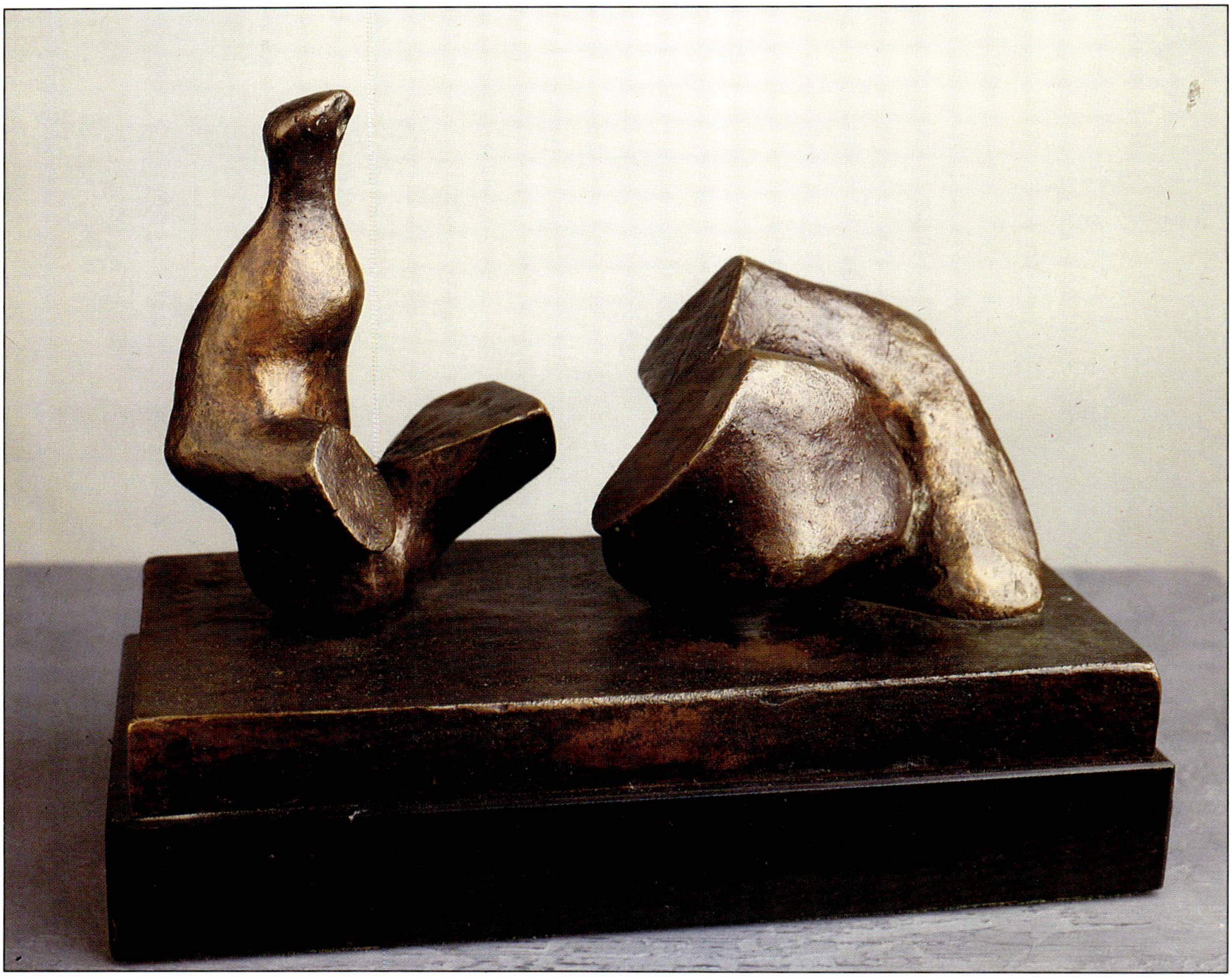

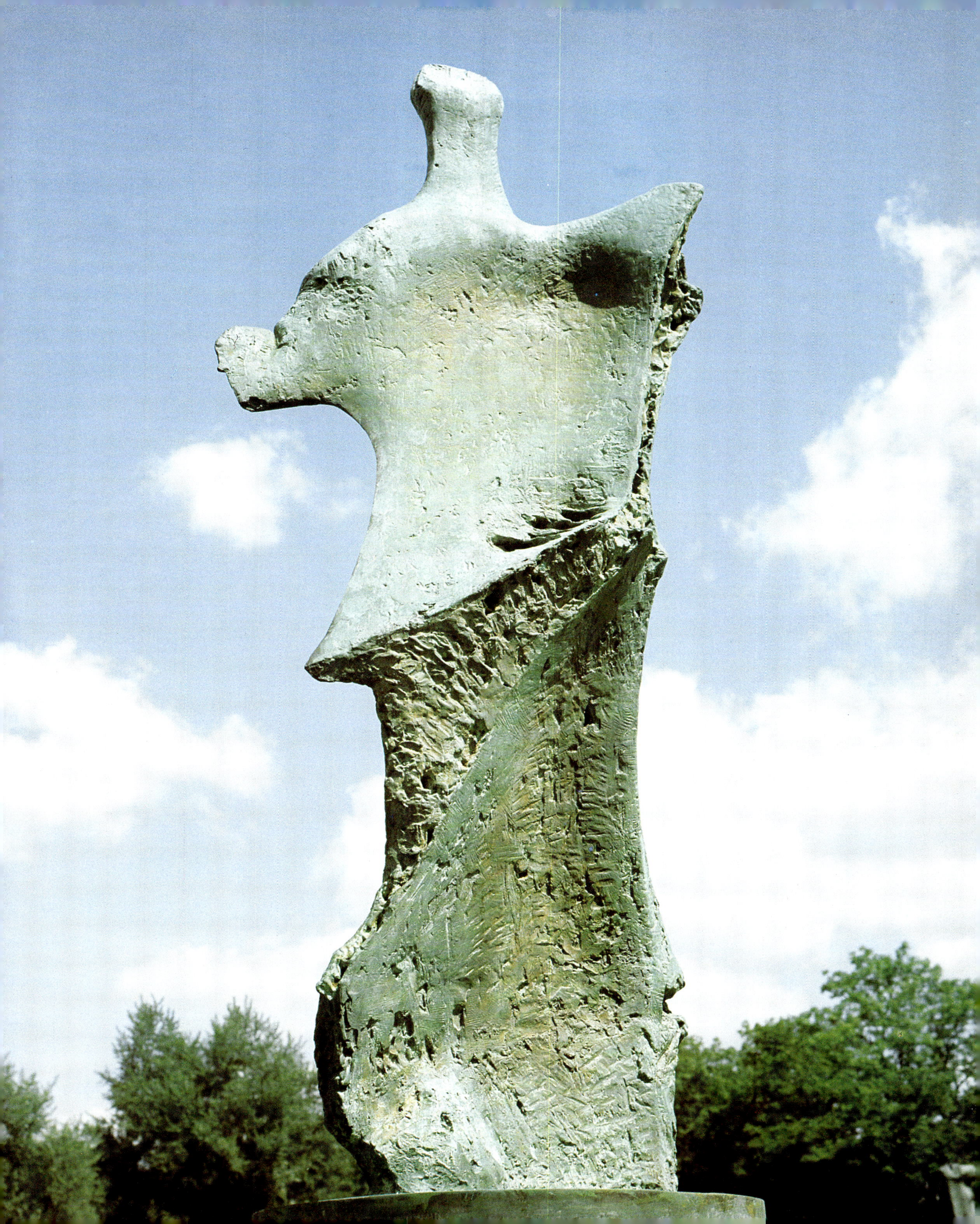

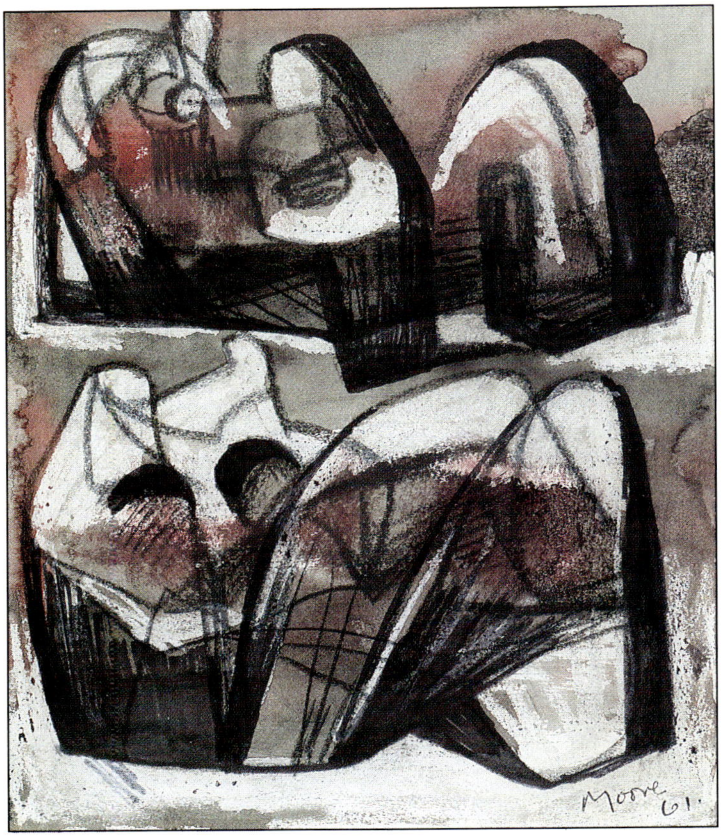

115

Page from Sketchbook 1961-62

Two Reclining Figures 1961

pencil, wax crayon, pastel,
watercolour wash,
felt-tipped pen, chalk
292 x 242mm
HMF 3029

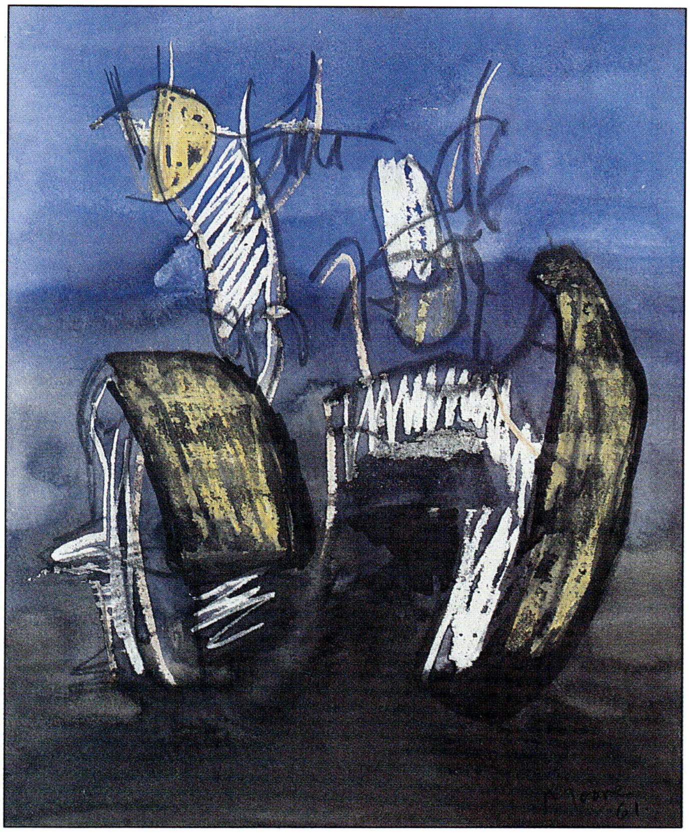

116

Page from Sketchbook 1961-62

Two Reclining Figures 1961

pencil, white wax crayon, coloured crayons, watercolour wash, washed charcoal, felt-tipped pen

291 x 239mm

HMF 3052

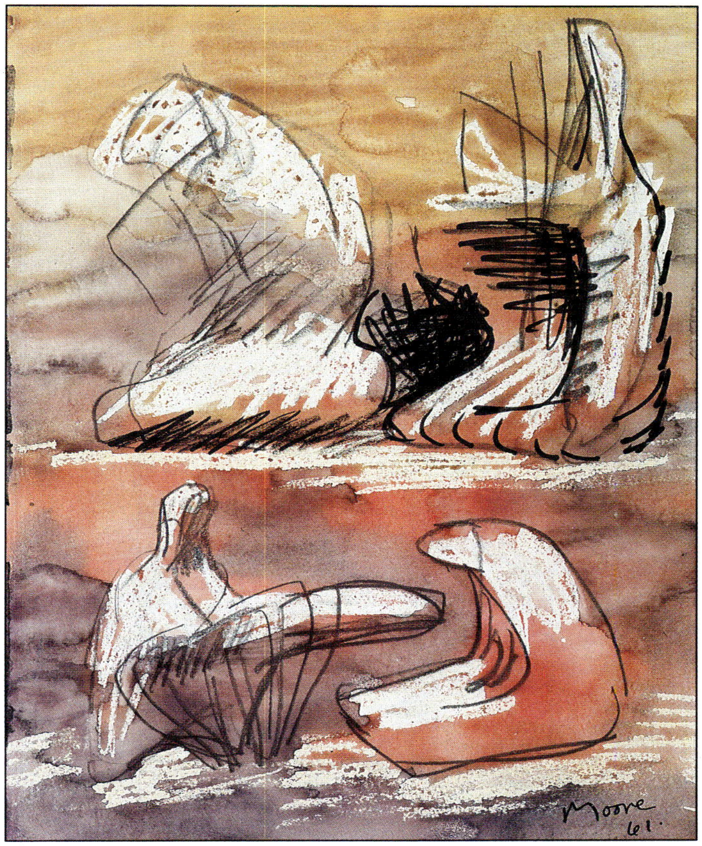

117

Page from Sketchbook 1961-62

Two Reclining Figures 1961

white wax crayon, watercolour wash, ink, crayon

292 x 242mm

HMF 3053

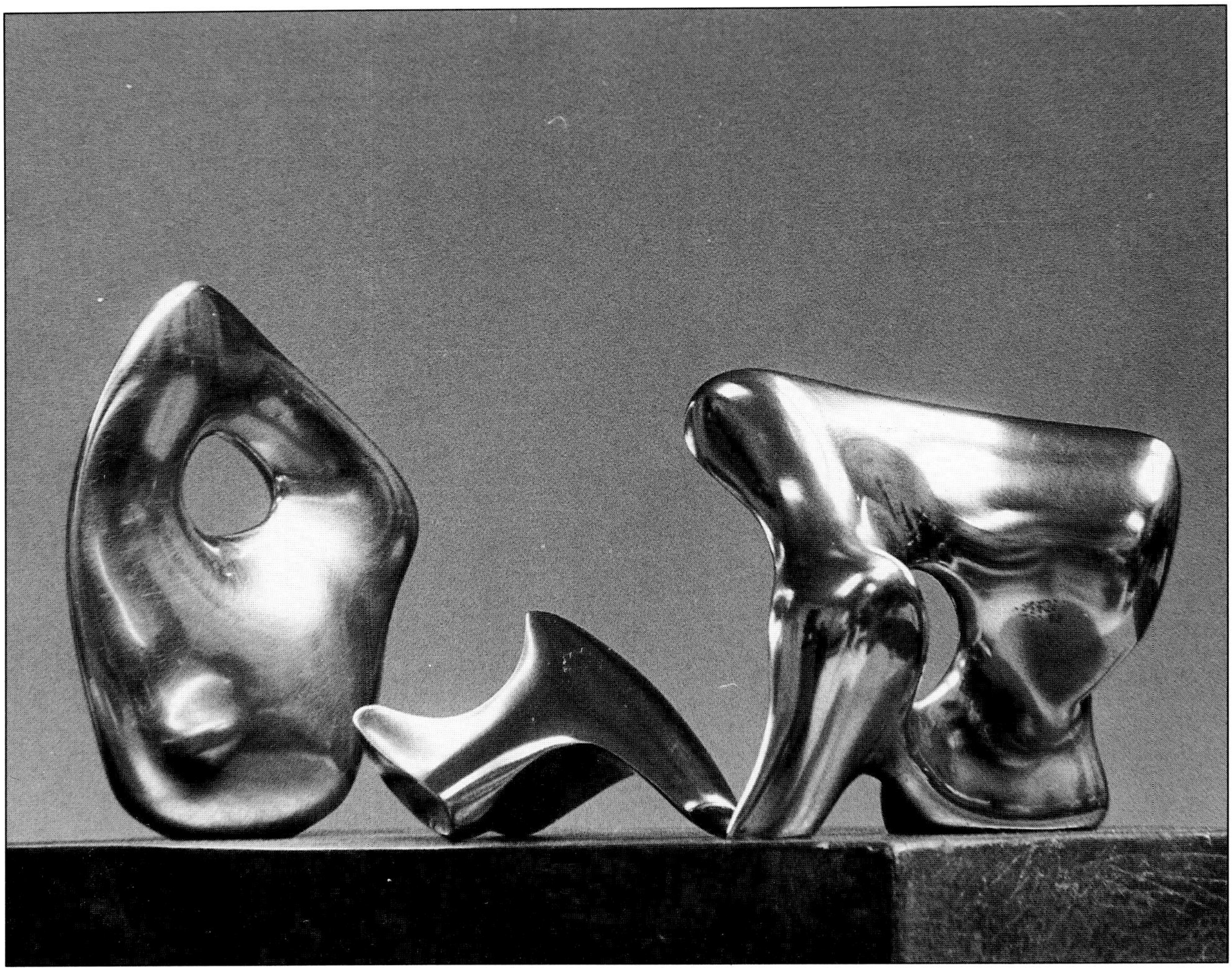

My two and three piece sculptures have the space between each part which to me is the same as spacing the knee from the foot. This space between each piece is terribly important and is as much a form or a shape just as much as the actual material.

118
Three Piece Reclining Figure: Maquette No.2: Polished 1962
L 21.6cm bronze edition of 9
LH 501

119

Sculptural Form 1962

H 25.4cm bronze edition of 9

LH 505b

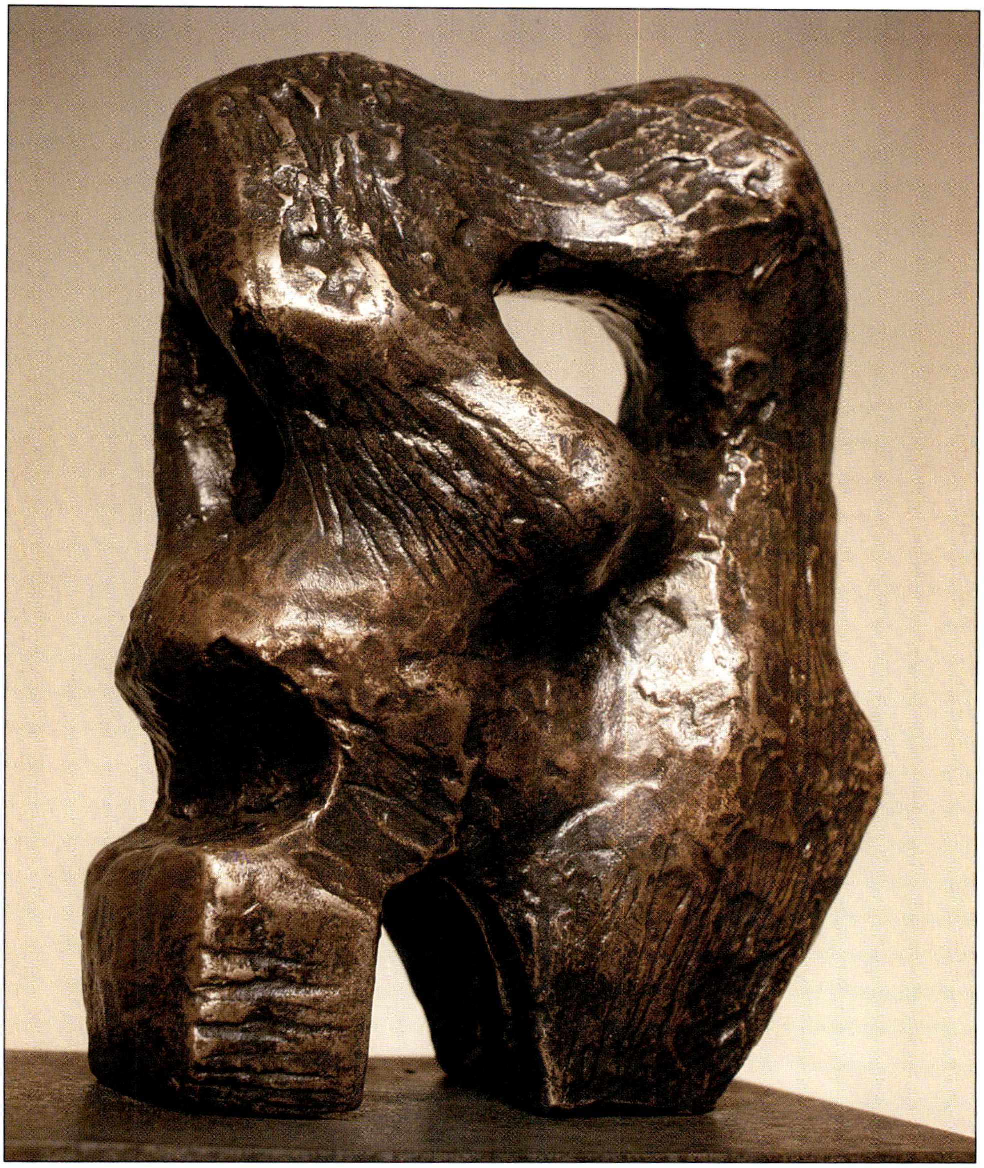

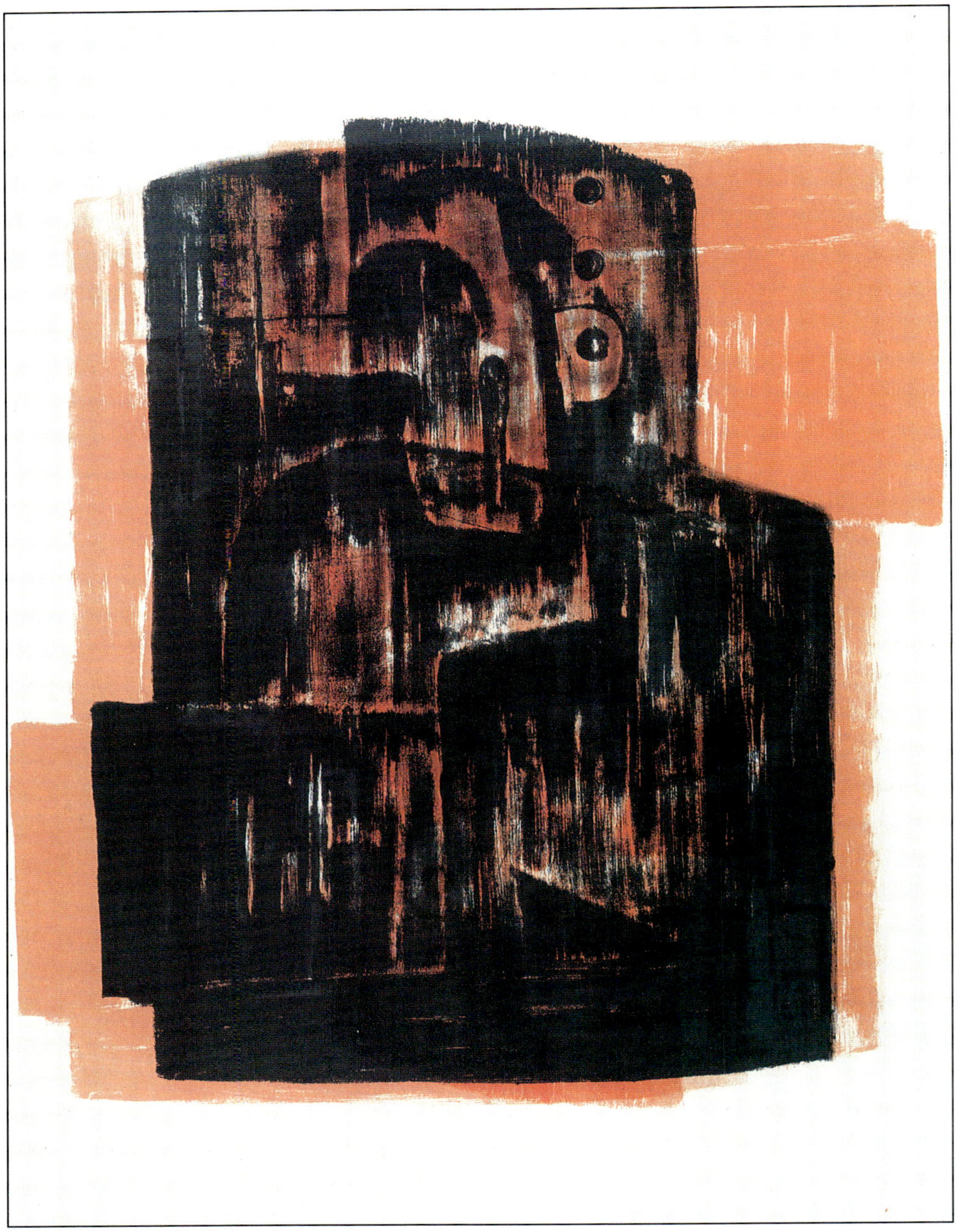

120
Black on Red Image 1963
lithograph in two colours
521 x 482mm
CGM 42

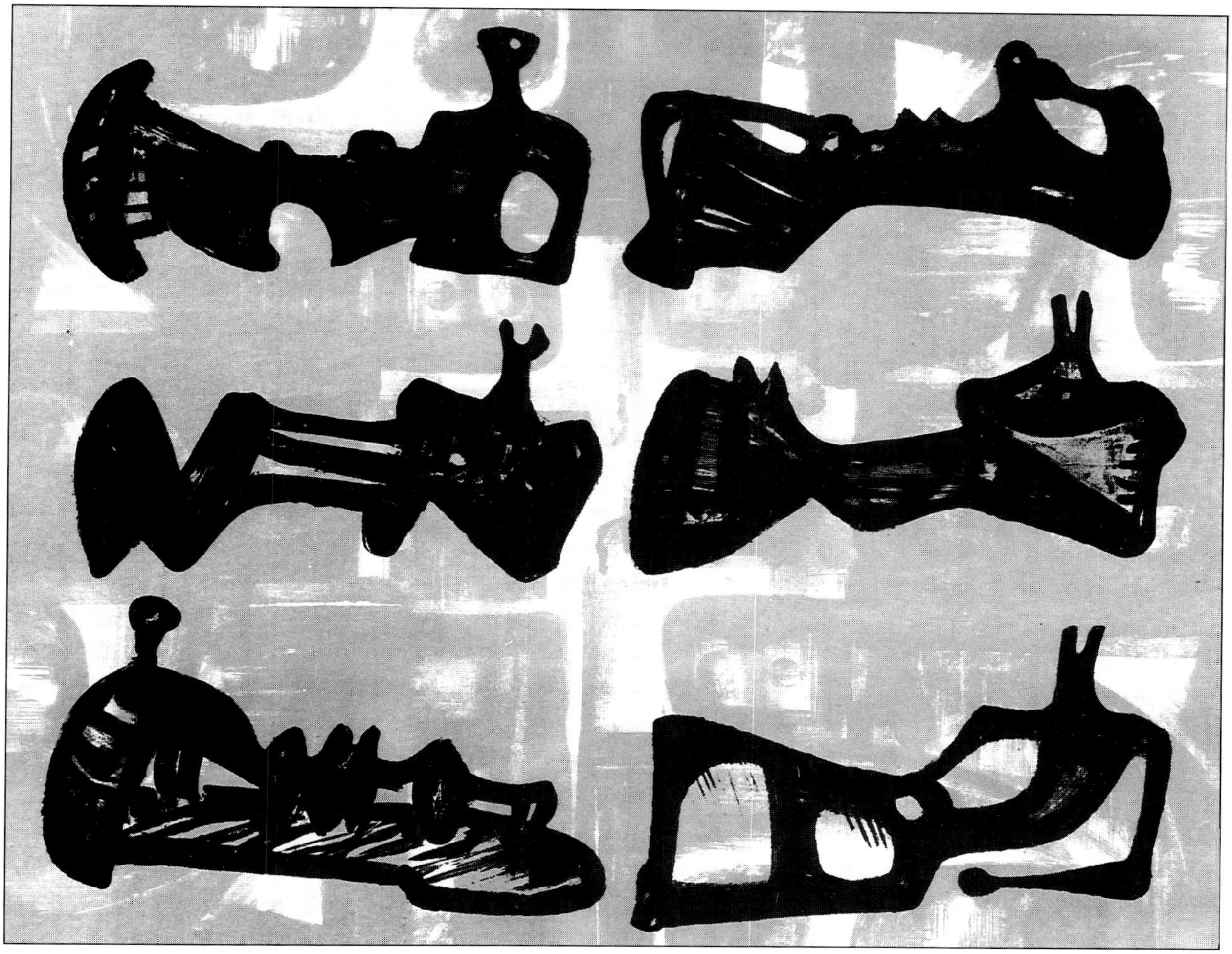

121
Six Reclining Figures with Buff Background 1963
lithograph in two colours
457 x 585mm
CGM 50

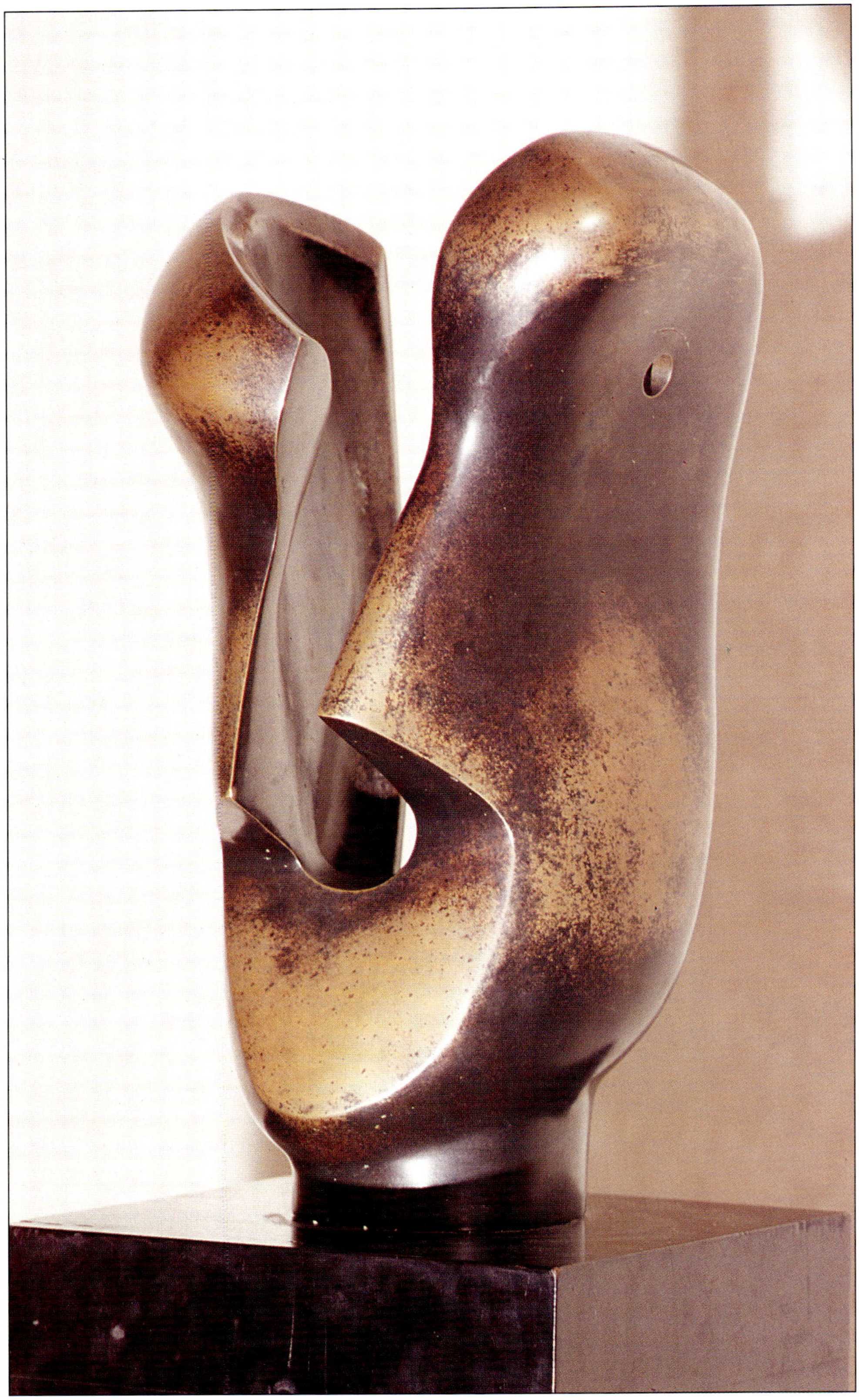

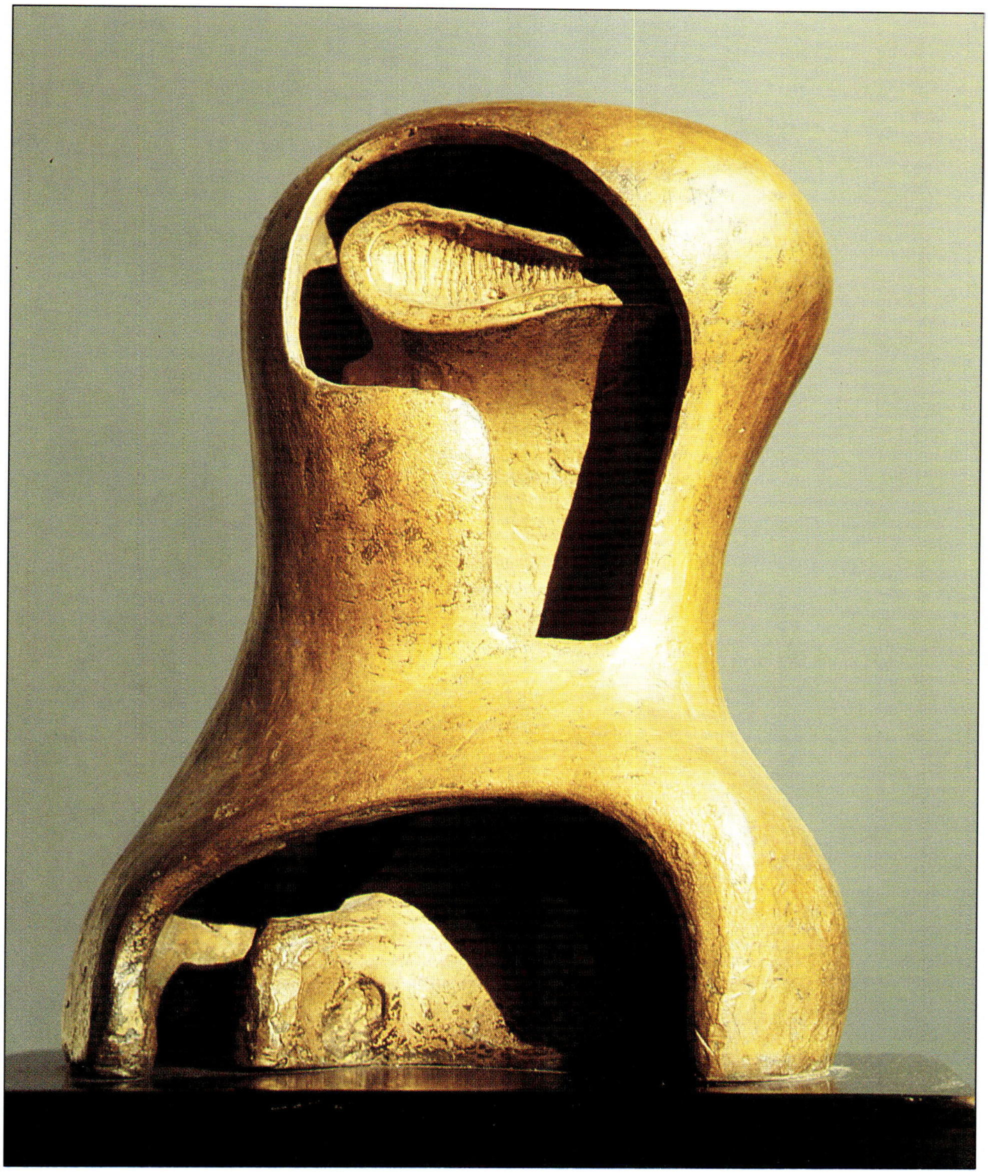

122
Divided Head 1963
H 35cm bronze edition of 9
LH 506

123
Head: Cyclops 1963
H 20.3cm bronze edition of 9
LH 507

124

Three Piece Reclining Figure: Holes 1963, cast 1977

L 22.2cm bronze edition of 9

LH 513a

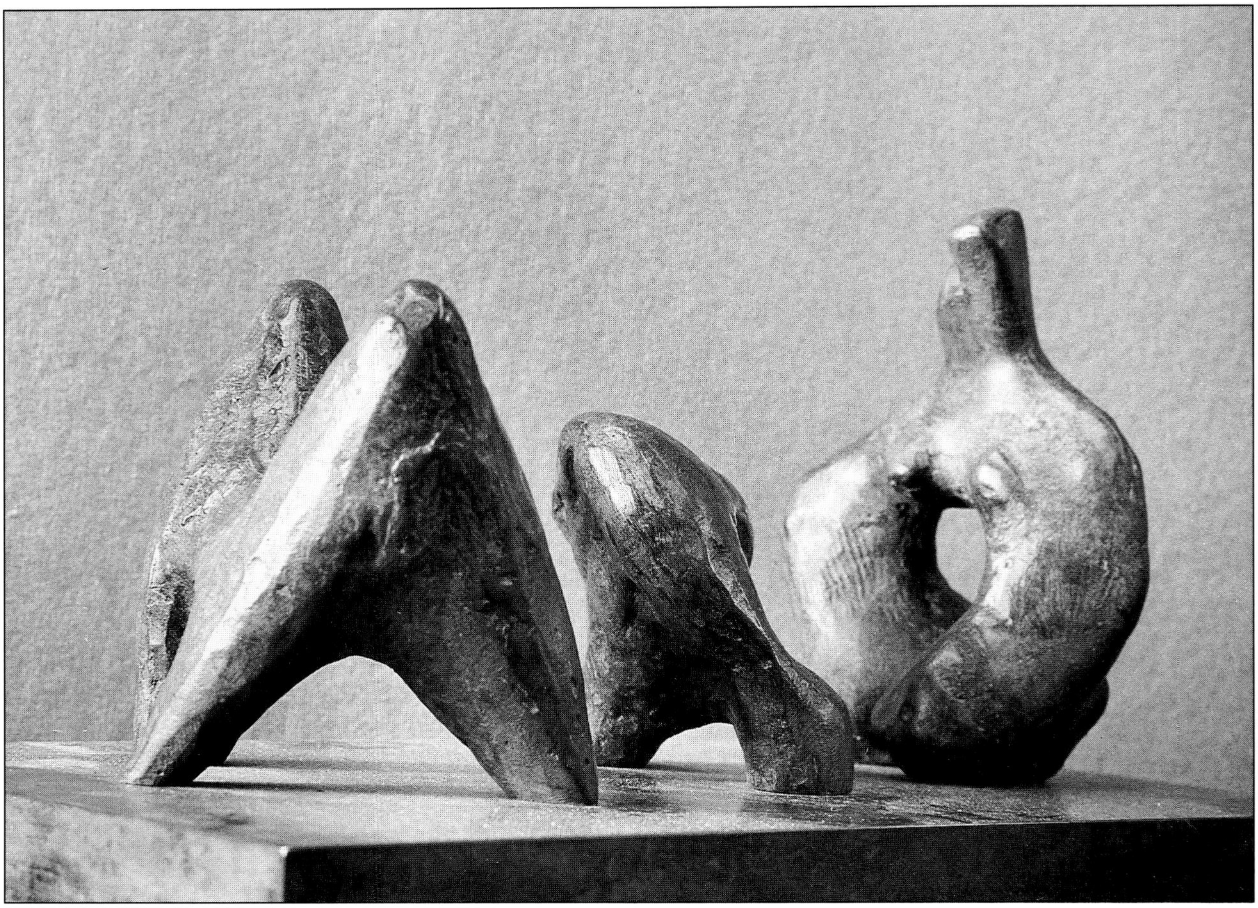

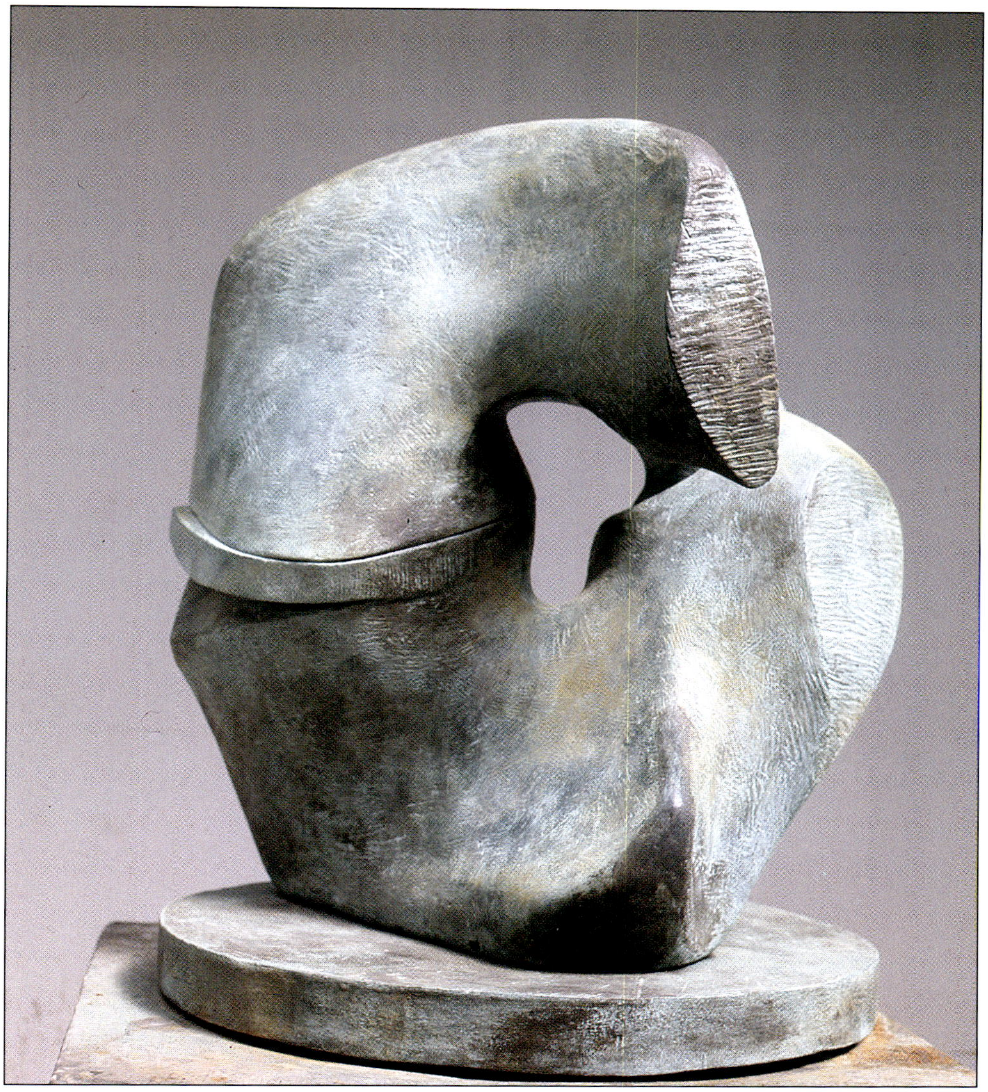

Locking Piece came about from two pebbles which I was playing with and which seemed to fit each other and lock together, and this gave me the idea of making a two-piece sculpture – not that the forms weren't separate but that they knitted together.

125
Working Model for Locking Piece 1962
H 106.5cm bronze edition of 9
LH 514

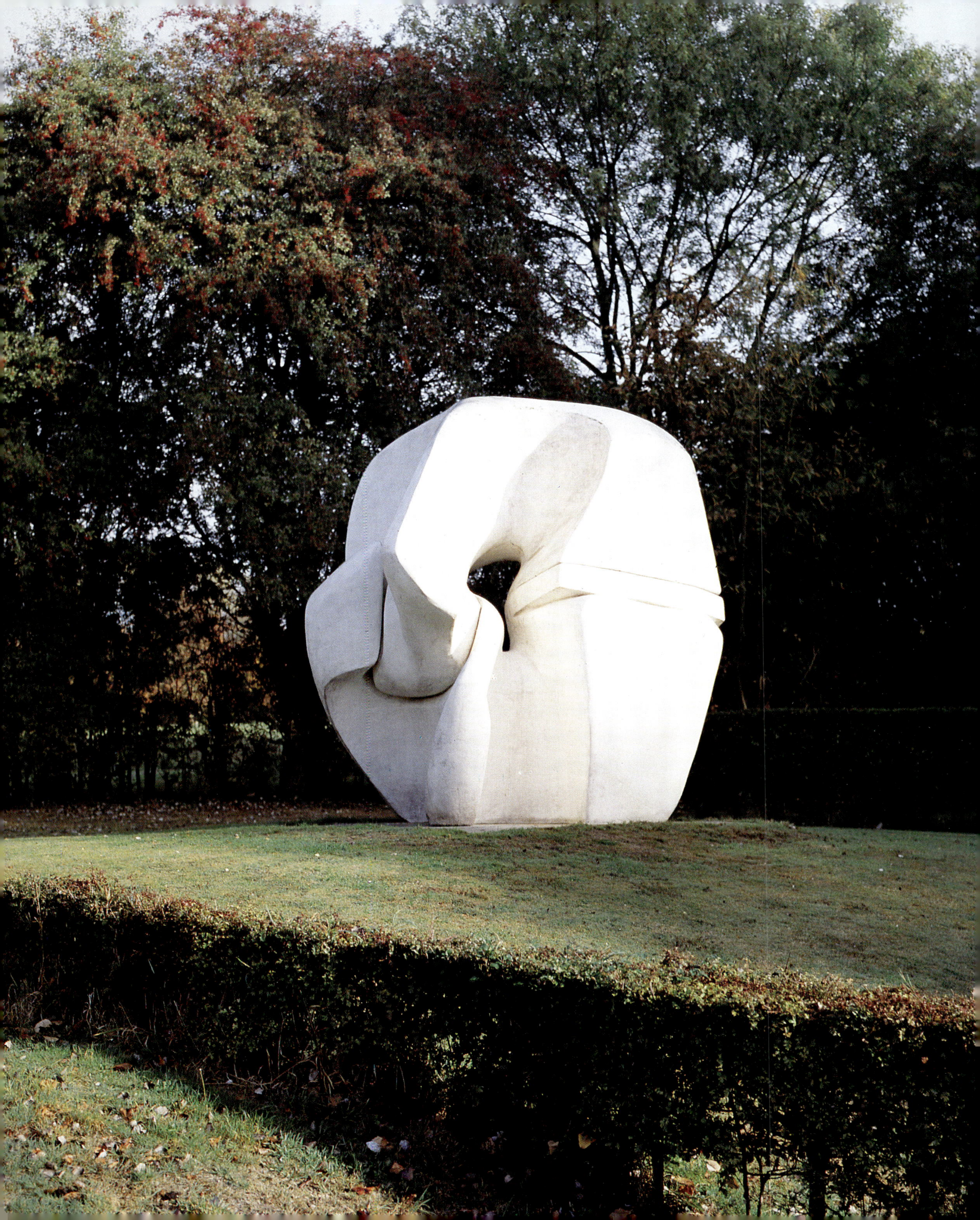

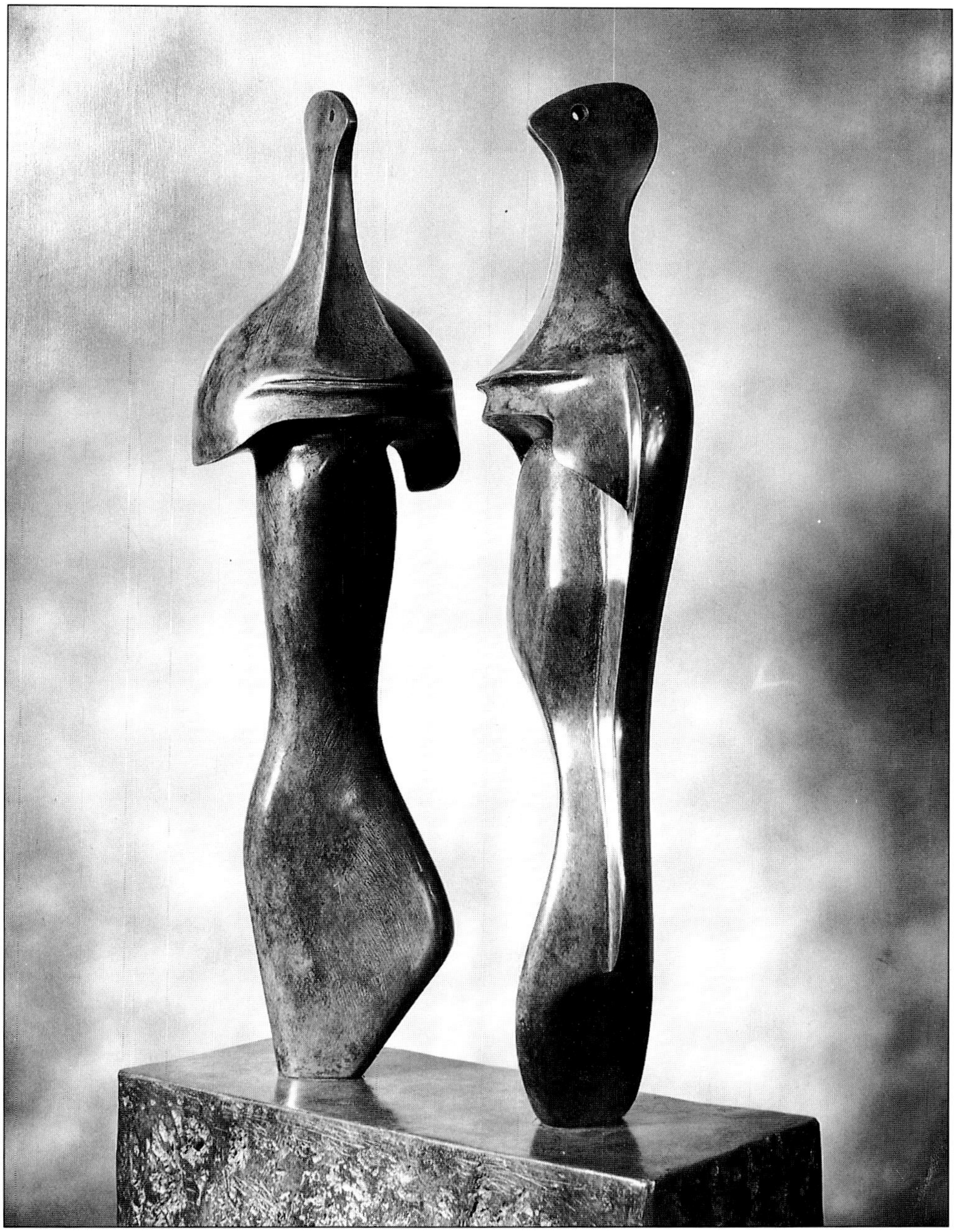

126
Locking Piece 1963-64
H 290cm fibreglass
LH 515

127
Two Three-Quarter Figures on Base cast 1984
H 101.5cm bronze edition of 9
LH 539b

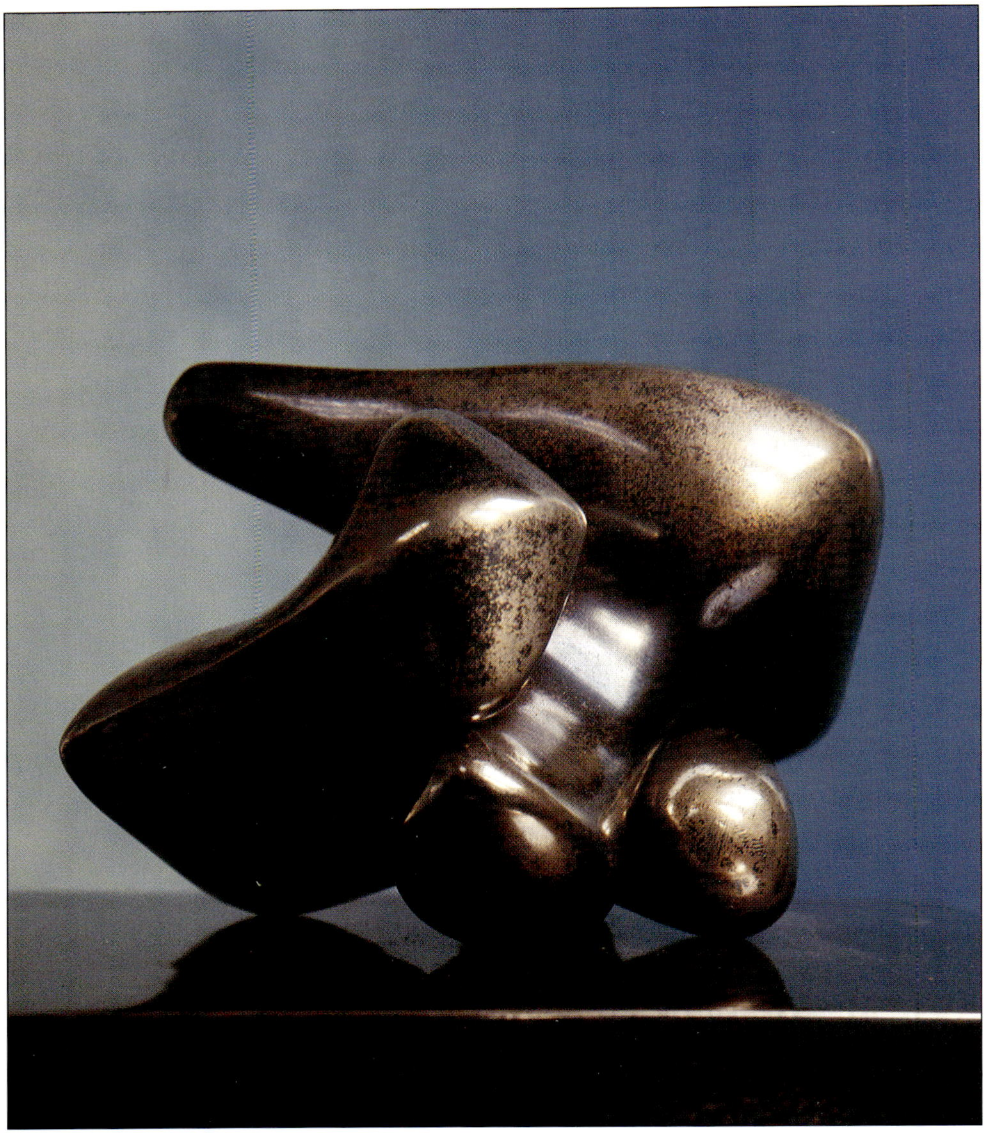

128

Maquette for Two Piece Sculpture No.11 1968

L 10cm bronze edition of 10

LH 582

129

Maquette for Spindle Piece 1968

H 17.1cm bronze edition of 9

LH 591

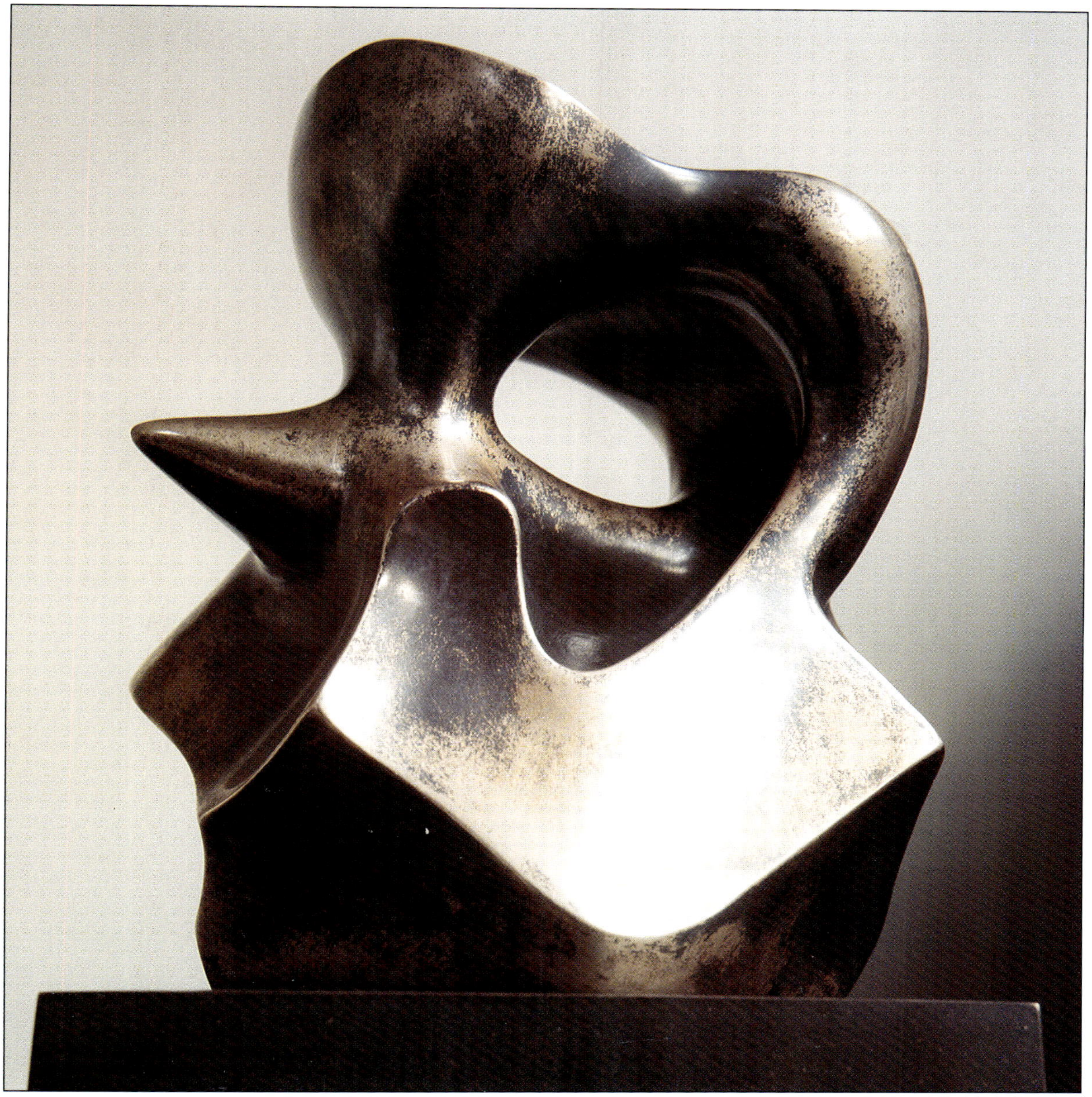

130

Working Model for Oval with Points

1968-69

H 110cm bronze edition of 12

LH 595

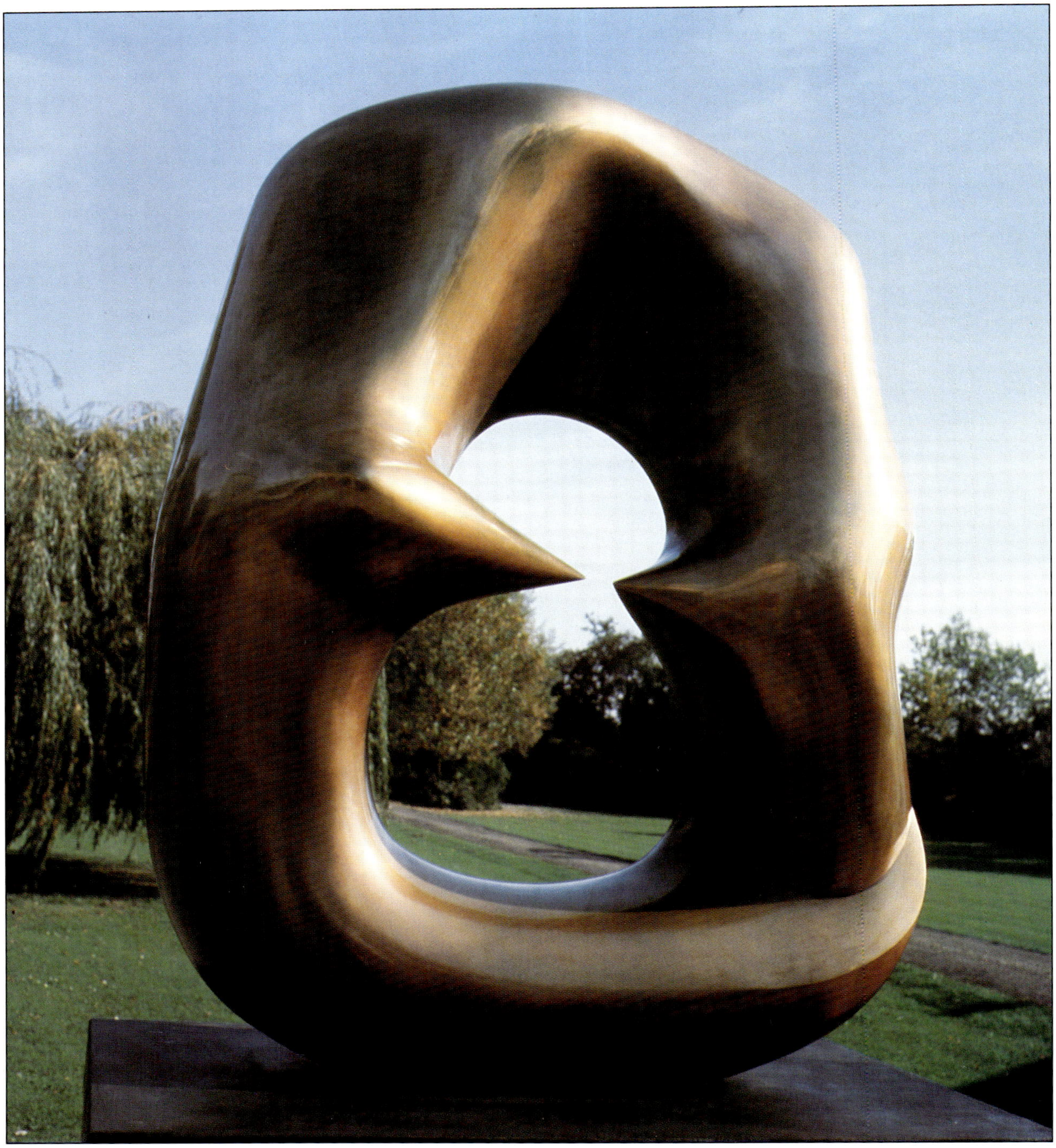

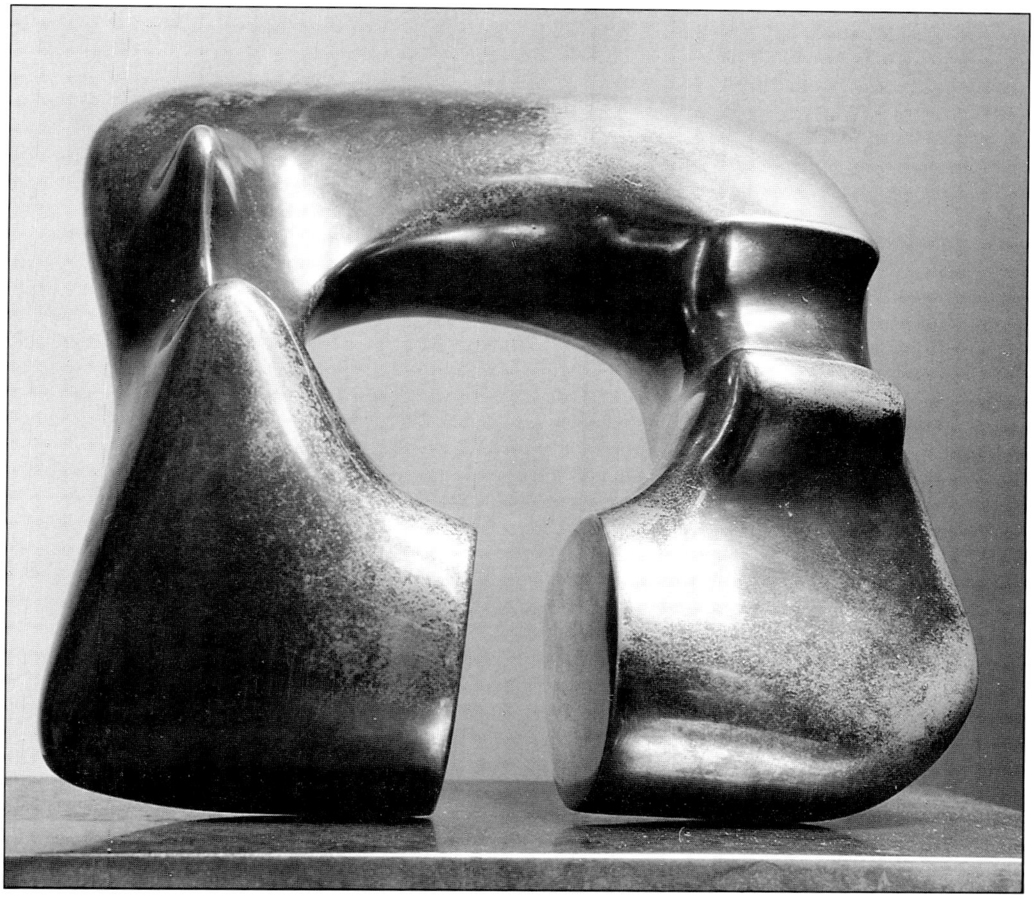

. . . this pointing has an emotional or physical action in it where things are just about to touch but don't. There is some anticipation of this action. Michelangelo used the same theme in his fresco on the ceiling of the Sistine chapel, of God creating Adam, in which the forefinger of God's hand is just about to touch and give life to Adam. It is also like the points in the sparking plug of a car, where the spark has to jump across the gap between the points.

131
Maquette for Square Form with Cut 1969
H 16.5cm bronze edition of 9
LH 597

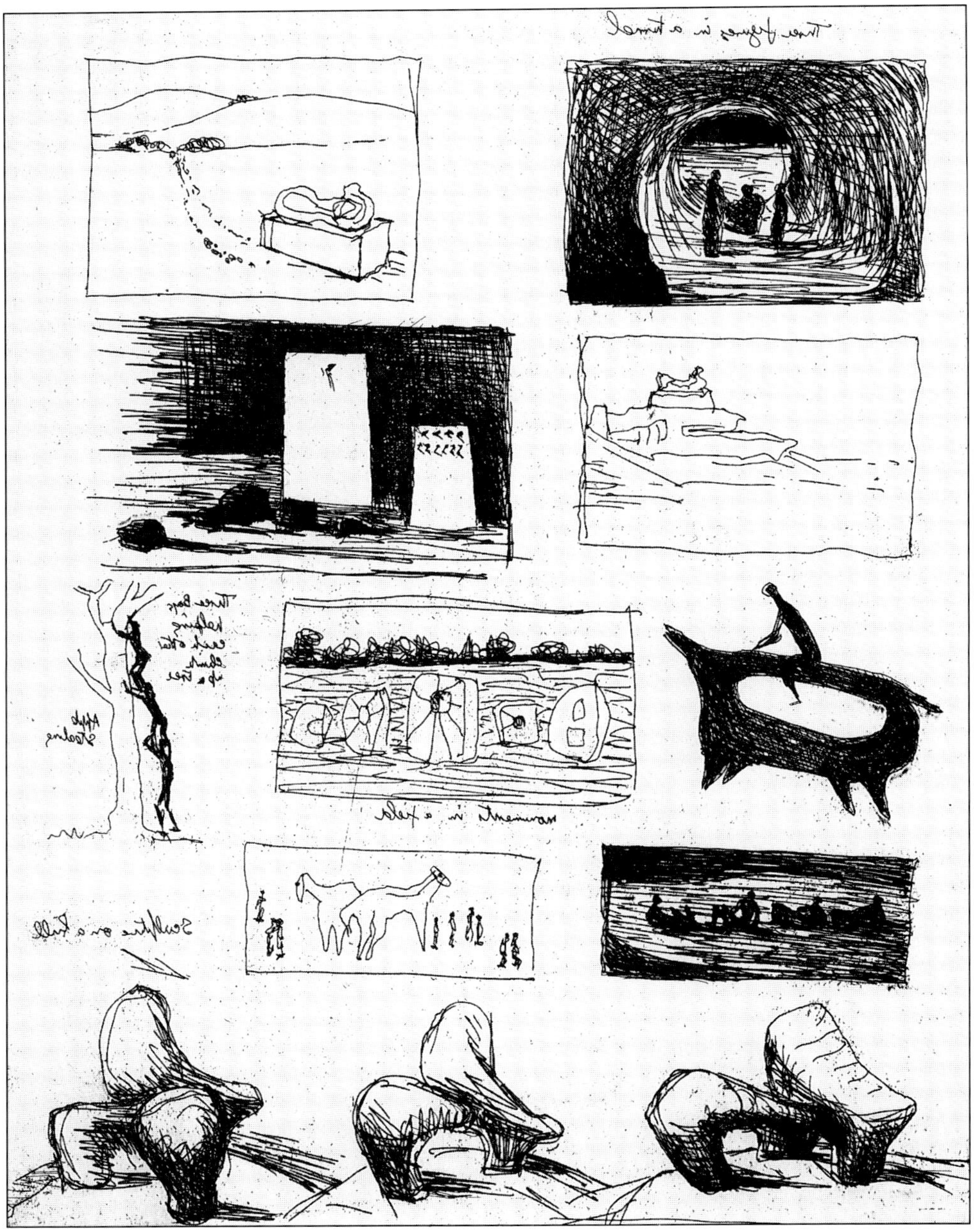

132

Ideas for Sculpture in Landscape 1969

etching

308 x 241mm

CGM 104

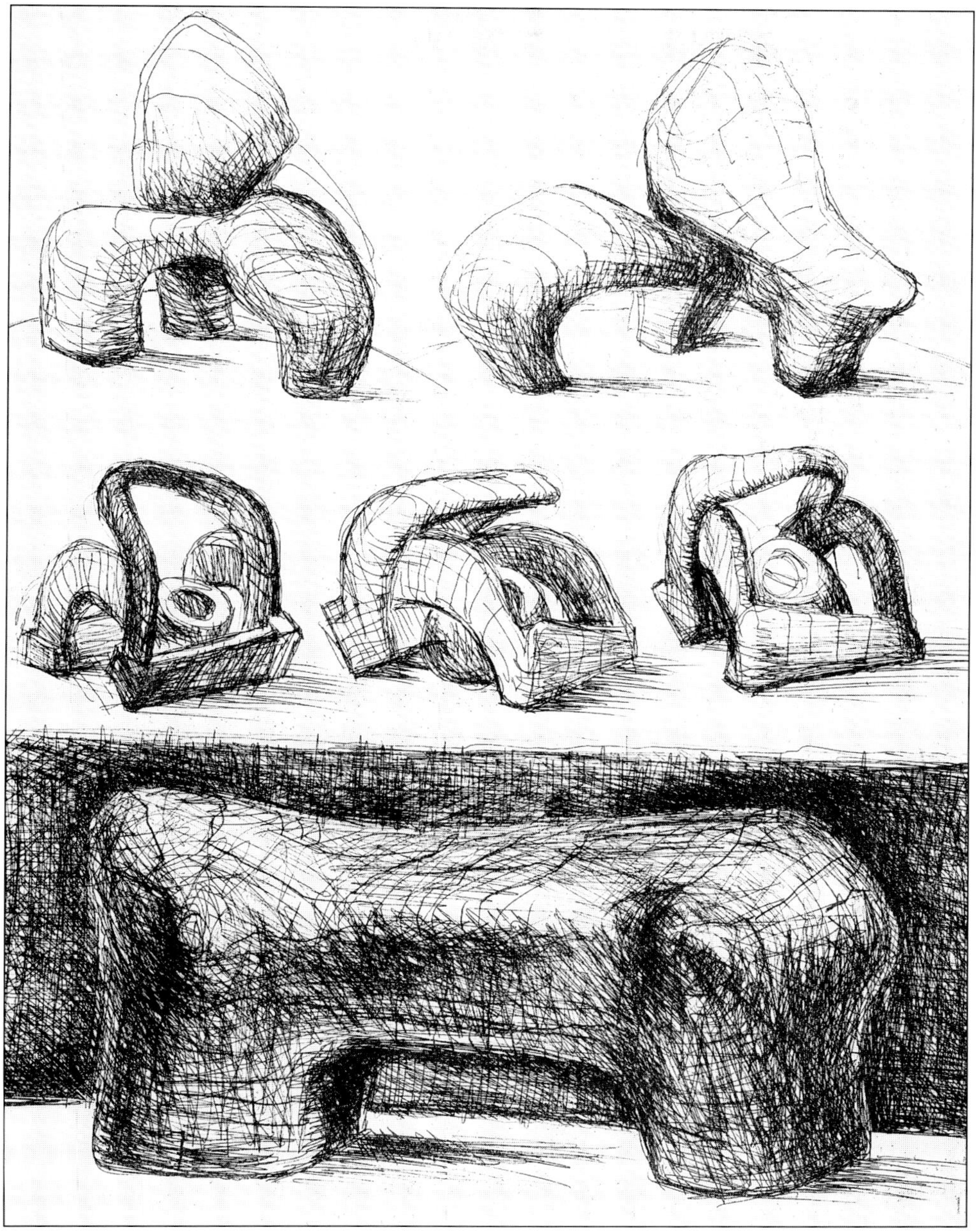

133

Projects for Hill Sculpture 1969

etching

308 x 241mm

CGM 105

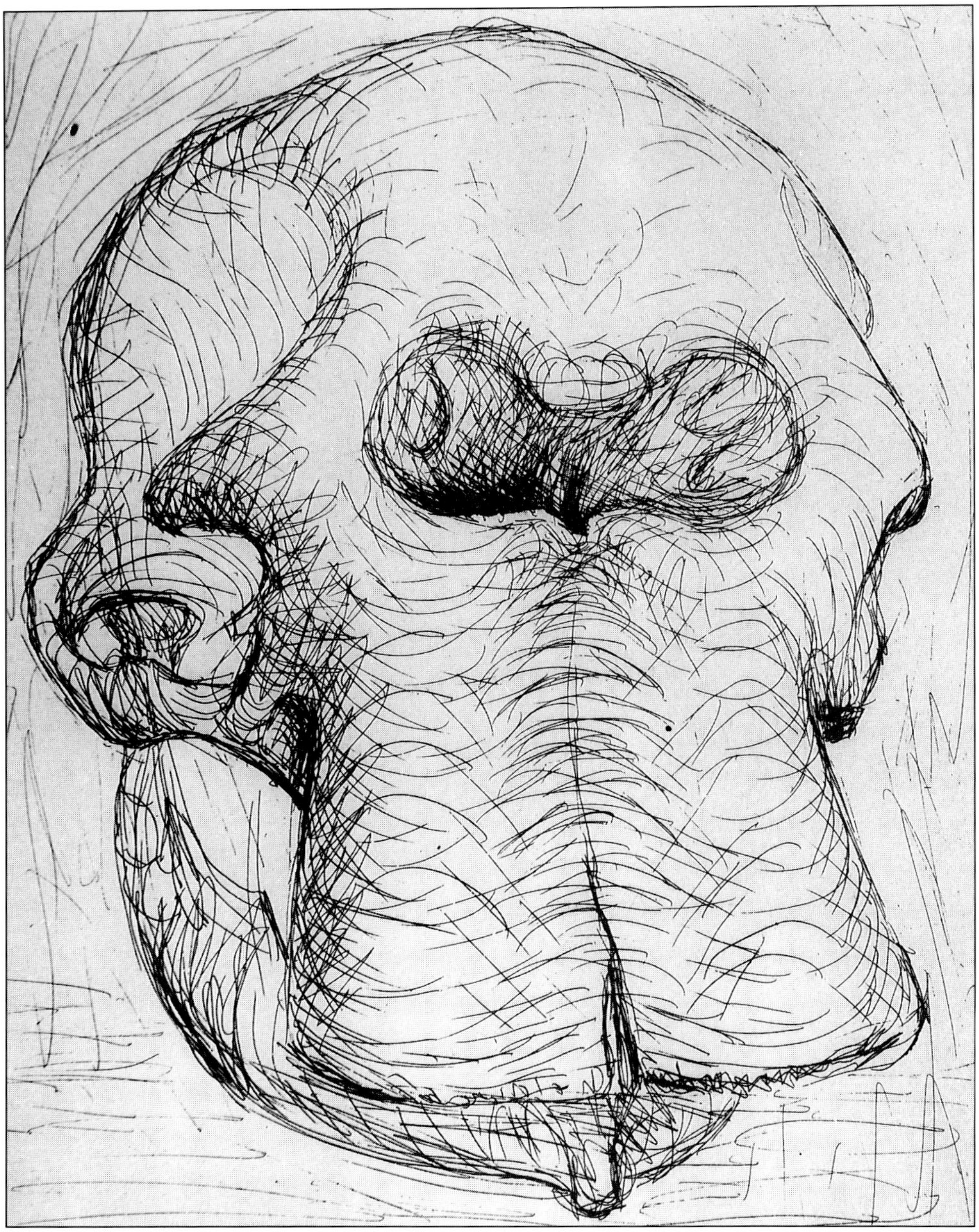

134
Elephant Skull, Plate I 1969
etching
254 x 200mm
CGM 114

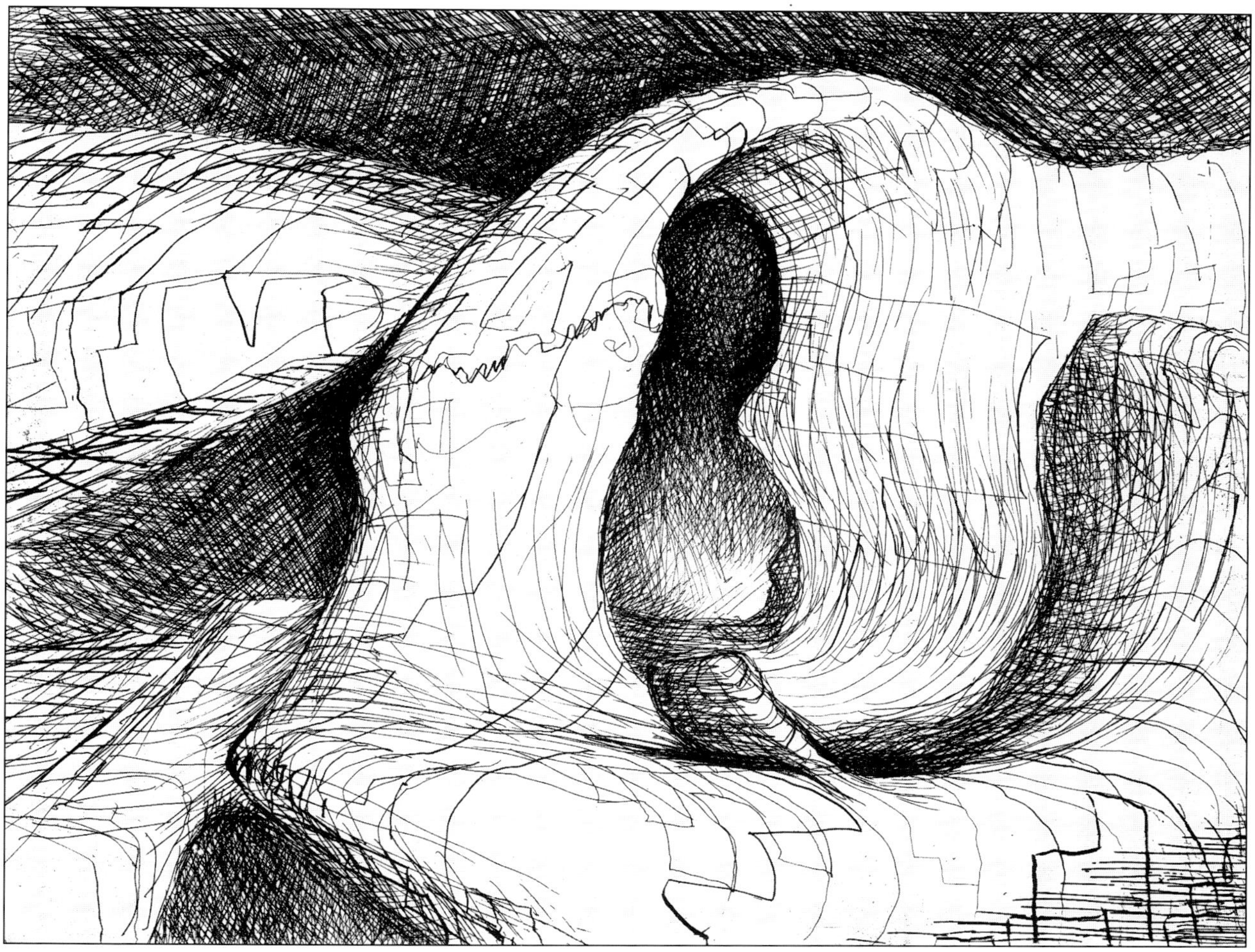

. . . I drew the whole skull to find out its general construction, gradually I became amazed at the complexity of it and my interest and excitement grew greater each day I worked. By bringing the skull very close to me and drawing various details I found so many contrasts of form and shape that I could begin to see in it great deserts and rocky landscapes, big caves in the sides of hills, great pieces of architecture, columns and dungeons, and so this series of etchings is really a mixture of observation and imagination.

135
Elephant Skull, Plate VIII 1969
etching
235 x 308mm
CGM 121

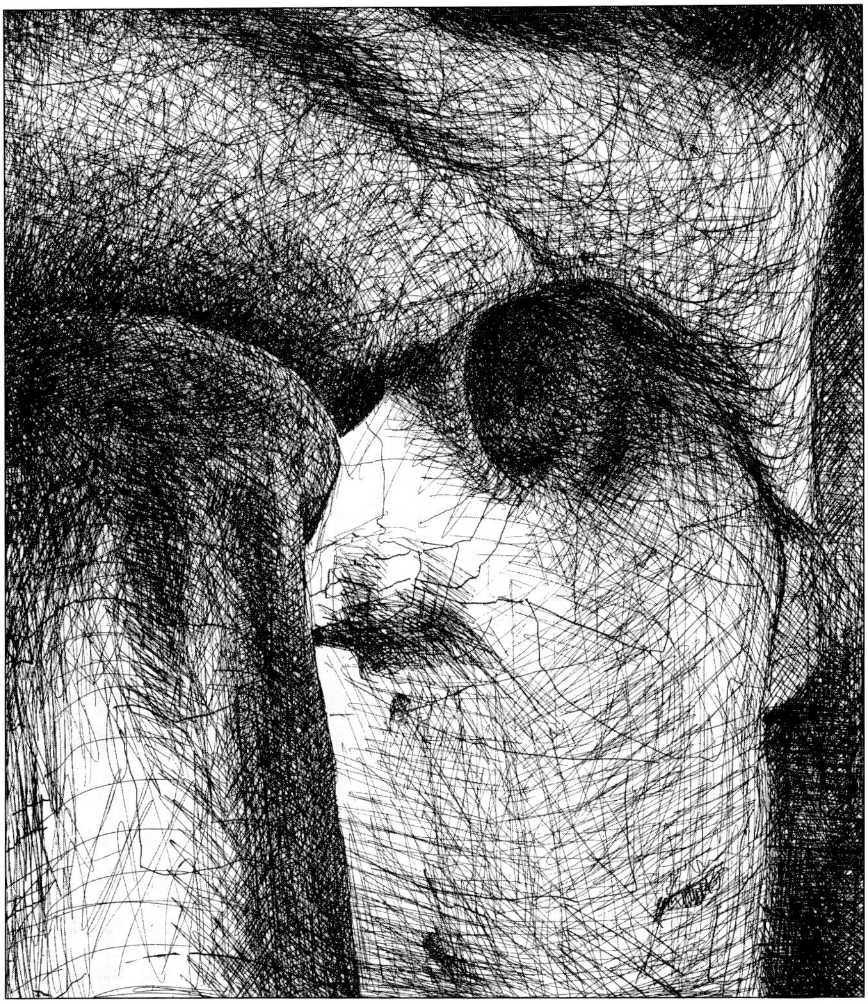

136

Elephant Skull, Plate XX 1969

etching

216 x 235mm

CGM 133

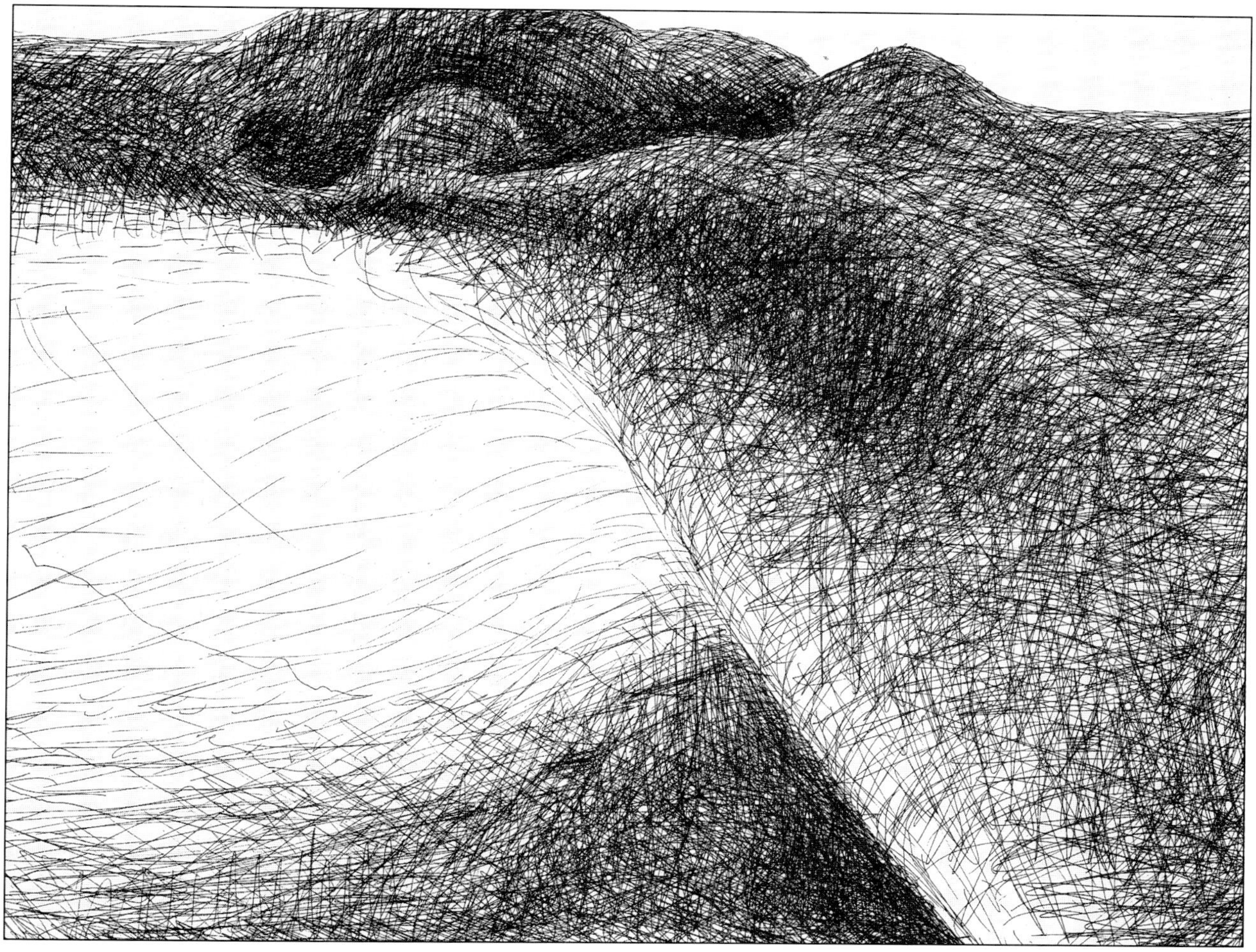

137

Elephant Skull, Plate XXII 1969

etching

235 x 308mm

CGM 135

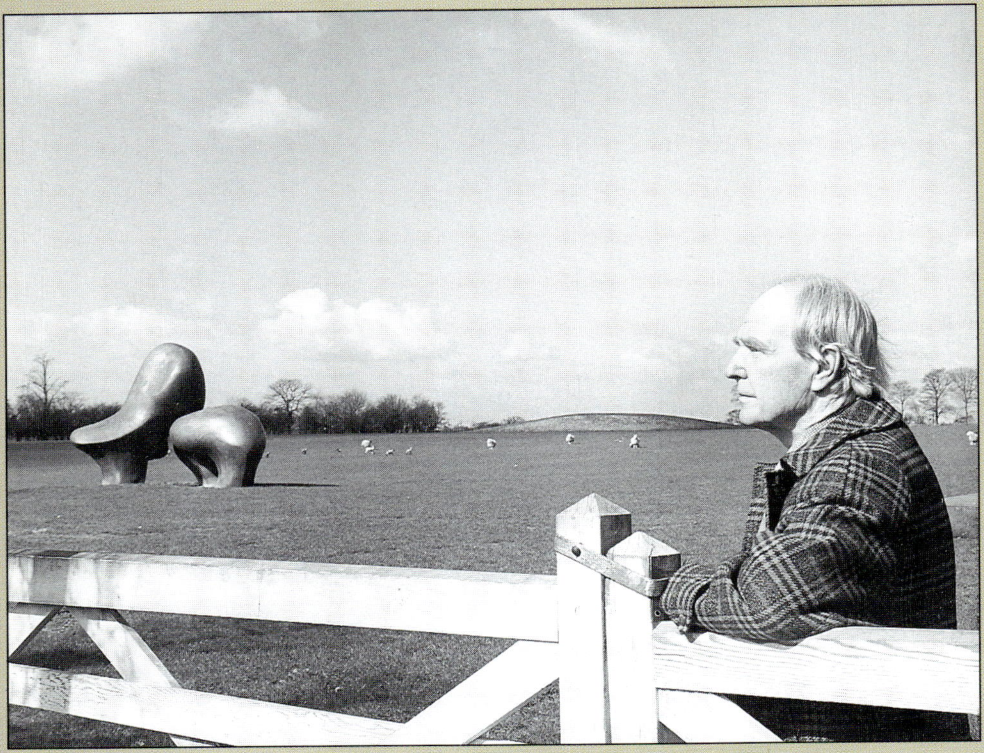

Henry Moore in the field behind his studios at Perry Green with **Sheep Piece** 1971-72 (LH 627; see cat.138).

1970s

In the 1970s Moore developed the printmaking that had become important to him in the previous decade. In 1969 the cave-like spaces within the skull of an elephant which he kept in his studio had inspired a portfolio of etchings (cats.134-137). He adopted a linear approach in admiration of the calligraphic style of drawings and etchings by Rembrandt. A series of etchings in a contrasting style, based on studies of Stonehenge (cats.146-148), convey his appreciation of the surface of the giant standing stones of that prehistoric temple. Sheep grazing in the field outside his studio provided a subject for etchings (cats.142-145) in yet another mode; he saw their rounded, sculptural forms as he had seen human life models as a young man.

Moore had imagined a sculpture on a hill as a shrouded rider on some unknown animal in an etching of 1969 (cat.132). These led to the more abstract shapes of cat.133 which, in turn, gave rise to *Sheep Piece* and *Hill Arches* (cats.138 and 139) in which the separate parts, formerly comprising a single reclining figure, join in a subtle interplay, suggesting the mating of elemental forms. He developed the theme of the reclining figure in the powerful invocation of woman, *Three Piece Reclining Figure: Draped* (see cat.155). Her instincts for offering protection are suggested by the curving leg form, doubling as drapery; her strength is conveyed by the second, bone-like leg; but the rocky, supranatural torso goes beyond woman, to nature herself, seen as an elemental mother.

During the 1970s the artist also reconsidered earlier themes. *Reclining Figure: Angles* (cat.163) is reminiscent of the *Draped Reclining Figure* of 1952-53 (cat.98), but she has woken out of a reverie and turns her head, as though startled. *Mother and Child: Towel* (cat.171) contrasts with the maquette for a Madonna and Child (cat.70), but in the late group only the child is life-like and the mother has become an archetypal figure, with exaggerated lap and abstracted head. By reconciling figure and abstraction Moore continued to give us a new awareness of Creation.

138

Working Model for Sheep Piece 1971

L 142cm bronze edition of 9

LH 626

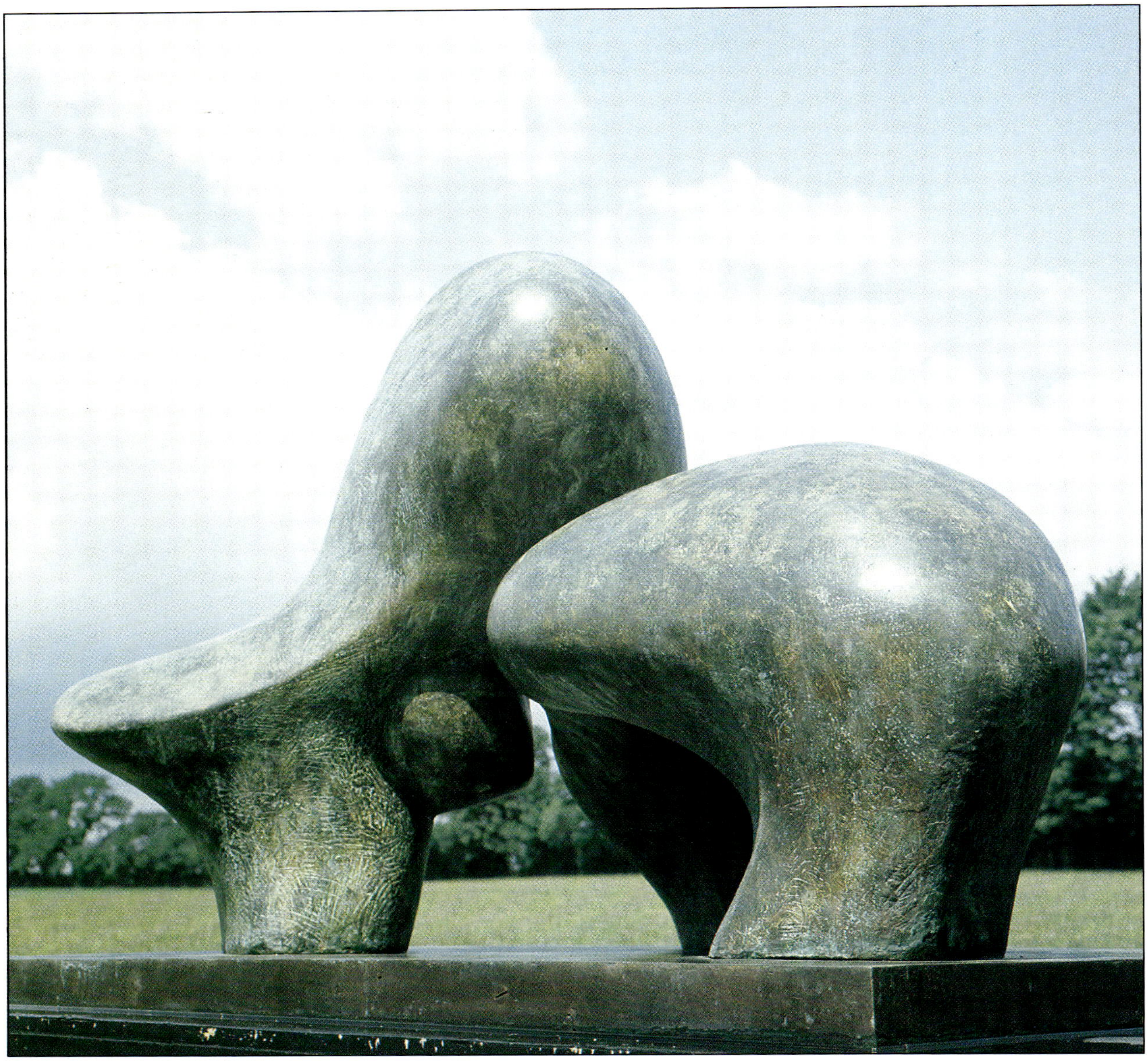

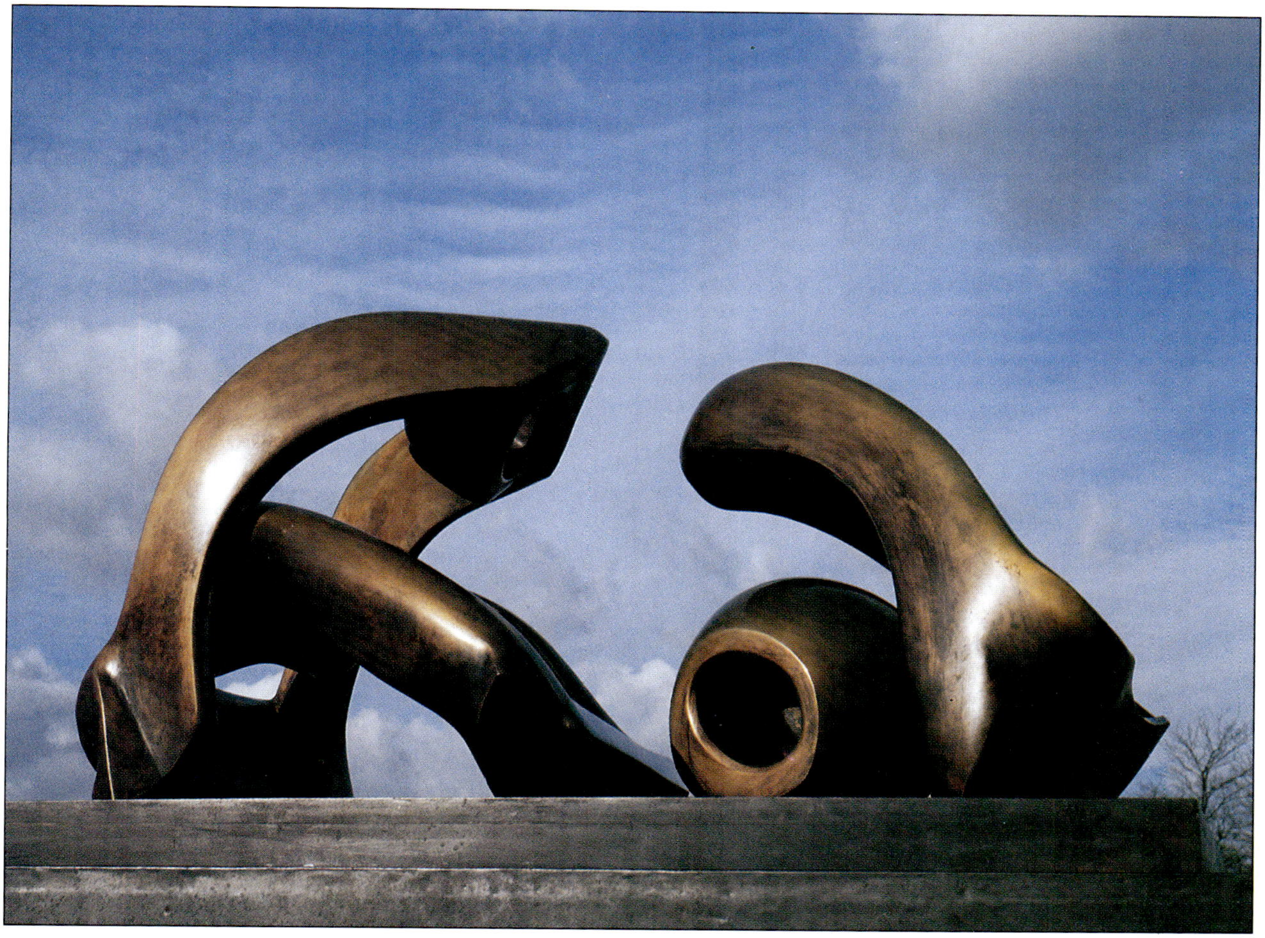

Appreciation of sculpture depends upon the ability to respond to form in three dimensions. That is perhaps why sculpture has been described as the most difficult of all arts; certainly it is more difficult than the arts which involve appreciation of flat forms, shape in only two dimensions. Many more people are 'form-blind' than colour-blind.

139
Working Model for Hill Arches 1972
L 109cm bronze edition of 9
LH 635

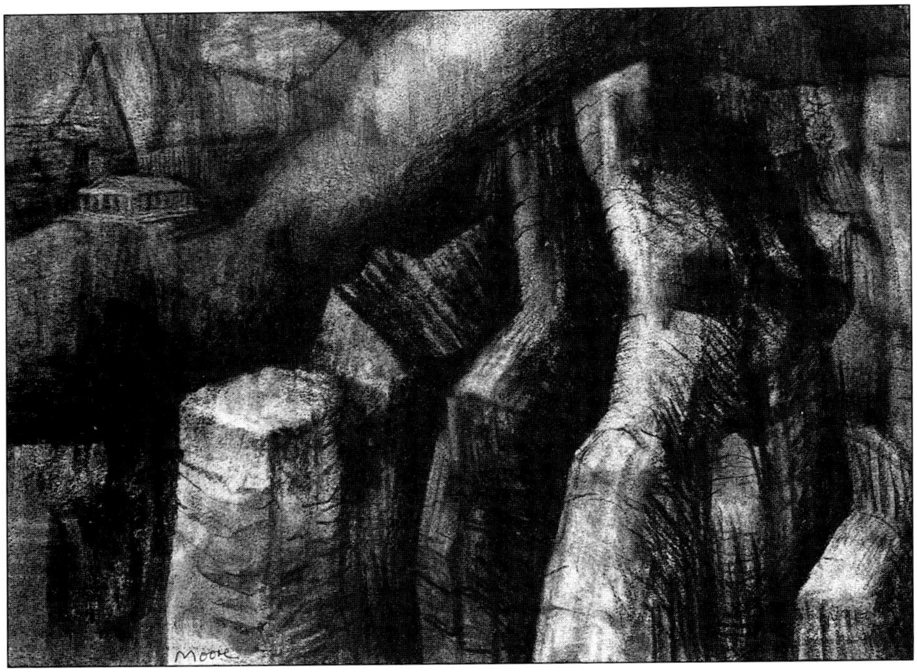

140
Classical Landscape with Temple *c.*1972
charcoal, black crayon, white chalk
213 x 290mm
HMF 3436

141
Three Seated Women and Children 1971
grey wash, charcoal, black chalk, red chalk or pastel, pencil
394 x 572mm
HMF 3313

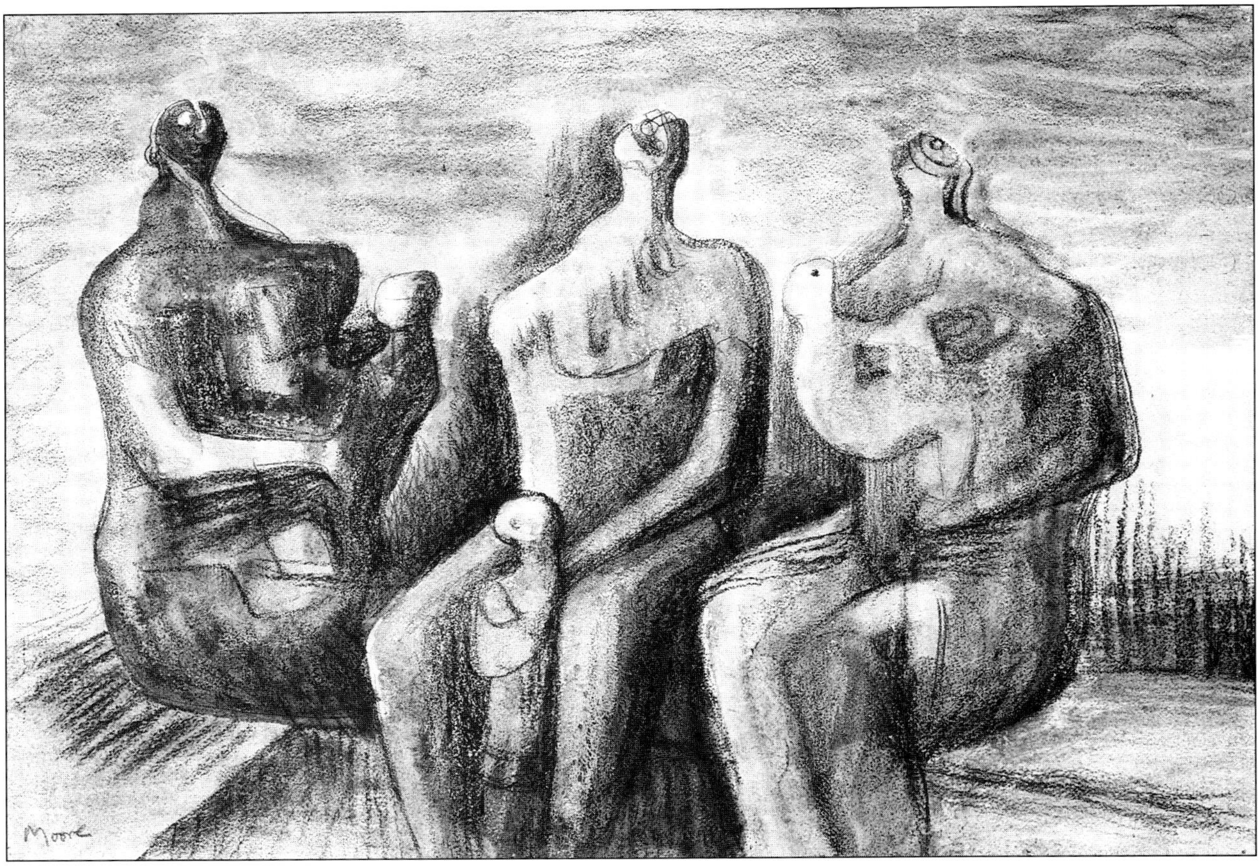

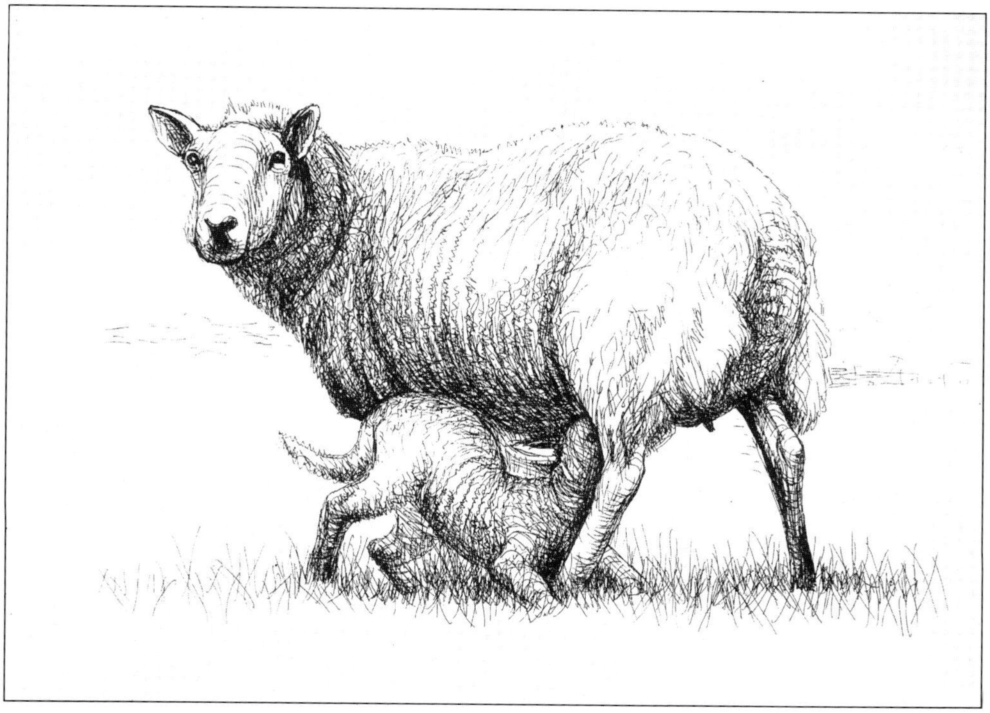

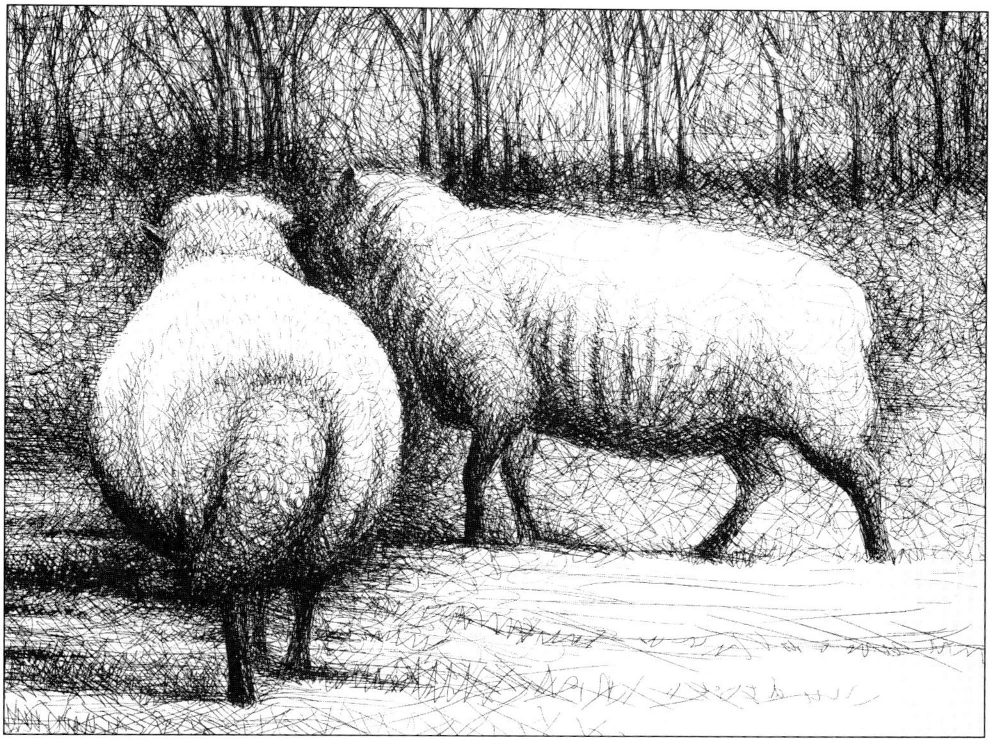

142
Sheep with Lamb I 1972
etching and drypoint
149 x 206mm
CGM 196

143
Sheep 1972
etching and drypoint
191 x 254mm
CGM 201

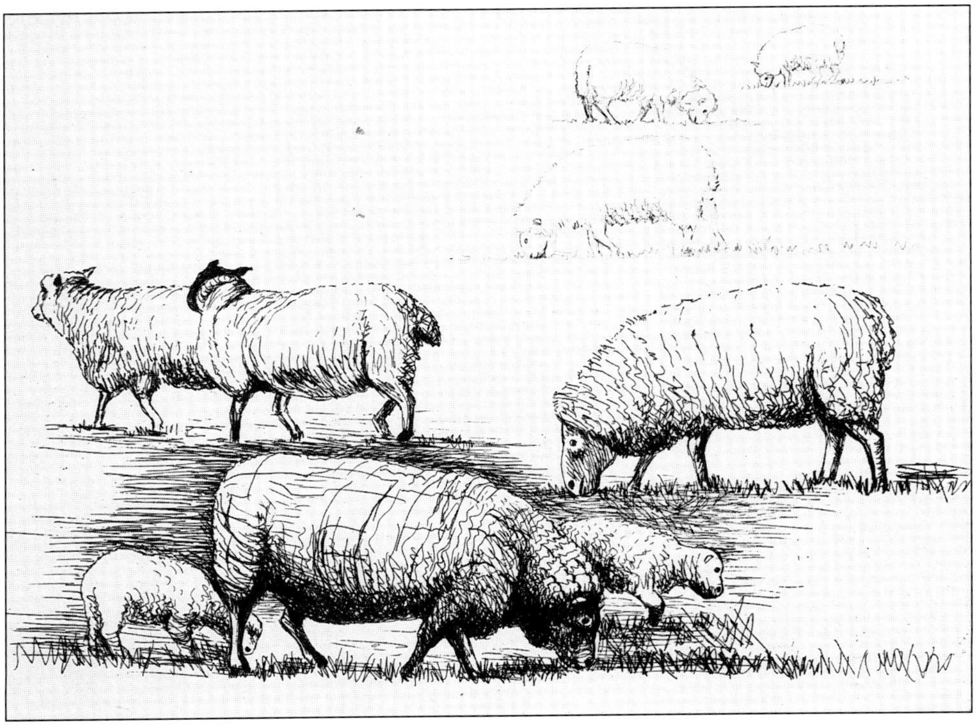

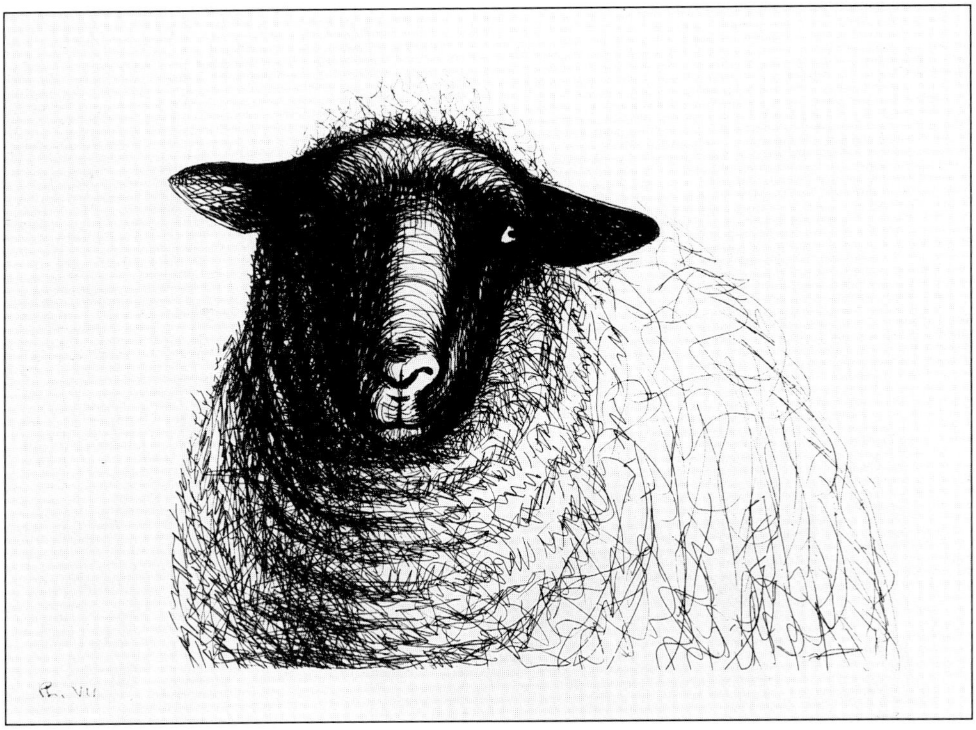

144
Sheep in Field 1974
etching and drypoint
190 x 255mm
CGM 226

145
Head 1974
etching and drypoint
190 x 254mm
CGM 228

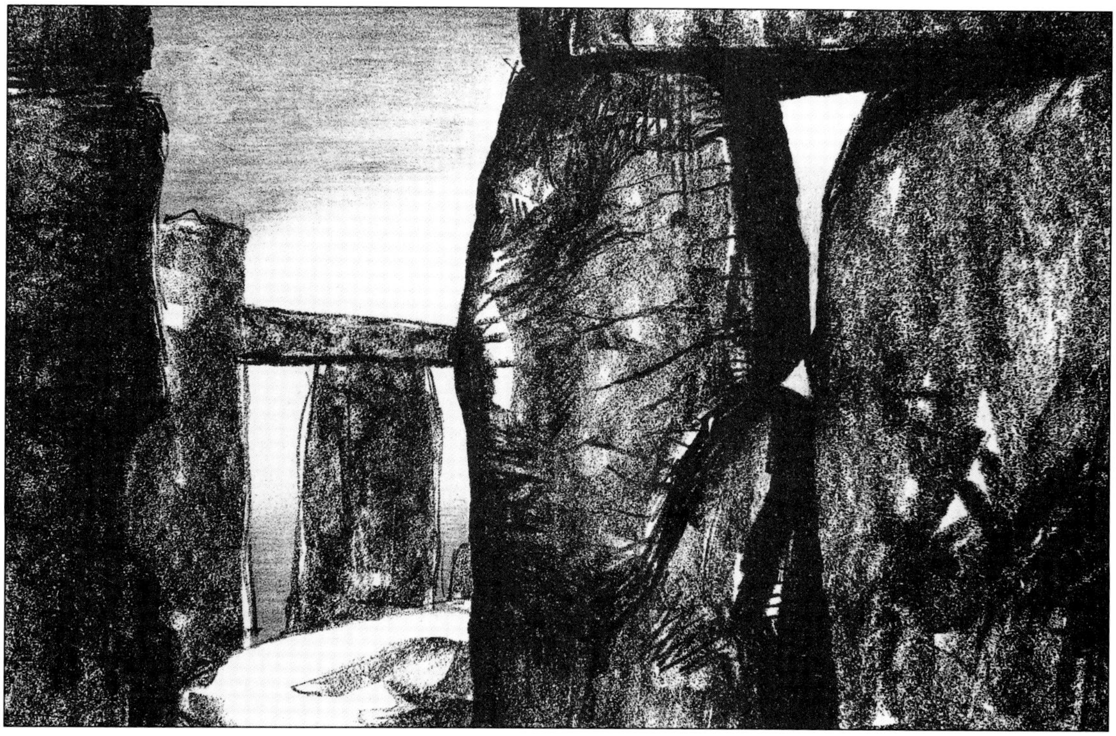

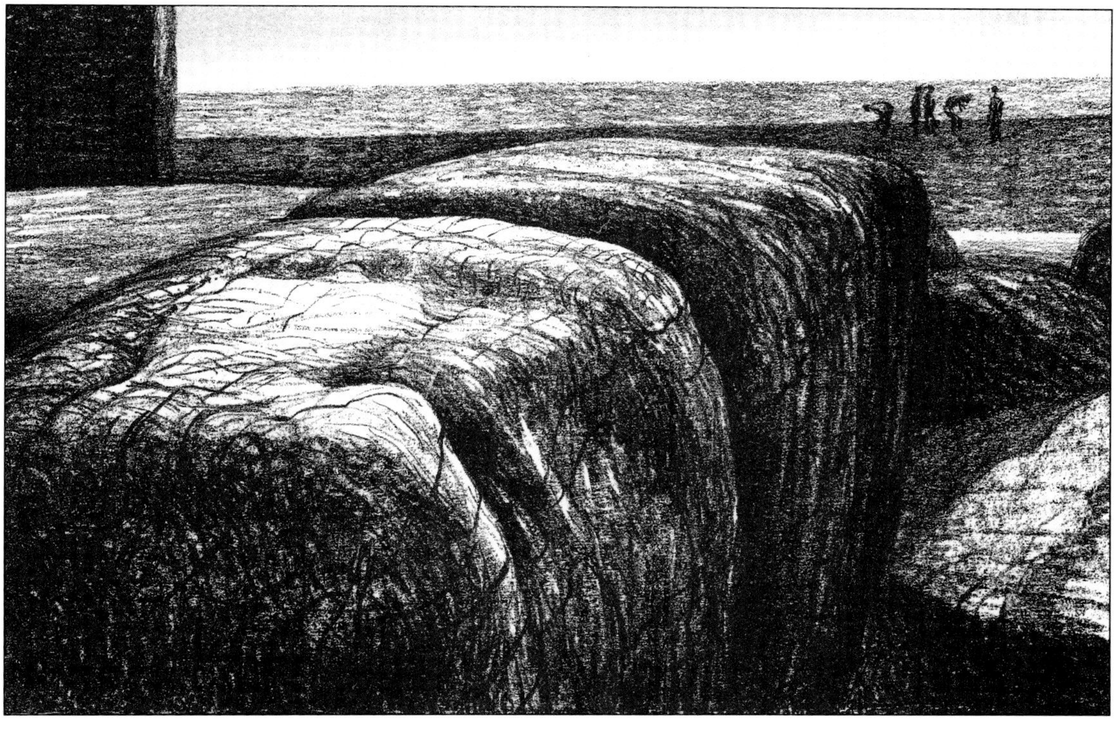

146

Stonehenge IV 1973

lithograph

289 x 435mm

CGM 211

147

Stonehenge IV 1973

lithograph in two colours

292 x 457mm

CGM 213

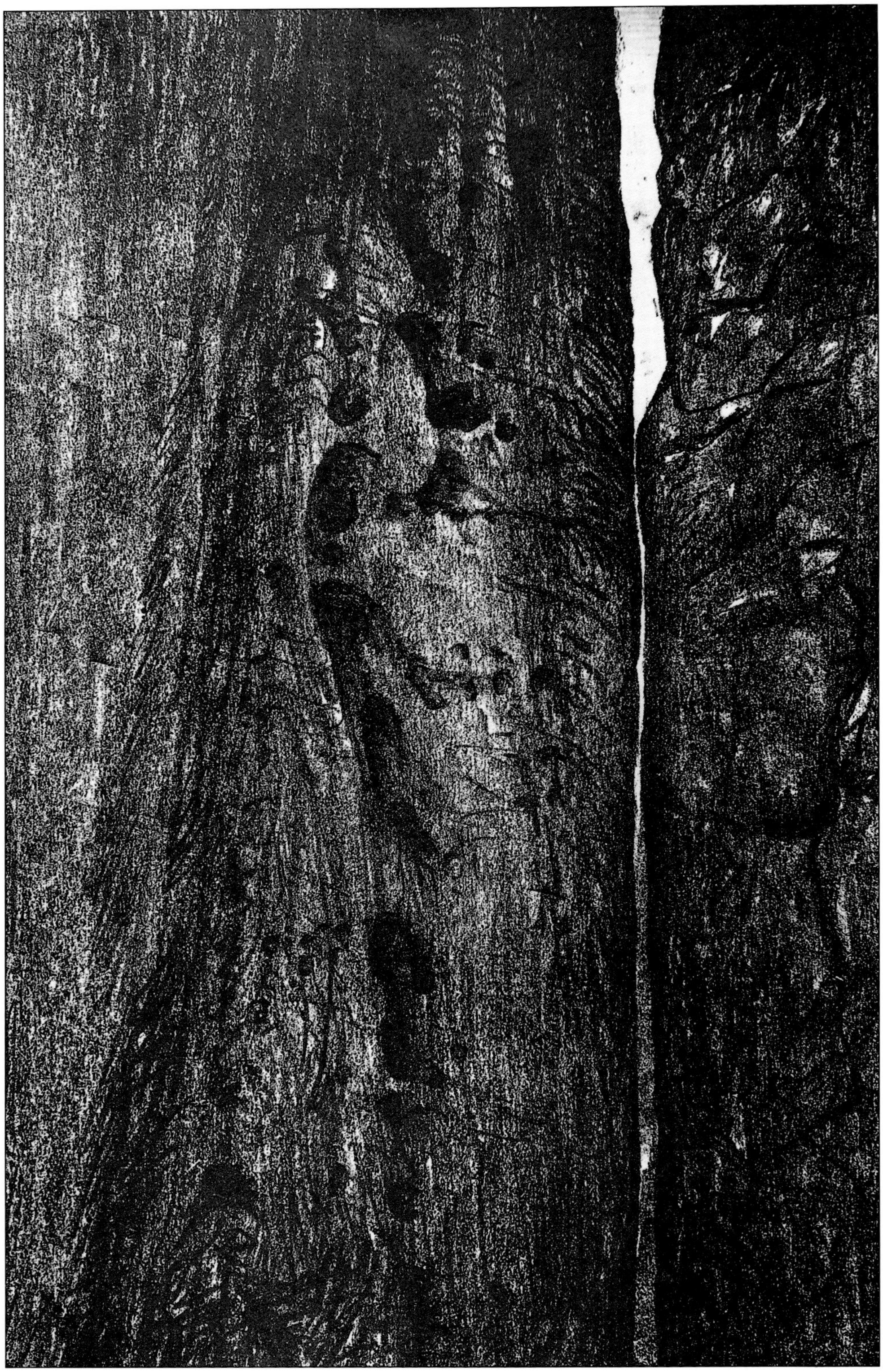

148
Stonehenge X 1973
lithograph
454 x 292mm
CGM 217

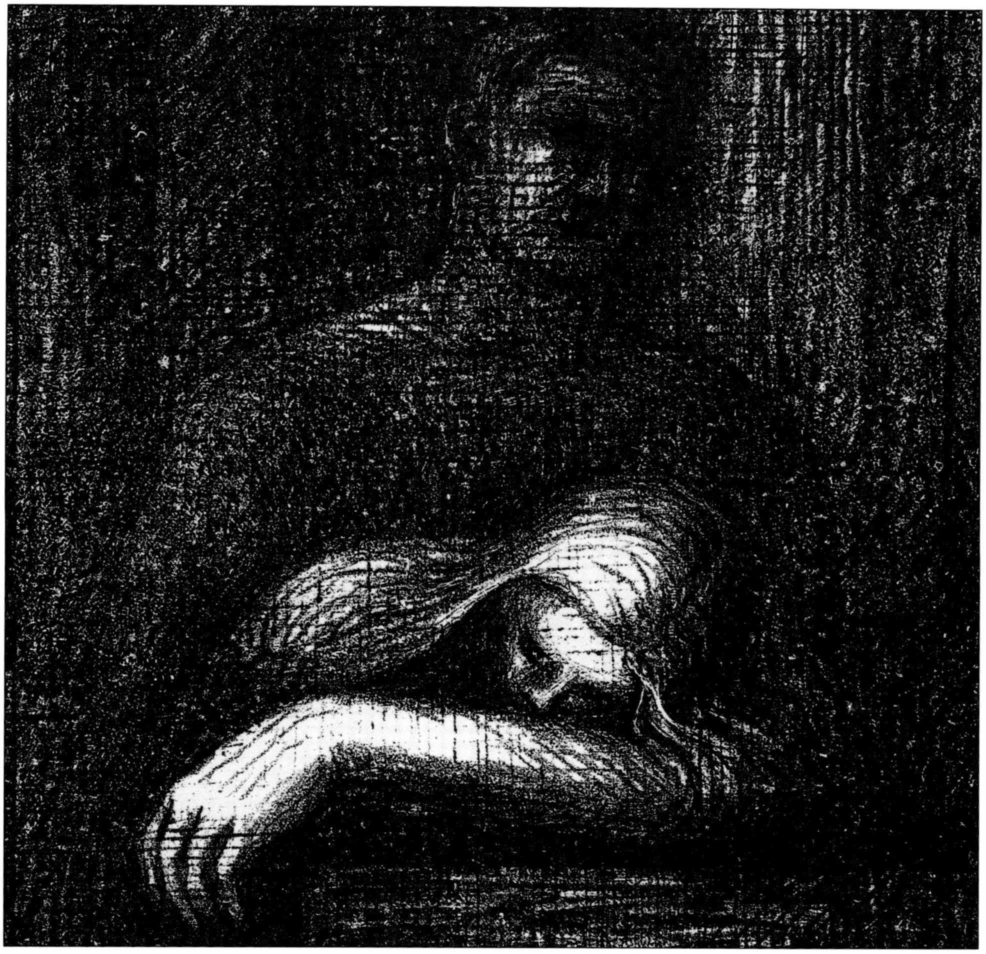

The Stonehenge series of drawings and lithographs and the Auden illustrations were done only a few months apart. The Stonehenge drawings gave me a taste for using deep blacks and increased my feeling for the medium of lithography . . . lithography, after all, is drawing on stone.

149
Lullaby Sleeping Head 1973
lithograph
273 x 292mm
CGM 250

150

Multitude II 1973

lithograph

292 x 270mm

CGM 253

151

Maquette for Goslar Warrior 1973

L 24.5cm bronze edition of 9

LH 640

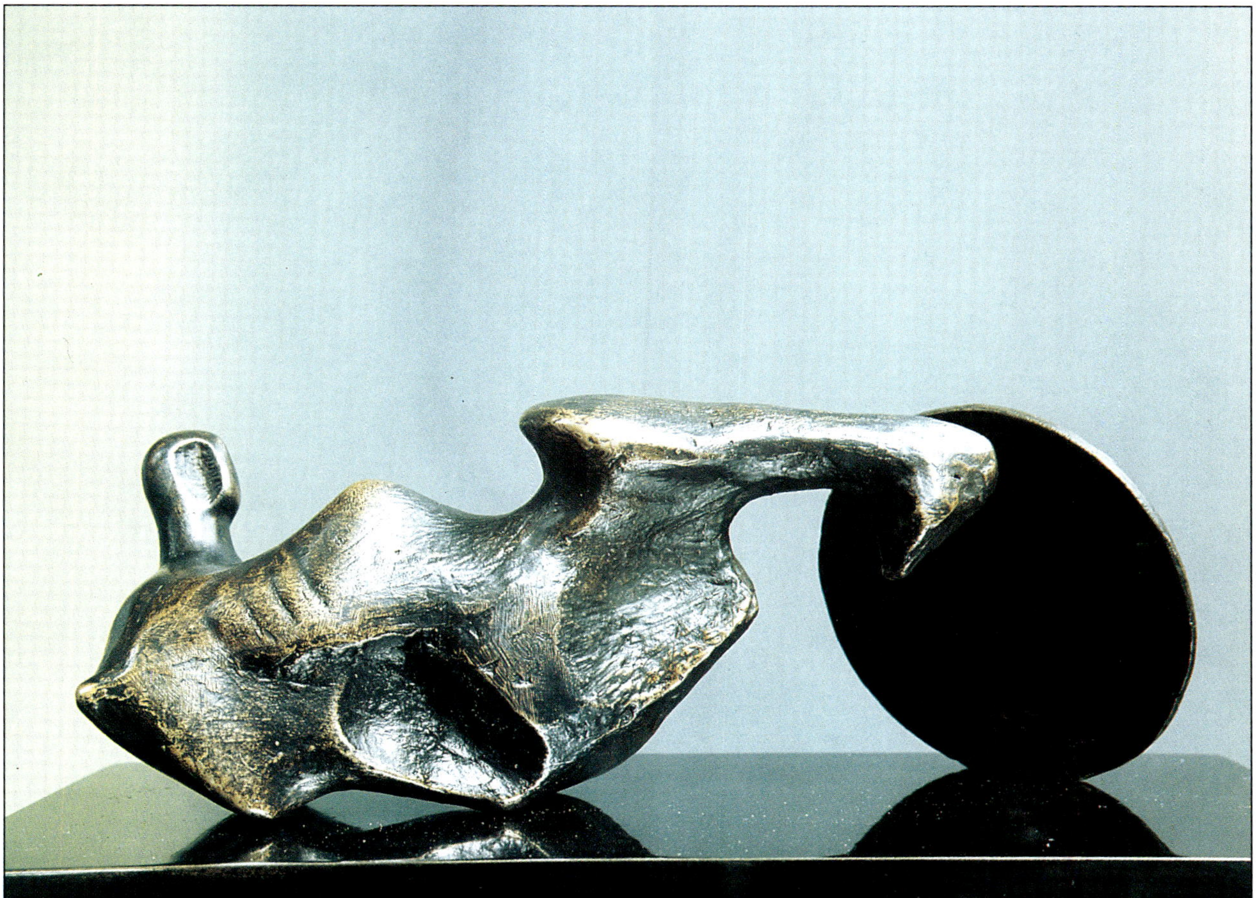

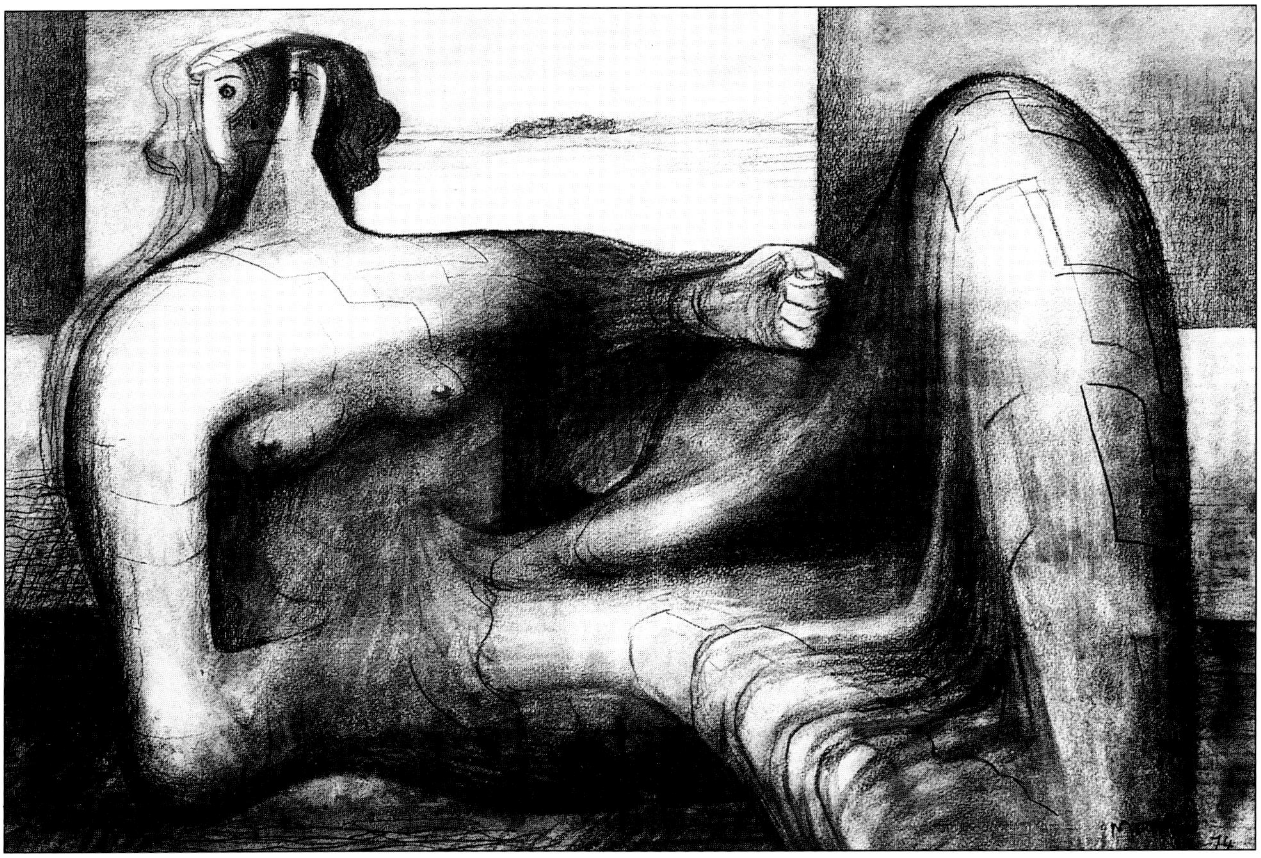

Reclining Woman in a Setting 1974
charcoal, pastel, watercolour wash,
black conté, black chinagraph
330 x 483mm
HMF 73-4(17)

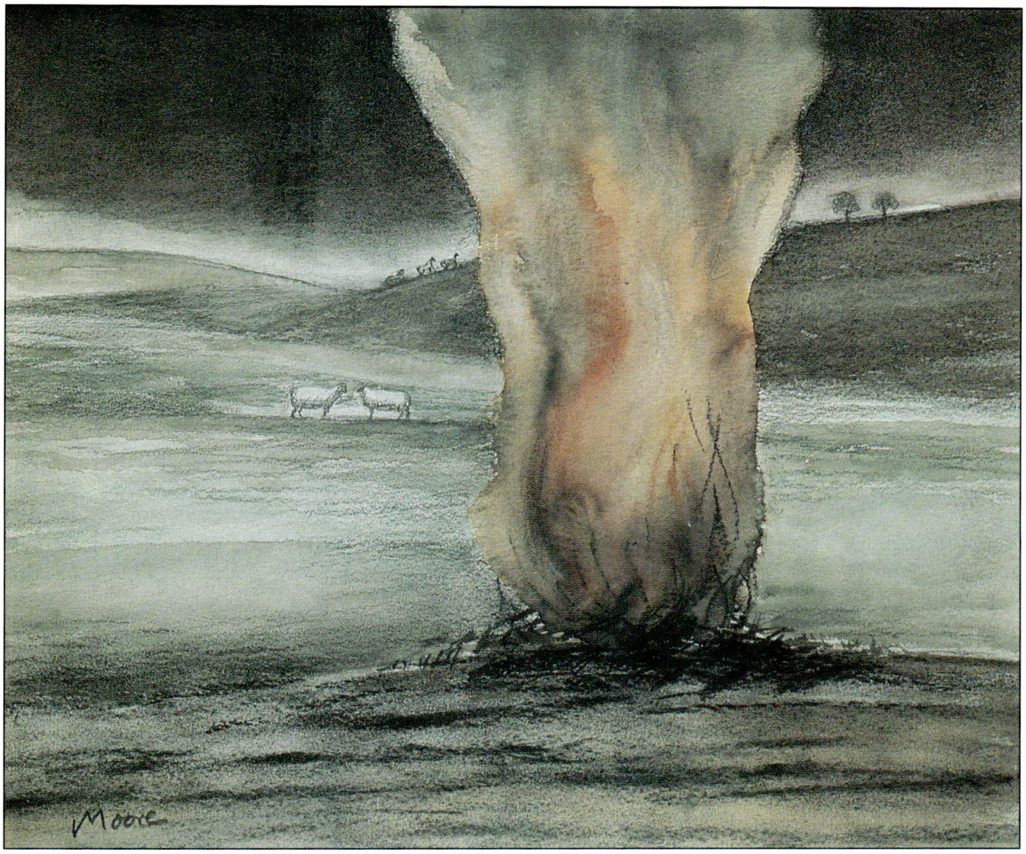

The bonfire drawings, like those of trees, have a connection with my ideas about sculpture: from a static base, the flames move upwards with a twisting rhythm.

153
Landscape with Bonfire IX 1975
pencil, watercolour, wash,
pastel, black chalk
275 x 330mm
HMF 75(27)

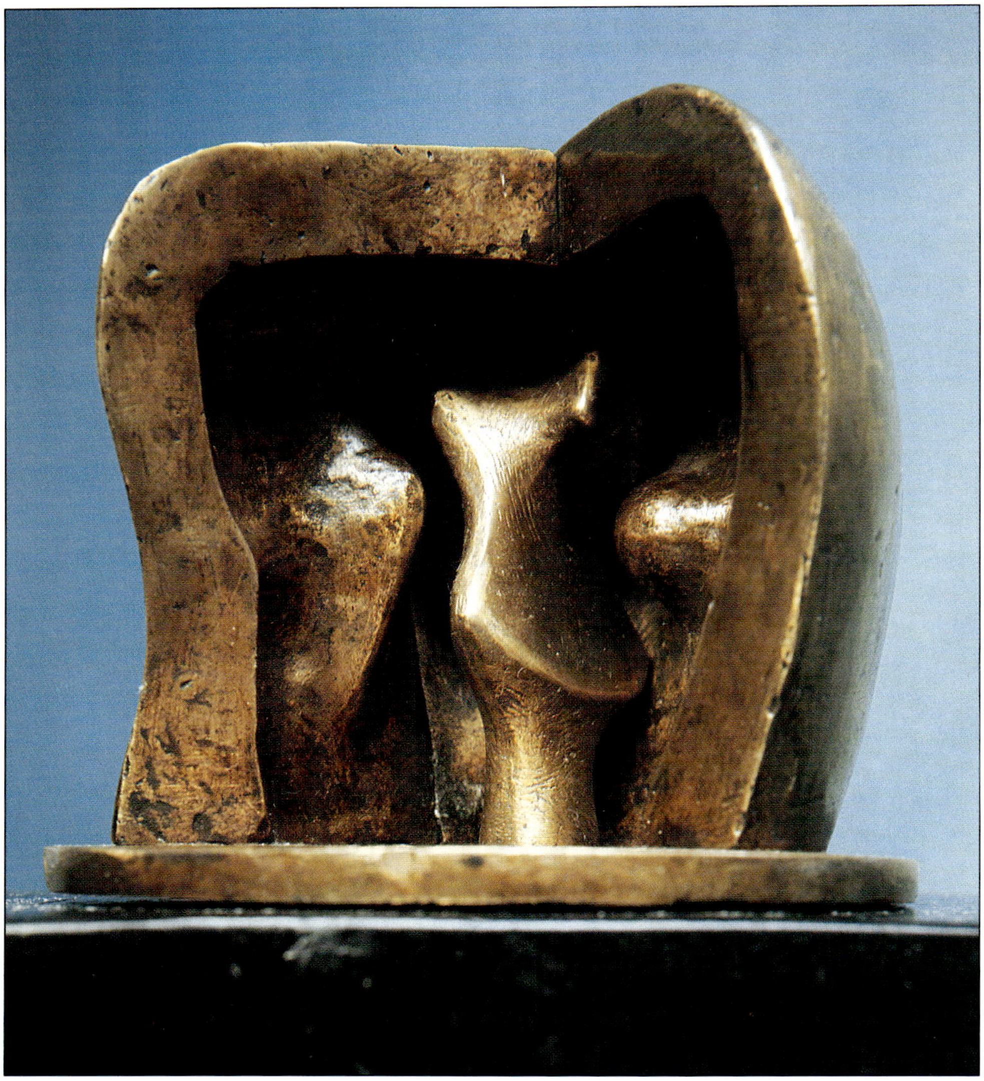

154

Maquette for Helmet Head No.6 1975

H 11cm bronze edition of 7

LH 650

155

Working Model for Three Piece Reclining Figure: Draped 1975

L 112cm bronze edition of 9

LH 654

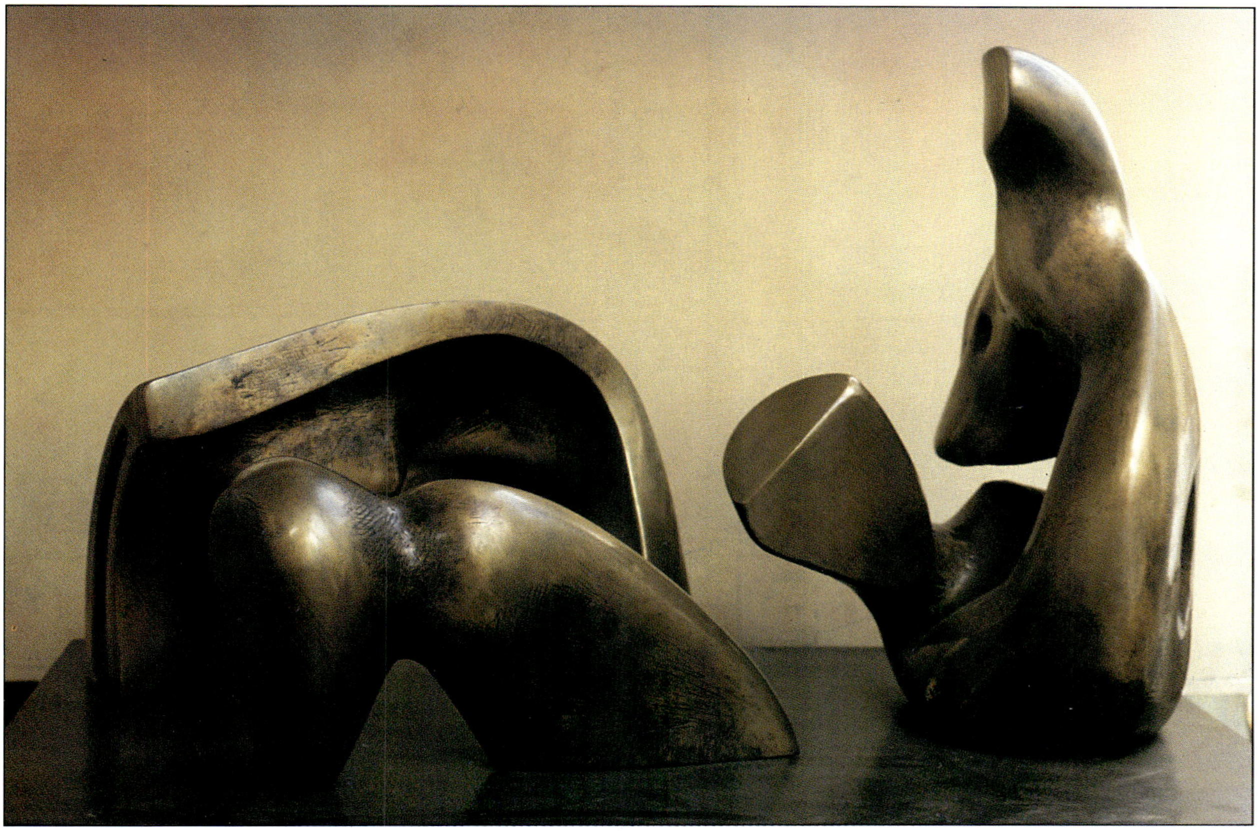

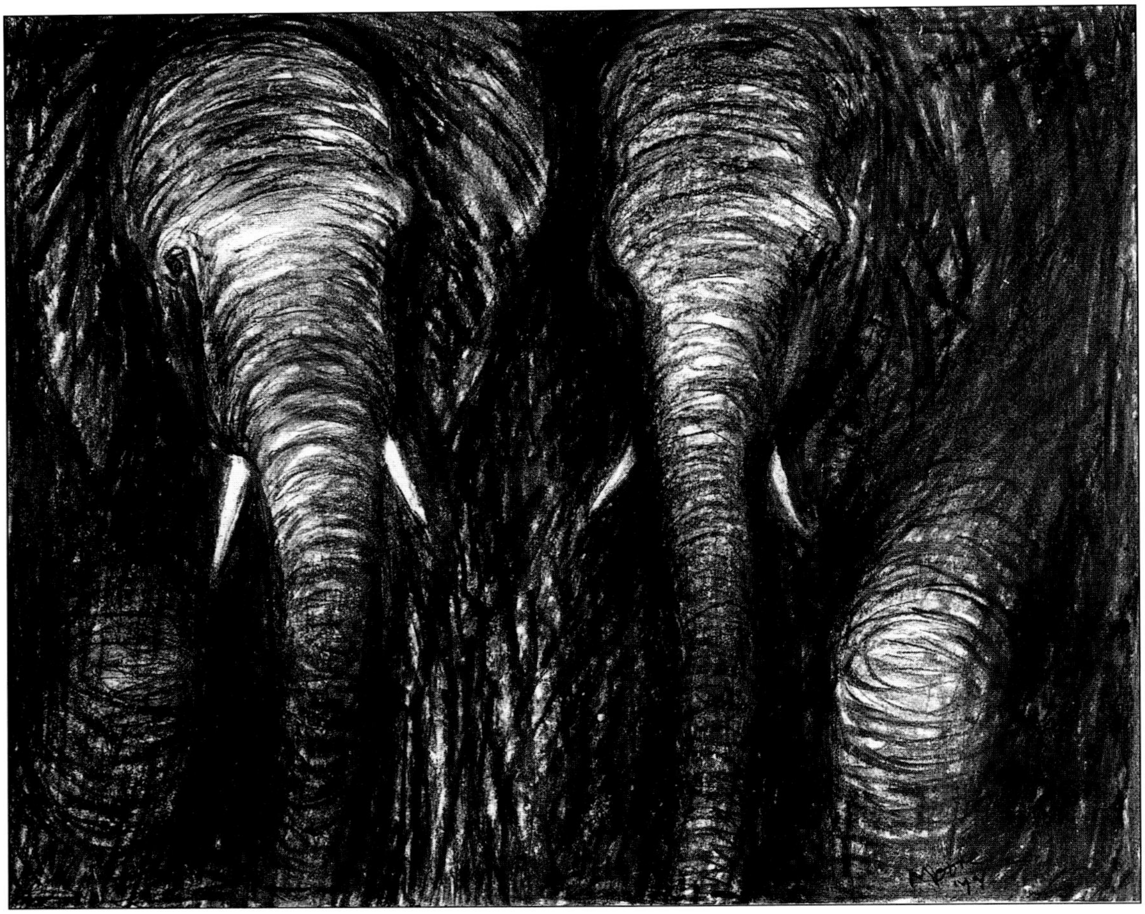

156
Forest Elephants 1977
charcoal, chalk
307 x 386mm
HMF 77(14)

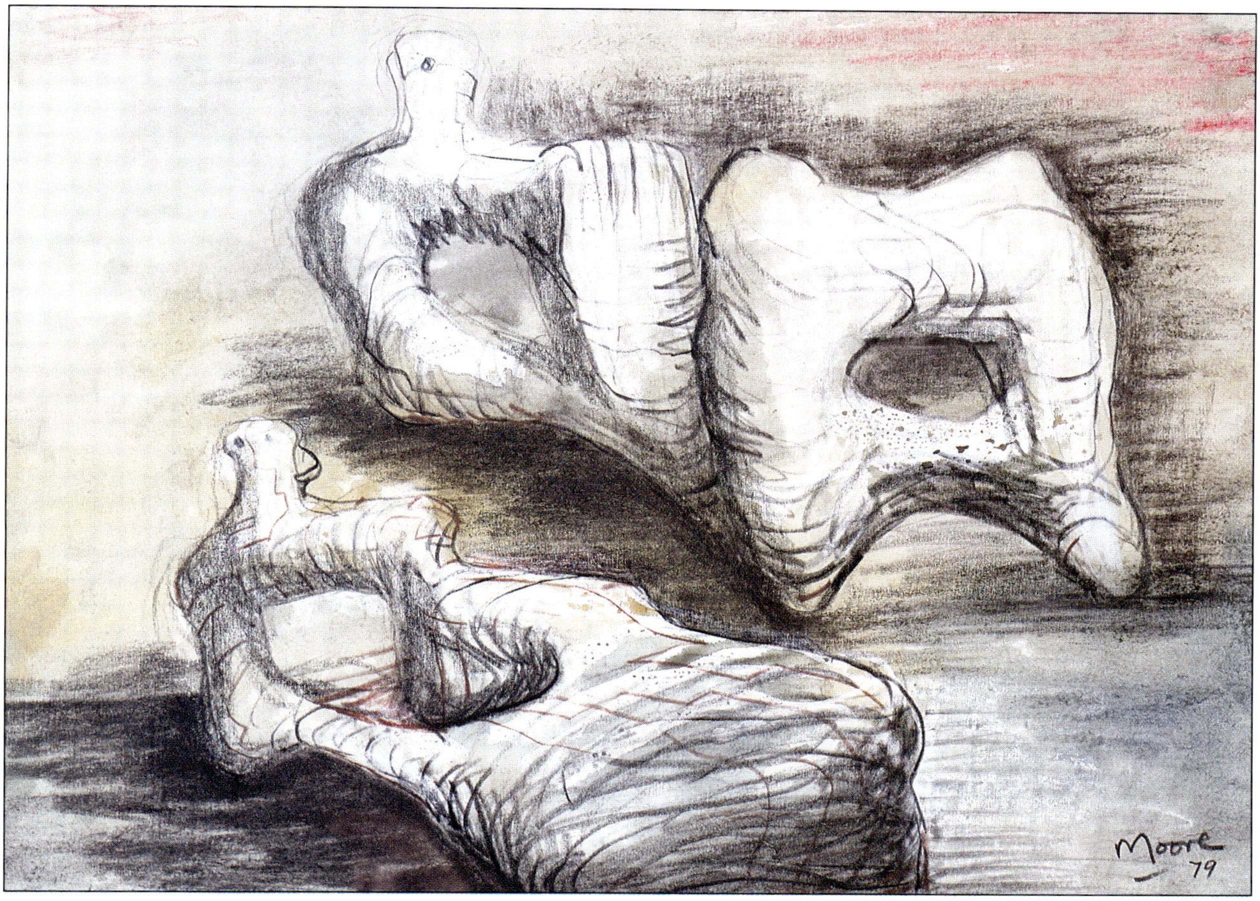

157
Two Reclining Figures:
Ideas for Sculpture 1979
charcoal, chalk, wax crayon,
watercolour wash
347 x 480mm
HMF 79(60)

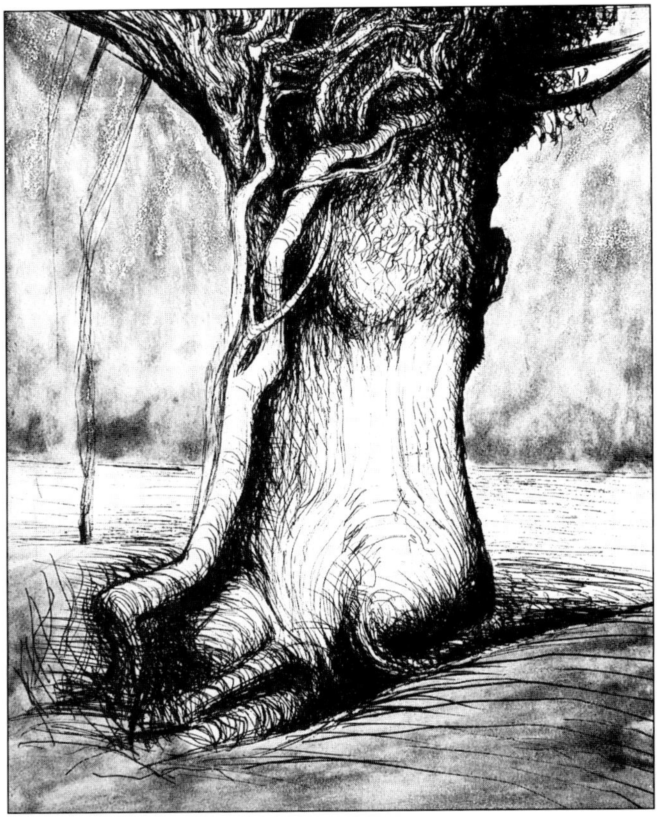

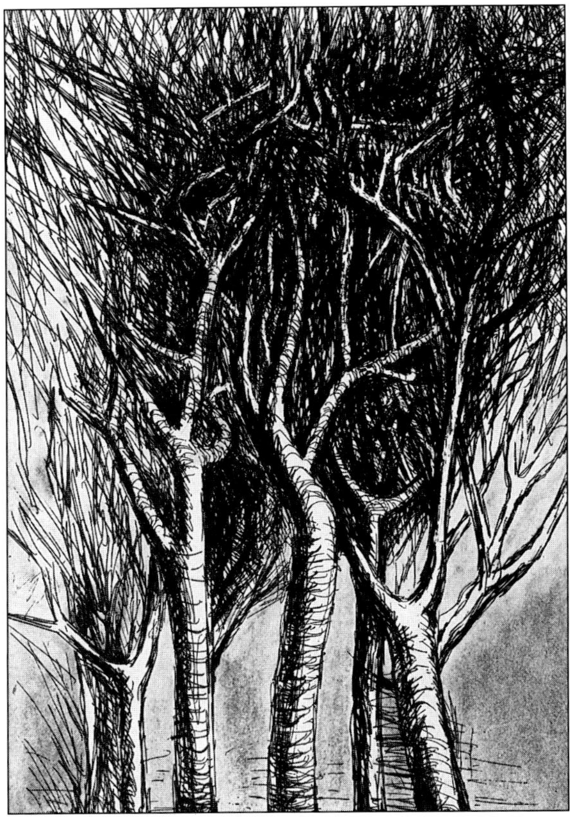

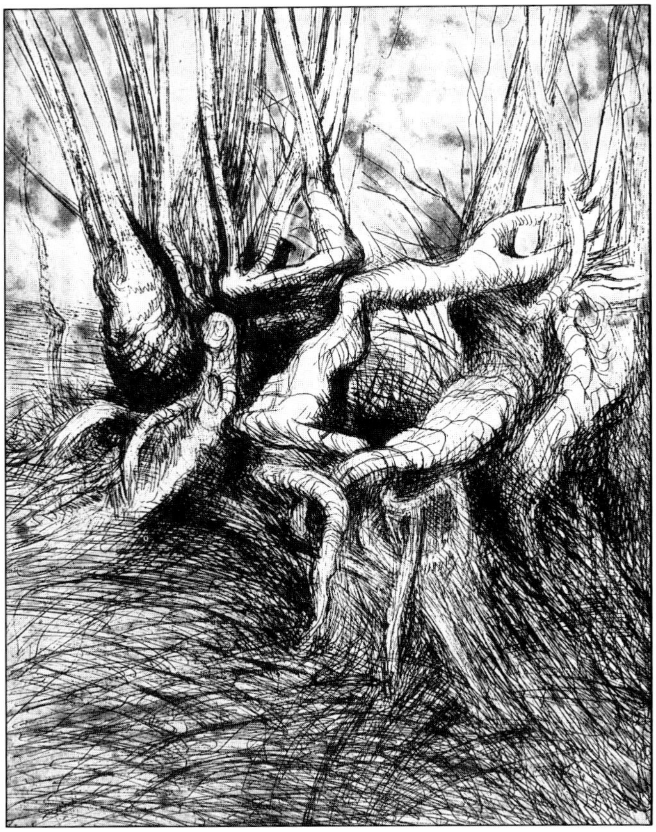

158
Trees I: Bole and Creeper 1979
etching and aquatint in three colours
238 x 188mm
CGM 547

159
Trees II: Upright Branches 1979
etching, drypoint and aquatint
in two colours
232 x 159mm
CGM 548

160
Trees IV: Tortured Roots 1979
etching, drypoint and aquatint
in two colours
242 x 188mm
CGM 550

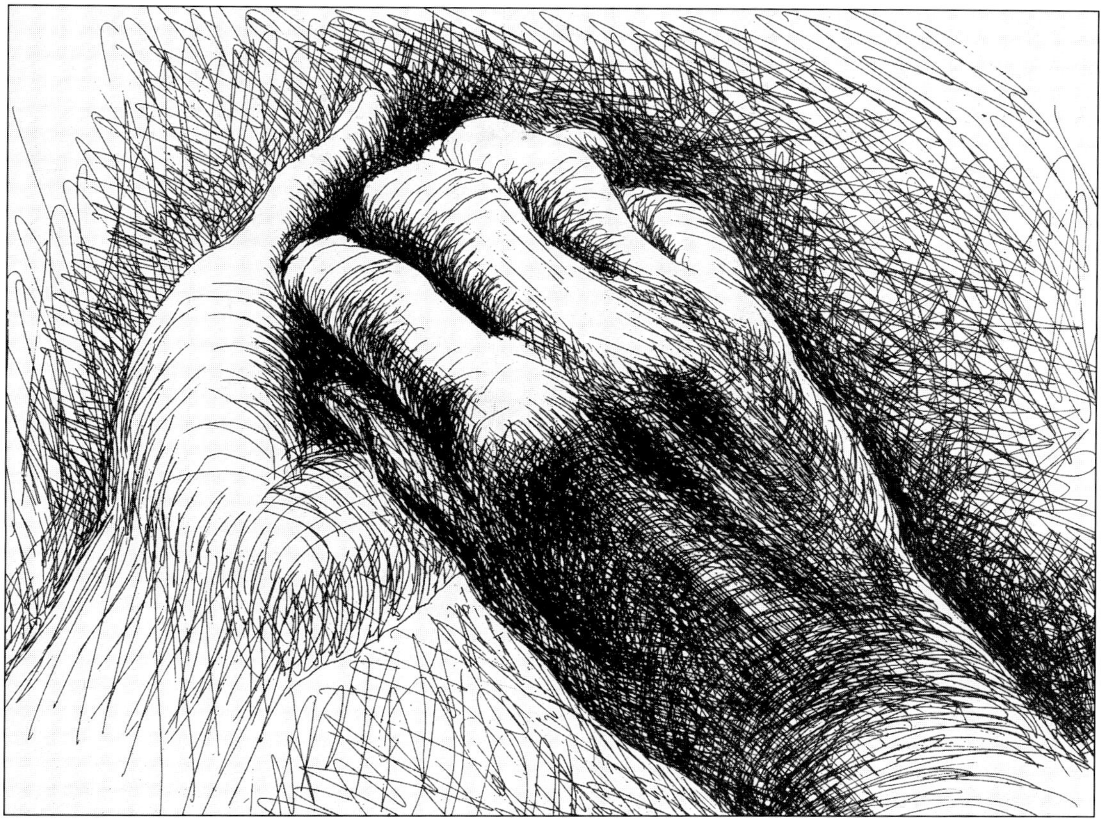

If one likes drawing hands, as I do, the nearest model is one's own two hands . . . Hands, to me, are – after the head and face – the most expressive part of the human figure.

161
The Artist's Hand II 1979
etching
190 x 254mm
CGM 554

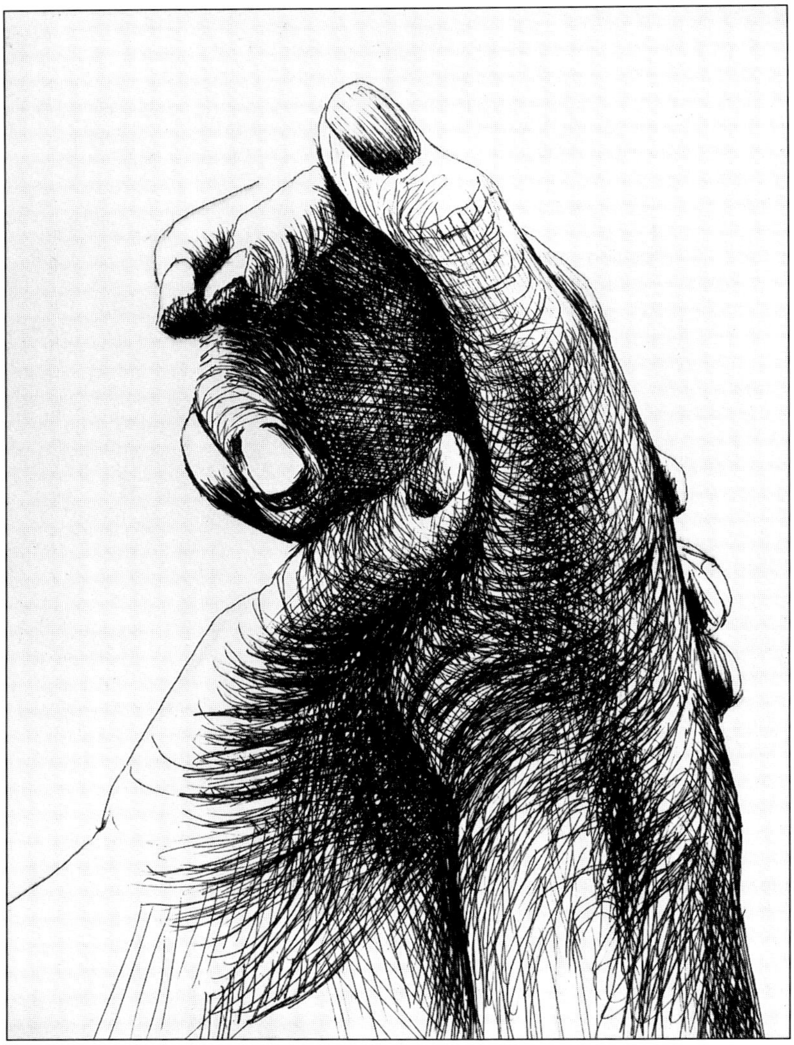

162
The Artist's Hand IV 1979
etching
225 x 168mm
CGM 556

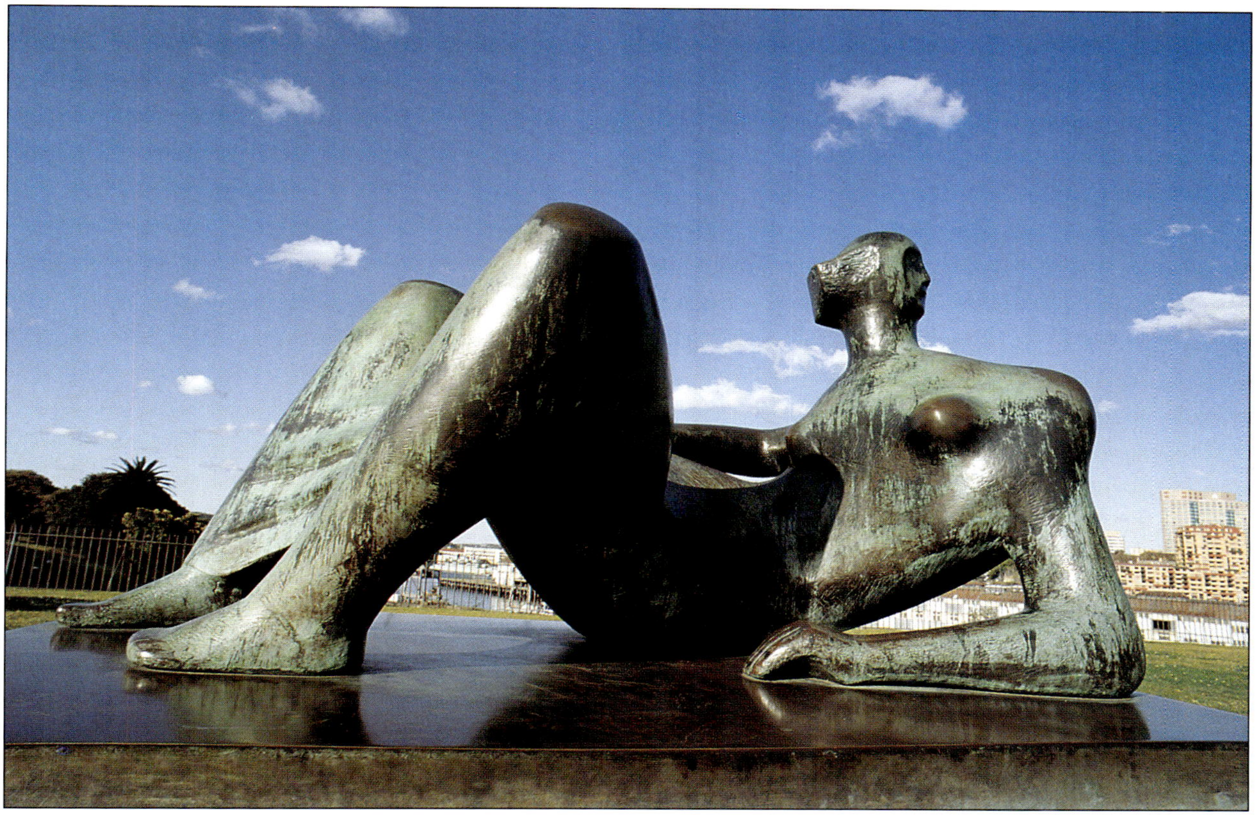

163
Reclining Figure: Angles 1979
L 218cm bronze edition of 9
Art Gallery of New South Wales,
Sydney
LH 675

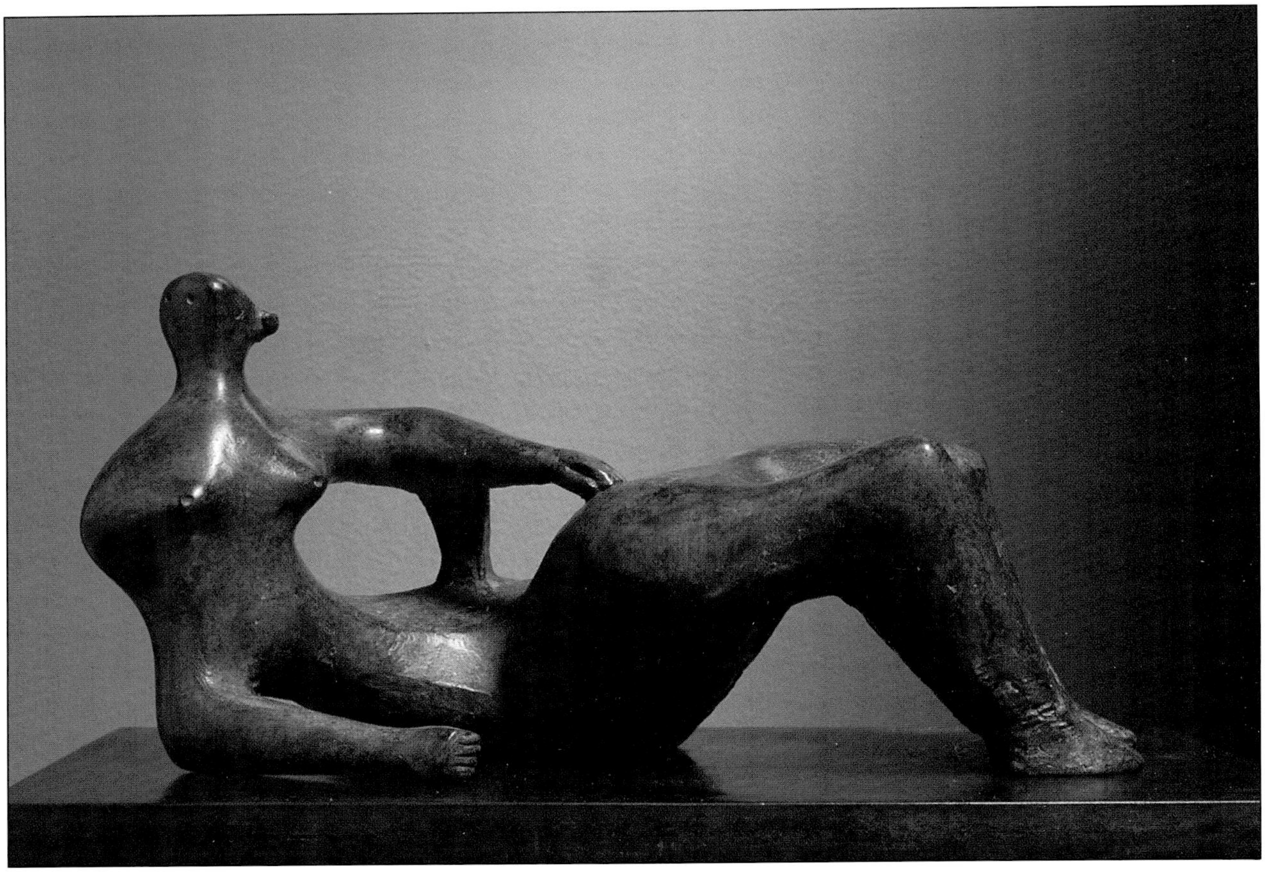

164
Maquette for Reclining Figure: Prop 1975
L 27.9cm bronze edition of 9
LH 676

165

Two Piece Reclining Figure: Thin 1976

L 24.8cm bronze edition of 9

LH 692

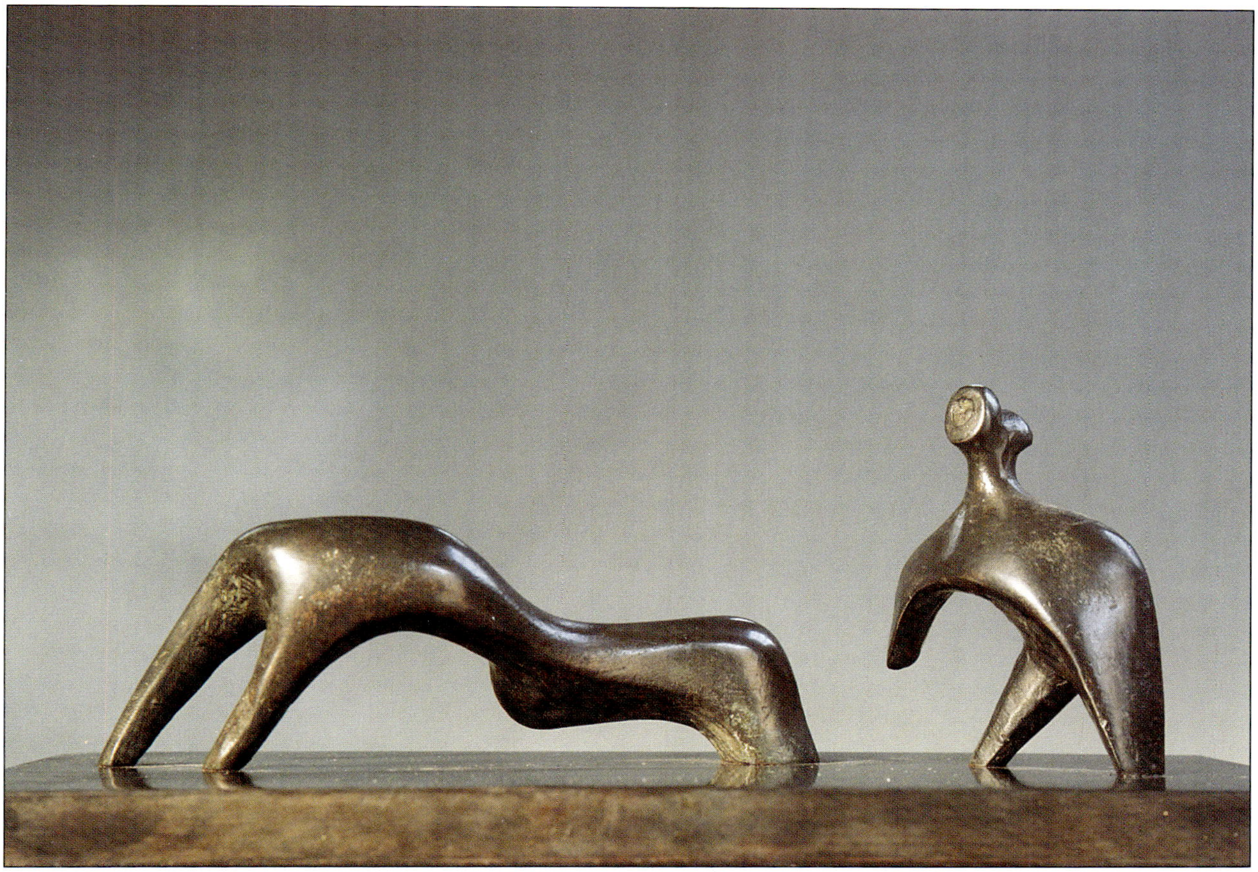

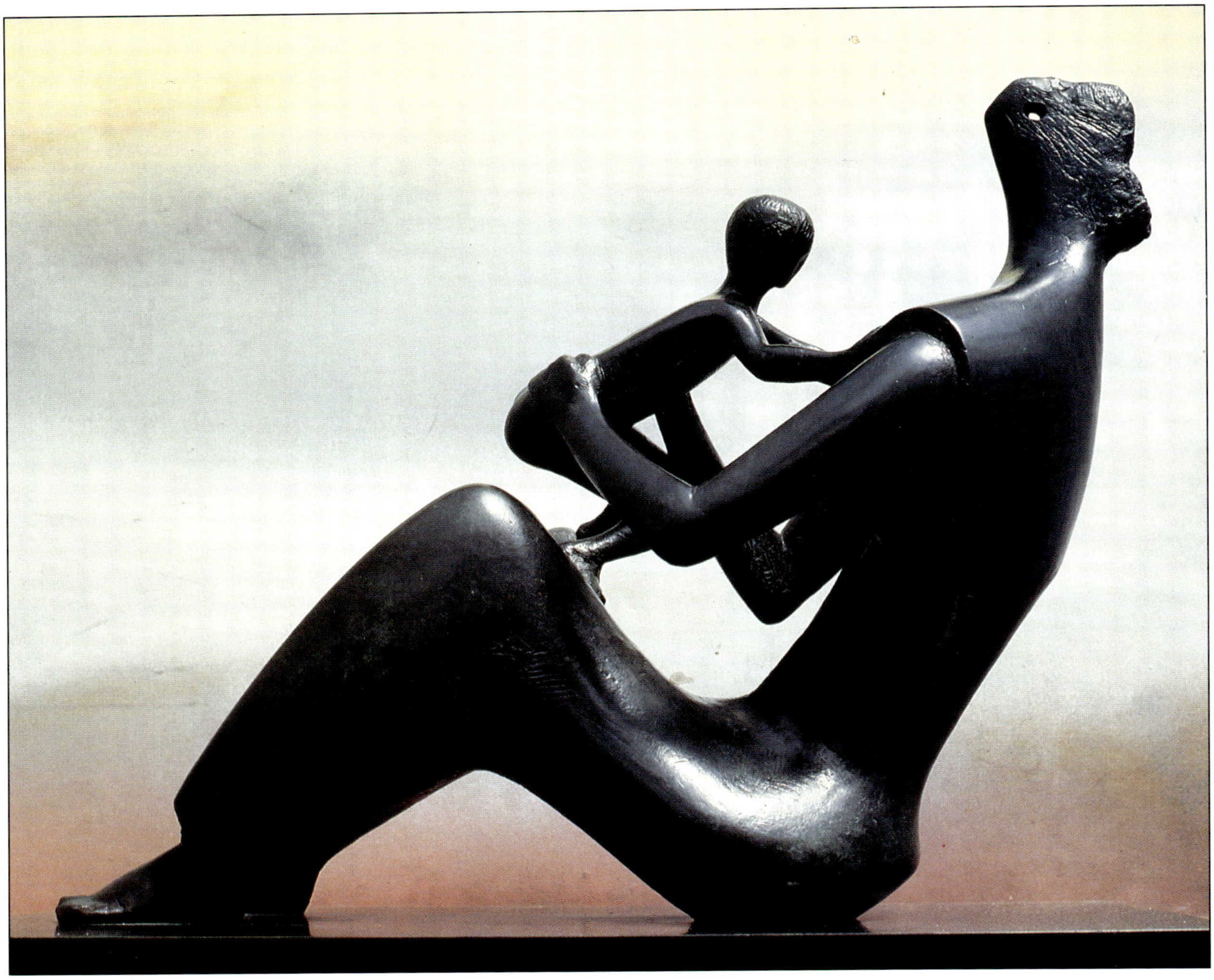

166

Mother and Child: Arms 1976-80

L 80cm bronze edition of 9

LH 698

167

Working Model for Draped Reclining Figure 1976-79

L 99cm bronze edition of 9

LH 705

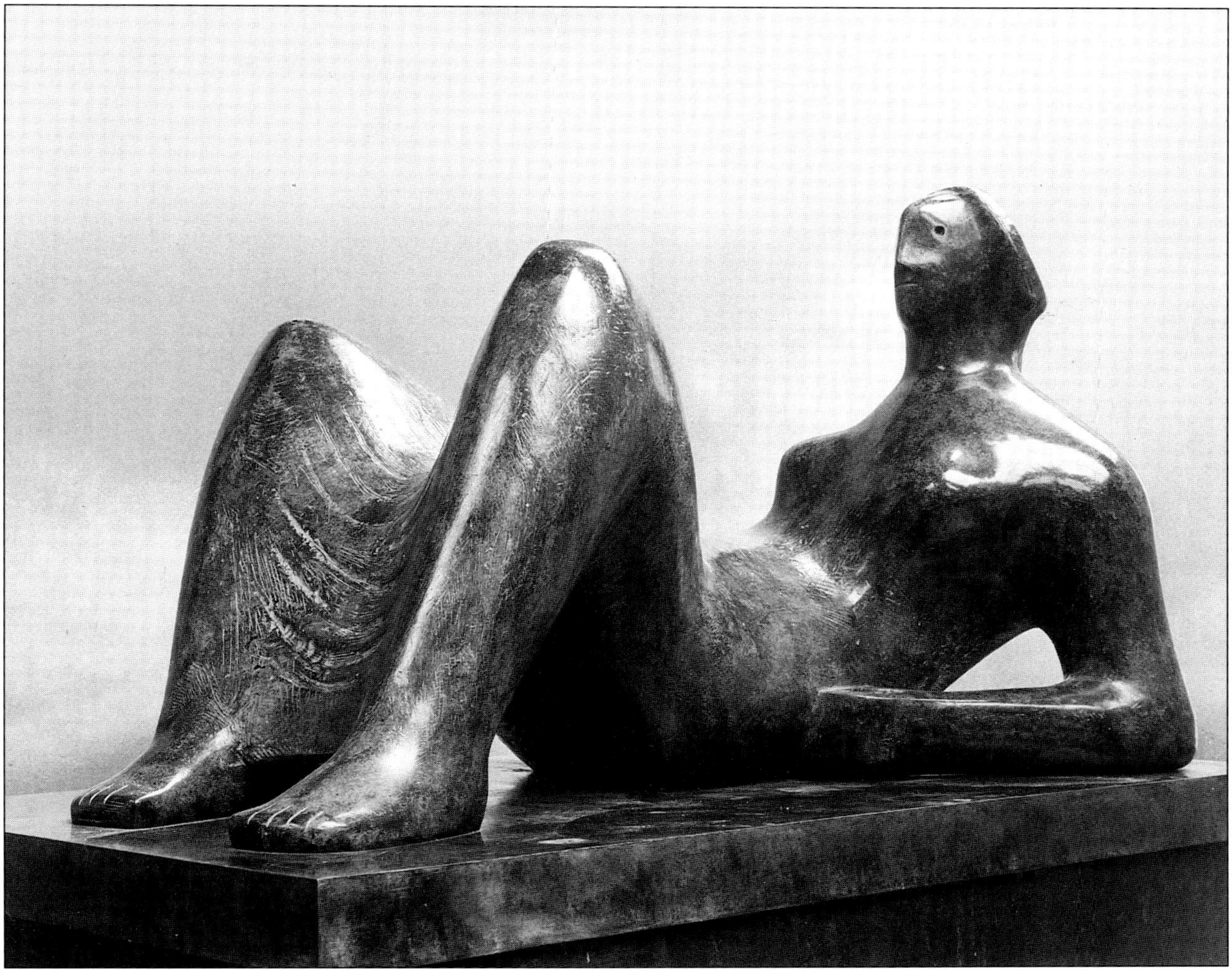

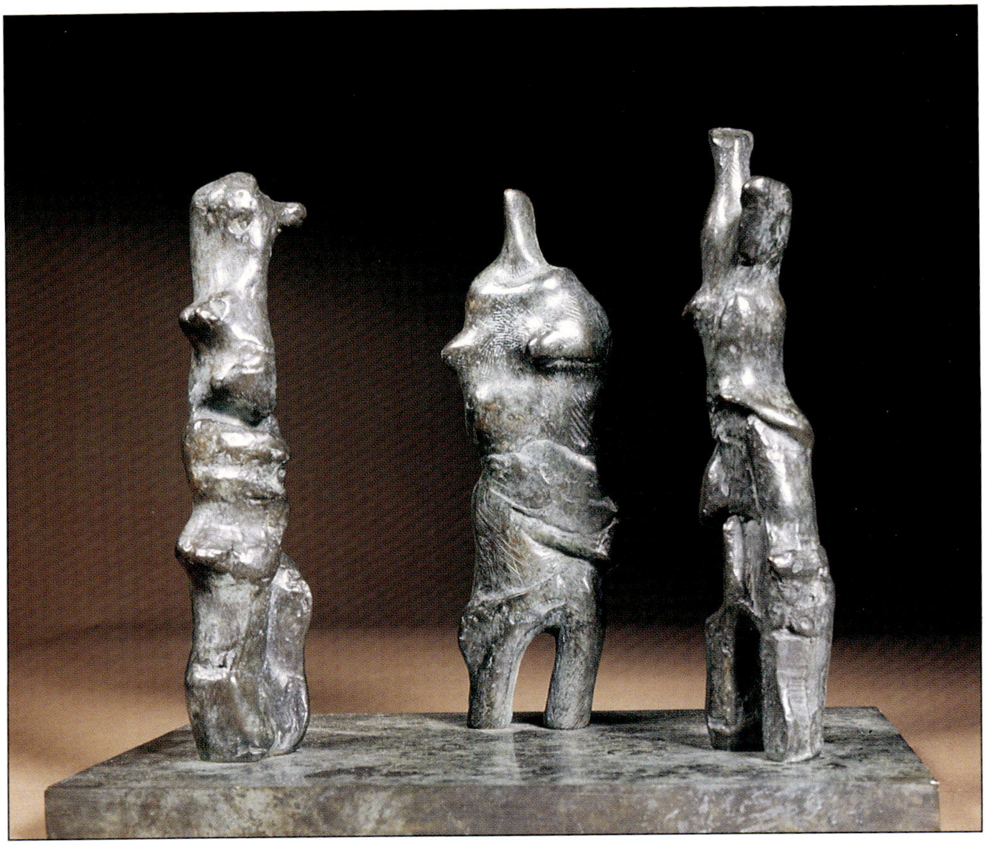

You see, there is a difference between scale and size. A small sculpture only three or four inches big can have about it a monumental scale, so that if you photographed it against a blank wall in which you had nothing to refer it to but only itself – or you photographed it against the sky against infinite distance – a small thing only a few inches big might seem, if it has monumental scale, to be any size.

168
Three Upright Motives 1977
H 20cm bronze edition of 7
LH 715

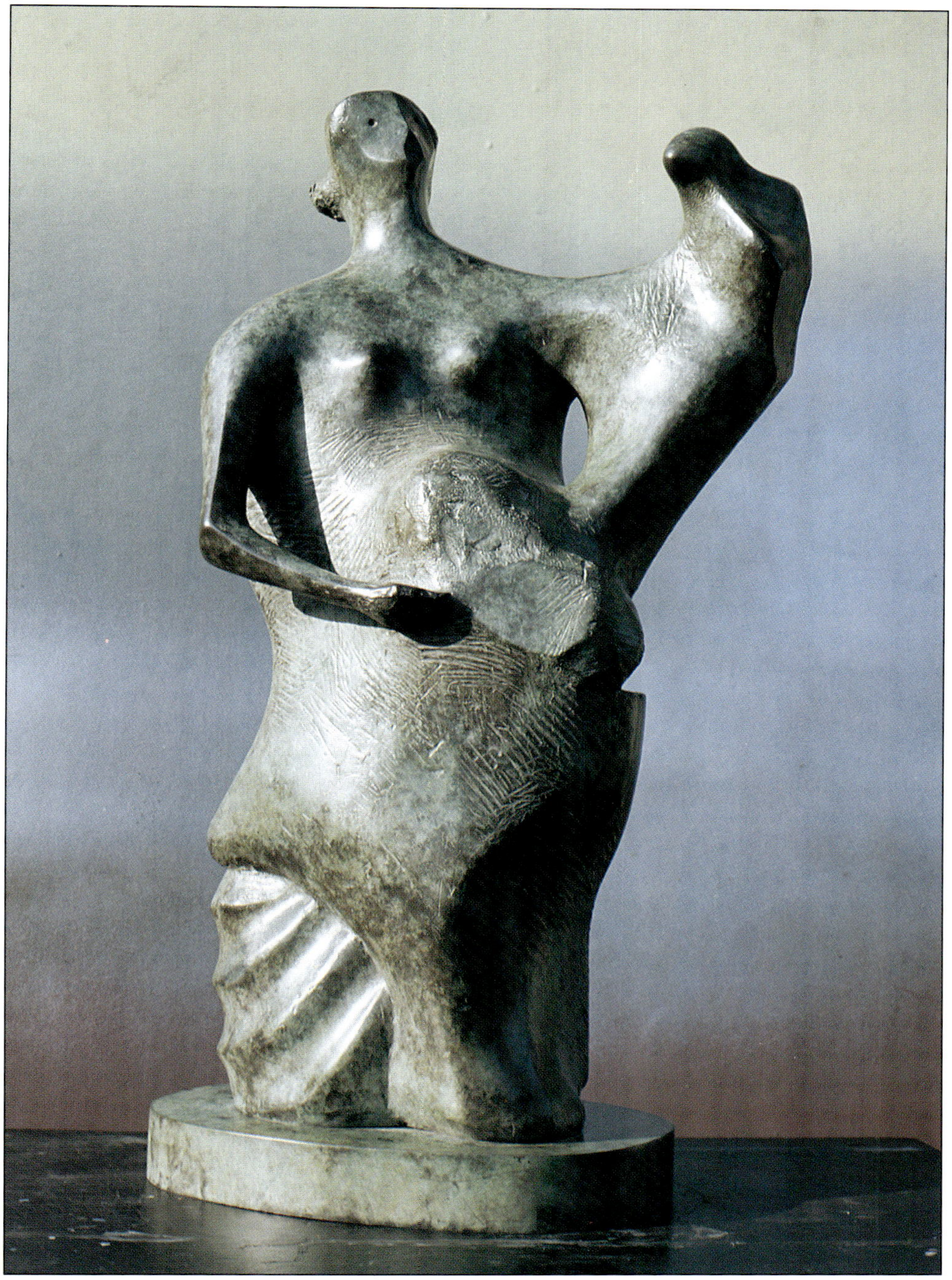

169

Working Model for Mother and Child: Upright 1978

H 57.8cm bronze edition of 9

LH 731

170

Mother and Child 1978

L 84cm stalactite

LH 754

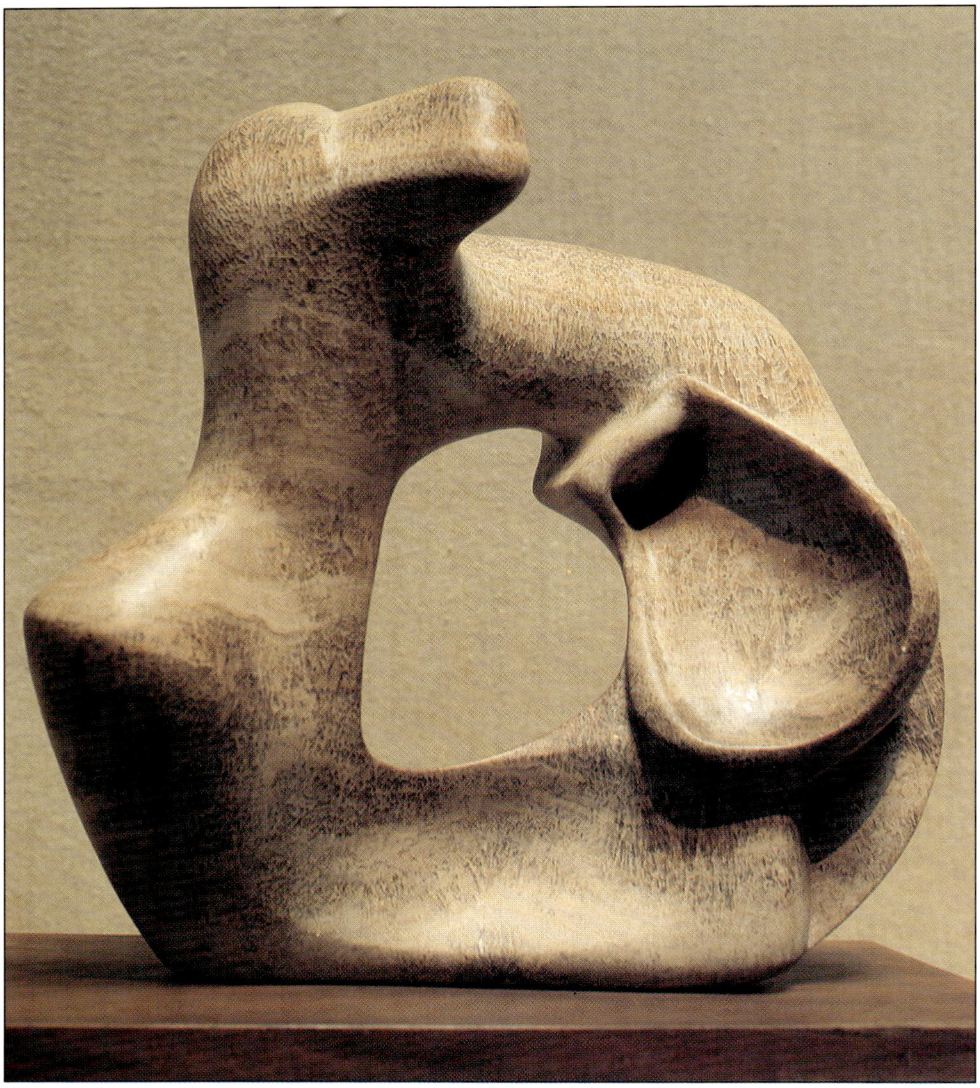

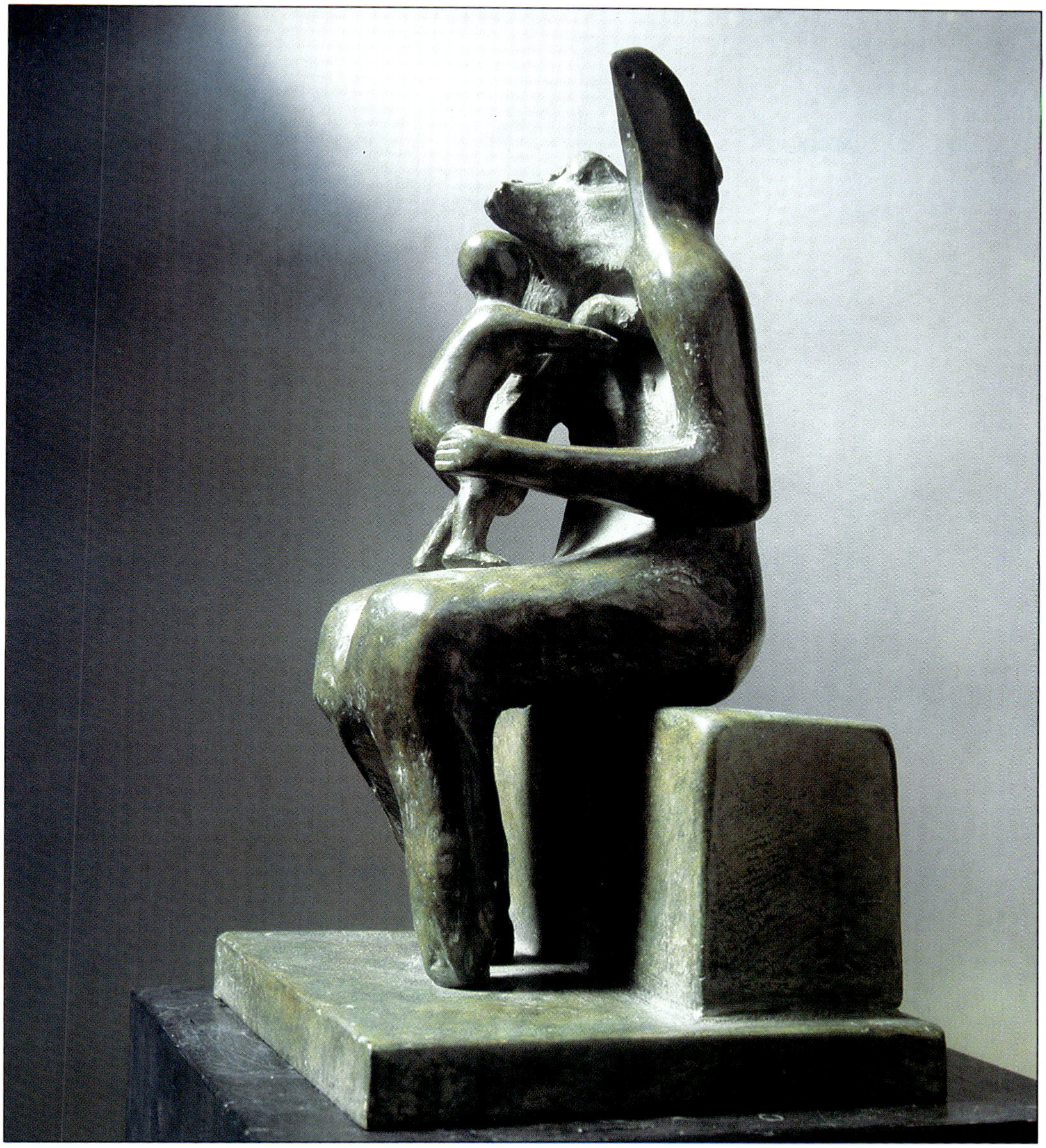

171

Mother and Child: Towel 1979

H 27cm bronze edition of 9

LH 763

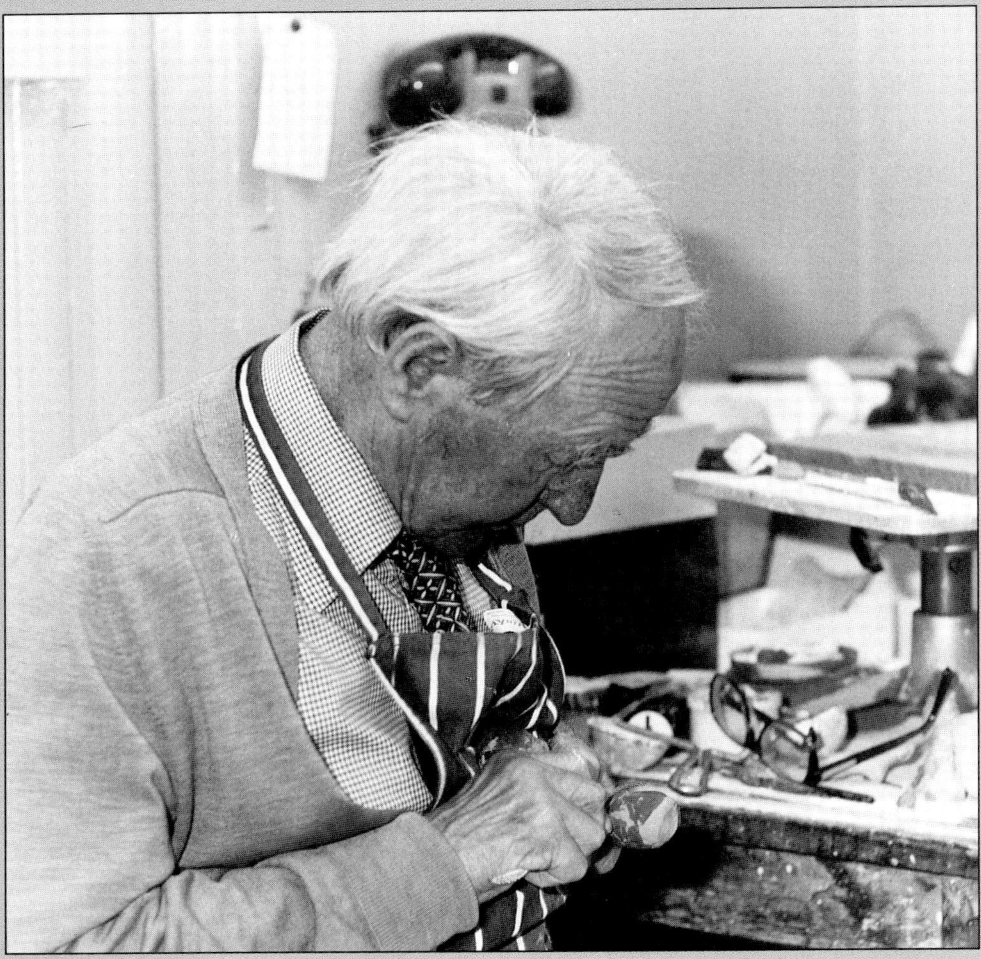

Henry Moore working in
his maquette studio, 1981.

1980s

Besides etching, Moore continued drawing in the 1980s, as much for enjoyment as for inspiration for sculpture. In his theatrical *Sculptor Looking at Rock Formation* (cat.172) he stressed the analogy between the human form and living rock, whereas in his only representation of a stage (cat.179) he reduced the figures to mask-like beings.

In his late sculpture Moore still sought to create for the viewer an equivalent of psychological awareness of the human at the cost of literal representation. Figures such as cats.180 and 182 are contorted, as though they are wrestling with their identity: they have escaped from their role as an equivalent to landscape, but they remain unsure of their role as human beings. They seem to represent the dilemma of the continuance of human life on a planet that man has made so hostile. Even by the 1970s the surest relationship for Moore was the mother and child, though the viewer's imagination is pushed to the limits in the abstracted carving *Mother and Child* in stalactite (cat.170). The close psychological bond expressed in abstract forms in the 1930s (cat.36) is, however, enhanced by the greater concession to natural form in cat.169 and the far more representational *Mother and Child: Arms* (cat.166).

Moore had already imagined a reclining mother and child in a drawing of 1928 (cat.14); he returned to the motif in 1973 with *Reclining Woman in a Setting* (cat.152), in which the mother's body swivels forward, revealing cave-like formations. Such cavities become the shelter for the infant in the sculpture *Draped Reclining Mother and Baby* (cat.181).

Enlargements from maquettes were now made in polystyrene, a light but soft material that replaced plaster in the last decades of Moore's life. Like a block of stone, polystyrene can be carved direct, though in polystyrene it is not always easy to achieve the subtlety of curvature or the variations in surface texture which had been so characteristic of Moore's bronzes cast from plaster models.

In spite of increasing pressure to provide monuments for sites all over the world, Moore preserved his vision; he retained his unique view of humanity and Nature and their interrelationship, however tenuous; he still transposed his ideas without telling a story. To the end of his working life he retained the freshness of vision, true to his ideals and to his background, distracted by neither fame nor fortune.

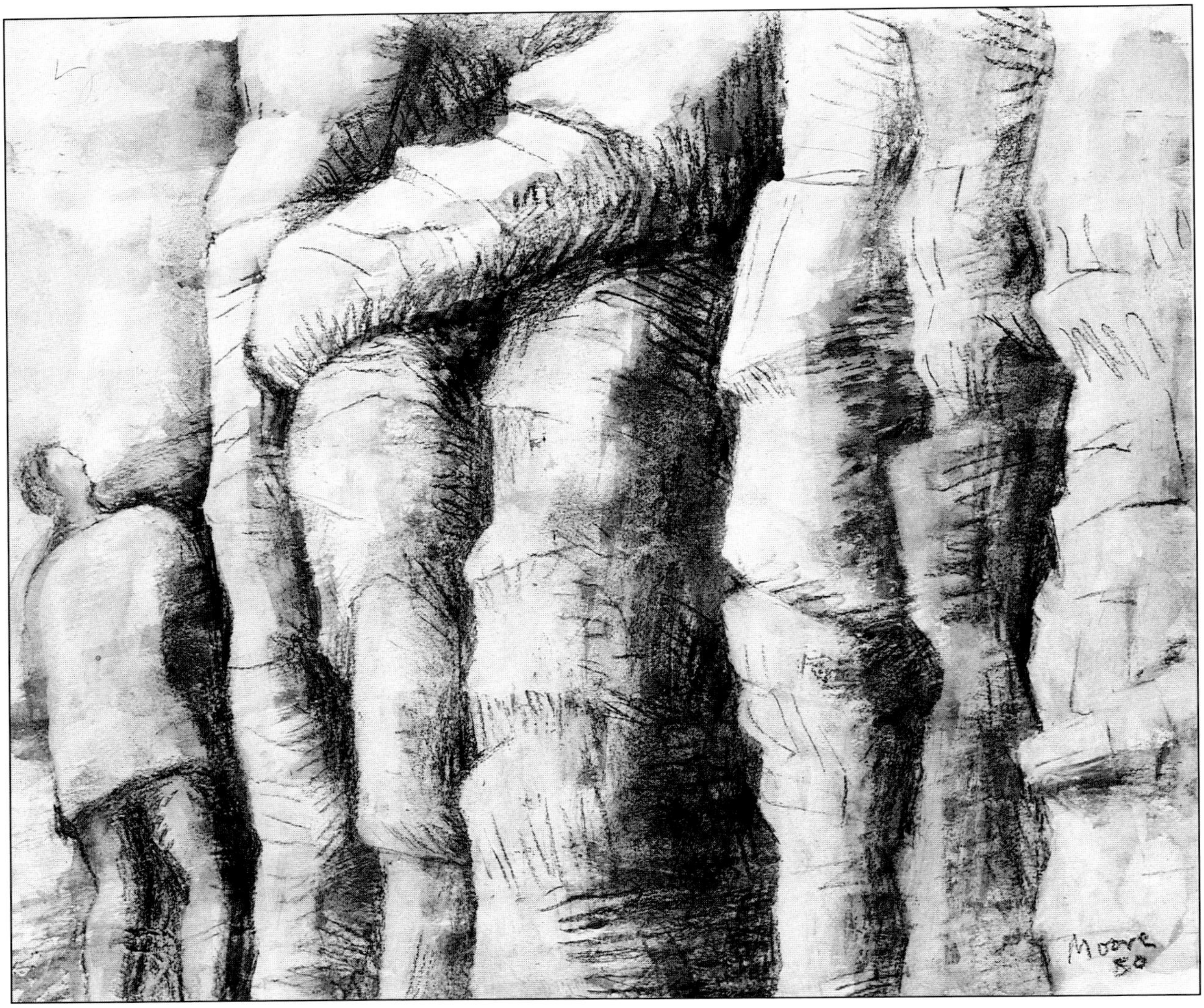

172
Sculptor Looking at Rock Formation 1980
charcoal, gouache on watercoloured paper
335 x 400mm
HMF 80(217)

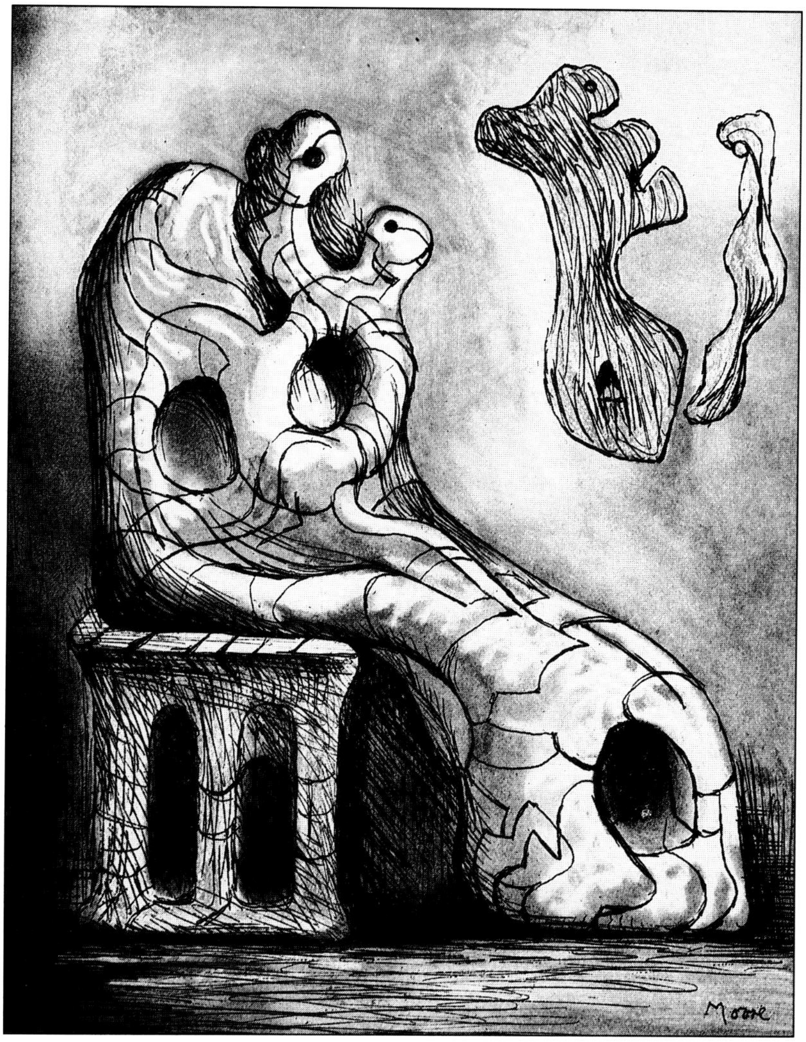

173

Seated Mother and Child 1980-81
etching, aquatint and roulette
in six colours
346 x 261mm
CGM 588

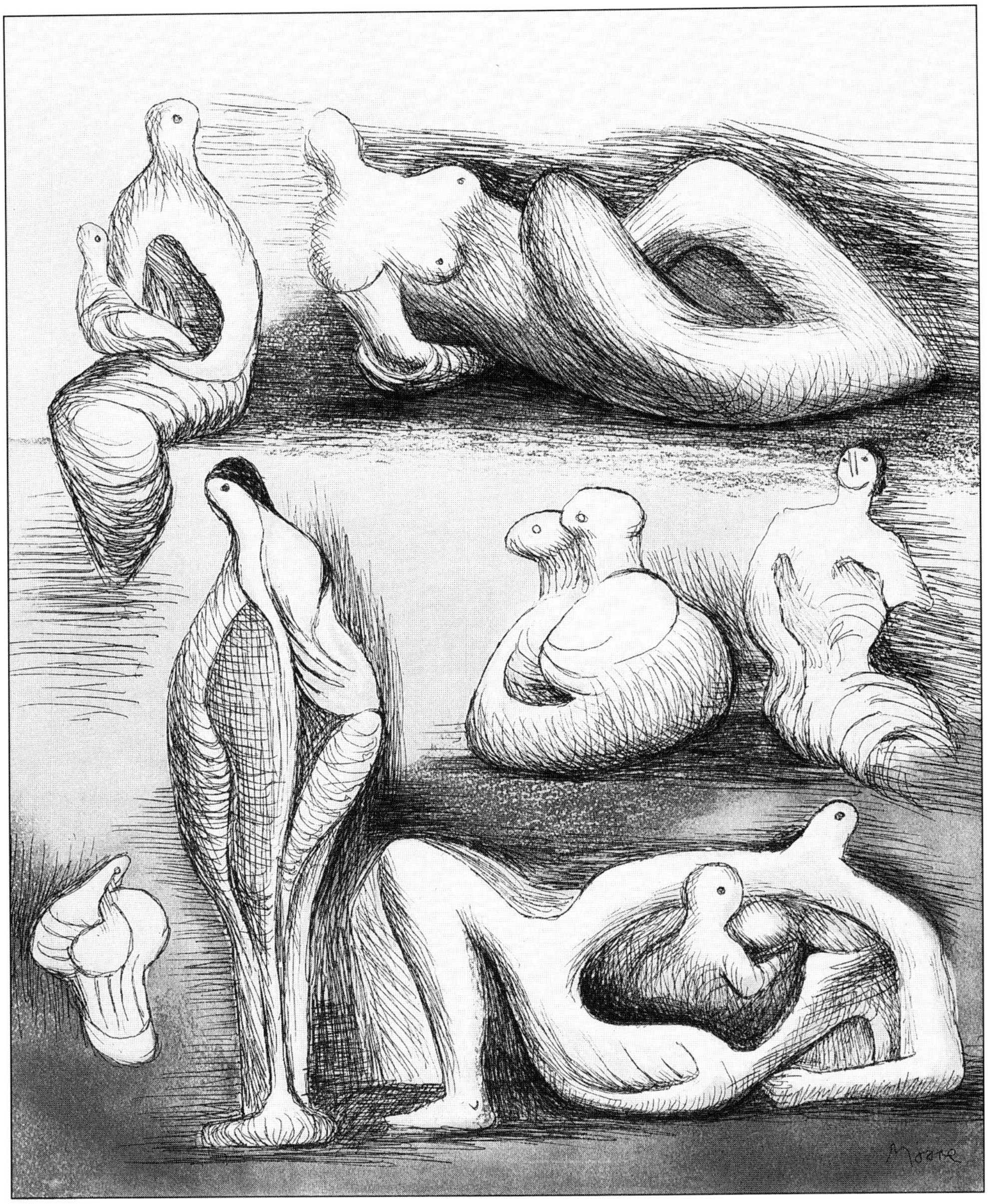

174

Seven Sculpture Ideas I 1980-81
etching, aquatint and roulette
in ten colours
362 x 293mm
CGM 589

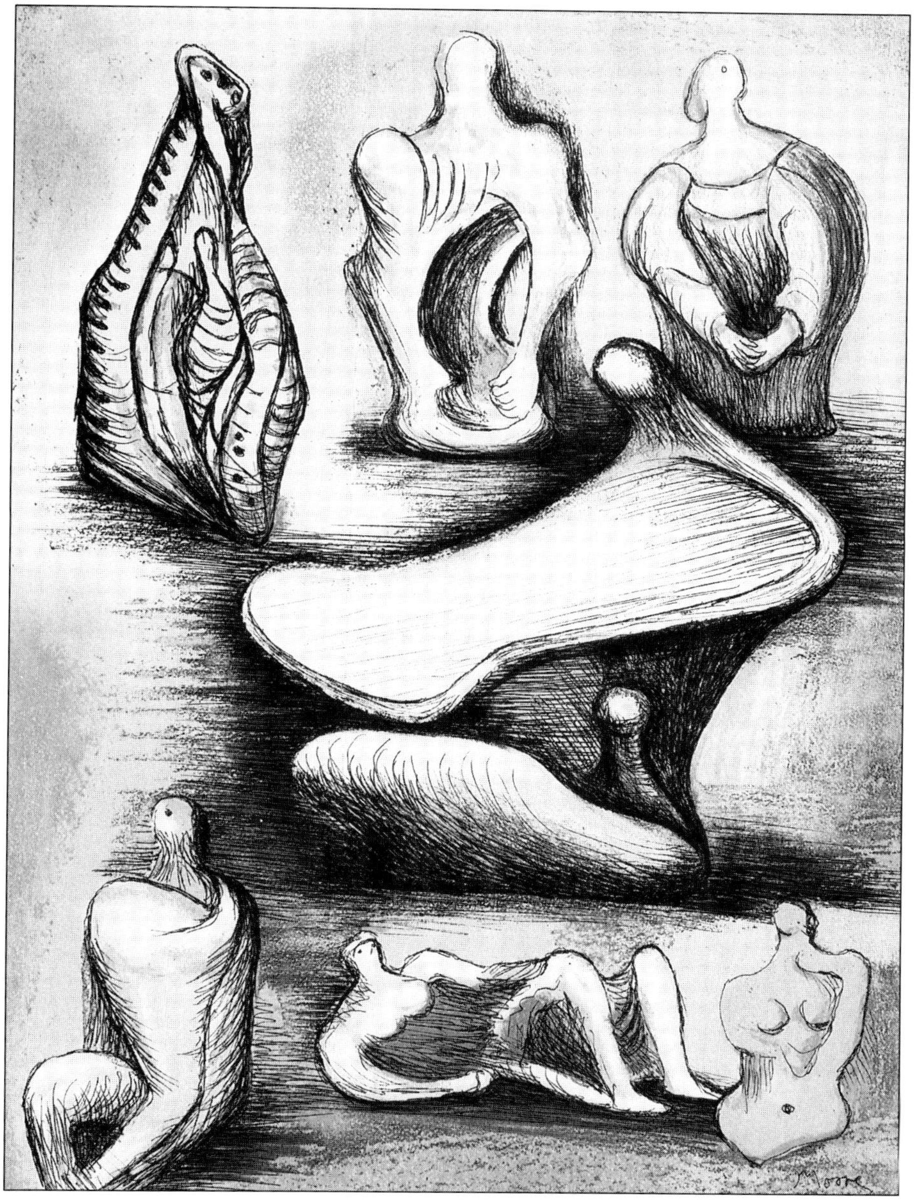

175

Seven Sculpture Ideas II 1980-81

etching, aquatint and roulette
in twelve colours

378 x 282mm

CGM 590

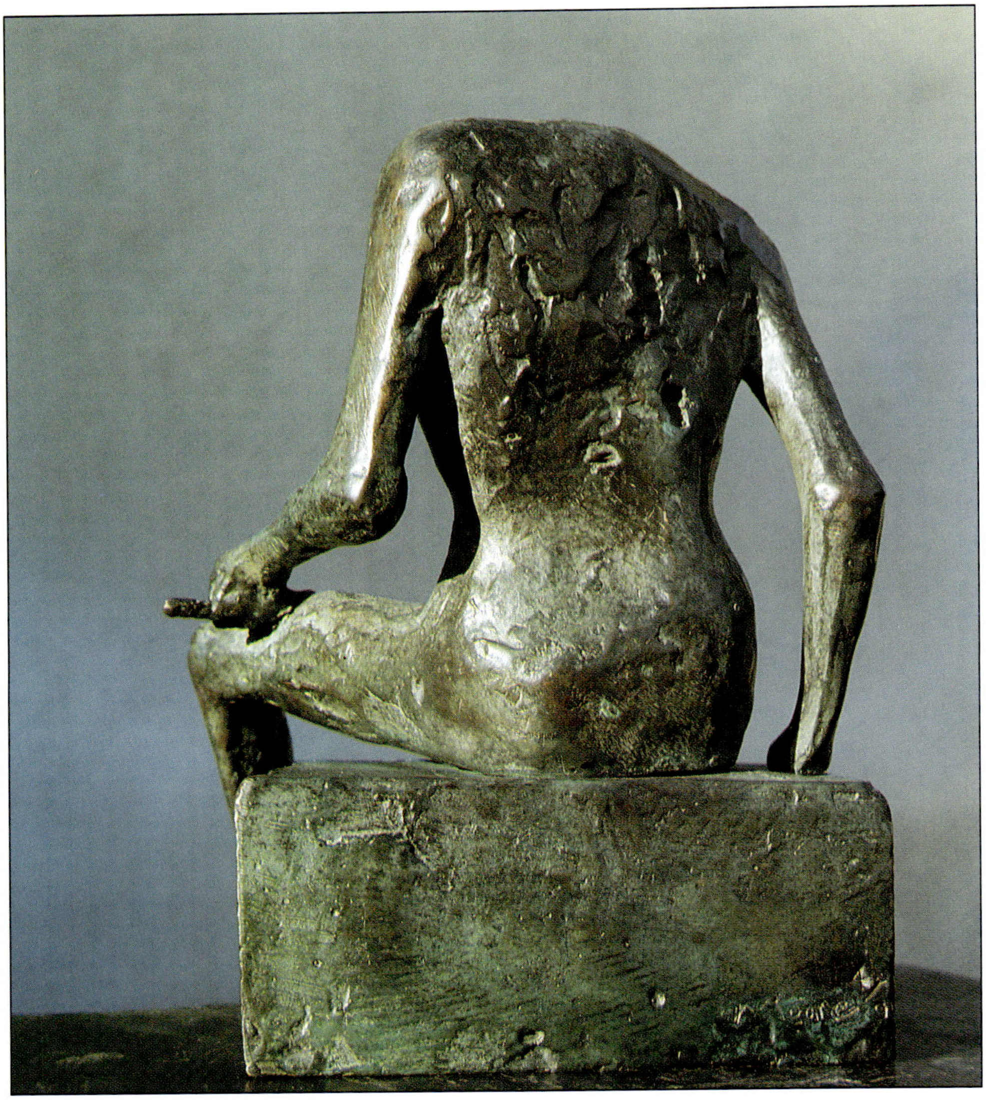

176
Male Torso *c.*1969, cast 1980
H 16cm bronze edition of 9
LH 795

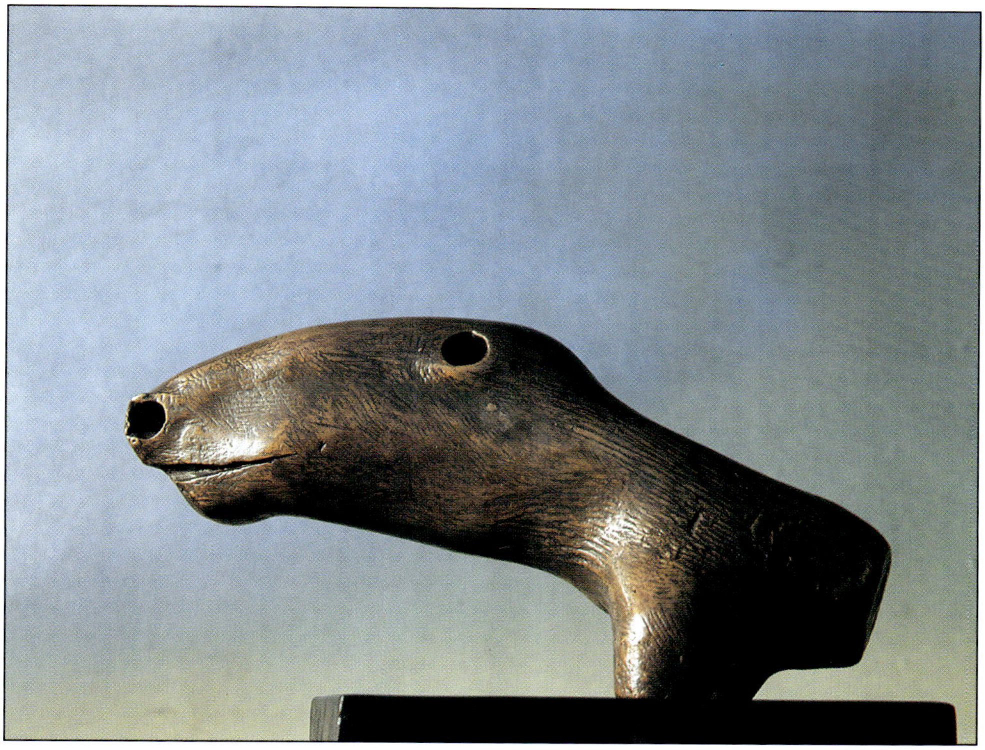

Animals for me have characters similar to many human beings. Sometimes I feel free when working on an animal idea because I can invent an imaginary animal. I would find it less natural to try to invent a new human.

177
Horse's Head 1980
L 19.7cm bronze edition of 7
LH 801

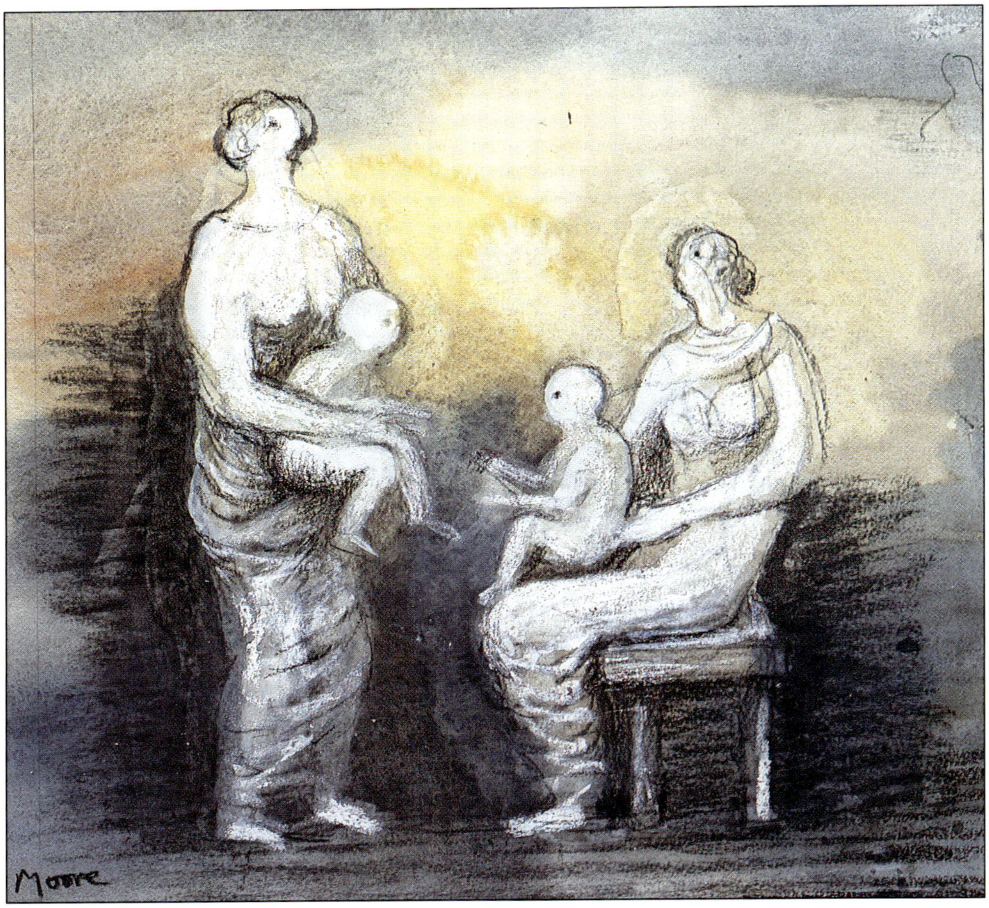

178

Standing and Seated Mothers with Children 1981

charcoal, white wax crayon, watercolour wash, black chinagraph, gouache

345 x 371mm

HMF 81(388)

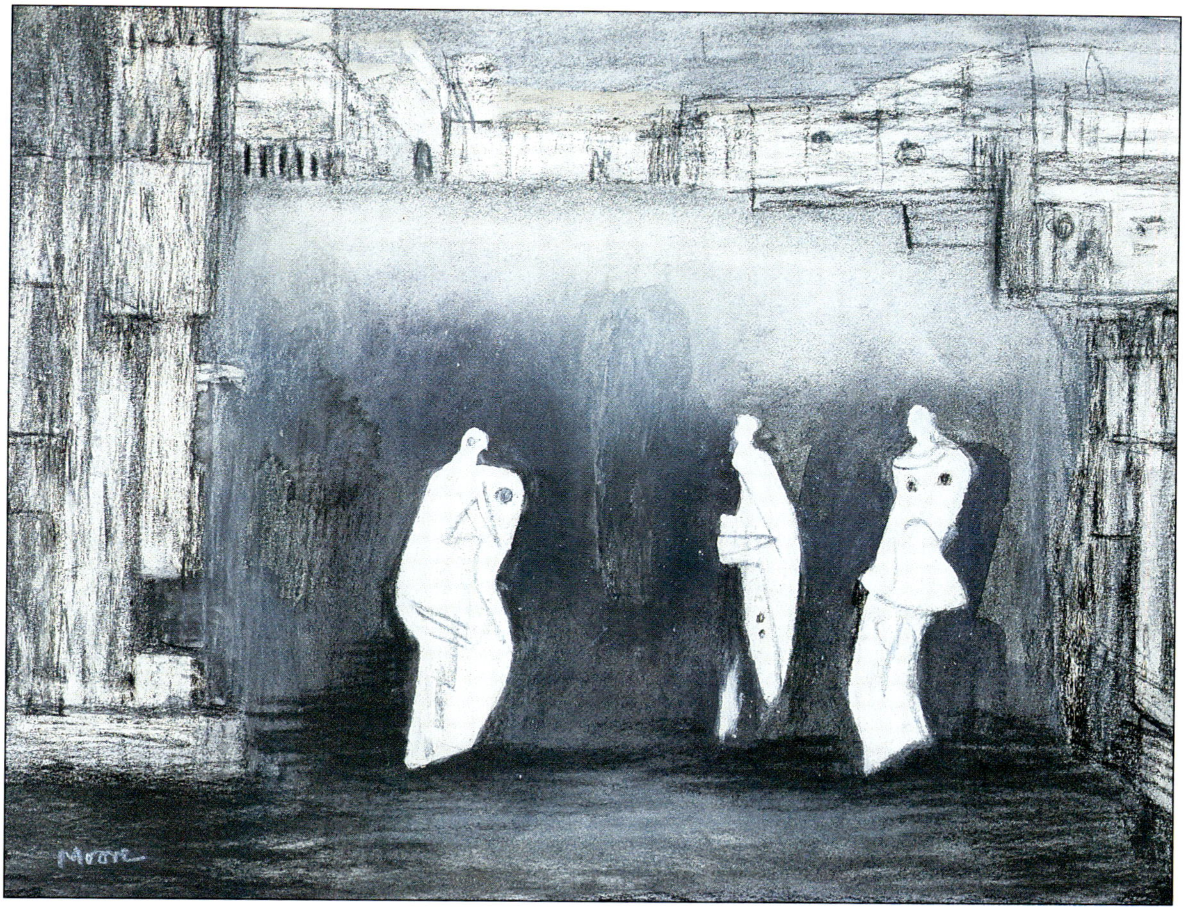

179

Three Figures on a Stage 1981

black chalk, charcoal, white wax crayon,
ink and watercolour wash, gouache

301 x 387mm

HMF 81(227)

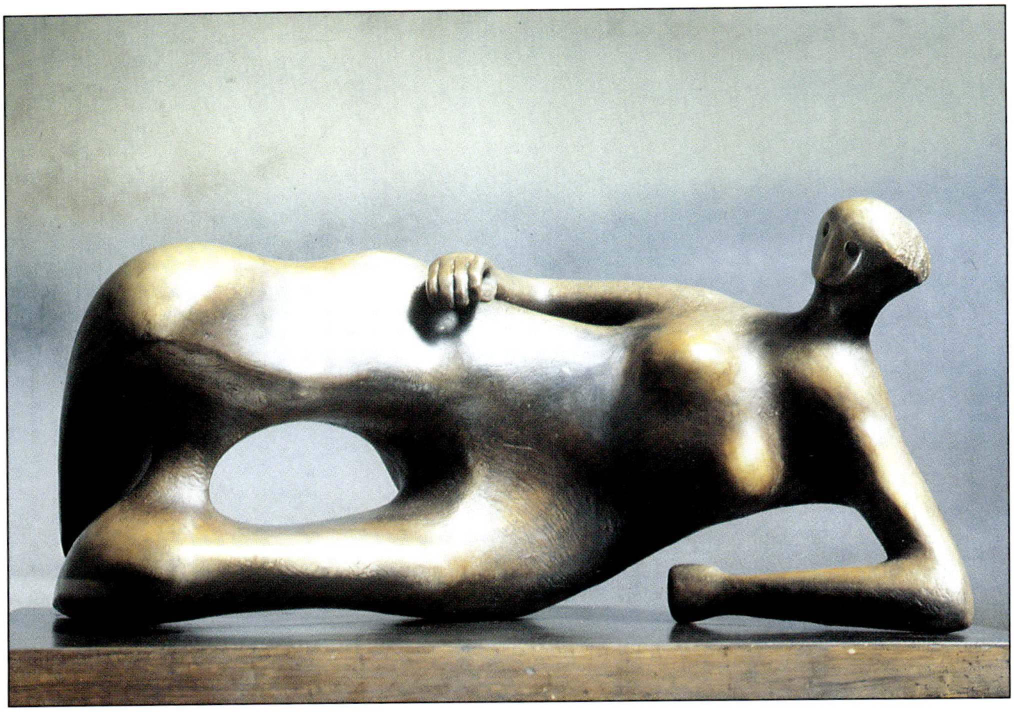

Sculpture should always at first sight have some obscurities, and further meanings. People should want to go on looking and thinking; it should never tell all about itself immediately. Initially both sculpture and painting must need effort to be fully appreciated or else it is just an empty immediacy like a poster, which is designed to be read by people on top of a bus in half a second. In fact all art should have some more mystery and meaning to it than is apparent to a quick observer.

180
Working Model for Reclining Woman: Elbow 1981
L 86.5cm bronze edition of 9
LH 809

181

Draped Reclining Mother and Baby 1982

L 265.5cm bronze

LH 822

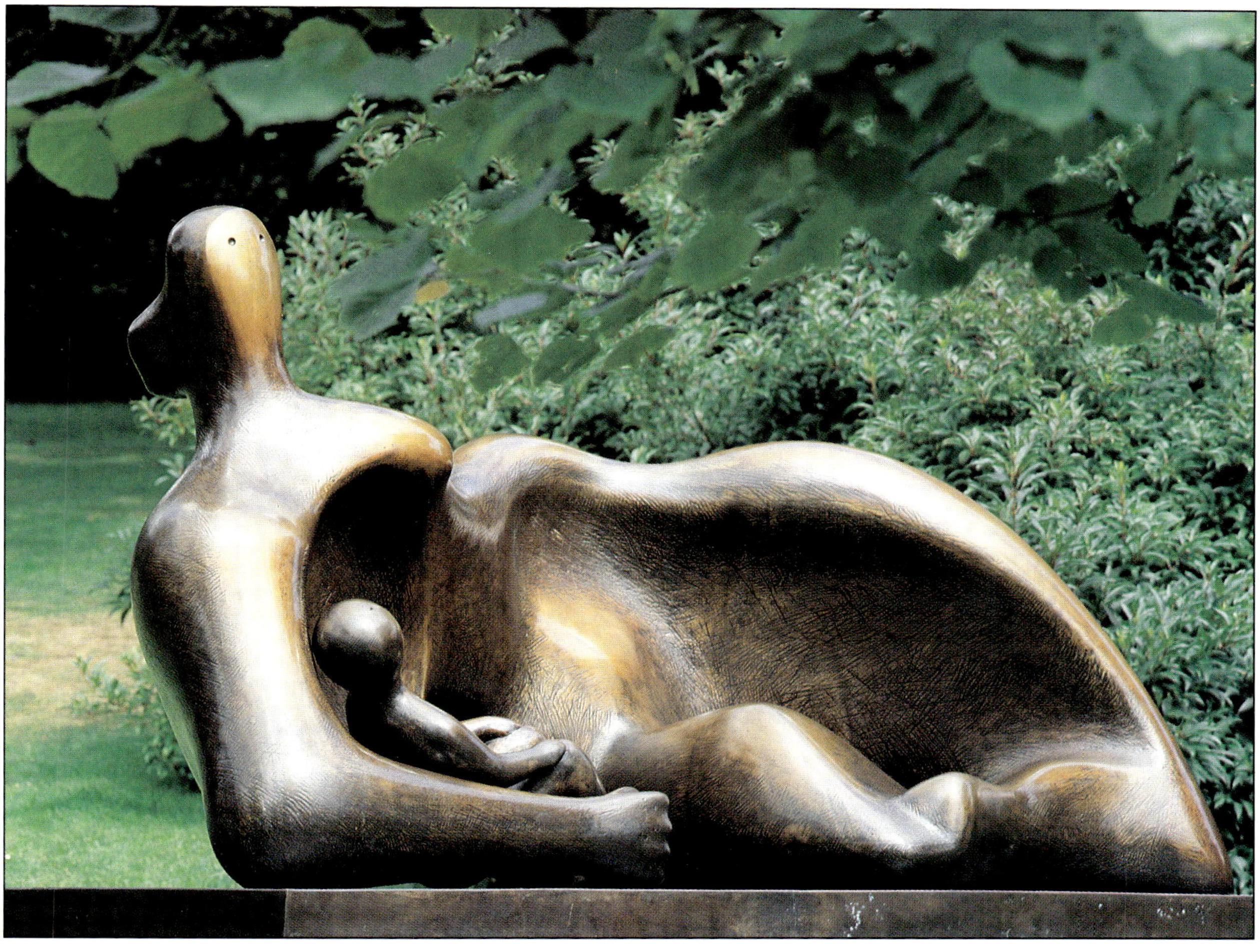

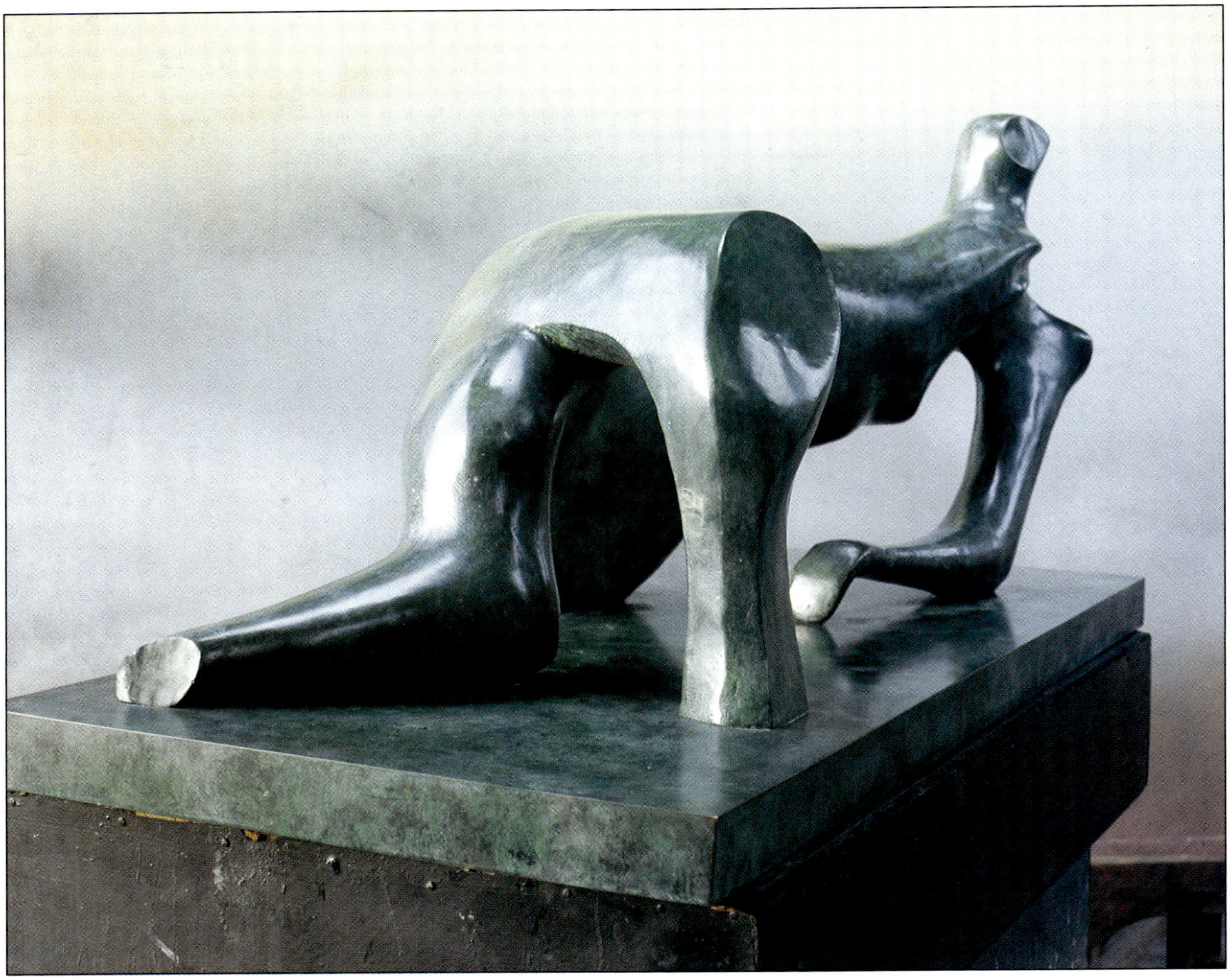

182

Reclining Figure: Open Pose 1982

L 91.5cm bronze edition of 9

LH 832

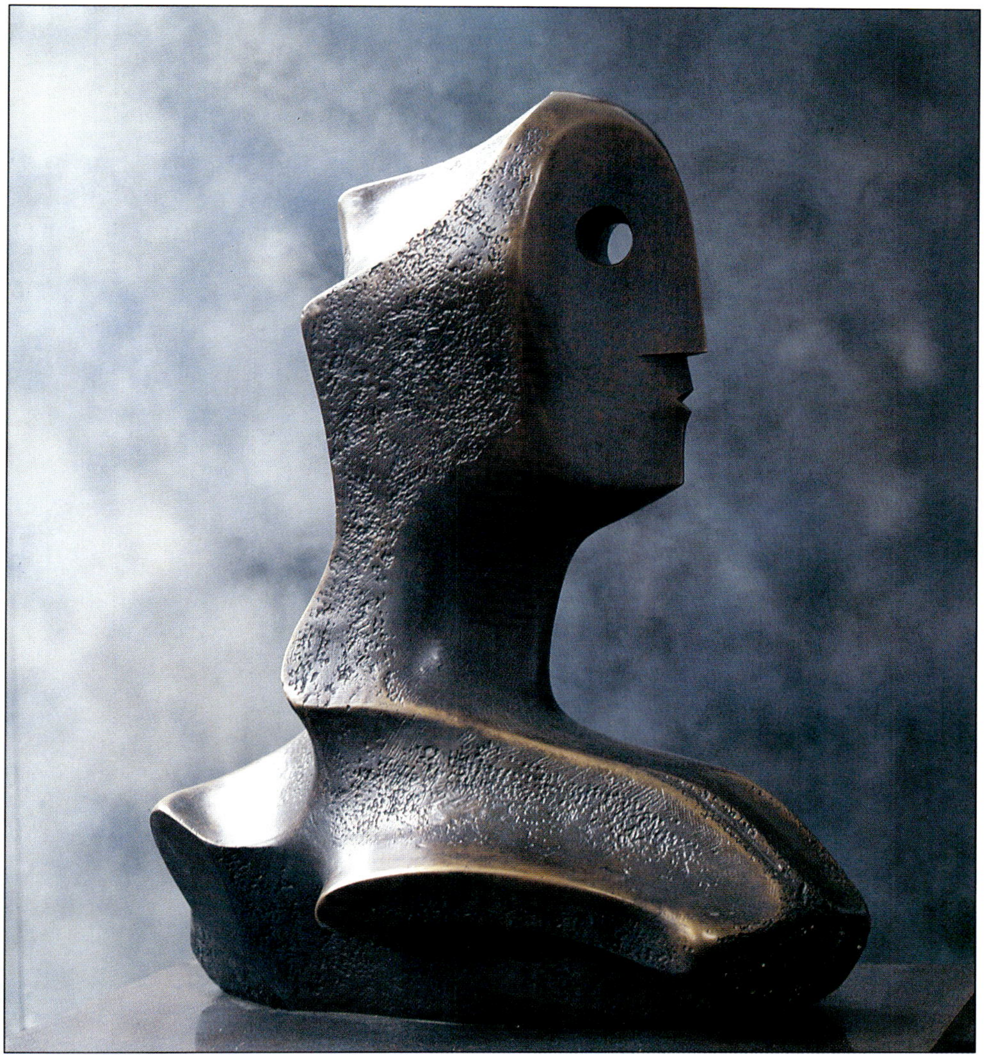

183
Head 1984
H 62.2cm bronze edition of 9
LH 918

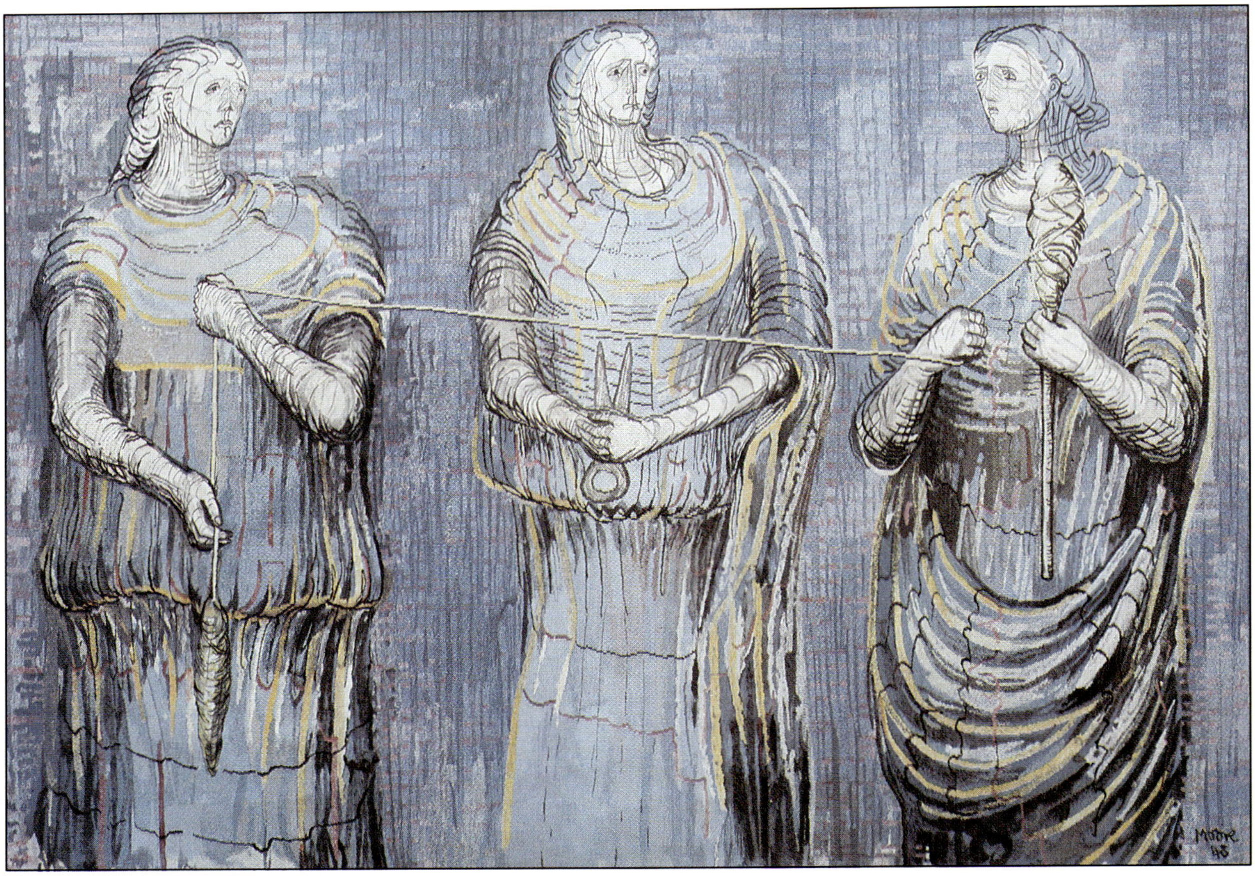

If it were just going to be a colour reproduction I wouldn't be interested. It is because it is a translation from one medium into another and has to be different that you get the surprise. It is not like a bronze-caster who has to produce an absolutely exact copy or it's thrown away; the beauty of tapestry is that it is different, an interpretation, and that is to me the excitement and the pleasure.

184
Three Fates 1983-84
Tapestry woven in 1983-84
at West Dean College from
a drawing executed by
Henry Moore in 1943
243 x 350cm
TAP 27

Selected Bibliography

CATALOGUES RAISONNÉS

Henry Moore: Complete Sculpture, 6 vols. Lund Humphries / Zwemmer, London 1944-88.

Henry Moore: Catalogue of Graphic Work, 4 vols. Cramer, Geneva 1973-88.

SELECTED PUBLICATIONS

Berthoud, Roger: **The Life of Henry Moore**. Faber, London; E.P. Dutton, New York 1987.

Clark, Kenneth: **Henry Moore Drawings**. Thames and Hudson, London; Harper and Row, New York 1974.

The Drawings of Henry Moore, ed. Alan G. Wilkinson. Garland, New York 1984.

Grigson, Geoffrey: **Henry Moore**. Penguin Books, Harmondsworth 1943.

Grohmann, Will: **The Art of Henry Moore**. First published by Rembrandt Verlag, Berlin 1960; Thames and Hudson, London; Abrams, New York 1960.

Hall, Donald: **Henry Moore: The Life and Work of a Great Sculptor**. Gollancz, London; Harper and Row, New York 1960.

Henry Moore at the British Museum, introduction and commentary by Henry Moore, photographs by David Finn. British Museum Publications, London 1981; Abrams, New York 1982.

Henry Moore: Drawings, ed. Ann Garrould. Thames and Hudson, London; Rizzoli, New York 1988.

Henry Moore: Energy in Space, photographs by John Hedgecoe. Bruckmann, Munich; New York Graphic Society, Boston 1974.

Henry Moore Maquettes, text by Erich Steingräber. Pantheon Edition, Studio Bruckmann, Munich 1978.

Henry Moore: Mother and Child Etchings, introduction by Gail Gelburd. Raymond Spencer Company, Much Hadham 1988.

Henry Moore on Sculpture, ed. Philip James. Macdonald, London 1966; Viking, New York 1967, revised 1971.

Henry Moore: Sculpture, ed. David Mitchinson, introduction by Franco Russoli. Polígrafa, Barcelona; Macmillan, London; Rizzoli, New York 1981.

Henry Moore: Unpublished Drawings, ed. David Mitchinson. Fratelli Pozzo, Turin; Abrams, New York 1971.

Neumann, Erich: **The Archetypal World of Henry Moore**. Routledge, London; Pantheon Books, New York 1959; Harper and Row, New York 1965; Princeton University Press, Princeton, New Jersey 1985.

Packer, William: **Henry Moore: An Illustrated Biography**, with photographs by Gemma Levine. Weidenfeld and Nicolson, London; Grove Press, New York 1985.

Read, Herbert: **Henry Moore: A Study of His Life and Work**. Thames and Hudson, London 1965; Praeger, New York 1966.

Read, John: **Henry Moore: Portrait of an Artist**. Whizzard Press / André Deutsch, London; Hacker, New York 1979.

Russell, John: **Henry Moore**. Allen Lane, London; Putnam, New York 1968; revised edition, Penguin Books, Harmondsworth 1973.

Strachan, Walter: **Henry Moore: Animals**. Aurum Press / Bernard Jacobson, London 1983.

MAJOR EXHIBITION CATALOGUES

Henry Moore, text by James Johnson Sweeney. Museum of Modern Art / Simon and Schuster, New York 1947.

Sculpture and Drawings by Henry Moore, text by David Sylvester. Arts Council of Great Britain, London 1951.

Henry Moore: Sculpture 1950-1960, text by Bryan Robertson. Whitechapel Art Gallery, London 1960.

Henry Moore, text by David Sylvester. Arts Council of Great Britain, London; Praeger, New York 1968.

Henry Moore. Rijksmuseum Kröller-Müller, Otterlo / Museum Boymans-Van Beuningen, Rotterdam 1968.

Henry Moore Exhibition in Japan, 1969, text by David Thompson. Mainichi Newspapers, Tokyo 1969.

Moore e Firenze, ed. Giovanni Carandente. Il Bisonte, Florence 1972, revised 1979.

Henry Moore in America, text by Henry J. Seldis. Los Angeles County Museum of Art, Los Angeles / Praeger, New York; Phaidon, London 1973.

Henry Moore by Henry Moore Exhibition, text by John Russell. Mainichi Newspapers, Tokyo 1974.

Henry Moore: Skulptur, Teckning, Grafik 1923-1975, text by Anne Seymour. Henie-Onstad Kunstsenter, Hovikodden / Kulturhuset, Stockholm / Nordjyllands Kunstmuseum, Ålborg 1975.

Expo Henry Moore, ed. Georg Müller. Zürcher Forum, Zurich 1976.

The Drawings of Henry Moore, text by Alan G. Wilkinson. Art Gallery of Ontario, Toronto 1977; Tate Gallery, London 1978.

Henry Moore: Sculptures et Dessins, introduction by DominiqueBozo. Editions des musées nationaux, Paris 1977.

Henry Moore: 80th Birthday Exhibition. Bradford Art Galleries and Museums, Bradford 1978.

Henry Moore at the Serpentine, text by David Sylvester. Arts Council of Great Britain, London 1978.

The Henry Moore Gift, introduction by John Russell. Tate Gallery, London 1978.

Henry Moore: Maquetten, Bronzen, Handzeichnungen, text by Gerhard Bott. Eduard Roether Verlag, Darmstadt 1979.

Henry Moore. Samsung Foundation of Art and Culture, Seoul 1982.

Henry Moore en Mexico: Escultura, Dibujo, Grafica de 1921 a 1987. Instituto Nacianal de Bellas Artes-Cultura, Mexico City 1982.

Henry Moore, text by José María Salvador. Museo de Arte Contemporáneo, Caracas 1983.

Notes

MAJOR EXHIBITION CATALOGUES
continued

Henry Moore: 60 Years of His Art, text by William S. Lieberman. Metropolitan Museum of Art, New York; Thames and Hudson, London 1983.

Henry Moore: Skulpturen, Zeichnungen, Grafiken. Habarta Kunsthandel & Verlag, Vienna 1983.

Henry Moore: Shelter and Coal Mining Drawings, text by Julian Andrews. Ministerium für Kultur der Deutschen Demokratischen Republik, Berlin 1984.

Henry Moore: Mutter und Kind. Skulpturenmuseum Glaskasten, Marl 1984.

The Art of Henry Moore, texts by David Mitchinson and William Packer. Metropolitan Art Museum, Tokyo; Art Museum, Fukuoka 1986.

Henry Moore: New Delhi 1987, ed. Ann Elliott and David Mitchinson, text by Norbert Lynton. National Gallery of Modern Art, New Delhi; British Council, London 1987.

Mother and Child: The Art of Henry Moore, ed. Gail Gelburd. Hofstra Museum and University, Hempstead, New York 1987.

Henry Moore, ed. Susan Compton. Royal Academy of Arts / Weidenfeld and Nicolson, London; Scribner's, New York 1988.

Henry Moore, ed. David Mitchinson. Fondation Pierre Gianadda, Martigny / Electa, Milan 1989.

Henry Moore: The Human Dimension, text by Norbert Lynton. First published in Russian by the British Council, London 1991; English edition HMF Enterprises Ltd in association with the British Council, 1991; Finnish edition Helsingin kaupungin taidemuseo, Helsinki 1991.

NICK WATERLOW

1 **Henry Moore on Sculpture**, ed. Philip James, Macdonald, London 1966, p.96.

2 Herbert Read, **'The Drawings of Henry Moore'**, *Art in Australia*, 1 September 1941, p.14.

3 Henry Moore, **Heads, Figures and Ideas**, Rainbird, London 1958, unpaginated.

4 William Packer, **Henry Moore: An Illustrated Biography**, Weidenfeld and Nicolson, London 1985, p.69.

5 John McPhee, **'Peter Bellew, Obituary'**, *Art and Australia*, vol. 24, no.3, Autumn 1987, p.340.

6 Herbert Read, p.12.

7 Herbert Read, p.12.

8 Herbert Read, p.12.

9 Bernard Smith, **'Henry Moore 1948'**, *Hermes*, magazine of the University of Sydney, 1948. Reprinted in *The Critic as Advocate*, Oxford University Press, Melbourne 1989, p.85-95.

10 Bernard Smith, p.86. Ref. Herbert Read (ed.), **Unit One: The Modern Movement in English Architecture, Painting and Sculpture,** Cassell, London 1934.

11 Henry Moore, **'The Sculptor's Aims'** quoted in Bernard Smith p.87.

12 Bernard Smith, p.88.

13 Bernard Smith, p.93.

14 Bernard Smith, p.94.

15 Bernard Smith diary entry, 18 January 1949.

16 Bernard Smith, *Melbourne Age*, 1963, p.8.

17 Lenton Parr in conversation with the author, Melbourne, January 1992.

18 Roger Berthoud, **The Life of Henry Moore**, Faber and Faber, London 1987, p.208.

19 **Daily Telegraph**, 19 September 1956; quoted in Roger Berthoud, p.268.

20 Henry Moore, **'The Sculptor Speaks'**, *Listener,* 18 August 1937.

21 Henry Moore, **'Primitive Art'**, *Listener,* 24 April 1941.

SUSAN COMPTON

1 Henry Moore, **'The Romanesque Carvings'**, *Chichester 900*, Chichester Cathedral 1975; quoted in Fiona MacCarthy, *Eric Gill*, London and Boston 1989, p.28. The titles of the reliefs are *The Raising of Lazarus* and *Christ Arriving at Bethany*.

2 Henry Moore, **'The Sculptor Speaks'**, *Listener*, 18 August 1937.

3 An account of the newspaper campaign waged by the *Morning Star* that resulted in Moore resigning from the Royal College of Art is given in Roger Berthoud, **The Life of Henry Moore**, Faber and Faber, London 1987, pp.106-8.

4 T.S. Eliot, Stanza ix, **'Choruses from the Rock'**, *Collected Poems 1909-1935*, Faber and Faber, London 1936.

5 Henry Moore, **'Madonna and Child (Northampton) 1943-44'**, in *Henry Moore on Sculpture*, ed. Philip James, Macdonald, London 1968.

6 Commissioning letter, 24 May 1949, Arts Council of Great Britain archives, quoted by Richard Cork, **'An art of the open air: Moore's major public sculpture'**, in Susan Compton, *Henry Moore*, Royal Academy of Arts / Weidenfeld and Nicolson, London 1988, p.20. The Festival of Britain was organised to celebrate the centenary of the Great Exhibition of 1851, best known for the Crystal Palace built in Hyde Park which housed it; the Festival of Britain was held on the South Bank of the River Thames, and its remaining monument is the Royal Festival Hall.

7 Henry Moore, statement in *Sculpture in the Open Air*, London County Council third international exhibition of sculpture, Holland Park, London 1954.

8 Gaudier's statement was originally published in his **Manifesto** in the Vorticist magazine *Blast*, no.1, 1914. See Charles Harrison, **English Art and Modernism 1900-1939**, London 1981, and **British Art in the Twentieth Century**, ed. Susan Compton, London 1987.

9 Eric Neumann, **The Archetypal World of Henry Moore**, trans. from German by R.F.C. Hull, Pantheon Books, New York 1959, pp.127-8.

10 Edward Sackville-West, **The Rescue**, Secker and Warburg, London 1945.

11 Goethe, **Prométhée,** Nicaise, Paris 1950, lithographs printed by Mourlot; catalogued in *Henry Moore: The Graphic Work 1932-1971*, ed. Gérald Cramer, Alistair Grant and David Mitchinson, Gérald Cramer, Geneva 1973.

12 See Alan G.Wilkinson, **The Drawings of Henry Moore**, Tate Gallery, London / Art Gallery of Ontario, Toronto 1977, p.44, fig.60; Wilkinson reproduces the pot from Ernst Fuhrmann, *Peru II*, Folkwang-Verlag, Hagen and Darmstadt 1922.

13 Sackville-West, **The Rescue** (see note 10 above), p.12.